ANNUAL EDITIONS

Drugs, Society, and Behavior 12/13
Twenty-Seventh Edition

EDITORS

Mary H. Maguire
California State University—Sacramento

Dr. Mary Maguire is an Associate Professor of Criminal Justice at California State University Sacramento, one of the largest Criminal Justice programs in the United States. She teaches Criminology, Research Methods, and Contemporary Issues in Criminal Justice. She has an MA in Psychology, an MSW, and a PhD. in Social Work and Social Research. Dr. Maguire has fifteen years of professional experience in behavioral health. She has twelve years of research experience measuring clinical models and behaviors of high-risk populations, including best practices forthose with mental illness and co-occurring substance abuse. She is published in the area of policing, corrections, and criminal justice policy.

Clifford Garoupa
Fresno City College

Mr. Garoupa received his Bachelor of Arts degree from California State University Fresno in Sociology, his Master's degree in Sociology from The Ohio State University, and his Juris Doctor degree from The San Joaquin College of Law. He worked for many years in the criminal justice system, both in law enforcement and criminal defense, primarily as an investigator but also as a consultant, particularly in homicide and serious drug cases. During his academic career, he has not only served in an advisory capacity to members of Congress, but also was appointed to the Fresno County Drug and Alcohol Advisory Board, acting for five years as that Board's Chairman. He has been interviewed on National Public Radio concerning European Harm Reduction Policy and Practice, particularly the implementation and effect of drug decriminalization in Portugal. He is the former Program Coordinator for the Drug and Alcohol Counseling program at Fresno City College, which is one of the largest such educational programs in California. He currently teaches both Sociology and Drug Studies.

ANNUAL EDITIONS: DRUGS, SOCIETY, AND BEHAVIOR, TWENTY-SEVENTH EDITION

Published by McGraw-Hill, a business unit of The McGraw-Hill Companies, Inc., 1221 Avenue
of the Americas, New York, NY 10020. Copyright © 2013 by The McGraw-Hill Companies, Inc.
All rights reserved. Printed in the United States of America. Previous edition(s) 2008, 2009, 2012.
No part of this publication may be reproduced or distributed in any form or by any means, or stored
in a database or retrieval system, without the prior written consent of The McGraw-Hill Companies,
Inc., including, but not limited to, in any network or other electronic storage or transmission, or
broadcast for distance learning.

Some ancillaries, including electronic and print components, may not be available to customers
outside the United States.

This book is printed on acid-free paper.

Annual Editions® is a registered trademark of The McGraw-Hill Companies, Inc.

Annual Editions is published by the **Contemporary Learning Series** group within the
McGraw-Hill Higher Education division.

1 2 3 4 5 6 7 8 9 0 QDB/QDB 1 0 9 8 7 6 5 4 3 2

ISBN 978-0-07-805123-4
MHID 0-07-805123-1
ISSN 1091-9945 (print)
ISSN 2158-8856 (online)

Managing Editor: *Larry Loeppke*
Senior Developmental Editor: *Dave Welsh*
Permissions Coordinator: *Rita Hingtgen*
Marketing Specialist: *Alice Link*
Project Manager: *Melissa Leick*
Design Coordinator: *Margarite Reynolds*
Cover Graphics: *Studio Montage, St. Louis, Missouri*
Buyer: *Susan K. Culbertson*
Media Project Manager: *Sridevi Palani*

Compositor: Laserwords Private Limited
Cover Images: Dave Moyer (inset); Ingram Publishing (background)

www.mhhe.com

Editors/Academic Advisory Board

Members of the Academic Advisory Board are instrumental in the final selection of articles for each edition of ANNUAL EDITIONS. Their review of articles for content, level, and appropriateness provides critical direction to the editors and staff. We think that you will find their careful consideration well reflected in this volume.

ANNUAL EDITIONS: Drugs, Society, and Behavior 12/13
27th Edition

Editors/Academic Advisory Board continued

Preface

In publishing ANNUAL EDITIONS we recognize the enormous role played by the magazines, newspapers, and journals of the public press in providing current, first-rate educational information in a broad spectrum of interest areas. Many of these articles are appropriate for students, researchers, and professionals seeking accurate, current material to help bridge the gap between principles and theories and the real world. These articles, however, become more useful for study when those of lasting value are carefully collected, organized, indexed, and reproduced in a low-cost format, which provides easy and permanent access when the material is needed. That is the role played by ANNUAL EDITIONS.

Humanity has developed an ambiguous relationship with substances we have come to define as drugs, particularly those drugs that alter human consciousness and behavior, psychoactive drugs. The use of such substances has resulted in a social circumstance whereby societies struggle to control human behaviors motivated and altered by their use. Although we consider modern society to function based upon logic, science, and reason, closer scrutiny of policy, regulation, and control belies this belief. In effect, such attempts at regulation face an enormous biological and psychological challenge: we humans are designed to alter our consciousness, or to use another term familiar to drug use, to "get high". As a result, to a significant degree, our societies face a seemingly insurmountable challenge: to control and/or manipulate human behavior with regard to drug using or consciousness-altering behaviors. To this end, societies have, presumably in an attempt to protect their members, developed what they perceive to be rational control mechanisms to protect people from themselves.

Unfortunately the historical foundations upon which drug regulation and control are based, especially in the United States, have their roots in racism and discrimination. This further complicates society's attempts to address, in a logical and coherent sense, what type of role or relationship humans should have with these substances. The reality of our modern world concerning drugs is unequivocal. Despite repeated resolutions by the United State's government in an attempt to achieve a "Drug Free America," and the staggering amount of money spent in the attempt to achieve that end, drugs are ubiquitous in American society; they are here to stay. What has come to be defined as deviant and antisocial behaviors in our attempts to "denormalize" drug use has, in fact, resulted in these activities becoming testimony to people's inherent creativity in their never-ending pursuit of states of altered consciousness. When this penchant to "get high" is combined with the precociousness inherent in our species, one ends up with the current circumstance: new substances are discovered regularly, either by scientific research or common curiosity, and the ritual of consciousness alteration begins anew. We currently find ourselves in a conundrum concerning drugs. For whatever reason, none of which are based upon science or rationality, some drugs are considered to be acceptable and appropriate, while others are seen to be highly dangerous and a threat. One does not need to be a psychopharmacologist or toxicologist to realize that there is very little difference, for instance, between ethyl alcohol and heroin. As a result, we readily accept and condone the use of one (alcohol) while declaring "war" against the other (heroin). The same situation exists with regard to tobacco, a compound that is among the most toxic and highly addictive known. For these reasons, oftentimes it is in fact impossible to make sense of how modern societies have come to view and address drug using behavior. We hope that the materials presented in this book offer the reader some insight and perspective with regard to understanding the role that drugs play in today's world and how we have come to our current situation concerning drugs and drug use.

The articles contained in *Annual Editions: Drugs, Society, and Behavior 12/13* are a collection of issues and perspectives designed to provide the reader with a framework for examining current drug-related issues of facts. The book is designed to offer students something to think about and something with which to think. It is a unique collection of materials of interest to the casual as well as the serious student of drug-related social phenomena. Unit 1 addresses the significance that drugs have in affecting diverse aspects of American life. It emphasizes the often-overlooked reality that drugs—legal and illegal—have remained a pervasive dimension of past as well as present American history. The unit begins with examples of the multiple ways in which Americans have been and continue to be affected by both legal and illegal drugs. Unit 2 examines the ways drugs affect the mind and body that result in dependence and addiction. Unit 3 examines the major drugs of use and abuse, along with issues relative to understanding the individual impacts of these drugs on society. It addresses the impacts produced by the use of legal and illegal drugs and emphasizes the alarming nature of widespread prescription drug abuse. Unit 4 reviews the dynamic nature of drugs as it relates to changing patterns and trends of use. It gives special attention this year to drug trends among youth, particularly those related to prescription drug abuse. Unit 5 focuses on the social costs of drug abuse and why the costs overwhelm many American institutions. Unit 6 illustrates the complexity in creating and implementing drug policy, such as that associated with medical marijuana and that associated with foreign drug control policy. Unit 7 concludes the book with discussions of current strategies for preventing and treating drug abuse. Can we deter people from harming themselves with drugs, and can we cure people addicted to drugs? What works and what does not work? Special attention is given to programs that address at-risk youth and programs that reduce criminal offender rehabilitation and recidivism. *Annual Editions: Drugs, Society, and Behavior 12/13* contains a number of features that are designed to make the volume user-friendly. These include a *table of contents* with abstracts that summarize each article and key concepts in boldface, a *topic guide* to help locate articles on specific individuals or subjects, *Internet References* that can be used to further explore the topics, and Critical Thinking study questions at the end of each article to help students better understand what they have read.

Mary Maguire, Clifford Garoupa
Editors

The Annual Editions Series

VOLUMES AVAILABLE

Adolescent Psychology

Aging

American Foreign Policy

American Government

Anthropology

Archaeology

Assessment and Evaluation

Business Ethics

Child Growth and Development

Comparative Politics

Criminal Justice

Developing World

Drugs, Society, and Behavior

Dying, Death, and Bereavement

Early Childhood Education

Economics

Educating Children with Exceptionalities

Education

Educational Psychology

Entrepreneurship

Environment

The Family

Gender

Geography

Global Issues

Health

Homeland Security

Human Development

Human Resources

Human Sexualities

International Business

Management

Marketing

Mass Media

Microbiology

Multicultural Education

Nursing

Nutrition

Physical Anthropology

Psychology

Race and Ethnic Relations

Social Problems

Sociology

State and Local Government

Sustainability

Technologies, Social Media, and Society

United States History, Volume 1

United States History, Volume 2

Urban Society

Violence and Terrorism

Western Civilization, Volume 1

World History, Volume 1

World History, Volume 2

World Politics

Contents

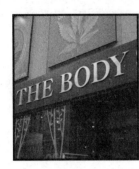

UNIT 1
Living with Drugs

Unit Overview   **xx**

The concepts in bold italics are developed in the article. For further expansion, please refer to the Topic Guide.

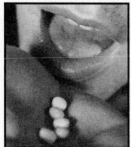

UNIT 2
Understanding How Drugs Work—Use, Dependency, and Addiction

The concepts in bold italics are developed in the article. For further expansion, please refer to the Topic Guide.

UNIT 3
The Major Drugs of Use and Abuse

The concepts in bold italics are developed in the article. For further expansion, please refer to the Topic Guide.

UNIT 4
Other Trends in Drug Use

UNIT 5
Measuring the Social Costs of Drugs

The concepts in bold italics are developed in the article. For further expansion, please refer to the Topic Guide.

UNIT 6
Creating and Sustaining Effective Drug Control Policy

UNIT 7
Prevention, Treatment, and Education

The concepts in bold italics are developed in the article. For further expansion, please refer to the Topic Guide.

The concepts in bold italics are developed in the article. For further expansion, please refer to the Topic Guide.

Correlation Guide

The *Annual Editions* series provides students with convenient, inexpensive access to current, carefully selected articles from the public press. *Annual Editions: Drugs, Society, and Behavior 12/13* is an easy-to-use reader that presents articles on important topics such as *drug lifestyle, drug types, drug-use trends, drug policy,* and many more. For more information on *Annual Editions* and other *McGraw-Hill Contemporary Learning Series* titles, visit **www.mhhe.com/cls.**

This convenient guide matches the units in **Annual Editions: Drugs, Society, and Behavior 12/13** with the corresponding chapters in three **of our best-selling McGraw-Hill Health** textbooks by Hart et al., Goode, and Fields

Annual Editions: Drugs, Society, and Behavior 12/13	Drugs, Society, and Human Behavior, 14/e by Hart et al.	Drugs in American Society, 8/e by Goode	Drugs in Perspective, 8/e by Fields
Unit 1: Living with Drugs	**Chapter 1:** Drug Use: An Overview **Chapter 2:** Drug Use as a Social Problem	**Chapter 1:** Drug Use: A Sociological Perspective	**Chapter 1:** Putting Drugs in Perspective
Unit 2: Understanding How Drugs Work—Use, Dependency, and Addiction	**Chapter 4:** The Nervous System **Chapter 5:** The Actions of Drugs	**Chapter 2:** Drug Use: A Pharmacological Perspective	**Chapter 3:** Drug-Specific Information **Chapter 4:** Assessment of Substance Abuse, Dependence, and Addiction
Unit 3: The Major Drugs of Use and Abuse	**Chapter 6:** Stimulants **Chapter 7:** Depressants and Inhalants **Chapter 9:** Alcohol **Chapter 10:** Tobacco **Chapter 11:** Caffeine **Chapter 12:** Dietary Supplements and Over-the-Counter Drugs **Chapter 13:** Opioids **Chapter 14:** Hallucinogens **Chapter 15:** Marijuana **Chapter 16:** Performance-Enhancing Drugs	**Chapter 3:** Drugs in the News Media **Chapter 7:** Alcohol and Tobacco **Chapter 8:** Marijuana, LSD, and Club Drugs **Chapter 9:** Stimulants: Amphetamine, Methamphetamine, Cocaine, and Crack **Chapter 10:** Heroin and Narcotics **Chapter 11:** The Pharmaceutical Neuroleptics: Sedatives, Hypnotics, Tranquilizers, Antipsychotics, and Antidepressants	**Chapter 3:** Drug-Specific Information
Unit 4: Other Trends in Drug Use	**Chapter 1:** Drug Use: An Overview **Chapter 2:** Drug Use as a Social Problem **Chapter 3:** Drug Products and Their Regulations	**Chapter 1:** Drug Use: A Sociological Perspective **Chapter 3:** Drugs in the News Media **Chapter 5:** Historical Trends in Drug Consumption **Chapter 12:** Controlling Drug Use: The Historical Context	**Chapter 1:** Putting Drugs in Perspective **Chapter 2:** Why Do People Abuse Drugs?
Unit 5: Measuring the Social Costs of Drugs	**Chapter 2:** Drug Use as a Social Problem	**Chapter 1:** Drug Use: A Sociological Perspective **Chapter 12:** Controlling Drug Use: The Historical Context **Chapter 13:** Drugs and Crime: What's the Connection? **Chapter 14:** The Illicit Drug Industry **Chapter 15:** Law Enforcement, Drug Courts, Drug Treatment **Chapter 16:** Legalization, Decriminalization, and Harm Reduction	**Chapter 1:** Putting Drugs in Perspective **Chapter 2:** Why Do People Abuse Drugs? **Chapter 5:** Substance Abuse and Family Systems **Chapter 10:** Prevention of Substance Abuse Problems **Chapter 11:** Disorders Co-occurring with Substance Abuse **Chapter 12:** Alcohol/Drug Recovery and Relapse Prevention
Unit 6: Creating and Sustaining Effective Drug Control Policy	**Chapter 3:** Drug Products and Their Regulations **Chapter 17:** Preventing Substance Abuse	**Chapter 15:** Law Enforcement, Drug Courts, Drug Treatment **Chapter 16:** Legalization, Decriminalization, and Harm Reduction	**Chapter 10:** Prevention of Substance Abuse Problems **Chapter 12:** Alcohol/Drug Recovery and Relapse Prevention
Unit 7: Prevention, Treatment, and Education	**Chapter 17:** Preventing Substance Abuse **Chapter 18:** Treating Substance Abuse and Dependence	**Chapter 15:** Law Enforcement, Drug Courts, Drug Treatment **Chapter 16:** Legalization, Decriminalization, and Harm Reduction	**Chapter 10:** Prevention of Substance Abuse Problems **Chapter 12:** Alcohol/Drug Recovery and Relapse Prevention

Topic Guide

This topic guide suggests how the selections in this book relate to the subjects covered in your course. You may want to use the topics listed on these pages to search the Web more easily.

On the following pages a number of websites have been gathered specifically for this book. They are arranged to reflect the units of this Annual Editions reader. You can link to these sites by going to www.mhhe.com/cls

All the articles that relate to each topic are listed below the bold-faced term.

Internet References

The following Internet sites have been selected to support the articles found in this reader. These sites were available at the time of publication. However, because websites often change their structure and content, the information listed may no longer be available. We invite you to visit www.mhhe.com/cls for easy access to these sites.

Annual Editions: Drugs, Society, and Behavior 12/13

General Sources

Higher Education Center for Alcohol and Other Drug Prevention
www.edc.org/hec

The U.S. Department of Education established the Higher Education Center for Alcohol and Other Drug Prevention to provide nationwide support for campus alcohol and other drug prevention efforts. The Center is working with colleges, universities, and preparatory schools throughout the country to develop strategies for changing campus culture, to foster environments that promote healthy lifestyles, and to prevent illegal alcohol and other drug use among students.

Mind for Better Health
www.mind.org.uk/help/diagnoses_and_conditions

This site provides information on a wide range of subjects from addiction and dependency to mental health problems. It also has information on legislation.

Narconon
www.youthaddiction.com

This site contains drug information, information on addiction, rehab information, online consultations, and other related resources.

National Clearinghouse for Alcohol and Drug Information
ncadi.samhsa.gov

This site provides information to teens about the problems and ramifications of drug use and abuse. There are numerous links to drug-related informational sites.

NSW Office of Drug Policy Home Page
www.druginfo.nsw.gov.au

This is an Australian government-based website with a great deal of drug-related information. The site includes information about illicit drugs (amphetamines, pseudoephedrine, GHB, heroin, ketamine, rohypnol, marijuana, paramethoxyamphetamines [PMA], steroids, cocaine, hallucinogens, inhalants, ecstasy, ritalin, and psychostimulants), information and resources, treatment services, law and justice, illicit drug diversion, and medical cannabis. It also includes statistics on drug use in Australia.

ONDCP (Office of National of Drug Control Policy)
www.whitehousedrugpolicy.gov

This site contains a vast amount of drug-related information, resources, and links. Included is information about drug policy, drug facts, publications, related links, prevention, treatment, science and technology, enforcement, state and local along with international facts, and policies, and programs. The site is easy to use and understand.

U.S. Department of Health and Human Services
http://ncadi.samhsa.gov/research

This site contains links and resources on various topics that include, but are not limited to, substance abuse and Mental Health Data Archive, OAS Short Reports (on such drugs as marijuana, crack cocaine, inhalants, club drugs, heroin, alcohol, and tobacco). Also included are government studies and an online library and databases.

United Nations Office on Drugs and Crime
www.unodc.org/unodc/index.html

This site includes information on the following drug-related topics in addition to many other topics: treatment and addiction and illicit drug facts. Also available on this site are recent and archive press releases and multimedia presentations.

UNIT 1: Living with Drugs

Freevibe Drug Facts
www.freevibe.com/Drug_Facts/why_drugs.asp#1

This website contains information on drug facts with links on drug information, why people take drugs, the physical effects and drug-related behavior, drug recognition, and discussions of addiction. The site also includes personal accounts by addicts.

Guide4Living Independent Health Information Online
www.guide4living.com/drugabuse

This site examines the use and abuse of a wide range of substances. It also provides personal stories, information on rehabilitation facilities, and a place for feedback.

Harm Reduction Coalition
www.harmreduction.org

This site provides valuable information about various harm reduction programs operating within the United States. Needle exchange programs, methadone maintenance, and also information about how harm reduction differs from criminalization of drug using behavior.

National Council on Alcoholism and Drug Dependence, Inc
www.ncadd.org

According to its website, the National Council on Alcoholism and Drug Dependence provides education, information, help, and hope in the fight against the chronic, and sometimes fatal, disease of alcoholism and other drug addictions.

Parents. The Anti-Drug
www.theantidrug.com

Tips and links for helping children avoid drugs can be found at this site. Also provided is help in parenting with drug-related issues such as how to advise young persons about the drug-related influences of peer pressure.

UNIT 2: Understanding How Drugs Work—Use, Dependency, and Addiction

AddictionSearch.com
www.addictionsearch.com

Check this site out for information on addiction and rehabilitation. Some of the other features of this site are the use of statistics, identification of social issues, resources for treatment, facility listings for the United States, and analysis of types of addictions by race, sex, and age of human populations.

Addiction Treatment Forum
www.atforum.com

News on addiction research and reports on substance abuse are available here.

nternet References

American Psychological Association's Addiction Related Publications

ttp://search.apa.org/search?query=&facet=classification:Addictions&
mited=true&section=pubs

This site is a good resource with several articles and information mostly on alcohol.

British Broadcasting Company Understanding Drugs

ww.bbc.co.uk/health/conditions/mental_health/drugs_use.shtml

This is a good reference for information about drug use, addiction, and dependence. Includes links.

Centre for Addiction and Mental Health (CAMH)

ww.camh.net

One of the largest addictions facilities in Canada, CAMH advances an understanding of addiction and translates this knowledge into resources that can be used to prevent problems and to provide effective treatments.

Dealing with Addictions

ttp://kidshealth.org/teen/your_mind/problems/addictions.html

This site contains information on addictions and includes a quiz on substance abuse. Categories are entitled Your Mind, Your Body, Sexual Health, Food and Fitness, Drugs and Alcohol, Diseases and Conditions, Infections, School and Jobs, Staying Safe, and questions and answers. Much of this site is available in Spanish.

Drugs and the Body: How Drugs Work

ww.doitnow.org/pdfs/223.pdf

This site pinpoints some basic but critical points in a straightforward manner. It explains how drugs can be administered, the processes through the body, effects, and changes over time. Included are drug-related information resources and links.

National Alcoholism Drug Information Center

ttp://addictioncareoptions.com

Get help and information about drug addition, alcoholism abuse, and top-rated addiction treatment centers.

The National Center on Addiction and Substance Abuse at Columbia University

ww.casacolumbia.org

The National Center on Addiction and Substance Abuse at Columbia University is a unique think/action tank that brings together all of the professional disciplines (health policy, medicine and nursing, communications, economics, sociology and anthropology, law and law enforcement, business, religion, and education) needed to study and combat all forms of substance abuse—illegal drugs, pills, alcohol, and tobacco—as they affect all aspects of society.

National Institute on Drug Abuse (NIDA)

ww.nida.nih.gov

NIDA's mission is to lead the nation in bringing the power of science to bear on drug abuse and addiction.

Public Agenda

ww.publicagenda.org/articles/illegal-drugs

A guide on illegal drugs has links that include understanding the issues, public opinions, and additional resources. Includes several links for each of these groups.

Understanding Addiction—Regret, Addiction and Death

ttp://teenadvice.about.com/library/weekly/aa011501a.htm

This site has several resources and articles related to drug use by young persons.

UNIT 3: The Major Drugs of Use and Abuse

The American Journal of Psychiatry

http://ajp.psychiatryonline.org/cgi/content/abstract/155/8/1016

This site contains a study on female twins and cannabis.

Multidisciplinary Association for Psychedelic Studies (MAPS)

www.maps.org

This site discusses current research into the possible medical uses of some psychedlic drugs and marijuana.

National Institute on Drug Abuse

www.drugabuse.gov

This is the National Institute on Drug Abuse website that identifies the major drugs of use and abuse. It provides resources and information for students, parents, and teachers, as well as reports on drug trends.

Office of Applied Studies

www.oas.samhsa.gov

Data and statistics on the major drugs of use and abuse along with reports on the effects of these drugs focusing on the emotional, social, psychological, and physical aspects are contained at this site. Also available are extensive survey findings on drug use related to evolving patterns of drug abuse.

QuitNet

www.quitnet.org

The QuitNet helps smokers control their nicotine addiction. This site operates in association with the Boston University School of Public Health.

Streetdrugs.org

www.streetdrugs.org

This site provides a great deal of information on street drugs. It is designed to target different audiences—teachers, parents, students, and law enforcement. On this site one can find information on the top ten most misused drugs in the world today, a comprehensive drug index, and information on signs of a drug abuser.

UNIT 4: Other Trends in Drug Use

Drug Story.org

www.drugstory.org/drug_stats/druguse_stats.asp

This site contains lots of information—"Hard Facts, Real Stories, Informed Experts"; information on drugs and their effects. Also covered are prevention and treatment, drugs and crime, drug trafficking, drug use statistics,

Marijuana as a Medicine

http://mojo.calyx.net/~olsen

Monitoring the Future

www.monitoringthefuture.org

Located at this site is a collaboration of drug trend data tables from 2005 focusing on students in the eighth, tenth, and twelfth grades; also described are trends in the availability of drugs, the attitudes of users, and the use of major drugs.

Prescription Drug Abuse

www.prescription-drug-abuse.org

This is a website designed to provide information on where and when to get help for drug abuse. It also has a decent amount of information outlining what prescription drug abuse is and the particular ones that are abused, links to additional articles, and information on who is abusing the drugs.

Internet References

Prescriptions Drug Use and Abuse
www.fda.gov/fdac/features/2001/501_drug.htm

This site contains lots of resources and links related to prescription drug use and abuse.

SAMHSA
www.drugabusestatistics.samhsa.gov/trends.htm

This link is to the office of applied studies, where you can link to numerous drug-related resources. It includes the latest and most comprehensive drug survey information in the United States.

United States Drug Trends
www.usdrugtrends.com

Provided at this site are drug trends for each state in the United States, such as information where each drug is most likely to be used in each state, cost of the drug, and where the drug supply is coming from.

UNIT 5: Measuring the Social Costs of Drugs

BMJ.com a publishing group
http://bmj.bmjjournals.com/cgi/content/abridged/326/7383/242/a

Drug Enforcement Administration
www.usdoj.gov/dea

The mission of the Drug Enforcement Administration is to enforce the controlled substances laws and regulations

Drug Policy Alliance
www.drugpolicy.org/database/index.html

News about drug policies and articles critiquing the real social and economic costs associated with drug abuse versus the cost of the drug war policies can be found here.

Drug Use Cost to the Economy
www.ccm-drugtest.com/ntl_effcts1.htm

European Monitoring Center for Drugs and Addiction
www.emcdda.europa.eu/html.cfm/index1357EN.html

A collection of research studies, based out of the European Union, on how much governments spend to tackle their drug problem.

National Drug Control Policy
www.ncjrs.org/ondcppubs/publications/policy/ndcs00/chap2_10.html

This site contains information about the consequences of illegal drug use, including economic loss, drug-related death, drug related medical emergencies, spreading of infectious diseases, homelessness, and drug use in the workplace.

The November Coalition
www.november.org

The November Coalition is a growing body of citizens whose lives have been gravely affected by the present drug policy. This group represents convicted prisoners, their loved ones, and others who believe that United States drug policies are unfair and unjust.

TRAC DEA Site
http://trac.syr.edu/tracdea/index.html

The Transactional Records Access Clearinghouse (TRAC) is a data gathering, data research, and data distribution organization associated with Syracuse University. According to its website, the purpose of TRAC is to provide the American people—and institutions of oversight such as Congress, news organizations, public interest groups, businesses, scholars, and lawyers—with comprehensive information about the activities of federal enforcement and regulatory agencies and the communities in which they take place.

United Nations Chronicle—online edition
www.un.org/Pubs/chronicle/1998/issue2/0298p7.html

This site contains information about the global nature of drugs.

UNIT 6: Creating and Sustaining Effective Drug Control Policy

Drug Policy Alliance
www.drugpolicy.org

This site explores and evaluates drug policy in the United States and around the world.

DrugText
www.drugtext.org

The DrugText library consists of individual drug-related libraries with independent search capabilities.

Effective Drug Policy: Why Journey's End Is Legalisations
www.drugscope.org.uk

This site contains the drug scope policy and public affairs in the United Kingdom.

Harm Reduction Coalition
www.harmreduction.org

The Higher Education Center for Alcohol and Other Drug Prevention
www.edc.org/hec/pubs/policy.htm

Setting and Improving Policies for Reducing Alcohol and Other Drug Problems on Campus: A Guide for School Administrators.

The National Organization on Fetal Alcohol Syndrome (NOFAS)
www.nofas.org

NOFAS is a nonprofit organization founded in 1990 dedicated to eliminating birth defects caused by alcohol consumption during pregnancy and improving the quality of life for those individuals and families affected. NOFAS is the only national organization focusing solely on fetal alcohol syndrome (FAS), the leading known cause of mental retardation.

National NORML Homepage
www.norml.org

This is the home page for the National Organization for the Reform of Marijuana Laws.

Transform Drug Policy Foundation
www.tdpf.org.uk

Transform Drug Policy Foundation exists to promote sustainable health and well-being by bringing about a just, effective, and humane system to regulate and control drugs at local, national, and international levels. Available on the website are media news articles—both recent and archived—links to other websites related to drug policy, and many other resources.

UNIT 7: Prevention, Treatment, and Education

American Council for Drug Education
www.acde.org

This site educates employers, parents, teachers, and health professionals about drugs and includes information on recognizing the signs and symptoms of drug use.

nternet References

D.A.R.E.
ww.dare-america.com

This year 33 million schoolchildren around the world—25 million in the United States—will benefit from D.A.R.E. (Drug Abuse Resistance Education), the highly acclaimed program that gives kids the skills they need to avoid involvement in drugs, gangs, or violence. D.A.R.E. was founded in 1983 in Los Angeles.

he Drug Reform Coordination Network (DRC)
ww.drcnet.org

According to its home page, the DRC Network is committed to reforming current drug laws in the United States.

Drug Watch International
ww.drugwatch.org

Drug Watch International is a volunteer nonprofit information network and advocacy organization that promotes the creation of healthy drug-free cultures in the world and opposes the legalization of drugs. The organization upholds a comprehensive approach to drug issues involving prevention, education, intervention/treatment, and law enforcement/interdiction.

Hazelden
ww.hazelden.org

Hazelden is a nonprofit organization providing high-quality, affordable rehabilitation, education, prevention, and professional services and publications in chemical dependency and related disorders.

Join Together
ww.jointogether.org

Contained here are multiple types of resources and web links regarding youth drug prevention for parents, teachers, community members, public officials, and faith leaders.

KCI (Koch Crime Institute) The Anti-Meth Site
ww.kci.org/meth_info/faq_meth.htm

This site contains Frequently Asked Questions on methamphetamine. Very interesting.

Marijuana Policy Project
www.mpp.org

The purpose of the Marijuana Policy Project is to develop and promote policies to minimize the harm associated with marijuana.

National Institute on Drug Abuse
www.nida.nih.gov/Infofacts/TreatMeth.html

Information on effective drug treatment approaches, costs for treating drug addiction, and the different treatment options (inpatient, outpatient, group, etc.) can all be found at this site.

Office of National Drug Control Policy (ONDCP)
www.whitehousedrugpolicy.gov

The principal purpose of ONDCP is to establish policies, priorities, and objectives for the nation's drug control program, the goals of which are to reduce illicit drug use, manufacturing, and trafficking; drug-related crime and violence; and drug-related health consequences.

The Partnership for Drug-Free America
www.drugfree.org/#

The Partnership for a Drug-Free America is a private, nonprofit organization that unites communications professionals, renowned scientists, and parents in the mission to reduce illicit drug abuse in America. Drugfree.org is a drug abuse prevention and treatment resource, existing to help parents and caregivers effectively address alcohol and drug abuse with their children. This website gives families the tools, information, and support they need to help their children lead healthy, drug-free lives.

United Nations International Drug Control Program (UNDCP)
www.undcp.org

The mission of UNDCP is to work with the nations and the people of the world to tackle the global drug problem and its consequences.

UNIT 1

Living with Drugs

Unit Selections

Learning Outcomes

After reading this Unit, you should be able to:

• Explain why history is important when attempting to understand contemporary drug-related events.

• Compare how the U.S. response to drug-related issues compares to those occurring in other countries.

• Describe what role the media plays in U.S. society's perception of drug-related events.

• Explain how national crises such as the war in Iraq and economic instability have influenced patterns of drug abuse.

• Determine what use marijuana may have in treating age-related diseases.

Student Website

www.mhhe.com/cls

Internet References

Freevibe Drug Facts
www.freevibe.com/Drug_Facts/why_drugs.asp#1
Guide4Living Independent Health Information Online
www.guide4living.com/drugabuse
Harm Reduction Coalition
www.harmreduction.org
National Council on Alcoholism and Drug Dependence, Inc.
www.ncadd.org
Parents. The Anti-Drug
www.theantidrug.com

When attempting to define the U.S. drug experience, one must examine the past as well as the present. Very often, drug use and its associated phenomena are viewed through a contemporary looking glass relative to our personal views, biases, and perspectives. Although today's drug scene is definitely a product of recent historical trends such as the crack trade of the 1980s, the methamphetamine problem, and the turn toward the expanded non-medical use of prescription drugs, it is also a product of the distant past. This past and the lessons it has generated, although largely unknown, forgotten, or ignored, provide one important perspective from which to assess our current status and to guide our future in terms of optimizing our efforts to manage the benefits and control the harm from legal and illegal drugs.

The U.S. drug experience is often defined in terms of a million individual realities, all meaningful and all different. In fact, these realities often originated as pieces of our historical, cultural, political, and personal past that combine to influence present-day drug-related phenomena significantly. The contemporary U.S. drug experience is the product of centuries of human attempts to alter or sustain consciousness through the use of mind-altering drugs. Early American history is replete with accounts of the exorbitant use of alcohol, opium, morphine, and cocaine. Further review of this history clearly suggests the precedents for Americans' continuing pursuit of a vast variety of stimulant, depressant, and hallucinogenic drugs. Drug wars, drug epidemics, drug prohibitions, and escalating trends of alarming drug use patterns were present throughout the early history of the United States. During this period, the addictive properties of most drugs were largely unknown. Today, the addictive properties of almost all drugs are known. So why is it that so many drug-related lessons of the past repeat themselves in the face of such powerful new knowledge? Why does Fetal Alcohol Syndrome remain as the leading cause of mental retardation in infants? How is it that the abuse of drugs continues to defy the lessons of history? How big is the U.S. drug problem and how is it measured?

One important way of answering questions about drug abuse is by conducting research and analyzing data recovered through numerous reporting instruments. These data are in turn used to assess historical trends and make policy decisions in response to what has been learned. For example, one leading source of information about drug use in America is the annual federal Substance Abuse and Mental Health Services Administration's National Survey on Drug Use and Health. It currently reports that there continues to be more than 19 million Americans over 12 years of age who are current users of illicit drugs. The most widely used illicit drug is marijuana with approximately 14 million users—a figure that has remained constant for the past five years. Approximately 51 percent of Americans over 12 are drinkers of alcohol; over 43 percent of full-time enrolled college students are binge drinkers (defined as consuming five or more drinks during a single drinking occasion). Approximately 29 percent of Americans over 12 use tobacco. Almost 23 million people are believed to be drug-dependent on alcohol or illicit drugs. There are approximately five million people using prescription painkillers for nonmedical reasons—an alarming trend. The size of the economy associated with drug use is staggering;

© The McGraw-Hill Companies, Inc./John Flournoy, photographer

Americans continue to spend more than $70 billion a year on illegal drugs alone.

Drugs impact our most powerful public institutions on many fronts. Drugs are *the* business of our criminal justice system, and drugs compete with terrorism, war, and other major national security concerns as demanding military issues. Over $3 billion per year is committed to the Department of Homeland Security to strengthen drug-related land and maritime border interdictions. The cost of illegal street drugs is up, and the post-9/11 national security infrastructure is impacting historical patterns of trafficking. And the relationship between drug trafficking and terrorism has focused added military emphasis on drug fighting. As the war in Iraq, Afghanistan, and Pakistan continues, U.S. drug agents in those countries are increasing efforts to contain the expanding heroin trade, a major source of funding for the Taliban. As you read through the pages of this book, the pervasive nature of drug-related influences on everyday life will become more apparent.

The lessons of our drug legacy are harsh, whether they are the subjects of public health or public policy. Methamphetamine is now recognized as having produced consequences equal to or surpassing those of crack. The entire dynamic of illicit drug use is changing. Once quiet rural towns, counties, and states have reported epidemics of methamphetamine abuse over the past 10 years, and these suggest comparisons to the inner-urban crack epidemics of the 1980s. The current level of drug-related violence in Mexico is out of control and is firmly in control of the U.S. drug market. This issue is the most dangerous emerging drug problem.

Families, schools, and workplaces continue to be impacted by the many facets of drug abuse. One in three Americans has a close relationship to someone who abuses drugs. It is only because of war, terrorism, and a struggling economy that more public attention toward drug problems has been diverted. The articles and graphics contained in this unit illustrate the evolving nature of issues influenced by the historical evolution of legal and illegal drug use in America. The changing historical evolution of drug-related phenomena is reflected within the character of all issues and controversies addressed by this book. Unit presents examples of the contemporary and diverse nature of current problems, issues, and concerns about drugs and how they continue to impact all aspects of public and private life. The drug-related events of today continue to forecast the drug-related events of tomorrow. The areas of public health, public policy, controlling crime, and education exist as good examples for discussion. As you read this and other literature on drug-related events, the dynamics of past and present drug-related linkages will become apparent.

History of Alcohol and Drinking around the World

David J. Hanson

Alcohol is a product that has provided a variety of functions for people throughout all history. From the earliest times to the present, alcohol has played important role in religion and worship. Historically, alcoholic beverages have served as sources of needed nutrients d have been widely used for their medicinal, antiseptic, d analgesic properties. The role of such beverages as irst quenchers is obvious and they play an important role enhancing the enjoyment and quality of life. They can a social lubricant, can facilitate relaxation, can provide armacological pleasure, and can increase the pleasure of ting. Thus, while alcohol has always been misused by a inority of drinkers, it has proved to be beneficial to most.

ncient Period

'hile no one knows when beverage alcohol was first used, was presumably the result of a fortuitous accident that curred at least tens of thousands of years ago. However, e discovery of late Stone Age beer jugs has established the ct that intentionally fermented beverages existed at least early as the Neolithic period (cir. 10,000 B.C.) (Patrick, 52, pp. 12–13), and it has been suggested that beer may ve preceded bread as a staple (Braidwood et al, 1953; Katz d Voigt, 1987); wine clearly appeared as a finished product in Egyptian pictographs around 4,000 B.C (Lucia, 1963a, 216).

The earliest alcoholic beverages may have been made from rries or honey (Blum *et al,* 1969, p. 25; Rouech, 1960, 8; French, 1890, p. 3) and winemaking may have originated the wild grape regions of the Middle East. Oral tradition corded in the Old Testament (Genesis 9:20) asserts that oah planted a vineyard on Mt. Ararat in what is now eastern rkey. In Sumer, beer and wine were used for medicinal irposes as early as 2,000 B.C (Babor, 1986, p. 1).

Brewing dates from the beginning of civilization in ancient gypt (Cherrington, 1925, v. 1, p. 404) and alcoholic beverges were very important in that country. Symbolic of this is e fact that while many gods were local or familial, Osiris, the god of wine, was worshiped throughout the entire country (Lucia, 1963b, p. 152). The Egyptians believed that this important god also invented beer (King, 1947, p. 11), a beverage that was considered a necessity of life; it was brewed in the home "on an everyday basis" (Marciniak, 1992, p. 2).

Both beer and wine were deified and offered to gods. Cellars and winepresses even had a god whose hieroglyph was a winepress (Ghaliounqui, 1979, p. 5). The ancient Egyptians made at least seventeen varieties of beer and at least 24 varieties of wine (Ghaliounqui, 1979, pp. 8 and 11). Alcoholic beverages were used for pleasure, nutrition, medicine, ritual, remuneration (Cherrington, 1925, v. 1, p. 405) and funerary purposes. The latter involved storing the beverages in tombs of the deceased for their use in the after-life (King, 1947, p. 11; Darby, 1977, p. 576).

Numerous accounts of the period stressed the importance of moderation, and these norms were both secular and religious (Darby, 1977, p. 58). While Egyptians did not generally appear to define inebriety as a problem, they warned against taverns (which were often houses of prostitution) and excessive drinking (Lutz, 1922, pp. 97, 105–108). After reviewing extensive evidence regarding the widespread but generally moderate use of alcoholic beverage, the historian Darby makes a most important observation: all these accounts are warped by the fact that moderate users "were overshadowed by their more boisterous counterparts who added 'color' to history" (Darby, 1977, p. 590). Thus, the intemperate use of alcohol throughout history receives a disproportionate amount of attention. Those who abuse alcohol cause problems, draw attention to themselves, are highly visible and cause legislation to be enacted. The vast majority of drinkers, who neither experience nor cause difficulties, are not noteworthy. Consequently, observers and writers largely ignore moderation.

Beer was the major beverage among the Babylonians, and as early as 2,700 B.C. they worshiped a wine goddess and other wine deities (Hyams, 1965, pp. 38–39). Babylonians regularly used both beer and wine as offerings to their gods (Lutz, 1922, pp. 125–126). Around 1,750 B.C, the famous Code of Hammurabi devoted attention to alcohol. However, there were no penalties for drunkenness; in fact, it was not even mentioned. The concern was fair commerce in alcohol (Popham, 1978, pp. 232–233). Nevertheless, although it was not a crime, it would appear that the Babylonians were critical of drunkenness (Lutz, 1922, pp. 115–116).[1]

A variety of alcoholic beverages have been used in China since prehistoric times (Granet, 1957, p. 144). Alcohol was considered a spiritual (mental) food rather than a material (physical) food, and extensive documentary evidence attests to the important role it played in the religious life (Hucker, 1975, p. 28; Fei-Peng, 1982, p. 13). "In ancient times people always drank when holding a memorial ceremony, offering sacrifices to gods or their ancestors, pledging resolution before going into battle, celebrating victory, before feuding and official executions, for taking an oath of allegiance, while attending the ceremonies of birth, marriage, reunions, departures, death, and festival banquets" (Fei-Peng, 1982, p. 13).

A Chinese imperial edict of about 1,116 B.C. makes it clear that the use of alcohol in moderation was believed to be prescribed by heaven. Whether or not it was prescribed by heaven, it was clearly beneficial to the treasury. At the time of Marco Polo (1254–1324) it was drunk daily (Gernet, 1962, p. 139) and was one of the treasury's biggest sources of income (Balazs, 1964, p. 97).

Alcoholic beverages were widely used in all segments of Chinese society, were used as a source of inspiration, were important for hospitality, were an antidote for fatigue, and were sometimes misused (Samuelson, 1878, pp. 19–20, 22, 26–27; Fei-Peng, 1982, p. 137; Simons, 1991, pp. 448–459). Laws against making wine were enacted and repealed forty-one times between 1,100 B.C. and A.D. 1,400. (Alcoholism and Drug Addiction Research Foundation of Ontario, 1961, p. 5). However, a commentator writing around 650 B.C. asserted that people "will not do without beer. To prohibit it and secure total abstinence from it is beyond the power even of sages. Hence, therefore, we have warnings on the abuse of it" (quoted in Rouecbe, 1963, p. 179; similar translation quoted in Samuelson, 1878, p. 20).

While the art of wine making reached the Hellenic peninsula by about 2,000 B.C. (Younger, 1966, p. 79), the first alcoholic beverage to obtain widespread popularity in what is now Greece was mead, a fermented beverage made from honey and water. However, by 1,700 B.C., wine making was commonplace, and during the next thousand years wine drinking assumed the same function so commonly found around the world: It was incorporated into religious rituals, it became important in hospitality, it was used for medicinal purposes and it became an integral part of daily meals (Babor, 1986, pp. 2–3). As a beverage, it was drunk in many ways: warm and chilled, pure and mixed with water, plain and spiced (Raymond, 1927, p. 53).

Contemporary writers observed that the Greeks were among the most temperate of ancient peoples. This appears to result from their rules stressing moderate drinking, their praise of temperance, their practice of diluting wine with water, and their avoidance of excess in general (Austin, 1985, p. 11). An exception to this ideal of moderation was the cult of Dionysus, in which intoxication was believed to bring people closer to their deity (Sournia, 1990, pp. 5–6; Raymond, 1927, p. 55).

While habitual drunkenness was rare, intoxication at banquets and festivals was not unusual (Austin, 1985, p. 11). In fact, the symposium, a gathering of men for an evening of conversation, entertainment and drinking typically ended in intoxication (Babor, 1986, p. 4). However, while there are no references in ancient Greek literature to mass drunkenness among the Greeks, there are references to it among foreign peoples (Patrick, 1952, p. 18). By 425 B.C., warnings against intemperance, especially at symposia, appear to become more frequent (Austin, 1985, pp. 21–22).

Xenophon (431–351 B.C.) and Plato (429–347 B.C.) both praised the moderate use of wine as beneficial to health and happiness, but both were critical of drunkenness, which appears to have become a problem. Hippocrates (cir. 460–370 B.C.) identified numerous medicinal properties of wine, which had long been used for its therapeutic value (Lucia, 1963a, pp. 36–40). Later, both Aristode (384–322 B.C.) and Zeno (cir. 336–264 B.C.) were very critical of drunkenness (Austin, 1985, pp. 23, 25, and 27).

Among Greeks, the Macedonians viewed intemperance as a sign of masculinity and were well known for their drunkenness. Their king, Alexander the Great (336–323 B.C.), whose mother adhered to the Dionysian cult, developed a reputation for inebriety (Souria, 1990, pp. 8–9; Babor, 1986, p. 5).

The Hebrews were reportedly introduced to wine during their captivity in Egypt. When Moses led them to Canaan (Palestine) around 1,200 B.C., they are reported to have regretted leaving behind the wines of Egypt (Numbers 20:5); however, they found vineyards to be plentiful in their new land (Lutz, 1922, p. 25). Around 850 B.C., the use of wine was criticized by the Rechabites and Nazarites,[2] two conservative nomadic groups who practiced abstinence from alcohol (Lutz, 1922, p. 133; Samuelson, 1878, pp. 62–63).

In 586 B.C., the Hebrews were conquered by the Babylonians and deported to Babylon. However, in 539 B.C., the Persians captured the city and released the Hebrews from their Exile (Daniel 5:1–4). Following the Exile, the Hebrews developed Judaism as it is now known, and they can be said to have become Jews. During the next 200 years, sobriety increased and pockets of antagonism to wine disappeared. It became a common beverage for all classes and ages, including the very young; an important source of nourishment; a prominent part in the festivities of the people; a widely appreciated medicine; an essential provision for any fortress; and an important commodity. In short, it came to be seen as a necessary element in the life of the Hebrews (Raymond, 1927, p. 23).

While there was still opposition to excessive drinking, it was no longer assumed that drinking inevitably led to unkenness. Wine came to be seen as a blessing from God and a symbol of joy (Psalms 104; Zachariah 10:7). These changes in beliefs and behaviors appear to be related to a rejection of belief in pagan gods, a new emphasis on individual morality, and the integration of secular drinking behaviors into religious ceremonies and their subsequent modification (Austin, 1985, pp. 18–19; Patai, 1980, pp. 61–73; Keller, 1970, pp. 290–294). Around 525 B.C., it was ruled that the kiddush (pronouncement of the Sabbath) should be recited over a blessed cup of wine. This established the regular drinking of wine in Jewish ceremonies outside the Temple (Austin, 1985, p. 19).

King Cyrus of Persia frequently praised the virtue of the moderate consumption of alcohol (cir. 525 B.C.). However, ritual intoxication appears to have been used as an adjunct to decision making and, at least after his death, drunkenness was not uncommon (Austin, 1985, p. 19).

Between the founding of Rome in 753 B.C. until the third century B.C., there is consensus among historians that the Romans practiced great moderation in drinking (Austin, 1985, p. 17). After the Roman conquest of the Italian peninsula and the rest of the Mediterranean basin (509 to 133 B.C.), the traditional Roman values of temperance, frugality and simplicity were gradually replaced by heavy drinking, ambition, degeneracy and corruption (Babor, 1986, p. 7; Wallbank & Taylor, 1954, p. 163). The Dionysian rites (Bacchanalia, in Latin) spread to Italy during this period and were subsequently outlawed by the Senate (Lausanne, 1969, p. 4; Cherrington, 1925, v. 1, pp. 251–252).

Practices that encouraged excessive drinking included drinking before meals on an empty stomach, inducing vomiting to permit the consumption of more food and wine, and drinking games. The latter included, for example, rapidly consuming as many cups as indicated by a throw of the dice (Babor, 1986, p. 10).

By the second and first centuries B.C., intoxication was no longer a rarity, and most prominent men of affairs (for example, Cato the Elder and Julius Caesar) were praised for their moderation in drinking. This would appear to be in response to growing misuse of alcohol in society, because before that time temperance was not singled out for praise as exemplary behavior. As the republic continued to decay, excessive drinking spread and some, such as Marc Antony (d. 30 B.C.), even took pride in their destructive drinking behavior (Austin, 1985, pp. 28 and 32–33).

Early Christian Period

With the dawn of Christianity and its gradual displacement of the previously dominant religions, the drinking attitudes and behaviors of Europe began to be influenced by the New Testament (Babor, 1986, p. 11). The earliest biblical writings after the death of Jesus (cir. A.D. 30) contain few references to alcohol. This may have reflected the fact that drunkenness was largely an upper-status vice with which Jesus had little contact (Raymond, 1927, pp. 81–82). Austin (1985, p. 35) has pointed out that Jesus used wine (Matthew 15:11; Luke 7:33–35) and approved of its moderate consumption (Matthew 15:11). On the other hand, he severely attacked drunkenness (Luke 21:34, 12:42; Matthew 24:45–51). The later writings of St. Paul (d. 64?) deal with alcohol in detail and are important to Christian doctrine on the subject. He considered wine to be a creation of God and therefore inherently good (1 Timothy 4:4), recommended its use for medicinal purposes (1 Timothy 5:23), but consistently condemned drunkenness (1 Corinthians 3:16–17, 5:11, 6:10; Galatians 5:19–21; Romans 13:3) and recommended abstinence for those who could not control their drinking.[3]

However, late in the second century, several heretical sects rejected alcohol and called for abstinence. By the late fourth and early fifth centuries, the Church responded by asserting that wine was an inherently good gift of God to be used and enjoyed. While individuals may choose not to drink, to despise wine was heresy. The Church advocated its moderate use but rejected excessive or abusive use as a sin. Those individuals who could not drink in moderation were urged to abstain (Austin, 1985, pp. 44 and 47–48).

It is clear that both the Old and New Testaments are clear and consistent in their condemnation of drunkenness. However, some Christians today argue that whenever "wine" was used by Jesus or praised as a gift of God, it was really grape juice; only when it caused drunkenness was it wine. Thus, they interpret the Bible as asserting that grape juice is good and that drinking it is acceptable to God but that wine is bad and that drinking it is unacceptable. This reasoning appears to be incorrect for at least two reasons. First, neither the Hebrew nor Biblical Greek word for wine can be translated or interpreted as referring to grape juice. Secondly, grape juice would quickly ferment into wine in the warm climate of the Mediterranean region without refrigeration or modern methods of preservation (Royce, 1986, pp. 55–56; Raymond, 1927, pp. 18–22; Hewitt, 1980, pp. 11–12).

The spread of Christianity and of viticulture in Western Europe occurred simultaneously (Lausanne, 1969, p. 367; Sournia, 1990, p. 12). Interestingly, St. Martin of Tours (316–397) was actively engaged in both spreading the Gospel and planting vineyards (Patrick, 1952, pp. 26–27).

In an effort to maintain traditional Jewish culture against the rise of Christianity, which was converting numerous Jews (Wallbank & Taylor, 1954, p. 227), detailed rules concerning the use of wine were incorporated into the Talmud. Importantly, wine was integrated into many religious ceremonies in limited quantity (Spiegel, 1979, pp. 20–29; Raymond, 1927, 45–47). In the social and political upheavals that rose as the fall of Rome approached in the fifth century, concern grew among rabbis that Judaism and its culture were in increasing danger.[4] Consequently, more Talmudic rules were laid down concerning the use of wine. These included the amount of wine that could be drunk on the Sabbath, the way in which wine was to be drunk, the legal status of wine in any way connected with idolatry, and the extent of personal responsibility for behavior while intoxicated (Austin, 1985, pp. 36 and 50).

Roman abuse of alcohol appears to have peaked around mid-first century (Jellinek, 1976, pp. 1,736–1,739). Wine had become the most popular beverage, and as Rome attracted a large influx of displaced persons, it was distributed free or at cost (Babor, 1986, pp. 7–8). This led to occasional excesses at festivals, victory triumphs and other celebrations, as described by contemporaries. The four emperors who ruled from A.D. 37 to A.D. 69 were all known for their abusive drinking. However, the emperors who followed were known for their temperance, and literary sources suggest that problem drinking decreased substantially in the Empire. Although there continued to be some criticisms of abusive drinking over the next several hundred years, most evidence indicates a decline of such behavior (Austin, 1985, pp. 37–44, p. 46, pp. 48–50). The fall of Rome and the Western Roman Empire occurred in 476 (Wallbank & Taylor, 1954, pp. 220–221).

Around A.D. 230, the Greek scholar Athenaeus wrote extensively on drinking and advocated moderation. The extensive attention to drinking, famous drinks, and drinking cups (of which he described 100) reflected the importance of wine to the Greeks (Austin, 1985, pp. 45–46).

The Middle Ages

The Middle Ages, that period of approximately one thousand years between the fall of Rome and the beginning of the High Renaissance (cir. 1500), saw numerous developments in life in general and in drinking in particular. In the early Middle Ages, mead, rustic beers, and wild fruit wines became increasingly popular, especially among Celts, Anglo-Saxons, Germans, and Scandinavians. However, wines remained the beverage of preference in the Romance countries (what is now Italy, Spain and France) (Babor, 1986, p. 11).

With the collapse of the Roman Empire and decline of urban life, religious institutions, particularly monasteries, became the repositories of the brewing and winemaking techniques that had been earlier developed (Babor, 1986, p. 11). While rustic beers continued to be produced in homes, the art of brewing essentially became the province of monks, who carefully guarded their knowledge (Cherrington, 1925, v. 1, p. 405). Monks brewed virtually all beer of good quality until the twelfth century. Around the thirteenth century, hops (which both flavors and preserves) became a common ingredient in some beers, especially in northern Europe (Wilson, 1991, p. 375).[5] Ale, often a thick and nutritious soupy beverage, soured quickly and was made for local consumption (Austin, 1985, p. 54, pp. 87–88).

Not surprisingly, the monasteries also maintained viticulture. Importantly, they had the resources, security, and stability in that often-turbulent time to improve the quality of their

vines slowly over 1986, (p. 11). While most wine was ma[...] and consumed locally, some wine trade did continue in sp[...] of the deteriorating roads (Hyams, 1965, p. 151; Wilso[...] 1991, p. 371).

By the millennium, the most popular form of festiviti[...] in England were known as "ales," and both ale and be[...] were at the top of lists of products to be given to lords f[...] rent. As towns were established in twelfth-century German[...] they were granted the privilege of brewing and selling be[...] in their immediate localities. A flourishing artisan brewi[...] industry developed in many towns, about which there w[...] strong civic pride (Cherrington, 1925, v. 1, p. 405; Aus[...] 1985, pp. 68, 74, 82–83).

The most important development regarding alcoh[...] throughout the Middle Ages was probably that of distill[...] tion. Interestingly, considerable disagreement exists concer[...] ing who discovered distillation and when the discovery w[...] made.[6] However, it was Albertus Magnus (1193–1280) wh[...] first clearly described the process which made possible t[...] manufacture of distilled spirits (Patrick, 1952, p. 29). Know[...] edge of the process began to spread slowly among monk[...] physicians and alchemists, who were interested in distill[...] alcohol as a cure for ailments. At that time it was called aq[...] vitae, "water of life,"[7] but was later known as brandy. The latt[...] term was derived from the Dutch brandewijn, meaning bur[...] (or distilled) wine (Seward, 1979, p. 151; Roueche, 196[...] pp. 172–173).

The Black Death and subsequent plagues, which began [...] the mid-fourteenth century, dramatically changed people[...] perception of their lives and place in the cosmos. With [...] understanding or control of the plagues that reduced t[...] population by as much as 82% in some villages, "proce[...] sions of flagellants mobbed city and village streets, hopin[...] by the pains they inflicted on themselves and each other, [...] take the edge off the plagues they attributed to God's wra[...] over human folly" (Slavin, 1973, pp. 12–16).

Some dramatically increased their consumption of alc[...] hol in the belief that this might protect them from the myst[...] rious disease, while others thought that through moderati[...] in all things, including alcohol, they could be saved. It wou[...] appear that, on balance, consumption of alcohol was hig[...] For example, in Bavaria, beer consumption was probab[...] about 300 liters per capita a year (compared to 150 lite[...] today) and in Florence wine consumption was about t[...] barrels per capita a year. Understandably, the consumpti[...] of distilled spirits, which was exclusively for medicinal p[...] poses, increased in popularity (Austin, 1985, pp. 104–10[...] 107–108).

As the end of the Middle Ages approached, the popula[...] ity of beer spread to England, France and Scotland (Aust[...] pp. 118–119). Beer brewers were recognized officially [...] a guild in England (Monckton, 1966, pp. 69–70), and t[...] adulteration of beer or wine became punishable by death [...] Scotland (Cherrington, 1929, vol. 5, p. 2,383). Important[...]

e consumption of spirits as a beverage began to occur
Braudel, 1974, p. 171).

Early Modern Period

he early modern period was generally characterized by
creasing prosperity and wealth. Towns and cities grew in
ze and number, foreign lands were discovered and colo-
zed, and trade expanded. Perhaps more importantly, there
eveloped a new view of the world. The medieval empha-
s on other-worldliness—the belief that life in this world is
ly a preparation for heaven—slowly gave way, especially
nong the wealthy and well educated, to an interest in life in
e here and now (Wallbank & Taylor, 1954, p. 513).

The Protestant Reformation and rise of aggressive national
ates destroyed the ideal of a universal Church overseeing
Holy Roman Empire. Rationality, individualism, and sci-
nce heavily impacted the prevalent emotional idealism,
mmunalism, and traditional religion (Wallbank & Taylor,
954, pp. 513–518; Slavin, 1973, ch. 5–7).

However, the Protestant leaders such as Luther, Calvin,
e leaders of the Anglican Church and even the Puritans did
ot differ substantially from the teachings of the Catholic
hurch: alcohol was a gift of God and created to be used in
oderation for pleasure, enjoyment and health; drunkenness
as viewed as a sin (Austin, 1985, p. 194).

From this period through at least the beginning of the
ghteenth century, attitudes toward drinking were charac-
rized by a continued recognition of the positive nature of
oderate consumption and an increased concern over the
egative effects of drunkenness. The latter, which was gen-
ally viewed as arising out of the increased self-indulgence
the time, was seen as a threat to spiritual salvation and
cietal well being. Intoxication was also inconsistent with
e emerging emphasis on rational mastery of self and world
d on work and efficiency (Austin, 1985, pp. 129–130).

However, consumption of alcohol was often high. In the
xteenth century, alcohol beverage consumption reached
00 liters per person per year in Valladolid, Spain, and Polish
easants consumed up to three liters of beer per day (Braudel,
974, pp. 236–238). In Coventry, the average amount of beer
d ale consumed was about 17 pints per person per week,
mpared to about three pints today (Monckton, 1966, p. 95);
tionwide, consumption was about one pint per day per cap-
a. Swedish beer consumption may have been 40 times higher
an in modern Sweden. English sailors received a ration of
gallon of beer per day, while soldiers received two-thirds of
gallon. In Denmark, the usual consumption of beer appears
have been a gallon per day for adult laborers and sailors
Austin, 1985, pp. 170, 186, 192).

However, the production and distribution of spirits spread
owly. Spirit drinking was still largely for medicinal pur-
ses throughout most of the sixteenth century. It has been
id of distilled alcohol that "the sixteenth century created it;

the seventeenth century consolidated it; the eighteenth popu-
larized it" (Braudel, 1967, p. 170).

A beverage that clearly made its debut during the
seventeenth century was sparkling champagne. The credit
for that development goes primarily to Dom Perignon, the
wine-master in a French abbey. Around 1668, he used strong
bottles, invented a more efficient cork (and one that could
contain the effervescence in those strong bottles), and began
developing the technique of blending the contents. However,
another century would pass before problems, especially
bursting bottles, would be solved and sparkling champagne
would become popular (Younger, 1966, pp. 345–346; Doxat,
1971, p. 54; Seward, 1979, pp. 139–143).

The original grain spirit, whiskey, appears to have first been
distilled in Ireland. While its specific origins are unknown
(Magee, 1980, p. 7; Wilson, 1973, p. 7) there is evidence that
by the sixteenth century it was widely consumed in some
parts of Scotland (Roueche, 1963, pp. 175–176). It was also
during the seventeenth century that Franciscus Sylvius (or
Franz de la Boe), a professor of medicine at the University
of Leyden, distilled spirits from grain.

Distilled spirit was generally flavored with juniper ber-
ries. The resulting beverage was known as junever, the
Dutch word for "juniper." The French changed the name to
genievre, which the English changed to "geneva" and then
modified to "gin"[8] (Roueche, 1963, pp. 173–174). Originally
used for medicinal purposes, the use of gin as a social drink
did not grow rapidly at first (Doxat, 1972, p. 98; Watney,
1976, p. 10). However, in 1690, England passed "An Act for
the Encouraging of the Distillation of Brandy and Spirits
from Corn" and within four years the annual production of
distilled spirits, most of which was gin, reached nearly one
million gallons (Roueche, 1963, p. 174).

The seventeenth century also saw the Virginia colonists
continue the traditional belief that alcoholic beverages are a
natural food and are good when used in moderation. In fact,
beer arrived with the first colonists, who considered it essential to their well being (Baron, 1962, pp. 3–8). The Puritan
minister Increase Mather preached in favor of alcohol but
against its abuse: "Drink is in itself a good creature of God,
and to be received with thankfulness, but the abuse of drink
is from Satan; the wine is from God, but the Drunkard is
from the Devil" (quoted in Rorabaugh, 1979, p. 30). During
that century the first distillery was established in the colonies
on what is now Staten Island (Roueche, 1963, p. 178), cultivation of hops began in Massachusetts, and both brewing and
distilling were legislatively encouraged in Maryland (Austin,
1985, pp. 230 and 249).

Rum is produced by distilling fermented molasses, which
is the residue left after sugar has been made from sugar cane.
Although it was introduced to the world, and presumably
invented, by the first European settlers in the West Indies, no
one knows when it was first produced or by what individual.
But by 1657, a rum distillery was operating in Boston. It was

highly successful and within a generation the manufacture of rum would become colonial New England's largest and most prosperous industry (Roueche, 1963, p. 178).

The dawn of the eighteenth century saw Parliament pass legislation designed to encourage the use of grain for distilling spirits. In 1685, consumption of gin had been slightly over one-half million gallons (Souria, 1990, p. 20). By 1714, gin production stood at two million gallons (Roueche, 1963, p. 174). In 1727, official (declared and taxed) production reached five million gallons; six years later the London area alone produced eleven million gallons of gin (French, 1890, p. 271; Samuelson, 1878, pp. 160–161; Watney, 1976, p. 16).

The English government actively promoted gin production to utilize surplus grain and to raise revenue. Encouraged by public policy, very cheap spirits flooded the market at a time when there was little stigma attached to drunkenness and when the growing urban poor in London sought relief from the newfound insecurities and harsh realities of urban life (Watney, 1976, p. 17; Austin, 1985, pp. xxi–xxii). Thus developed the so-called Gin Epidemic.

While the negative effects of that phenomenon may have been exaggerated[9] (Sournia, 1990, p. 21; Mathias, 1959, p. xxv), Parliament passed legislation in 1736 to discourage consumption by prohibiting the sale of gin in quantities of less than two gallons and raising the tax on it dramatically.[10] However, the peak in consumption was reached seven years later, when the nation of six and one-half million people drank over 18 million gallons of gin. And most was consumed by the small minority of the population then living in London and other cities; people in the countryside largely remained loyal to beer, ale and cider (Doxat, 1972, pp. 98–100; Watney, 1976, p.17).

After its dramatic peak, gin consumption rapidly declined. From 18 million gallons in 1743, it dropped to just over seven million gallons in 1751 and to less than two million by 1758, and generally declined to the end of the century (Ashton, 1955, p. 243). A number of factors appear to have converged to discourage consumption of gin. These include the production of higher quality beer of lower price, rising corn prices and taxes which eroded the price advantage of gin, a temporary ban on distilling, a stigmatization of drinking gin, an increasing criticism of drunkenness, a newer standard of behavior that criticized coarseness and excess, increased tea and coffee consumption, an increase in piety and increasing industrialization with a consequent emphasis on sobriety and labor efficiency (Sournia, 1990, p. 22; King, 1947, p. 117; Austin, 1985, pp. xxiii–xxiv, 324–325, 351; Younger, 1966, p. 341).

While drunkenness was still an accepted part of life in the eighteenth century (Austin, 1985, p. xxv), the nineteenth century would bring a change in attitudes as a result of increasing industrialization and the need for a reliable and punctual work force (Porter, 1990, p. xii). Self-discipline was needed in place of self-expression, and task orientation had to replace relaxed conviviality. Drunkenness would come to be define as a threat to industrial efficiency and growth.

Problems commonly associated with industrializatio and rapid urbanization were also attributed to alcohol. Thu problems such as urban crime, poverty and high infant mortality rates were blamed on alcohol, although "it is likely tha gross overcrowding and unemployment had much to do wit these problems" (Soumia, 1990, p. 21). Over time, more an more personal, social and religious/moral problems woul be blamed on alcohol. And not only would it be enough t prevent drunkenness; any consumption of alcohol woul come to be seen as unacceptable. Groups that began by pro moting temperance—the moderate use of alcohol—woul ultimately become abolitionist and press for the complet and total prohibition of the production and distribution o beverage alcohol. Unfortunately, this would not eliminat social problems but would compound the situation by crea ing additional problems.

Summary and Conclusion

It is clear that alcohol has been highly valued and in continu ous use by peoples throughout history. Reflecting its vita role, consumption of alcohol in moderation has rarely bee questioned throughout most of recorded time. To the con trary, "Fermented dietary beverage . . . was so common a element in the various cultures that it was taken for granted a one of the basic elements of survival and self-preservation (Lucia, 1963b, p. 165). Indicative of its value is the fact th it has frequently been acceptable as a medium of exchang For example, in Medieval England, ale was often used to pa toll, rent or debts (Watney, 1974, p. 16).

From the earliest times alcohol has played an importa role in religion,"[11] typically seen as a gift of deities ar closely associated with their worship. Religious rejection alcohol appears to be a rare phenomenon. When it does occu such rejection may be unrelated to alcohol per se but refle other considerations. For example, the nomadic Rechabite rejected wine because they associated it with an unaccep able agricultural life style. Nazarites abstained only durin the period of their probation, after which they returned drinking (Sournia, 1990, p. 5; Samuelson, 1878, pp. 62–63 Among other reasons, Mohammed may have forbidden alc hol in order to further distinguish his followers from those other religions (Royce, 1986, p. 57).

Alcoholic beverages have also been an important sour of nutrients and calories (Braudel, 1974, p. 175). In ancie Egypt, the phrase "bread and beer" stood for all food and w also a common greeting. Many alcoholic beverages, such Egyptian bouza and Sudanese merissa, contain high leve of protein, fat and carbohydrates, a fact that helps expla the frequent lack of nutritional deficiencies in some popul tions whose diets are generally poor. Importantly, the leve of amino acids and vitamins increase during fermentatio

ihaliounqui, 1979, pp. 8–9). While modern food technol-
3y uses enrichment or fortification to improve the nutri-
on of foods, it is possible to achieve nutritional enrichment
aturally through fermentation (Steinkraus, 1979, p. 36).

Alcoholic beverages have long served as thirst quench-
s. Water pollution is far from new; to the contrary, sup-
ies have generally been either unhealthful or questionable
best. Ancient writers rarely wrote about water, except
a warning (Ghaliounqui, 1979, p. 3). Travelers crossing
hat is now Zaire in 1648 reported having to drink water
at resembled horse's urine. In the late eighteenth century
ost Parisians drank water from a very muddy and often
iemically polluted Seine (Braudel, 1967, pp. 159–161).
offee and tea were not introduced into Europe until the
id-seventeenth century, and it was another hundred or more
ars before they were commonly consumed on a daily basis
Austin, 1985, pp. 251, 254, 351, 359, 366).

Another important function of alcohol has been therapeu-
: or medicinal. Current research suggests that the moder-
e consumption of alcohol is preferable to abstinence. It
ppears to reduce the incidence of coronary heart disease
.g., Razay, 1992; Jackson *et al.*, 1991; Klatsky *et al.*,
990, p. 745; Rimm *et al.*, 1991; Miller *et al.*, 1990), cancer
.g., Bofetta & Garfinkel, 1990) and osteoporosis (e.g.,
avaler & Van Thiel, 1992), among many other diseases and
onditions, and to increase longevity (e.g., DeLabry *et al.*,
992). It has clearly been a major analgesic, and one widely
ailable to people in pain. Relatedly, it has provided relief
om the fatigue of hard labor.

Not to be underestimated is the important role alcohol has
rved in enhancing the enjoyment and quality of life. It can
serve as a social lubricant, can provide entertainment, can facilitate relaxation, can provide pharmacological pleasure and can
enhance the flavors of food (Gastineau *et al.*, 1979).

While alcohol has always been misused by a minority of
drinkers, it has clearly proved to be beneficial to most. In
the words of the founding Director of the National Institute
on Alcohol Abuse and Alcoholism, ". . . alcohol has existed
longer than all human memory. It has outlived generations,
nations, epochs and ages. It is a part of us, and that is fortu-
nate indeed. For although alcohol will always be the master
of some, for most of us it will continue to be the servant of
man" (Chafetz, 1965, p. 223).

References

Hanson, David J. *Preventing Alcohol Abuse: Alcohol, Culture and Control.* Wesport, CT: Praeger, 1995. www2.potsdam.edu/ hansondj/controversies/1114796842.html. Retrieved May 2, 2008

Marley, David. *Chemical Addiction, Drug Use, and Treatment.* MedScape Today 2001 www.medscape.com/viewarticle/418525. Retrieved May 2,2008

Critical Thinking

1. Why have patterns related to alcohol use remained consistent around the world for centuries?

2. Consider the theme(s) of alcohol use throughout history as
   presented in this article and describe how alcohol use today
   relates to those themes.

Adapted from **DAVID J. HANSON,** PhD *Preventing Alcohol Abuse: Alcohol, Culture and Control.* Westport, CT: Praeger, 1995.

Can Sips at Home Prevent Binges?

ERIC ASIMOV

Parents always want to share their passions with their children. Whether you're a fan of baseball or the blues, sailing or tinkering with old cars, few things are as rewarding as seeing a spark of receptivity in the eyes of the next generation.

It usually doesn't take. Most of the time kids—teenagers, anyway—would as soon snicker at their old man's obsessions as indulge him. Even so, I can't help hoping that my sons might share my taste in music and food, books and movies, ball teams and politics. Why should wine be any different?

It's the alcohol, of course, which makes wine not just tricky but potentially hazardous. Nonetheless, I would like to teach my sons—16 and 17—that wine is a wonderful part of a meal. I want to teach them to enjoy it while also drumming it into them that when abused, wine, like any other alcoholic beverage, can be a grave danger.

As they were growing up I occasionally gave them tastes from my glass—an unusual wine, perhaps, or a taste of Champagne on New Year's Eve. They've had sips at Seders and they see wine nightly at our dinner table. With both boys now in high school, I thought it was time to offer them the option of small tastes at dinner.

In European wine regions, a new parent might dip a finger in the local pride and wipe it lovingly across an infant's lips— "just to give the taste." A child at the family table might have a spoonful of wine added to the water, because it says, "You are one of us." A teenager might have a small glass of wine, introducing an adult pleasure in a safe and supervised manner. This is how I imagined it in my house.

But about a year ago, my wife attended a gathering on the Upper East Side sponsored by several high schools addressing the topic of teenagers and alcohol.

The highly charged discussion centered on the real dangers of binge drinking and peer pressure, of brain damage and parental over-permissiveness, and of the law.

One authority disparaged the European model, saying that teenage drinking in Europe—never mind which part—is much worse than it is in the United States. The underlying message was that nothing good comes from mixing alcohol and teenagers.

My wife was shaken. We agreed to hold off on the tasting plan. But I decided to try to get some answers myself.

I found ample evidence of the dangers of abusive drinking. Recent studies have shown that heavy drinking does mor damage to the teenage brain than previously suspected, whil the part of the brain responsible for judgment is not even full formed until the age of 25.

"If we were to argue that responsible drinking requires responsible brain, theoretically we wouldn't introduce alco hol until 25," said Dr. Ralph I. Lopez, a clinical professor pediatrics at Weill-Cornell Medical College who specializes adolescents.

The law specifies 21 as the age when people can buy an drink alcohol. Bill Crowley, a spokesman for the New Yor State Liquor Authority, confirmed that it was illegal to giv anyone underage a taste of an alcoholic beverage in a restau rant, cafe or bar. But in the home?

"We don't have any jurisdiction over what happens in th home," Mr. Crowley said. Of course, each state's laws diffe and lack of jurisdiction doesn't mean immunity. The police social service agencies could intervene if underage bingein were encouraged in the home. And when driving is a facto everything changes. But inside the home, the law, at least, seem to permit the small tastes that I had in mind.

Even so, are small tastes justified? Abundant research show the dangers of heavy drinking and the necessity of getting hel with teenage alcohol abuse. But little guidance is offered teaching teenagers about the pleasures of wine with a meal.

It would be easy to preach abstinence to children unt they're 21, but is it naive and even irresponsible to think th teenagers won't experiment? Might forbidding even a taste wine with a meal actually encourage secrecy and recklessnes

Some experts think so. Dr. Lopez began to offer his daught a little wine at dinner when she was 13.

"You have to look at a family and decide where alcohol fits he said. "If you demonstrate the beauty of wine, just as yc would Grandma's special pie, then it augments a meal. How ever, if there is an issue about drinking within a family then it a different situation."

If a family member had an alcohol problem, or if cocktai were served regularly for relaxation, he said, "That's a differe message than wine at the table."

I called Dr. Paul Steinberg, a psychiatrist in Washington, wl is the former director of counseling at Georgetown Universit

"The best evidence shows that teaching kids to drink respon-bly is better than shutting them off entirely from it," he told me. "You want to introduce your kids to it, and get across the oint that that this is to be enjoyed but not abused."

He said that the most dangerous day of a young person's life the 21st birthday, when legality is celebrated all too fervently. ntroducing wine as a part of a meal, he said, was a significant rotection against bingeing behavior.

What is the evidence? In 1983, Dr. George E. Vaillant, a rofessor of psychiatry at Harvard University, published "The atural History of Alcoholism," a landmark work that drew on 40-year survey of hundreds of men in Boston and Cambridge.

Dr. Vaillant compared 136 men who were alcoholics with en who were not. Those who grew up in families where alco-ol was forbidden at the table, but was consumed away from e home, apart from food, were seven times more likely to be coholics that those who came from families where wine was erved with meals but drunkenness was not tolerated.

He concluded that teenagers should be taught to enjoy wine ith family meals, and 25 years later Dr. Vaillant stands by his commendation. "The theoretical position is: driving a car, ooting a rifle, using alcohol are all dangerous activities," he ld me, "and the way you teach responsibility is to let parents ach appropriate use."

"If you are taught to drink in a ceremonial way with food, en the purpose of alcohol is taste and celebration, not inebria-on," he added. "If you are forbidden to use it until college then u drink to get drunk."

In a more recent study of 80 teenagers and 80 young adults in aly, Lee Strunin, a professor at the Boston University School Public Health, found that drinking wine in a family setting fered some protection against bingeing and may encourage oderate drinking. But she cautioned against extrapolating om Italy to the United States.

Her colleague, David Rosenbloom, director of the School of Public Health's Youth Alcohol Prevention Center, emphasized that family context was crucial. "Does the kid see the parents drunk?" he asked. "Does the kid understand expectations? Is there violence in the family setting?"

"It is certainly possible that in some family contexts the introduction of wine at family dinners could have a mild pro-tective factor," he said, adding that he believes that expecting abstinence is a perfectly reasonable parental position.

In the best of all possible worlds, I suppose, young adults would not touch alcohol until they turn 25 and then would instantly understand the pleasures of moderate consumption. It seems to me as silly to imagine that as it is to expect the same at 21.

Although the issue is not settled in my household, my cau-tious opinion now is that my teenage sons have more to gain than to lose by having a taste of wine now and then with dinner. By taste, I mean just that: a couple of sips, perhaps, not a full glass, and decidedly not for any of their friends, whose own parents must make their own decisions.

The years between ages 15 and 25 are dangerous straits, and it doesn't help to know that alcohol is associated with many of the hazards young adults face. Finding that sweet spot between sanctimony and self-centered frivolity is a parent's job. I think I'm there, but it's not quite comfortable.

Critical Thinking

1. What is the European model, so to speak, with regard to underage drinking?

2. Do you feel that limited exposure in a social context to alcohol is beneficial in preventing alcohol abuse later in life?

3. What is the difference between social drinking and binge drinking?

Tackling Top Teen Problem— Prescription Drugs

Taking prescription drugs makes you feel 'chill', a teenager recently told the Bulletin, "and nothing worries you.

GEORGE LAUBY AND KAMIE WHEELOCK

Many people ages 11 to 18 routinely take pills such as Vicodin, Percocet, Xanax, Klonopin, Adderal, Concerta, Ritalin or generic knockoffs of the same.

The illegal use of prescription drugs looms larger than problem drinking or marijuana use, North Platte High School Principal Jim Whitney said.

The drugs are stolen from medicine cabinets, parents' or grandparents' medicine cabinets, or from a friend's house, or even bought off the Internet.

Drugs are passed to friends, either for free or for money. Some pills are reportedly taken by the handful at so-called "pharma parties" where pills are reportedly dumped in a bowl for anyone and everyone, and chased down with beers.

"You are just messed up," a student said of the effects. "You don't even want to move. You just want to lay there and stare off into space."

"Prescription drug abuse has been around in different forms for a long time," Whitney said, "but in the last year and a half it has probably become more popular than alcohol."

In a 2007 Lincoln County survey, 12–14 percent of high school students said they had abused prescription drugs. The same survey found more than 3 percent of sixth graders abused the drugs, and more than 5 percent of eighth graders.

The number who get caught is much lower. Only 12 students have been caught with illegal prescription drugs this year at the high school, Whitney said. Nearly all of them were suspended.

Kids steal drugs not just to chill, but to sell. Many pills bring from $2–5 each. Oxycontin can bring $40 each, according to a high school user who asked to remain anonymous.

"Have you ever attended a pharma or pill party?" w asked the student.

"I wouldn't call them pill parties," she said, "but pretty much any party there's someone who has pills, is on pills. Recently a couple of people had some Adder and we were snorting it. Adderal is popular because makes it so you can drink more and you can stay up a night long."

Adderal is an amphetamine usually prescribed to tre attention deficit hyperactivity.

Taking the Call

The growing problem prompted a group of North Plat residents to fight back. Listeners are hearing hundreds radio announcements on virtually every North Platte rad station, alerting the public to the problem.

The group has distributed thousands of pamphle bundles of posters and dozens of banners.

They have set a day—April 25—aside to collect pr scription drugs, including syringes and over-the-count drugs. They will set up a drive-up drop point at the hi school.

The drugs will ultimately be incinerated.

They have lined up a team of powerful speakers wl will talk about the danger, the self-destruction that com with drug abuse.

The group of residents joined together during t Leadership Lincoln County program, wherein 20 peop spend a year learning about major businesses and publ services so they can get good things done.

In one part of the leadership program, the 20 split ir groups of 5–6 people. Each group was challenged develop a public project that will continue into the futu

The group–Wendy Thompson, Wanda Cooper, Sandy Ross, Bob Lantis, Patrick O'Neil and Connie Cook— kicked around ideas. After a visit with law enforcement officials they agreed to tackle the prescription drug problem at the urging of Capt. Jim Parish of the Nebraska State Patrol.

"The more we learned, the more we got involved," said Cook, a driving force in the project. "The information was riveting— and motivating. We learned about some kids at high school who got in trouble. Their parents were completely shocked. We were shocked. We had no idea."

"Now, we're passionate to do something constructive," Cook said. "It's amazing; every day we learn more and more."

"Have you taken other drugs?" the Bulletin asked another student.

"Yeah. I smoke weed like every day and used ecstasy once and I dabbled in coke for a couple of months last year and still do it every once in awhile," he said.

"I tried meth twice, but it made me crazy. I don't want to ever do very much of it; it's bad stuff. I've done mushrooms a couple times too, and of course alcohol is a drug too."

"I'm out of my alcoholic phase but I still drink on the weekends," he said. "I won't buy any drug except weed or alcohol but if someone's offering, I'll do pretty much anything. I'll never do heroin though, but I want to try acid in a few years just to see what it's like."

"Do a lot of your friends take pills?"

"Yeah, pretty much all of them. I have five friends that always have them. They take them pretty much every day."

"What do they think of it?"

"It's not considered a bad thing to do. Pills are the equivalent of smoking weed for people who can't smoke because they are on probation or just don't like pot. Like, the preppy kids do it because their parents would know if they smoked pot because they'd smell it. But most parents have no idea that their kids are getting messed up on pills."

Leadership Is Learning

The leadership group recently dropped posters and flyers at all of Lincoln County's schools, plus Stapleton.

At North Platte's middle schools, they asked the principals if they have caught kids using prescription drugs.

"They told us, 'As far as catching them, no, we've not caught them yet, but we know there are kids here who are stealing drugs so they can sell them to other kids," Cook said.

"We want this information out to the public," she said. "We know there is a need to educate those who are all the way from 101 years old to 10 years old. They need to know it's happening and how bad it is for kids, and the environment."

Cook said kids don't understand the dangers.

"What do you take the most?" we asked a North Platte high school student.

"I started out taking Xanax because I got as many as I wanted, for free. Then I had some Percocet. I loved those but they're too addictive to take for a long time. Most people take pain pills (Vicodin/Percocet), anxiety pills (Xanax/Klonopin), or attention deficit disorder pills (Adderal/Concerta/Ritalin)."

"How much would a kid spend on drugs in an average week?"

"People always gave them to me for free, but the average pill popper could probably spend $50–100 a week. The preppies can spend a lot from their lunch-gas-pocket money."

Harm to Creatures Large and Small

Even when the drugs are thrown away, they are usually flushed down the toilet.

Even when drugs are taken properly, traces enter the waste stream that eventually empties into nature, according to the Environmental Protection Agency.

The EPA is becoming more concerned. A study in Boulder, Colo. found female sucker fish outnumber males 5 to 1, and 50 percent of the males have female sex indicators, apparently from estrogen traces from pills for women.

Near Dallas, tiny amounts of Prozac have been found in the livers and brain cells of channel catfish and crappie.

Lots of Help

As part of the leadership project, Cook addressed the Lincoln County noon Rotary in mid-March. She cited national reports that the use of Oxycontin increased by 30 percent in one year—2007—among high school seniors. And she said one out of 10 high school seniors that year used Vicodin illegally.

Eighty-one percent of teens who abuse prescription or over-the-counter drugs combine them with alcohol, the national study said.

Hospital emergency room visits involving such drugs increased 21 percent in 2008. Nearly half of those visits were from patients 12 to 20 years old.

The number of teens going into drug treatment has increased 300 percent in the last 10 years.

As Cook painted the alarming picture of abuse and incapacitation, community members offered to help. So far, 24 individuals and businesses have stepped up to sponsor the local education and collection effort.

"The support is overwhelming," Cook said.

The Language of Pharming

Big boys, cotton, kicker–Various slang for prescription pain relievers.

Chill pills, french fries, tranqs–Various slang for prescription sedatives and tranquilizers.

Pharming (pronounced "farming")–From the word pharmaceutical. It means kids getting high by raiding their parents' medicine cabinets for prescription drugs.

Pharm parties–Parties where teens bring prescription drugs from home, mix them together into a big bowl (see 'trail mix'), and grab a handful. Not surprisingly, pharm parties are usually arranged while parents are out.

Pilz (pronounced "pills")–A popular term used to describe prescription medications. Can also include over-the-counter medications.

Recipe–Prescription drugs mixed with alcoholic or other beverages.

Trail mix–A mixture of various prescription drugs, usually served in a big bag or bowl at pharm parties.

"We heard you got into serious medical trouble once from taking too many drugs. Why didn't that stop you from taking more?" we asked a student.

"Well, I know I won't ever take that many again, and it did stop me for the most part. I was getting messed up every day. After that I didn't touch a pill for months. I switched to coke for a couple months, then pot when the person that always gave me coke got sent to rehab."

Featured Speaker—Former Abuser

Former Husker football All-American Jason Peter will speak to the public at the end of the drug collection day, April 25.

Peter, one of the nation's best defensive linemen in 1997, graduated from Nebraska and went to the NFL, where he earned $6.5 million from the Carolina Panthers. But he blew most of the money on illegal drugs, taking up to 80 pain killers a day.

Jason Peter's life finally crashed. A series of injuries took him off the NFL roster.

He managed to clean up and wrote a book, "Heros of the Underground" and now hosts an ESPN talk show from his hometown of Lincoln. He spends his spare time traveling, talking about the dangers of drug abuse.

"Prescription drugs are a lot more addictive than people realize," another North Platte student told the Bulletin.

"You can get into big-time trouble," he said. "Possession of a controlled substance is a felony. They can even charge you for each pill in your possession. If they think you're selling them you get possession of a controlled substance with intent to distribute, which is prison time."

National Obsession

"Our national pastime—self-destruction," writer Jerry Stahl said in a review of Jason Peter's book.

"We are a nation obsessed with pharmaceuticals," Cook said as she addressed the Rotary. "We spend vast sums to manage our health, and we pop pills to address every conceivable symptom. In this nation, we abuse prescription drugs . . . daily."

Persons 65 and older take one-third of all prescribed medications even though they comprise 13 percent of the population, Cook said. Older patients are more likely to have multiple prescriptions, which can lead to unintentional misuse, more drugs stored in medicine cabinets for kids to steal.

The leadership group advises to keep medicine containers closed, even locked. Keep a record of prescriptions and the amount on hand. Reinforce a message of caution and restraint to your children. Start early, long before adolescence. Build a solid foundation for resisting temptations and outside influences.

North Platte Therapist: Most Clients Abuse Prescriptions

Young people steal grandma's pills and distribute them at school. Senior citizens falsify prescriptions for more pain medication. Babysitters take pills from cabinets.

An Ohio real estate agent lost her license for pilfering pills from bathrooms at open houses.

The appeal is obvious—the drugs can be legally obtained, the stigma of going to a street pusher can be avoided, and the price isn't steep.

There are an estimated 800,000 websites which sell prescription drugs on the Internet and will ship them to households no questions asked.

Today, about one-third of all U.S. drug abuse is prescription drug abuse.

Approximately 1.9 million persons age 12 or older have used Oxycontin (pain reliever, like morphine) nonmedically at least once in their lifetime, according to Columbia University's National Center on Addiction and Substance Abuse.

Vicki Dugger, a therapist with New Beginnings Therapy Associates in North Platte, said about 75 percent of the patients she treats admitted abusing prescription drugs.

Dugger said many more people are aware of it today than in the 1980s and 1990s. Still, much more awareness is needed.

"There's a misconception that abusing prescription medication is not harmful," Dugger said. "The fact is, can have deadly results."

Dugger said. kids have died after attending pharming parties. She has some tips for parents to help keep their teenagers safe:

- Consider your own drug behavior and the message you are sending.
- Do a drug inventory. Forgotten or expired prescriptions or leftover over-the-counter meds could be appealing to kids, so get rid of them. Put new drugs away.
- Reach out and have a discussion. Dugger said research showed that kids who learn a lot about drug risks from their parents are up to half as likely to use drugs as kids who haven't had that conversation from mom and dad.
- Look on the computer. Try conducting your own web search to see how easily one can buy prescription meds without a prescription.
- Watch for warning signs. These may include unexplained disappearance of meds from medicine cabinets, declining grades, loss of interest in activities, changes in friends and behaviors, disrupted sleeping or eating patterns and more.

Dugger said she recently had a mother of a teen ask her about all the Musinex boxes around her house.

Musinex is a medication that is used for temporary relief of coughs caused by certain respiratory tract infections but teens have been known to abuse it by taking more than the recommended amounts to get high.

Dugger said she advised the mother to have a conversation with her teen immediately.

Critical Thinking

1. Do you see an abuse of prescription drugs among your friends or fellow classmates? How will you know when abuse exists?

2. What, in your opinion, needs to take place in the wider society to lessen dependency and prevent the abuse of prescription drugs?

The entire Bulletin staff contributed to this report. It was first published April 1 in the Bulletin print edition.

When Booze Was Banned but Pot Was Not

What can today's antiprohibitionists learn from their predecessors?

JACOB SULLUM

Of the 27 amendments to the U.S. Constitution, the 18th is the only one explicitly aimed at restricting people's freedom. It is also the only one that has ever been repealed. Maybe that's encouraging, especially for those of us who recognize the parallels between that amendment, which ushered in the nationwide prohibition of alcohol, and current bans on other drugs.

But given the manifest failure and unpleasant side effects of Prohibition, its elimination after 14 years is not terribly surprising, despite the arduous process required to undo a constitutional amendment. The real puzzle, as the journalist Daniel Okrent argues in his masterful new history of the period, is how a nation that never had a teetotaling majority, let alone one committed to forcibly imposing its lifestyle on others, embarked upon such a doomed experiment to begin with. How did a country consisting mostly of drinkers agree to forbid drinking?

The short answer is that it didn't. As a reveler accurately protests during a Treasury Department raid on a private banquet in the HBO series *Boardwalk Empire,* neither the 18th Amendment nor the Volstead Act, which implemented it, prohibited mere possession or consumption of alcohol. The amendment took effect a full year after ratification, and those who could afford it were free in the meantime to stock up on wine and liquor, which they were permitted to consume until the supplies ran out. The law also included exceptions that were important for those without well-stocked wine cellars or the means to buy the entire inventory of a liquor store (as the actress Mary Pickford did). Home production of cider, beer, and wine was permitted, as was commercial production of alcohol for religious, medicinal, and industrial use (three loopholes that were widely abused). In these respects Prohibition was much less onerous than our current drug laws. Indeed, the legal situation was akin to what toda would be called "decriminalization" or even a form o "legalization."

After Prohibition took effect, Okrent shows, attempt to punish bootleggers with anything more than a slap o the wrist provoked public outrage and invited jury nulli fication. One can imagine what would have happened i the Anti-Saloon League and the Woman's Christian Tem perance Union had demanded a legal regime in whic possessing, say, five milliliters of whiskey triggered mandatory five-year prison sentence (as possessing fiv grams of crack cocaine did until recently). The lack of pen alties for consumption helped reassure drinkers who vote for Prohibition as legislators and supported it (or did nc vigorously resist it) as citizens. Some of these "dry wets sincerely believed that the barriers to drinking erecte by Prohibition, while unnecessary for moderate imbib ers like themselves, would save working-class saloo patrons from their own excesses. Pauline Morton Sabir the well-heeled, martini-drinking Republican activist wh went from supporting the 18th Amendment to heading th Women's Organization for National Prohibition Reforn one of the most influential pro-repeal groups, apparentl had such an attitude.

In addition to paternalism, the longstanding America ambivalence toward pleasure in general and alcohol-fuele pleasure in particular helped pave the way to Prohibitior The Puritans were not dour teetotalers, but they wer anxious about excess, and a similar discomfort may hav discouraged drinkers from actively resisting dry demands But by far the most important factor, Okrent persuasivel argues, was the political maneuvering of the Anti-Saloo League (ASL) and its master strategist, Wayne Wheele who turned a minority position into the supreme law o

e land by mobilizing a highly motivated bloc of swing
oters.

Defining itself as "the Church in Action Against the
aloon," the clergy-led ASL reached dry sympathizers
rough churches (mostly Methodist and Baptist) across
e country. Okrent says the group typically could deliver
omething like 10 percent of voters to whichever candidate
ounded driest (regardless of his private behavior). This
ower was enough to change the outcome of elections, put-
ng the fear of the ASL, which Okrent calls "the mightiest
essure group in the nation's history," into the state and
deral legislators who would vote to approve the 18th
mendment. That doesn't mean none of the legislators who
oted dry were sincere; many of them—including Rich-
ond Hobson of Alabama and Morris Sheppard of Texas,
e 18th Amendment's chief sponsors in the House and
enate, respectively—were deadly serious about reform-
g their fellow citizens by regulating their liquid diets.
ut even the most ardent drys depended on ASL-energized
upporters for their political survival.

The ASL strategy worked because wet voters did not
ave the same passion and unity, while the affected busi-
ess interests feuded among themselves until the day their
dustry was abolished. Americans who objected to Pro-
bition generally did not feel strongly enough to make
at issue decisive in their choice of candidates, although
ey did make themselves heard when the issue itself was
ut to a vote. Californians, for example, defeated four
uccessive ballot measures that would have established
atewide prohibition before their legislature approved
e 18th Amendment in 1919.

As Prohibition wore on, its unintended consequences
rovided the fire that wets had lacked before it was
nacted. They were appalled by rampant corruption, black
arket violence, newly empowered criminals, invasions of
rivacy, and deaths linked to alcohol poisoned under govrnment order to discourage diversion (a policy that Sen.
dward Edwards of New Jersey denounced as "legalized
urder"). These burdens seemed all the more intolerable
ecause Prohibition was so conspicuously ineffective.
s a common saying of the time put it, the drys had
eir law and the wets had their liquor, thanks to myriad
uasi-legal and illicit businesses that Okrent colorfully
escribes.

Entrepreneurs taking advantage of legal loopholes
cluded operators of "booze cruises" to international
aters, travel agents selling trips to Cuba (which became
popular tourist destination on the strength of its proxim-
y and wetness), "medicinal" alcohol distributors whose
rochures ("for physician permittees only") resembled
ar menus, priests and rabbis who obtained allegedly
cramental wine for their congregations (which grew

dramatically after Prohibition was enacted), breweries
that turned to selling "malt syrup" for home beer production, vintners who delivered fermentable juice directly
into San Francisco cellars through chutes connected to
grape-crushing trucks, and the marketers of the Vino-
Sano Grape Brick, which "came in a printed wrapper
instructing the purchaser to add water to make grape
juice, but to be sure *not* to add yeast or sugar, or leave
it in a dark place, or let it sit too long before drinking it
because 'it might ferment and become wine.' " The outright lawbreakers included speakeasy proprietors such as
the Stork Club's Sherman Billingsley, gangsters such as
Al Capone, rum runners such as Bill McCoy, and big-
time bootleggers such as Sam Bronfman, the Canadian
distiller who made a fortune shipping illicit liquor to
thirsty Americans under the cover of false paperwork.
Their stories, as related by Okrent, are illuminating as
well as engaging, vividly showing how prohibition
warps everything it touches, transforming ordinary business transactions into tales of intrigue.

The plain fact that the government could not stop the
flow of booze, but merely divert it into new channels at
great cost, led disillusioned drys to join angry wets in
a coalition that achieved an unprecedented and never-
repeated feat. As late as 1930, just three years before
repeal, Morris Sheppard confidently asserted, "There is
as much chance of repealing the Eighteenth Amendment
as there is for a hummingbird to fly to the planet Mars
with the Washington Monument tied to its tail."

That hummingbird was lifted partly by a rising tide
of wet immigrants and urbanites. During the first few
decades of the 20th century, the country became steadily
less rural and less WASPy, a trend that ultimately made
Prohibition democratically unsustainable. Understanding this demographic reality, dry members of Congress
desperately delayed the constitutionally required reap-
portionment of legislative districts for nearly a decade
after the 1920 census. "The dry refusal to allow Congress
to recalculate state-by-state representation in the House
during the 1920s is one of those political maneuvers
in American history so audacious it's hard to believe it
happened," Okrent writes. "The episode is all the more
remarkable for never having established itself in the
national consciousness."

Other Prohibition-driven assaults on the Constitution
are likewise little remembered today. In 1922 the Court
reinforced a dangerous exception to the Fifth Amendment's Double Jeopardy Clause by declaring that the "dual
sovereignty" doctrine allowed prosecution of Prohibition
violators in both state and federal courts for the same
offense. In 1927 the Court ruled that requiring a bootleg-
ger to declare his illegal earnings for tax purposes did not

violate the Fifth Amendment's guarantee against compelled self-incrimination. And "in twenty separate cases between 1920 and 1933," Okrent notes, the Court carried out "a broad-strokes rewriting" of the case law concerning the Fourth Amendment's prohibition of "unreasonable searches and seizures." Among other things, the Court declared that a warrant was not needed to search a car suspected of carrying contraband liquor or to eavesdrop on telephone conversations between bootleggers (a precedent that was not overturned until 1967). Because of Prohibition's demands, Okrent writes, "long-honored restraints on police authority soon gave way."

That tendency has a familiar ring to anyone who follows Supreme Court cases growing out of the war on drugs, which have steadily whittled away at the Fourth Amendment during the last few decades. But unlike today, the incursions required to enforce Prohibition elicited widespread dismay. Here is how *The New York Times* summarized the Anti-Saloon League's response to the wiretap decision: "It is feared by the dry forces that Prohibition will fall into 'disrepute' and suffer 'irreparable harm' if the American public concludes that 'universal snooping' is favored for enforcing the Eighteenth Amendment."

The fear of a popular backlash was well-founded. From the beginning, Prohibition was resisted in the wetter provinces of America, where the authorities often declined to enforce it. Maryland never passed its own version of the Volstead Act, while New York repealed its alcohol prohibition law in 1923. Eleven other states eliminated their statutes by referendum in November 1932, months before Congress presented the 21st Amendment (which repealed the 18th) and more than a year before it was ratified.

This history of noncooperation is instructive in considering an argument that was often made by opponents of Proposition 19, the marijuana legalization initiative that California voters rejected in November. The measure's detractors claimed legalizing marijuana at the state level would run afoul of the Supremacy Clause, which says "this Constitution, and the laws of the United States which shall be made in pursuance thereof . . . shall be the supreme law of the land." Yet even under a prohibition system that, unlike the current one, was explicitly authorized by the Constitution, states had no obligation to ban what Congress banned or punish what Congress punished. In fact, state and local resistance to alcohol prohibition led the way to national repeal.

That precedent, while encouraging to antiprohibitionists who hope that federalism can help end the war on drugs, should be viewed with caution. For one thing,

federalism isn't what it used to be. Alcohol prohibiti￼ was enacted and repealed before the Supreme Court tran￼ formed the Commerce Clause into an all-purpose licen￼ to meddle, when it was taken for granted that the feder￼ government could not ban an intoxicant unless the Co￼ stitution was amended to provide such a power. While t￼ feds may not have the resources to wage the war on dru￼ without state assistance, under existing precedents the￼ clearly have the legal authority to try.

Another barrier to emulating the antiprohibitionists ￼ the 1920s is that none of the currently banned drugs is (￼ ever was) as widely consumed in this country as alcoh￼ That fact is crucial in understanding the contrast betwe￼ the outrage that led to the repeal of alcohol prohibiti￼ and Americans' general indifference to the damage do￼ by the war on drugs today. The illegal drug that com￼ closest to alcohol in popularity is marijuana, which su￼ vey data indicate most Americans born after World W￼ II have at least tried. That experience is reflected in ri￼ ing public support for legalizing marijuana, which hit ￼ record 46 percent in a nationwide Gallup poll conduct￼ the week before Proposition 19 was defeated.

A third problem for today's antiprohibitionists is t￼ deep roots of the status quo. Alcohol prohibition ca￼ and went in 14 years, which made it easy to distingui￼ between the bad effects of drinking and the bad effe￼ of trying to stop it. By contrast, the government has be￼ waging war on cocaine and opiates since 1914 and o￼ marijuana since 1937 (initially under the guise of enfor￼ ing revenue measures). Few people living today ha￼ clear memories of a different legal regime. That is on￼ reason why histories like Okrent's, which bring to life ￼ period when booze was banned but pot was not, are ￼ valuable.

Reflecting on the long-term impact of the vain attem￼ to get between Americans and their liquor, Okrent writ￼ "In 1920 could anyone have believed that the Eighteen￼ Amendment, ostensibly addressing the single subject ￼ intoxicating beverages, would set off an avalanche ￼ change in areas as diverse as international trade, spee￼ boat design, tourism practices, soft-drink marketing, an￼ the English language itself? Or that it would provoke t￼ establishment of the first nationwide criminal syndicat￼ the idea of home dinner parties, the deep engagement ￼ women in political issues other than suffrage, and th￼ creation of Las Vegas?" Nearly a century after the w￼ on other drugs was launched, Americans are only begi￼ ning to recognize its far-reaching consequences, most ￼ which are considerably less fun than a dinner party or ￼ trip to Vegas.

Critical Thinking

1. What exactly did the Eighteenth Amendment prohibit?
2. Describe the similarities and differences between alcohol prohibition and the current prohibition of illegal drugs.

3. Do you think that Prohibition was effective? Why or why not?

Senior editor JACOB SULLUM (jsullum@reason.com) is a nationally syndicated columnist and the author of *Saying Yes: In Defense of Drug Use* (Tarcher/Penguin).

om Reason Magazine, February 2011, pp. 56–59. Copyright © 2011 by Reason Foundation, 3415 S. Sepulveda Blvd., Suite 400, Los Angeles, CA 90034. www.reason.com

... Having a Great Detox

RUTH LA FERLA

In the weeks before Tara Conner handed over her crown as Miss USA, she talked to television reporters about her stay at a treatment center for drug addiction and alcoholism. At the insistence of Donald Trump, an owner of the beauty competition, Ms. Conner had sought treatment at the Caron center in Wernersville, Pa., a former resort hotel set on a pastoral 110 acres.

She emerged earlier this month the picture of vibrant health and cheer, describing the experience as "amazing, absolutely amazing, a lot of fun."

Taking in her ebullience, and her glossy good looks, a viewer might have been forgiven for craving a bit of whatever it was that Ms. Conner was having. She is, after all, but one in a coterie of high-profile personalities to have recently undergone well-publicized stays in substance abuse programs that have, to all appearances, less in common with traditional bare-bones detox centers than they do with a luxury spa or resort.

She is also among the latest to have apparently shed a debilitating addiction as lightly as she might have a few unwanted pounds.

Less than a decade ago, a stint in rehab was assumed to be a body- and soul-wrenching experience. A trip to even an elite facility like the Betty Ford Center in Rancho Mirage, Calif., was sufficiently shaming to keep under wraps—the psychic equivalent of a week in the stocks. Today a sojourn at a boutique establishment like Promises in Malibu, Calif., where until last week Britney Spears was tucked away, is openly discussed and in some quarters glamorized as a hip, if costly, refuge for the gilded set.

That idea is perpetuated—indeed aggressively promoted— by the marketers of a handful of high-end facilities, some of which advertise amenities on their websites like private rooms with 600-thread-count bedsheets, high-tech gyms, spa cuisine and ocean views. "There used to be a stigma to coming to a place like this," said Chris Prentiss, the director of Passages, another exclusive treatment center in Malibu. "Now it's like wearing a Ralph Lauren shirt."

Richard DeGrandpre, the author of *The Cult of Pharmacolog* (Duke University Press, 2006), an exploration of America's ever-changing relationship with drugs, ascribes the latest cachet of rehab to a prurient, even envious fascination with celebrity culture, one, he said, in which "rehab has become fashionable, almost to the point, ironically, of giving a person status."

No one seriously disputes that drug addiction and alcoholism are grave and potentially life-threatening. But among devotees of networks like E! Entertainment or the readers of *People* which report obsessively on rehab, there is no escaping the conclusion that rehabilitation programs have become a pampering hostelry for the privileged classes, some of whose members bounce in and out like tennis balls.

There are 8,000 programs claiming to treat substance abuse in the United States, according to the Center on Addiction and Substance Abuse at Columbia University. Only a fraction are short-term residential programs, which can cost $25,000 to $80,000 for a recommended one-month stay. That price, the directors say, covers intensive treatment, with some establishments having as many as 10 counselors and therapists per patient. As health insurance coverage of residential treatment has declined, the programs have courted an affluent, lustrous clientele, in large part by touting lavish appointments. Some seem to be promote recovery as a luxury holiday.

Members of glamour industries like fashion, film and publishing have been quick to pick up, and propagate, the message. Earlier this month *Us Weekly* published a feature laid out like a glossy travel brochure, portraying treatment as something akin to a visit to a five-star hotel.

"After Britney and Lindsay, so many of our staffers were saying, 'God, what's it going to take for me to go to rehab?'" recalled Janice Min, the editor. "Not to diminish what it takes to get clean, but to some of them, rehab sounded like a great escape from everyday life."

At the Valentino show in Paris last month, "Rehab," a popular ditty by Amy Winehouse, pulsed on the runway. Carlos Souza, a public relations executive for the fashion house, crooned some of the lyrics: "They tried to make me go; I said no, no, no." The song is "great, catchy and of the moment," he said. "I wouldn't say rehab is chic, but in the crazy society we live in, it is the new ashram weekend."

To those in the serious business of recovery, such a position is willfully naïve, at best a double-edged sword. The fanfare surrounding celebrities helps take the disgrace out of treatment, Doug Tieman, the director of the Caron center, acknowledged. But it also fosters the impression that "a daily massage or riding a horse is necessary to recovery." Caron offers both.

William Cope Moyers, the vice president for external affairs at Hazelden in Center City, Minn., and the author of *Broken*

Viking, 2006), an addiction memoir, said the tendency of equating recovery with rest and relaxation trivializes a serious illness.

Treatment "requires hard work and a willingness to confront our demons," Mr. Moyers said. "People who seek treatment as 0 days of R & R are only doing themselves and their families great disservice."

Addiction, he added, does not discriminate. "It is a disease that doesn't care whether you are glamorous or gory." Yet even low-frills residential clinics, which emphasize detoxification and therapy over nutrition and skin care, are inaccessible to the average American.

Hazelden spends about $3 million a year in patient aid, Mr. Moyers said, offering it primarily to employed middle-class patients with private health insurance. They are patients who have nothing in fame or riches compared with those depicted on television shows like *Dirt,* in which a Lohan-like pivotal character enters a boutique center hidden away in the Hollywood Hills; or the series *24,* which shows a fictionalized former first lady being treated in a well-cushioned, pastel-tinted bungalow.

But the Hard Rock resort in Las Vegas, which offers a series of "rehab nights" of poolside drinking and carousing, is among a number of businesses promoting the concept of rehab as an alternately laid back and stimulating retreat for the middle class.

In the popular culture, "rehab isn't just mainstream, it is seen as inevitable," said Martin Kaplan, the associate dean of the Annenberg School for Communication at the University of Southern California. Dr. Kaplan, a professor of popular culture, went on to observe that the current idealization of recovery is embedded in the popular psyche. It is an alluring new spin, he said, on the classic American narrative of transgression and redemption, by which "we tell ourselves that life is full of all kinds of twists, falls and dark moments, and that we occasionally need help beyond what we ourselves can provide."

For some that narrative has acquired an enviable gloss. Those suffering from addictions can comfort themselves that they share the same problems as Ms. Lohan or the designer Marc Jacobs, whose business partner announced this month that Mr. Jacobs was entering rehab. And outsiders can press their noses to the glass.

"I'm starting to feel a tad excluded—resentful even," Simon Doonan wrote caustically in a recent column in The New York Observer. "I want to eat spa cuisines with Britney and Mel and then do group therapy with Keith Urban."

In an interview, Mr. Doonan, the creative director of Barneys New York, elaborated: "It's almost to the point where you suspect that if you're not going into rehab, maybe you're not such an interesting person."

Referring to Isaiah Washington, a television actor who recently entered treatment in part as a public apology for uttering a gay slur, Mr. Doonan argued: "Rehab adds another dimension. It's a great profile-raiser."

And a classy comfort station. Facilities like Promises in Malibu, a home away from home to Matthew Perry and Charlie Sheen, compete on the Internet to court the cream. On its Website, the Wonderland Center, on Mulholland Drive in Los Angeles, with clients like Ms. Lohan and Mike Tyson, offers detox, psychotherapy and spiritual counseling supplemented by peaceful walks in nearby Runyan Canyon and "access to the same trainers and beauty consultants used by Hollywood celebrities."

Few programs advertise their cure rates. One study, in the journal *Psychology of Addictive Behaviors* in 1997, found that clients in short residential programs had a 69 percent decline in weekly cocaine use and a 58 percent reduction in heavy drinking in the year following treatment.

Such results can be misleading, said Joseph T. Califano, who heads the Center on Addiction at Columbia, since the figures tend to be based on the number of people completing the program. Many therapeutic communities have a dropout rate as high as 80 percent, he said.

At Passages, a $22 million Malibu estate on a bluff overlooking the Pacific, treatment means four to five hours a day of individual therapy, and perks include tennis lessons taught by a pro and meals prepared by a former head chef at Spago.

Mr. Prentiss, the director and a self-described metaphysician who favors sherbet-colored suits and likens the healing powers of Malibu itself to Lourdes, offers no excuses: "When you are charging close to $60,000 for a monthlong stay, you've got to have a facility that goes along with it."

"After all," he added dryly, "Britney Spears isn't going to stay in a shack."

Critical Thinking

1. How many substance abuse treatment programs are in operation in the United States?

2. Do you think that luxury treatment facilities are more effective or less effective than traditional treatment facilities? Why or why not?

3. Why do you think that "rehab" has become fashionable in the United States?

Scientists Are High on Idea That Marijuana Reduces Memory Impairment

EMILY CALDWELL

Columbus, Ohio–The more research they do, the more evidence Ohio State University scientists find that specific elements of marijuana can be good for the aging brain by reducing inflammation there and possibly even stimulating the formation of new brain cells.

The research suggests that the development of a legal drug that contains certain properties similar to those in marijuana might help prevent or delay the onset of Alzheimer's disease. Though the exact cause of Alzheimer's remains unknown, chronic inflammation in the brain is believed to contribute to memory impairment.

Any new drug's properties would resemble those of tetrahydrocannabinol, or THC, the main psychoactive substance in the cannabis plant, but would not share its high-producing effects. THC joins nicotine, alcohol and caffeine as agents that, in moderation, have shown some protection against inflammation in the brain that might translate to better memory late in life.

"It's not that everything immoral is good for the brain. It's just that there are some substances that millions of people for thousands of years have used in billions of doses, and we're noticing there's a little signal above all the noise," said Gary Wenk, professor of psychology at Ohio State and principal investigator on the research.

Wenk's work has already shown that a THC-like synthetic drug can improve memory in animals. Now his team is trying to find out exactly how it works in the brain.

The most recent research on rats indicates that at least three receptors in the brain are activated by the synthetic drug, which is similar to marijuana. These receptors are proteins within the brain's endocannabinoid system, which is involved in memory as well as physiological processes associated with appetite, mood and pain response.

This research is also showing that receptors in this system can influence brain inflammation and the production of new neurons, or brain cells.

"When we're young, we reproduce neurons and our memory works fine. When we age, the process slows down, so we have a decrease in new cell formation in normal aging. You nee those cells to come back and help form new memories, and w found that this THC-like agent can influence creation of tho cells," said Yannick Marchalant, a study coauthor and resear assistant professor of psychology at Ohio State.

> **Could people smoke marijuana to prevent Alzheimer's disease if the disease is in their family? We're not saying that, but it might actually work. What we are saying is it appears that a safe, legal substance that mimics those important properties of marijuana can work on receptors in the brain to prevent memory impairments in aging. So that's really hopeful, Wenk said.**

Marchalant described the research in a poster presentatic Wednesday (11/19/08) at the Society for Neuroscience meetin in Washington, D.C.

Knowing exactly how any of these compounds work in th brain can make it easier for drug designers to target specif systems with agents that will offer the most effective anti-agin benefits, said Wenk, who is also a professor of neuroscien and molecular virology, immunology and medical genetics.

"Could people smoke marijuana to prevent Alzheimer disease if the disease is in their family? We're not saying tha but it might actually work. What we are saying is it appea that a safe, legal substance that mimics those important prop erties of marijuana can work on receptors in the brain to pr vent memory impairments in aging. So that's really hopefu Wenk said.

One thing is clear from the studies: Once memory impair ment is evident, the treatment is not effective. Reducir inflammation and preserving or generating neurons must occur before the memory loss is obvious, Wenk said.

Marchalant led a study on old rats using the synthetic drug, called WIN-55212-2 (WIN), which is not used in humans because of its high potency to induce psychoactive effects.

The researchers used a pump under the skin to give the rats a constant dose of WIN for three weeks–a dose low enough to produce no psychoactive effects on the animals. A control group of rats received no intervention. In follow-up memory tests, in which rats were placed in a small swimming pool to determine how well they use visual cues to find a platform hidden under the surface of the water, the treated rats did better than the control rats in learning and remembering how to find the hidden platform.

"Old rats are not very good at that task. They can learn, but it takes them more time to find the platform. When we gave them the drug, it made them a little better at that task," Marchalant said.

In some rats, Marchalant combined the WIN with compounds that are known to block specific receptors, which then offers hints at which receptors WIN is activating. The results indicated the WIN lowered the rats' brain inflammation in the hippocampus by acting on what is called the TRPV1 receptor. The hippocampus is responsible for short-term memory.

With the same intervention technique, the researchers also determined that WIN acts on receptors known as CB1 and CB2, leading to the generation of new brain cells—a process known as neurogenesis. Those results led the scientists to speculate that the combination of lowered inflammation and neurogenesis is the reason the rats' memory improved after treatment with WIN.

The researchers are continuing to study the endocannabinoid system's role in regulating inflammation and neuron development. They are trying to zero in on the receptors that must be activated to produce the most benefits from any newly developed drug.

What they already know is THC alone isn't the answer.

"The end goal is not to recommend the use of THC in humans to reduce Alzheimer's," Marchalant said. "We need to find exactly which receptors are most crucial, and ideally lead to the development of drugs that specifically activate those receptors. We hope a compound can be found that can target both inflammation and neurogenesis, which would be the most efficient way to produce the best effects."

References

The National Institutes of Health supported this work.

Coauthors on the presentation are Holly Brothers and Lauren Burgess, both of Ohio State's Department of Psychology.

Critical Thinking

1. What role does chronic inflammation in the brain play in Alzheimer's disease?

2. What is THC and how does it affect the brain?

3. What is the endocannabinoid system? What is it responsible for in the brain?

UNIT 2

Understanding How Drugs Work—Use, Dependency, and Addiction

Unit Selections

Learning Outcomes

After reading this Unit, you should be able to:

- Explain why some people become dependent on certain drugs far sooner than other people.

- Describe how is it possible to predict one's own liability for becoming drug dependent.

- Describe multiple processes by which a person becomes addicted to alcohol and/or drugs.

- Outline and support an argument for which influences most predict addictive behavior.

Student Website

www.mhhe.com/cls

Understanding how drugs act upon the human mind and body is a critical component to the resolution of issues concerning drug use and abuse. An understanding of basic pharmacology is requisite for informed discussion on practically every drug-related issue and controversy. One does not have to look far to find misinformed debate, much of which surrounds the basic lack of knowledge of how drugs work. Different drugs produce different bodily effects and consequences. All psychoactive drugs influence the central nervous system, which, in turn, sits at the center of how we physiologically and psychologically interpret and react to the world around us. Some drugs, such as methamphetamine and LSD, have great, immediate influence on the nervous system, while others, such as tobacco and marijuana, elicit less-pronounced reactions. Almost all psychoactive drugs have their effects on the body, which are mitigated by the dosage level of the drug taken, the manner in which it is ingested, and the physiological and emotional state of the user. Cocaine smoked in the form of crack versus snorted as powder produces profoundly different physical and emotional effects on the user. However, even though illegal drugs often provide the most sensational perspective from which to view these relationships, the abuse of prescription drugs is being reported as an exploding new component of the addiction problem. Currently, the non-medical use of pain relievers such as oxycodone and hydrocodone is continuing at alarming rates. This trend has been increasing steadily since 1994, and it currently competes with methamphetamine abuse as the most alarming national trend of drug abuse. Currently, more than 5 million Americans use prescription pain medications for non-medical reasons. Molecular properties of certain drugs allow them to imitate and artificially reproduce certain naturally occurring brain chemicals that provide the basis for the drugs' influence. The continued use of certain drugs and their repeated alteration of the body's biochemical structure provide one explanation for the physiological consequences of drug use. The human brain is the quintessential master pharmacist and repeatedly altering its chemical functions by drug use is risky. Doing such things may produce profound implications for becoming addicted. For example, heroin use replicates the natural brain chemical endorphin, which supports the body's biochemical defense to pain and stress. The continued use of heroin is believed to deplete natural endorphins, causing the nervous system to produce a painful physical and emotional reaction when heroin is withdrawn. Subsequently, one significant motivation for continued use is realized. A word of caution is in order, however, when proceeding through the various explanations for what drugs do and why they do it. Many people, because of an emotional and/or political relationship to the world of drugs, assert a subjective predisposition when interpreting certain drugs' effects and consequences. One person is an alcoholic while another is a social drinker. People often argue, rationalize, and explain the perceived nature of drugs' effects based upon an extremely superficial understanding of diverse pharmacological properties of different drugs. A detached and scientifically sophisticated awareness of drug pharmacology may help strengthen the platform from which to interpret the various consequences of drug use. Drug addiction results as a continuum comprised of experimentation, recreational use, regular use, and abuse. The

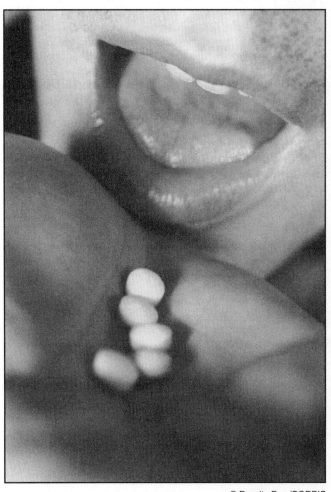

process is influenced by a plethora of physiological, psychological, and environmental factors. Although some still argue that drug dependence is largely a matter of individual behavior—something to be chosen or rejected—most experts agree that new scientific discoveries clearly define the roots of addiction to live within molecular levels of the brain. Powerful drugs, upon repeated administration, easily compromise the brain's ability to make decisions about its best interests.

One theory used to describe specific drugs as more addictive or less addictive explains a process referred to as "reinforcement." Simply explained, reinforcement is a form of psychological conditioning that results from a drug's influence on a person's brain. Reinforcement is the term used to describe a person's behavior that expresses the uncontrollable need to repeatedly introduce the drug to the body. Powerful drugs such as the stimulant cocaine and the depressant oxycodone influence the brain's reward pathway and promote behavior in which drug seeking is recognized by the brain as actions necessary for survival. Persons addicted to drugs known to be strongly reinforcing typically report that they care more about getting the drug than about anything else—even in the face of self-destruction. Drug addiction and the rate at which it occurs must compete with certain physiological and psychological, as well as environmental, variables that are unique to individuals. A drug user with a greater number of biological markers known to be associated with drug addiction, such as mental illness, alcoholism, and poor physical health, may encourage drug dependency sooner than a person with fewer biological markers. Similarly, a person's positive environmental associations, or "natural reinforcers," such as a strong family structure and healthy personal and professional relationships may not only make experimentation unappealing, it may delay a user's developing drug addiction. Subsequently, one's liability for drug addiction is closely associated with genetics, environment, and the use of psychoactive drugs. Understanding the concept of addiction requires an awareness of these factors. For many people, drug addiction and the reasons that contribute to it are murky concepts.

The articles in Unit 2 illustrate some of the current research and viewpoints on the ways that drugs act upon the human body. New science is suggesting that a new era has begun relative to understanding drugs and their pharmacological influence on the human body. This new science is critical to understanding the assorted consequences of drug use and abuse. Science has taken us closer to understanding that acute drug use changes brain function profoundly and that these changes may remain with the user long after the drug has left the system. New research investigating the liabilities produced by adolescent smoking tobacco suggests that even small amounts produce remarkable susceptibility for addiction. Subsequently, many new issues have emerged for drug and health-related public policy. Increasingly, drug abuse competes with other social maladies as public enemy number one. Further, the need for a combined biological, behavioral, and social response to this problem becomes more evident. Many healthcare professionals and healthcare educators, in addition to those from other diverse backgrounds, argue that research dollars spent on drug abuse and addiction should approach that spent on heart disease, cancer, and AIDS. The articles in Unit 2 provide examples of how some new discoveries have influenced our thinking about addiction. They also provide examples of how, even in light of new knowledge, breaking addictions is so very hard to do.

Internet References

AddictionSearch. com
www.addictionsearch.com

Addiction Treatment Forum
www.atforum.com

American Psychological Association's Addiction Related Publications
http://search.apa.org/search?query=&facet=classification:
Addictions&limited=true&section=pubs

British Broadcasting Company Understanding Drugs
www.bbc.co.uk/health/conditions/mental_health drugsuse.shtml

Centre for Addiction and Mental Health (CAMH)
www.camh.net

Dealing with Addictions
http://kidshealth.org/teen/your_mind/problems/addictions.html

Drugs and the Body: How Drugs Work
www.doitnow.org/pdfs/223.pdf

National Alcoholism Drug Information Center
http://addictioncareoptions.com

The National Center on Addiction and Substance Abuse at Columbia University
www.casacolumbia.org

National Institute on Drug Abuse (NIDA)
www.nida.nih.gov

Public Agenda
www.publicagenda.org/articles/illegal-drugs

Understanding Addiction—Regret, Addiction and Death
http://teenadvice.about.com/library/weekly/aa011501a.htm

Drug Addiction and Its Effects

Drug Abuse and Addiction

Many people do not understand why individuals become addicted to drugs or how drugs change the brain to foster compulsive drug abuse. They mistakenly view drug abuse and addiction as strictly a social problem and may characterize those who take drugs as morally weak. One very common belief is that drug abusers should be able to just stop taking drugs if they are only willing to change their behavior. What people often underestimate is the complexity of drug addiction—that it is a disease that impacts the brain and because of that, stopping drug abuse is not simply a matter of willpower. Through scientific advances we now know much more about how exactly drugs work in the brain, and we also know that drug addiction can be successfully treated to help people stop abusing drugs and resume their productive lives.

What Is Drug Addiction?

Addiction is a chronic, often relapsing brain disease that causes compulsive drug seeking and use despite harmful consequences to the individual that is addicted and to those around them. Drug addiction is a brain disease because the abuse of drugs leads to changes in the structure and function of the brain. Although it is true that for most people the initial decision to take drugs is voluntary, over time the changes in the brain caused by repeated drug abuse can affect a person's self control and ability to make sound decisions, and at the same time send intense impulses to take drugs.

It is because of these changes in the brain that it is so challenging for a person who is addicted to stop abusing drugs. Fortunately, there are treatments that help people to counteract addiction's powerful disruptive effects and regain control. Research shows that combining addiction treatment medications, if available, with behavioral therapy is the best way to ensure success for most patients. Treatment approaches that are tailored to each patient's drug abuse patterns and any co-occurring medical, psychiatric, and social problems can lead to sustained recovery and a life without drug abuse.

Similar to other chronic, relapsing diseases, such as diabetes, asthma, or heart disease, drug addiction can be managed successfully. And, as with other chronic diseases, it is not uncommon for a person to relapse and begin abusing drugs again. Relapse, however, does not signal failure—rather, it indicates that treatment should be reinstated, adjusted, or that alternate treatment is needed to help the individual regain control and recover.

What Happens to Your Brain When You Take Drugs?

Drugs are chemicals that tap into the brain's communication system and disrupt the way nerve cells normally send, receive, and process information. There are at least two ways that drugs are able to do this: (1) by imitating the brain's natural chemical messengers, and/or (2) by overstimulating the "reward circuit" of the brain.

Some drugs, such as marijuana and heroin, have a similar structure to chemical messengers, called neurotransmitters, which are naturally produced by the brain. Because of this similarity, these drugs are able to "fool" the brain's receptors and activate nerve cells to send abnormal messages.

Other drugs, such as cocaine or methamphetamine, can cause the nerve cells to release abnormally large amounts of natural neurotransmitters, or prevent the normal recycling of these brain chemicals, which is needed to shut off the signal between neurons. This disruption produces a greatly amplified message that ultimately disrupts normal communication patterns.

Nearly all drugs, directly or indirectly, target the brain's reward system by flooding the circuit with dopamine. Dopamine is a neurotransmitter present in regions of the brain that control movement, emotion, motivation, and feelings of pleasure. The overstimulation of this system, which normally responds to natural behaviors that are linked to survival (eating, spending time with loved ones, etc.), produces euphoric effects in response to the drugs. This reaction sets in motion a pattern that "teaches" people to repeat the behavior of abusing drugs.

As a person continues to abuse drugs, the brain adapts to the overwhelming surges in dopamine by producing less dopamine or by reducing the number of dopamine receptors in the reward circuit. As a result, dopamine's impact on the reward circuit is lessened, reducing the abuser's ability to enjoy the drugs and the things that previously brought pleasure. This decrease compels those addicted to drugs to keep abusing drugs in order to attempt to bring their dopamine function back to normal. And, they may now require larger amounts of the drug than they first did to achieve the dopamine high—an effect known as tolerance.

Long-term abuse causes changes in other brain chemical systems and circuits as well. Glutamate is a neurotransmitter that influences the reward circuit and the ability to learn. When the optimal concentration of glutamate is altered by drug abuse, the brain attempts to compensate, which can impair cognitive function. Drugs of abuse facilitate nonconscious (conditioned) learning, which leads the user to experience uncontrollable cravings when they see a place or person they associate with the drug experience, even when the drug itself is not available. Brain imaging studies of drug-addicted individuals show changes in areas of the brain that are critical to judgment, decisionmaking, learning and memory, and behavior control. Together, these changes can drive an abuser to seek out and take drugs compulsively despite adverse consequences—in other words, to become addicted to drugs.

Why Do Some People Become Addicted, While Others Do Not?

No single factor can predict whether or not a person will become addicted to drugs. Risk for addiction is influenced by a person's biology, social environment, and age or stage of development. The more risk factors an individual has, the greater the chance that taking drugs can lead to addiction. For example:

- **Biology.** The genes that people are born with—in combination with environmental influences—account for about half of their addiction vulnerability. Additionally, gender, ethnicity, and the presence of other mental disorders may influence risk for drug abuse and addiction.
- **Environment.** A person's environment includes many different influences—from family and friends to socioeconomic status and quality of life in general. Factors such as peer pressure, physical and sexual abuse, stress, and parental involvement can greatly influence the course of drug abuse and addiction in a person's life.
- **Development.** Genetic and environmental factors interact with critical developmental stages in a person's life to affect addiction vulnerability, and adolescents experience a double challenge. Although taking drugs at any age can lead to addiction, the earlier that drug use begins, the more likely it is to progress to more serious abuse. And because adolescents' brains are still developing in the areas that govern decisionmaking, judgment, and self-control, they are especially prone to risk-taking behaviors, including trying drugs of abuse.

Prevention Is the Key

Drug addiction is a preventable disease. Results from NIDA-funded research have shown that prevention programs that involve the family, schools, communities, and the media are effective in reducing drug abuse. Although many events and cultural factors affect drug abuse trends, when youths perceive drug abuse as harmful, they reduce their drug taking. It is necessary, therefore, to help youth and the general public to understand the risks of drug abuse and for teachers, parents, and healthcare professionals to keep sending the message that drug addiction can be prevented if a person never abuses drugs.

Critical Thinking

1. Drug addiction carries with it a stigma, and is often not thought of as a disease. Explain the reason behind this.
2. If drug addiction is a preventable disease, what do you think the future of drug abuse will look like?

From *Drug Abuse and Addiction*, February 26, 2008. National Institute on Drug Abuse.

Family History of Alcohol Abuse Associated with Problematic Drinking among College Students

Joseph W. LaBrie et al.

1. Introduction

Risky drinking among college students is of particular concern for university administrators and health professions. Researchers have attempted to isolate correlates of risky drinking. A family history of alcohol abuse (FH+) is a well-documented risk factor for heavy alcohol use and alcohol-related problems (Chalder, Elgar, & Bennett, 2006; Cotton, 1979; Hussong, Curran, & Chassin, 1998; Kuntsche Rehm, & Gmel, 2004; Pullen, 1994; Turnbull, 1994; Warner, White, & Johnson., 2007). About 20% of college students are FH+ (Perkins, 2002) and the college environment may be more harmful for those students predisposed to alcohol problems. A few studies have revealed considerably higher rates of alcohol use (Kushner & Sher, 1993; LaBrie, Kenney, Lac, & Migliuri, 2009; Pullen, 1994) and alcohol-related problems (Leeman, Fenton, & Volpicelli, 2007) among FH+ compared with FH− college students. In contrast, other studies have found no relationship between family history and problematic alcohol use among college students (Engs, 1990; MacDonald, Fleming, & Barry, 1991; Harrell, Slane, & Klump, 2009). Further, there have been conflicting results on the role gender plays among FH+ college students. Some have found FH+ males to be more susceptible to risky drinking and consequences than FH+ females (e.g. Andersson, Johnsson, Berglund, & Öjehagen, 2007; Jackson, Sher, Gotham, & Wood, 2001; Sher, Walitzer, Wood, & Brent, 1991), while Hartford, Parker and Grant (1992) found no such gender difference. Inconsistencies in existing research highlight the need to explicate how family history status may impact drinking behaviors and problems in collegiate populations.

Alcohol expectancies, the specific beliefs about the behavioral, emotional, and cognitive effects of alcohol (Leigh, 1987), are a potential psychosocial motivator of risky drinking. Stronger positive alcohol expectancies are associated with problem drinking (e.g. Anderson, Schweinsburg, Paulus, Brown, & Tapert, 2005; Brown, Goldman, & Christiansen, 1985).

Alcohol-outcome expectancies result from both personal experience with alcohol and from mirroring drinking behavior of individuals (Lundahl et al, 1997), and have thus been shown to differ by family history status in that FH+ individuals have endorsed stronger alcohol-related expectancies, particularly overall positive expectancies (Morean et al, 2009; Pastor & Evans, 2003). Further, FH+ individuals with stronger overall positive expectancies are most likely to experience alcohol-related problems (Conway, Swendsen, & Merikangas, 2003; VanVoorst & Quirk, 2003).

Much of the previous research on family history of alcohol abuse has focused on COAs (children of alcohols) during adolescence (Barnow, Schuckit, Lucht, John, & Freyberger, 2002; Brown, Creamer, & Stetson, 1987; Chalder et al., 2006; Nash, McQueen, & Bray, 2005; Sher et al., 1991) and middle–late adulthood (Beaudoin, Murray, Bond, & Barnes, 1997; Cloninger, Sigvardsson, & Bohman, 1996; Curran et al., 1999). Moreover, family history studies involving college students have suffered from various limitations, such as a relatively small sample size (e.g., Leeman et al., 2007; Pullen, 1994), single-sex samples (e.g. LaBrie et al., 2009; Harrell et al., 2009), or first-year student samples (e.g. Andersson et al., 2007, Gotham, Sher, & Wood, 2003; Jackson et al., 2001). The present study broadens previous research by offering unique insight into family history of alcohol abuse, alcohol-related behaviors and problems, and further examines the moderating effect of gender in family history status on alcohol consumption, alcohol expectancies, and alcohol-related consequences among a large, multisite, ethnically diverse sample of male and female college students.

2. Methods
2.1 Participants

Participants were recruited from two west-coast universities, a large, public institution with 30,000 undergraduates and a mid-sized private institution with approximately 5500 undergraduates. Of a randomly selected pool of 7000 students, 3753 (53.6%) consented to participate. Representative of the makeup of the corresponding institutions, participants' mean age was 19.88 ($SD = 1.36$) and the majority of the participants were female (61%). The sample consisted of 18.9% first-year students, 24.5% sophomores, 27.4% juniors, and 29.2% seniors. Racial representation was as follows: 57.4% Caucasian, 18.7% Asian, 10.7% Multiracial, 3.2% African American, and 10.0% reported other racial/ethnic groups. On average, participants consumed 6.04 ($SD = 8.58$) drinks over 1.59 ($SD = 1.53$) drinking days per week. Among the 67.5% of students who drank, they consumed an average of 8.94 ($SD = 9.11$) drinks per week and averaged 2.36 ($SD = 1.30$) drinking days.

2.2. Design and Procedure

At the start of the fall semester, 7000 students (3500 from each campus), received letters inviting them to participate in a study about alcohol use and perceptions of college-student drinking. The students were directed to a link for an online survey. After students clicked on the link and entered their individual pin, they were presented with a local IRB-approved consent form. Participants then completed a 20 min survey, for which they received a $20 compensation.

2.3 Measures

2.3.1. Demographics

Participants indicated their gender, age, most recent GPA, and race.

2.3.2. Family History

Participants indicated whether they had a biological relative that "has or has had a significant drinking problem—one that should or did lead to treatment." This measure was previously developed and successfully used by Miller & Marlatt (1984).

2.3.3. Alcohol Consumption

The Daily Drinking Questionnaire (DDQ: Collins, parks, & Marlan, 1985; Kivlahan, Marlatt, Fromme, & Coppel, 1990) asked students to report, from the past 30 days, the typical number of drinks they consumed each day of the week. Responses were summed to form a total drinks per week variable used in this analysis.

2.3.4. Negative Consequences

The 25-item Rutgers Alcohol Problem Index (RAPI, White & Labouvie, 1989) ($\alpha = .925$) assessed alcohol-related consequences. Using a 0 (*never*) to 4 (*more than 10 times*) scale, participants indicated how many times in the past three months they had experienced each stated circumstance (e.g., "Caused shame or embarrassment to someone," "Passed out or fainted suddenly," or "Felt that you had a problem with school.").

2.3.5. Alcohol Expectancies and Evaluations

The Comprehensive Effects of Alcohol (CEOA; Fromme, Stroot, & Kaplan, 1993) is a two-part questionnaire consisting of 76 items. In Part 1, representing items tapping expectancies, participants indicated expectations concerning how he or she may act or feel under the influence of alcohol (e.g., "I would enjoy sex more," "I would act sociable"; 1 = "disagree" 4 = "agree"). In Part 2, representing evaluations, participants subjectively evaluated the effects of alcohol with the same 38 items as Part 1 of the questionnaire (e.g., "Enjoying sex more," "Feeling sociable" 1 = "bad" 3 = "neutral" 5 = "good"). Each of the expectancies and evaluations components may be further divided into positive factors (sociability, tension reduction, liquid courage, and sexuality) and negative factors (cognitive behavioral impairment, risk and aggression, and self-perception).

3. Results

A family history of alcohol abuse was reported by 35.0% of the total sample, and FH+ participants were more likely to have drank in the past year than their FH− peers (81% vs 74%; $\chi^2 = 9.63$, $p < .001$). Independent sample t-tests, separately conducted for males and females, revealed several systematic differences between FH+ and FH− respondents (Table 1). Among males, FH+ respondents averaged significantly higher than their FH− counterparts on drinks per week, negative consequences, overall positive expectancies, positive expectancies concerned with tension reduction and liquid courage, as well as positive evaluations concerned with tension reduction. Among females, FH+ respondents reported significantly higher drinks per week, negative consequences, overall positive expectancies, as well as positive expectancies concerned with sociability, tension reduction, and sexuality in comparison to the FH− participants. Typically, FH+ females reported negative evaluations (risk and aggression, and self-perception) to be worse than did FH− females.

Additional analyses show that, among males, FH+ participants drank 45.7% more drinks per week and experienced 43.6% more negative consequences than those classified as FH−. Among females, however, FH+ individuals consumed 14.4% more drinks and experienced 23.6% more negative consequences than their FH− counterparts. Such results, taken together, suggest that a family history of alcohol abuse may adversely impact males more than females in the college environment.

An ANCOVA model, controlling for age, GPA, race, overall positive and negative expectancies, and overall positive and negative evaluations, was performed to predict drinks per week. Family history status (FH+ or FH−) and respondent gender (male or female) served as the independent factors. After ruling out the statistical contribution of the covariates, main effects were found for both family history and gender, and their interaction also emerged (Table 2). This statistical interaction, presented in Figure 1, revealed that the difference between FH+ and FH− on drinking was more pronounced in males than females, and that FH+ males were especially vulnerable to higher levels of alcohol consumption.

A second ANCOVA model was conducted to predict alcohol negative consequences. Age, GPA, race, and drinks per week were entered as covariates, and family history and gender served

Table 1 Mean Difference on Drinking Variable by Family History, for Males and Females

Measure	Males					Females				
	FH+ (n = 435)		FH– (n = 1008)			FH+ (n = 875)		FH– (n = 1420)		
	M	(SD)	M	(SD)	t-test	M	(SD)	M	(SD)	t-test
Drinks per week	10.75	(12.83)	7.38	(10.43)	5.21***	4.94	(6.04)	4.32	(5.68)	2.48*
Negative consequences	6.72	(9.10)	4.68	(8.77)	5.21***	4.55	(6.64)	3.68	(6.03)	3.11**
Overall positive expectancies	2.55	(0.55)	2.47	(0.58)	2.16*	2.42	(0.58)	2.35	(0.59)	2.73**
Sociability	2.94	(0.68)	2.88	(0.70)	1.50	2.96	(0.73)	2.87	(0.73)	2.74**
Tension reduction	2.63	(0.71)	2.53	(0.74)	2.39*	2.32	(0.72)	2.24	(0.72)	2.53*
Liquid courage	2.48	(0.69)	2.39	(0.72)	2.14*	2.29	(0.71)	2.25	(0.73)	1.18
Sexuality	2.13	(0.73)	2.09	(0.73)	0.93	2.12	(0.76)	2.05	(0.75)	2.11*
Overall negative expectancies	2.28	(0.52)	2.28	(0.59)	0.07	2.20	(0.56)	2.20	(0.58)	0.21
Cognitive behavioral imp.	2.64	(0.60)	2.63	(0.65)	0.32	2.64	(0.65)	2.62	(0.68)	0.73
Risk and aggression	2.31	(0.71)	2.26	(0.73)	1.21	2.10	(0.74)	2.11	(0.74)	–0.40
Self-perception	1.89	(0.64)	1.95	(0.72)	–1.34	1.87	(0.69)	1.87	(0.69)	0.25
Overall positive evaluations	3.48	(0.84)	3.40	(0.83)	1.75	3.18	(0.85)	3.19	(0.86)	–0.39
Sociability	3.84	(0.93)	3.80	(0.92)	0.85	3.66	(0.94)	3.65	(0.95)	0.27
Tension reduction	3.82	(1.00)	3.67	(0.97)	2.55*	3.41	(0.99)	3.40	(1.00)	0.26
Liquid courage	2.95	(0.91)	2.90	(0.90)	0.98	2.72	(0.90)	2.79	(0.91)	–1.79
Sexuality	3.32	(1.07)	3.21	(1.02)	1.69	2.92	(1.08)	2.92	(1.05)	–0.20
Overall negative evaluations	1.89	(0.57)	1.92	(0.62)	–0.89	1.68	(0.50)	1.76	(0.55)	–3.45***
Cognitive behavioral imp.	1.82	(0.64)	1.82	(0.68)	0.04	1.62	(0.56)	1.63	(0.58)	–0.19
Risk and aggression	2.13	(0.83)	2.15	(0.84)	–0.39	1.92	(0.76)	2.07	(0.81)	–4.25***
Self-perception	1.71	(0.64)	1.79	(0.71)	–1.85	1.49	(0.55)	1.58	(0.61)	–3.49***

*p<.05. **p<.01. ***p<.001.

as the independent variables. After the variance attributed to the covariates were accounted for in the model, family history remained statistically significant, but no gender main effect or interaction was discovered (Table 2).

4. Discussion

The present investigation uses a large multisite sample and corroborates extant literature by identifying family history as a significant risk factor for alcohol misuse and related consequences among male and female college students (Kushner & Sher, 1993; Leeman et al., 2007; LaBrie et al., 2009; Pullen, 1994). More specifically, this study extends previous research by finding that, whether attributable to genetics or environmental upbringing, familial ties to alcoholism were considerably more hazardous for males than females in regard to excessive alcohol consumption. Compared to FH– same-sex peers, FH+ males drank 41% more drinks per week and FH+ females drank 14% more drinks per week. Notably, results covaried out other important predictors

of drinking (e.g. age, GPA, race) to better assess how FH status and gender may be related to drinking in college, over and above such variables. By highlighting family history positive college students' heightened susceptibility to risky drinking and consequences, and male FH+ students' enhanced risk for alcohol misuse, the current results may help college personnel identify and target prevention efforts to at-risk students. Preventative interventions taking place early in college with FH+ students might help them better understand their heightened alcohol-related vulnerabilities and provide them with tools and motivation to reduce potential harm.

In addition, findings both confirm and extend relevant research examining the role that alcohol expectancies play in FH+ college students' alcohol behaviors and outcomes. Not only did students reporting familial alcohol abuse endorse significantly greater overall positive expectancies than same-sex FH– counterparts, but FH+ female respondents evaluated the negative effects of alcohol to be substantially "more bad" than FH– females. This paradoxical finding, in which women exposed to familial alcohol

Table 2 ANCOVA Models Predicting Drinks Per Week and Negative Consequences

Variable	df	MS	F test
DV: drinks per week			
Covariates			
Age	1	137.51	2.29
GPA	1	209.84	3.49
Race	1	5207.62	86.57***
Overall positive expectancies	1	10,846.35	108.31***
Overall negative expectancies	1	6536.75	108.67***
Overall positive evaluations	1	6.15	0.10
Overall negative evaluations	1	2833.10	47.10***
Family history	1	1032.70	17.17***
Gender	1	8485.34	141.06***
Family history × gender	1	1025.75	17.05***
DV: negative consequences			
Covariates			
Age	1	95.33	2.34
GPA	1	452.91	11.09***
Race	1	423.66	10.39**
Drinks per week	1	43,439.92	1063.97***
Family history	1	460.67	11.28
Gender	1	130.98	3.21
Family history × gender	1	2.71	0.07

Note: race (1 = Caucasian, 0 = non-Caucasian).
* $p < .05.$ ** $p < .01.$ *** $p < .001.$

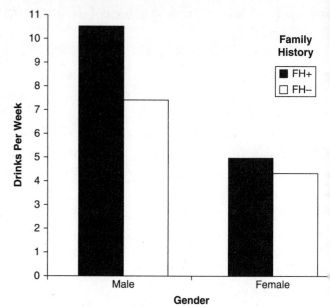

Figure 1 Family history status × gender interaction on drink per week

abuse judged alcohol's negative evaluations to be worse, yet were more likely to agree that drinking personally yielded positive effects (i.e., expectancies) may suggest that FH+ women may not equate their own drinking with that of alcoholic family members and thus may feel immune to the negative evaluations they themselves associate with alcohol. More concerning, however, is the possibility that these findings may be indicative of cognitive dissonance, whereby highly endorsed positive expectancies contribute to continued drinking, often heavy drinking, in students even though they have been exposed to, and thus recognize, the negative aspects of drinking. By rationalizing alcohol misuse through heightened expectancies, FH+ college females may be able to reduce dissonance and fulfill strong, possibly genetically predisposed desires to imbibe. Regardless, FH+ students' apparent awareness of the negative effects of alcohol use through their own familial experience may be a promising avenue for intervening. Intervention with these students should allow them to reflect on and be mindful of their experiences with these negative effects, thereby building motivation to avoid these same consequences while challenging positive alcohol expectancies.

The present findings are limited in that they do not account for environmental risk factors known to co-occur with FH status (e.g., histories of physical or sexual abuse or attraction to high-risk student groups) and that may confound the relationship between FH+ status and both alcohol expectancies and misuse. Future studies assessing such risk factors may be warranted. Another limitation of the current study is the use of one, nonspecific classification of FH+ status. Future research may benefit from distinguishing first, second, and third degree affiliation to alcohol abuse (e.g. parent vs. grandparent or aunt/uncle), gender of the relative with alcohol problems (e.g. mother vs. father), or familial history density (i.e., whether an individual has more than one family member with an alcohol problem). A more defined classification of FH status may also reveal environmental risk factors; for instance, the extent to which residential exposure to alcoholism may heighten risk.

The current study reveals that FH+ students make up a substantial percentage (35%) of the college population and that these students are at increased risk for problematic drinking and consequences as compared to their FH– peers. Despite this and previous research in concert with the current findings, preventative interventions targeting FH+ students are lacking. Both researchers and college health personnel may wish to invest resources in targeting these individuals.

References

Anderson, K. G., Schweinsburg, A., Paulus, M., Brown, S. A., & Tapert, S. (2005). Examining personality and alcohol expectancies using functional magnetic resonance imaging (fMRI) with adolescents. *Journal of Studies on Alcohol, 66,* 323–331.

Article 8. Family History of Alcohol Abuse Associated with Problematic Drinking among College Students

Andersson, C., Johnsson, K., Berglund, M., & Öjehagen, A. (2007). Alcohol involvement in Swedish university freshmen related to gender, age, serious relationship and family history of alcohol problems. *Alcohol and Alcoholism, 42*(5), 448–455.

Barnow, S., Schuckit, M., Lucht, M., John, U., & Freyberger, H. J. (2002). The importance of positive family history of alcoholism, parental rejection and emotional warmth, behavioral problems and peer substance use for alcohol problems in teenagers: a path analysis. *Journal of Studies on Alcohol, 63*, 305–315.

Beaudoin, C. M., Murray, R. P., Bond, J., Jr., & Barnes, G. E. (1997). Personality characteristics of depressed or alcoholic adult children of alcoholics. *Personality and Individual Differences, 23*, 559–567.

Brown, S. A., Creamer, V. A., & Stetson, B. A. (1987). Adolescent alcohol expectancies in relation to personal and parental drinking patterns. *Journal of Abnormal Psychology, 96*, 117–121.

Brown, S., Goldman, M., & Christiansen, B. (1985). Do alcohol expectancies mediate drinking patterns of adults? *Journal of Consulting and Clinical Psychology, 53*(4), 512–519.

Chalder, M., Elgar, F. J., & Bennett, P. (2006). Drinking and motivations to drink among adolescent children of parents with alcohol problems. *Alcohol & Alcoholism, 41*(1), 107–113.

Cloninger, C. R., Sigvardsson, S., & Bohman, M. (1996). Type I and Type II Alcoholism: an update. *Alcohol Health and Research World, 20*, 18–23.

Collins, R. L., Parks, G. A., & Marlett, A. (1985). Social determinants of alcohol consumption: the effects of social interaction and model status on self-administration of alcohol. *Journal of Consulting and Clinical Psychology, 53*(2), 189–200.

Conway, K. P., Swendsen, J. D., & Merikangas, K. R. (2003). Alcohol expectancies, alcohol consumption, and problem drinking. *The moderating role of family history. Addictive Behaviors, 28*, 823–836.

Cotton, N. S. (1979). The familial incidence of alcoholism: a review. *Journal of Studies on Alcohol, 40*(1), 89–116.

Curran, G. M., Stoltenberg, S. F., Hill, E. M., Mudd, S. A., Blow, F. C., & Zucker, R. A. (1999). Gender differences in the relationship among SES, family history of alcohol disorders and alcohol dependence. *Journal of Studies on Alcohol, 60*, 825–832.

Engs, R. (1990). Family background of alcohol abuse and its relationship to alcohol consumption among college students: an unexpected finding. *Journal of Studies on Alcohol, 51*(6), 542–547.

Fromme, K., Stroot, E., & Kaplan, D. (1993). Comprehensive effects of alcohol: development and psychometric assessment of a new expectancy questionnaire. *Psychological Assessment, 5*(1), 19–26.

Gotham, H. J., Sher, K. J., & Wood, P. K. (2003). Alcohol involvement and development task completion during young adulthood. *Journal of Studies on Alcohol, 64*, 32–42.

Harford, T., Parker, D., & Grant, B. (1992). Family history, alcohol use and dependence symptoms among young adults in the United States. *Alcoholism: Clinical and Experimental Research, 16*(6), 1042–1046.

Harrell, Z., Slane, J., & Klump, K. (2009). Predictors of alcohol problems in college women: the role of depressive symptoms, disordered eating, and family history of alcoholism. *Addictive Behaviors, 34*(3), 252–257.

Hussong, A. M., Curran, P. J., & Chassin, L. (1998). Pathways of risk for accelterated heavy alcohol use among adolescent children of alcohol parents. *Journal of Abnormal Child Psychology, 26*(6), 453.

Kivlahan, D. R., Marlatt, G. A., Fromme, K., & Coppel, D. B. (1990). Secondary prevention with college drinkers: evaluation of an alcohol skills training program. *Journal of Consulting and Clinical Psychology, 58*, 805–810.

Kuntsche, E., Rehm, J., & Gmel, G. (2004). Characteristics of binge drinkers in Europe. *Social Science & Medicine, 59*, 113–127.

Kushner, M. G., & Sher, K. J. (1993). Comorbidity of alcohol and anxiety disorders among college students: effects of gender and family history of alcoholism. *Addictive Behaviors, 18*, 543–552.

Jackson, K. M., Sher, K. J., Gotham, H. J., & Wood, P. K. (2001). Transition into and out of large-effect drinking in young adulthood. *Journal of Abnormal Psychology, 110*(3), 378–391.

LaBrie, J. W., Kenney, S. R., Lac, A., & Migliuri, S. M. (2009). Differential drinking patterns of family history positive and family history negative first semester college females. *Addictive Behaviors, 34*, 190–196.

Leeman, R., Fenton, M., & Volpicelli, J. (2007). Impaired control and undergraduate problem drinking. *Alcohol & Alcoholism, 42*(1), 42–48.

Leigh, B. C. (1987). Evaluations of alcohol expectancies: do they add to prediction of drinking patterns? *Psychology of Addictive Behaviors, 1*(3), 135–139.

Lundahl, L., Davis, T., Adesso, V., & Lukas, S. (1997). Alcohol expectancies: effects of gender, age, and family history of alcoholism. *Addictive Behaviors, 22*(1), 115–125.

MacDonald, R., Fleming, M., & Barry, K. (1991). Risk factors associated with alcohol abuse in college students. *American Journal of Drug and Alcohol Abuse, 17*(4), 439–449.

Miller, W. R., & Marlatt, G. A. (1984). Brief drinking profile. Odessa, FL: Psychological Assessment Resources.

Morean, M. E., Corbin, W. R., Sinha, R., & O'Malley, S. S. (2009). Parental history of anxiety and alcohol-use disorders and alcohol expectancies as predictors of alcohol-related problems. *Journal of Studies on Alcohol and Drugs, 70*, 227–236.

Nash, S. G., McQueen, A., & Bray, J. H. (2005). Pathways to adolescent alcohol use: family environment, peer influence, and parental expectations. *Journal of Adolescent Health, 37*, 19–28.

Pastor, A. D., & Evans, S. M. (2003). Alcohol outcome expectancies and risk for alcohol use problems in women with and without a family history of alcoholism. *Drug and Alcohol Dependence, 70*, 201–214.

Perkins, H. W. (2002). Surveying the damage: a review of research on consequences of alcohol misuse in college populations. *Journal of Studies on Alcohol, 14*, 91–100.

Pullen, L. M. (1994). The relationship among alcohol abuse in college students and selected psychological/demographic variables. *Journal of Alcohol and Drug Education, 40*(1), 36–50.

Sher, K. J., Walitzer, K. S., Wood, P. K., & Brent, E. E. (1991). Characteristics of children of alcoholics: putative risk factors, substance use and abuse, and psychopathology. *Journal of Abnormal Psychology, 100*, 427–448.

Turnbull, J. E. (1994). Early background variables as predictors of adult alcohol problems in women. *International Journal of the Addictions, 29*, 707–728.

VanVoorst, W. A., & Quirk, S. W. (2003). Are relations between parental history of alcohol problems and changes in drinking moderated by positive expectancies? *Alcoholism: Clinical and Experimental Research, 26,* 25–30.

White, H., & Labouvie, E. (1989). Towards the assessment of adolescent problem drinking. *Journal of Studies on Alcohol, 50*(1), 30–37.

Warner, L. A., White, H. R., & Johnson, V. (2007). Alcohol initiation experiences and family history of alcoholism as predictors of problem-drinking trajectories. *Journal of Studies on Alcohol and Drugs, 68,* 56–65.

Critical Thinking

1. Explain why FH+ women may experience cognitive dissonance regarding their own use of alcohol.

2. Would having this information available influence college student's behavior?

Acknowledgment—Support for this research was provided by Nationa Institute of Alcohol Abuse and Alcoholism grant R01-AA012547.

Adolescent Substance Abuse:

America's #1 Public Health Problem

A Report of the National Court Appointed Special Advocate Association

Introduction and Executive Summary

This report finds that adolescent smoking, drinking, misusing prescription drugs and using illegal drugs is, by any measure, a public health problem of epidemic proportion, presenting a clear and present danger to millions of America's teenagers and severe and expensive long-range consequences for our entire population. This report is a wake-up call for all of us, regardless of whether we seek to win the future by investing in our youth or seek to cut public spending to avoid a back-breaking financial burden on our children and grandchildren. The findings and recommendations in this report offer common ground and opportunity to help achieve both objectives.

This report finds that:

- Three-fourths of high school students (75.6 percent, 10.0 million)[1] have used addictive substances including cigarettes, alcohol, marijuana or cocaine.
- Almost half of high school students (46.1 percent, 6.1 million) are current[2] users of these substances.
- Of high school students who have ever smoked a cigarette, had a drink of alcohol or used other drugs, 19.4 percent have a clinical substance use disorder,[3] as do 33.3 percent of current users.[4]

And these estimates are low; none includes adolescents who are incarcerated in the juvenile justice system or the large numbers of adolescents who have dropped out of high school.[5] Rates of substance use and substance use disorders are even higher in these populations than among high school students generally.

Teen users are at significantly higher risk of developing an addictive disorder compared to adults, and the earlier they began using, the higher their risk. Nine out of 10 people who meet the clinical criteria for substance use disorders involving nicotine, alcohol or other drugs began smoking, drinking or using other drugs before they turned 18. People who begin using any addictive substance before age 15 are six and a half times as likely to develop a substance use disorder as those who delay use until age 21 or older (28.1 percent vs. 4.3 percent).

Alcohol is the most preferred addictive substance among high school students:

- 72.5 percent of high school students have drunk alcohol,
- 46.3 percent have smoked cigarettes,
- 36.8 percent have used marijuana and
- 14.8 percent have misused controlled prescription drugs.[6]

Two-thirds (65.1 percent) of high school students have used more than one substance.

The fact that 75.6 percent of high school students have used addictive substances and 46.1 percent are current users dwarfs the prevalence rates of many other risky health behaviors considered to be of epidemic proportion among teens in the U.S. For example, 34.2 percent of teens[7] are overweight or obese;[8] 18.3 percent[9] have ever experienced symptoms of depression; and 28.1 percent of 9th graders and 19.9 percent of 12th graders have been victims of bullying.[10] Substance use also frequently co-occurs with these and other health problems that teens face.[11]

The Consequences

The immediate consequences of teen substance use are devastating, ranging from injuries and unintended pregnancies; to medical conditions such as asthma, depression, anxiety, psychosis and impaired brain function; to reduced academic performance and educational achievement; to criminal involvement and even death.

And, these consequences extend beyond teen users to those who breathe in their cigarette smoke; those assaulted, injured or killed by teens who are drunk or high; those who contract sexually transmitted diseases or experience unplanned pregnancies; and to babies born to teen mothers who smoke, drink or use other drugs during pregnancy.

It does not take heavy or dependent use to experience life-altering and potentially fatal consequences. Driving a car under the influence of alcohol or other drugs can lead to disability or death. One occasion of drinking or other drug use can result in a dangerous fight or having unprotected sex. It can take as few as one or two episodes of smoking to show symptoms of nicotine dependence or one dose of cocaine to die from a heart attack. And all of these tragic outcomes also create substantial costs to society.

The financial costs of teen substance use and addiction;[12] include, for example, an estimated $68.0 billion associated with underage drinking alone and $14.4 billion associated with substance-related juvenile justice programs annually. In the long run, the consequences of adolescent substance use and addiction place enormous burdens on our health care, criminal justice, family court, education and social service systems.

Total costs to federal, state and local governments of substance use among the entire U.S. population are at least $467.7 billion per year—almost $1,500 for every person in America—driven primarily by those who began their use as teens. These costs are the result of accidents, diseases, crimes, child neglect and abuse, unplanned pregnancies, homelessness, unemployment and other outcomes of our failure to prevent substance use and treat this health condition. Addiction, whether to nicotine, alcohol or other drugs, is a complex brain disease that can be treated, but when left untreated, the consequences and their costs escalate.

It is time for America to deal with our Nation's number one public health problem: substance abuse and addiction. While we must provide treatment for those in need, the best cure is prevention.

—Jim Ramstad
Former Member of Congress (MN-3)

The Making of an Epidemic

This report finds that the tragedy is not that we don't know what to do; rather, it is that we simply fail to do it. We know that risky substance use and addiction is the leading cause of preventable death and disability in the United States, and in most cases it begins in the teen years. Adolescence is, in fact, *the* critical period for the onset of substance use and its potentially debilitating consequences for two reasons:

- The regions of the brain that are critical to decision making, judgment, impulse control, emotion and memory are not yet fully developed in adolescence, making teens more prone than adults to taking risks, including experimenting with tobacco, alcohol and other drugs.
- Because the teen brain is still developing, addictive substances physically alter its structure and function faster and more intensely than in adults,[13] interfering with brain development, further impairing judgment and heightening the risk of addiction.

While adolescence itself increases the chances that teens will use addictive substances, American culture further increases that risk. Teens are highly vulnerable to the wide-ranging social influences that subtly condone or more overtly encourage their use of these substances. These influences include the acceptance of substance use by parents, schools and communities; pervasive advertising of these products; media portrayals of substance use as benign or even glamorous, fun and relaxing; and the widespread availability of tobacco, alcohol, marijuana and controlled prescription drugs. Our teens are awash in a sea of addictive substances, while adults send mixed messages at best, wink and look the other way, or blatantly condone or promote their use. In so doing, we normalize behavior that undermines the health and futures of our teens.

Adding to the recipe for teen substance use, many teens have other challenges in their lives that make them more inclined to use addictive substances, more vulnerable to the ubiquitous cultural influences promoting use or that hike the risk of progression from substance use to addiction. These challenges include being the victim of neglect, abuse or other trauma, suffering from mental health disorders that frequently co-occur with substance use and inheriting a genetic predisposition to addiction.

The science of addiction and evidence of its consequences is clear enough to conclude that there is no recommended level of safe use of addictive substances by teens.

The CASA Study

This report documents the nature and origin of the largest preventable—and most costly—health problem in America. It reveals the latest information about how substance use and addiction affect the teen brain and neurochemistry; lays out the extent of the problem of teen substance use and addiction; and describes the health, safety and social consequences. It examines the broad factors within American culture that drive adolescent substance use and explores the range of individual factors that compounds these risks for many vulnerable teens. It summarizes what research demonstrates can be done to prevent and reduce the problem; describes the chasm between this knowledge and what health care providers, parents, schools, communities and policymakers are actually doing and explores the barriers to bridging this gap and implementing effective substance use prevention and control policies. Finally, it provides concrete and evidence-based recommendations for health care professionals, parents, policymakers, educators, the media, researchers and teens themselves to act in the face of the body of knowledge presented in this report.

CASA's work for this report involved nationally representative online surveys of 1,000 high school students, 1,000 parents of high school students (75 percent from the same households as the student respondents) and 500 school personnel (including teachers, principals, counselors and coaches); extensive in-depth analyses of seven national data sets; interviews with approximately 50 leading experts in a broad range of fields related to this report; five focus groups with students, parents and school personnel; and a review of more than 2,000 scientific articles and reports.[14]

Other Key Findings

Despite considerable declines in overall reported rates of current substance use since 1999, progress appears to have stalled and rates may once again be on the rise. The use of smokeless tobacco has been increasing since 2003. Declines in past 30 day cigarette smoking are slowing significantly, and national data suggest that current use of marijuana and controlled prescription drugs may be inching up.

The overall decline in substance use rates also may obfuscate dangerous patterns of substance use; for example, high school students drink more drinks when they drink (4.9 drinks per day) than any other age group, including 18–25 year olds (4.4 drinks per day).

While most teens responding to CASA's survey of high school students conducted for this study report that they believe substance use to be very dangerous, almost half of them are current users. Further, a quarter of them (24.7 percent) see marijuana as a harmless drug and 16.9 percent think of it as a medicine. Teens who hold favorable views of the benefits of substance use—such as being cool or popular weight control, self-medication, stress relief or coping—are more likely to smoke, drink and use other drugs than those who hold less favorable beliefs or stronger perceptions of risk.

Adolescent Substance Use Hikes the Risk of Addiction

One in eight high school students (11.9 percent, 1.6 million) have a diagnosable clinical substance use disorder involving nicotine, alcohol or other drugs. Because the adolescent brain is more sensitive to the addictive properties of nicotine, alcohol and other drugs, the younger a person is when he or she begins to use addictive substances, the greater the risk of developing the disease of addiction.

Every year that the onset of substance use is delayed until the mid-20s—about the time when the human brain is more fully developed—the risk of developing a substance use disorder is reduced. One in four people who used *any* addictive substance before they turned 18 have a substance use disorder, compared with one in 25 who first used any of these substances at age 21 or older.

Adolescent substance use and its often tragic consequences, including addiction, can be prevented. Parents should be outraged that we are letting this happen to our children.

—*Senator Leticia Van de Putte*
Texas State Senate

Teen Substance Use Compromises Academic Performance, Safety and Health

Teen substance use contributes to some of the most glaring barriers to health and productivity facing the current generation of teenagers in the United States. For example:

- Teen tobacco, alcohol and marijuana users are at least twice as likely as nonusers to have poor grades and teen marijuana users are approximately twice as likely as nonusers to drop out of high school.

- In 2009, one in 10 (9.7 percent) high school students reported driving after drinking alcohol in the past month.
- More than one in five (21.6 percent) sexually-active high school students report having used alcohol or other drugs before their last sexual experience; one in five teens and young adults report having unprotected sex after drinking or using other drugs.
- In 2009, 32.0 percent of all substance related reports in emergency department visits made by patients ages 12 to 17 were alcohol related and 18.7 percent were marijuana related.
- Substance use is a major contributor to the three leading causes of death among adolescents—accidents, homicides and suicides—and increases the risk of numerous potentially fatal health conditions, including cancers, heart disease and respiratory illnesses.
- Smoking is related to impaired lung growth, asthma-related symptoms and declines in lung function in adolescence; regular cigarette smoking increases the risk of lung cancer, breast cancer, emphysema, bronchial disorders and cardiovascular diseases.
- Alcohol-induced damage has been observed in the brains of binge-drinking teens. Teens with alcohol use disorders have more self-reported health problems (including problems with sleep, eating and vision) and more abnormalities during physical examinations (including in the abdominal region as well as in their respiratory and cardiovascular systems) than those without alcohol use disorders.
- Heavy or chronic marijuana use is associated with a host of cognitive impairments and with structural and functional brain changes. Regular use of marijuana can hike the risk of respiratory illnesses including chronic cough, bronchitis and lung infections.

Even relatively low levels of substance use can have disastrous consequences for teens, including accidents, violence, unsafe sexual activity, cardiac and respiratory problems and even death.

The consequences of adolescent substance use extend to all teens, even those who are not using. A significant proportion of high school students reports knowing someone personally who has gotten into trouble with parents, their school or the authorities (41.0 percent); who has gotten into an accident (26.8 percent); whose ability to perform school or work activities has been disturbed (24.5 percent); who has been injured or harassed (19.4 percent each); who has had an unintended pregnancy (13.8 percent); who has experienced physical abuse (11.1 percent); and who has been sexually assaulted or raped (7.0 percent) due to someone else's substance use.

American Culture Drives Teen Substance Use

Strong parental disapproval of substance use can help offset cultural messages promoting substance use, but too many parents by their own attitudes or behaviors further increase the chances that their teens will use:

As parents, siblings, neighbors and leaders, we must work together and remain vigilant in our efforts to generate greater awareness about the dangers of substance misuse and the suffering, violence and death that far too often results when our children use alcohol and other drugs. We must encourage our teens to make the right choices, resist peer pressure and recognize that substance use by teens can have life-altering and tragic consequences.

—*Lucille Roybal-Allard*
Congresswoman (CA-34)

- Nearly half (46.1 percent) of children under age 18 (34.4 million) live in a household where someone age 18 or older engages in risky substance use;[15] 45.4 percent (33.9 million) live with a *parent* who is a risky substance user.

- More than one in six (17.8 percent) children under age 18 (13.3 million) live in a household where someone age 18 or older has a substance use disorder;[16] 16.9 percent (12.6 million) live with a *parent* who has the disorder.

- Less than half (42.6 percent) of parents list refraining from smoking cigarettes, drinking alcohol, using marijuana, misusing prescription drugs or using other illicit drugs as one of their top three concerns for their teens, and 20.8 percent characterize marijuana as a harmless drug.

Disapproval from the larger community in which teens live also can help protect teens; however, substance-related images are pervasive in neighborhood-based advertising and retail sales across the country, sending the message that substance use is a normal part of life. Greater numbers of tobacco and alcohol retail outlets in a community relate to increased risk of adolescent substance use.

Depictions of smoking and drinking in television shows and movies popular with teens also are pervasive. The odds of becoming a tobacco user are more than doubled by exposure to tobacco marketing and media images of tobacco use. Alcohol advertising is related to young people's attitudes and expectations regarding drinking and to their risk of alcohol use.

If teens exposed to these messages decide to try smoking, drinking or using other drugs, they have little trouble obtaining these products. The majority of 10th graders say that it would be easy for them to get cigarettes (76.1 percent), alcohol (80.9 percent) or marijuana (69.3 percent). The most common sources of tobacco, alcohol and other drugs are friends and family.

Some Teens Face Personal Challenges that Compound Their Risk of Substance Use and Addiction

These include:

- A genetic predisposition toward developing an addiction or a family history of substance use disorders,

- Adverse childhood events, such as abuse, neglect or other trauma,
- Co-occurring mental health problems,
- Peer victimization or bullying, and
- Engagement in other health- and safety-risk behaviors such as early or unsafe sex, unhealthy weight control behaviors, risky driving or violent or aggressive behavior.

Not only are these teens more likely to use addictive substances and to develop substance use disorders, but many of them also are more likely to start using substances at a young age,[77] to use multiple addictive substances and to progress more quickly to heavy use and addiction.

Certain sub-groups of adolescents—such as those who are in the child welfare system, drop out of high school, are involved with the criminal justice system or have a minority sexual identity—also are at elevated risk for substance use, addiction and their health and social consequences.

Prevention: We Know What Works but Fail to Act

As with any other behavioral health problem, effective prevention starts at home. Teens at reduced risk for substance use live in homes where parents model healthy behavior, create a nurturing family environment, play an active role in their children's lives, communicate openly and honestly about substance use and set and enforce clear rules. They also have the companionship and guidance of positive adult role models, strong attachments to their schools or communities and goals for the future. Those who participate in clubs, community service or volunteer activities or are involved in religious or spiritual practice are at reduced risk as well.

Beyond the family, key public health measures are critical to prevent adolescent substance use, including:

- Helping the public understand that teen substance use is a health concern and understand the consequences of adolescent substance use, factors that increase the risk that teens will use, the link between early use and addiction, ways to prevent adolescent substance use and how best to respond if a problem is identified.
- Incorporating screening and early intervention into routine health care practice and into health services offered through schools, child welfare programs and juvenile justice systems.
- Reducing underage access to addictive products including increasing the cost of smoking and drinking through higher tobacco and alcohol taxes.
- Limiting teens' exposure to pro-substance use advertising and media messages.
- Providing targeted prevention and intervention services to teens at high risk for substance use.

In spite of this knowledge about what works, many parents and other adults continue to think of teen substance use as an inevitable and relatively harmless rite of passage and continue to send teens mixed messages about the acceptability of substance

se. Addictive substances remain easily available to teens. Pro-
ibstance use media messages bombard young people through
rint, electronic, visual and audio media. Public policy efforts to
irb use are limited and often pale in comparison with compet-
ig efforts by the tobacco and alcohol industries. Schools and
ommunities frequently implement prevention programs that
re not effective or enforce policies that compound the problem.
nd, the health care profession misses a critical opportunity to
creen, identify and intervene with teen substance users before
eir use progresses to addiction and to offer quality treatment
those who already have a substance use disorder.

reatment: We Know What Works but
ail to Provide Care

range of effective treatments for adolescent substance use
isorders have been developed, including cognitive-behavioral
chniques and motivational enhancement therapies. Programs
iore likely to be effective are built on strong evidence, are
mily-oriented, are developmentally appropriate and are deliv-
ed by qualified health care professionals. Yet programs to
eat teens with substance use disorders are few and far between
id, of the programs that do exist, few are tailored to the unique
eeds of teens. Access to treatment is constrained further by
ost, limited insurance coverage and an inadequate referral
ream from health care providers who are not well informed of
propriate and effective treatment options.

Of the 13.2 million high school students in the United
tates, 1.6 million meet clinical criteria for an alcohol or other
rug use disorder involving nicotine, alcohol or other drugs, yet
nly 99,913 (6.4 percent of those with an alcohol or other drug
se disorder[17]) have received treatment[18] in the past year. Even
ie 28.0 percent of treatment facilities nationwide that offer
ecialized programs for adolescents generally provide sub-
ptimal care.

Teen substance use disorders are in most cases only
ildressed after teens are deeply into trouble: a common source
f referral to addiction treatment is through the criminal justice
rstem (48.2 percent of referrals). Only 11.2 percent of adoles-
ents referred to treatment are referred by schools and only 4.7
ercent are referred by a health care professional.

Recommendations and Next Steps

he first challenge to implementing effective prevention and
eatment strategies is helping Americans understand that teen
ibstance use is a preventable public health problem and addic-
on is a treatable disease. A widespread misunderstanding of
ie problem of adolescent substance use leaves parents in the
ark about how to keep their teens safe, results in insufficient
aining of health care professionals and contributes to the lack
f insurance reimbursement.

The economic interests of the tobacco, alcohol and phar-
iaceutical industries too often overshadow the public health
oncern, and the self-interest of groups resisting smoking
strictions or promoting the decriminalization or legalization
f marijuana for personal use or the lowering of the minimum
gal drinking age further national ambivalence about adoles-
ent substance use.

It is well past time to put into action reasonable and practical
solutions. In the face of the abundance of evidence regarding
what works in prevention and treatment, CASA presents the
following recommendations to help our nation make a dramatic
shift in how we think about and address teen substance use and
addiction:[19]

Parents

Parents are the single strongest influence—for better or
worse—on their teens' choices to smoke, drink or use other
drugs. Parents must recognize that substance use is a real and
present threat to their teens' health, safety and future and take
steps to prevent it. Parents set rules and expectations to protect their children from many harms, such as requiring that they
wear seat belts, not text while driving, be sexually abstinent or
avoid unprotected sex, or limit their junk food intake. Requiring their teens to refrain from tobacco, alcohol or other drug
use is just as important and could have significant lifesaving
outcomes.

Parents should get the facts; set a good example; restrict
access to addictive substances; communicate clear, consistent
no-use messages; consistently enforce rules; monitor their
teens; require that their health care providers address this issue
in the context of routine professional care; and get help fast at
the earliest signs of trouble. Parents should set the norms of
behavior for their teens and for other parents as well.

Health Care Professionals

Health care professionals have an obligation to address a public
health problem that affects three quarters of teens and a medical
condition that affects one in eight of them by integrating addiction services into mainstream health care. As with all other
health conditions that teens face, the role of health care professionals related to teen substance use is to educate, prevent,
screen, diagnose, treat or refer for specialty care. To effect this
change, health care professionals also should work to expand
treatment capacity in the medical system, require education and
training in addiction services and press government and private
health care insurers to reimburse for adolescent substance use
screenings, brief interventions and treatment.

By taking these actions, health care providers can help
change cultural norms about the acceptability of adolescent
tobacco, alcohol and other drug use, interrupt the progression
from use to addiction and reduce the enormous health and
social consequences.

Policymakers

Policymakers can reduce the cultural influences that drive adolescent substance use by implementing public awareness campaigns; curbing teen access to addictive substances by raising
taxes on tobacco and alcohol products, expanding tobacco bans
and raising the minimum age for purchase of tobacco products to 21; and by limiting adolescents' exposure to tobacco
and alcohol advertising. They also can use the leverage of government systems to expand access to quality prevention and
treatment services for adolescents—particularly those at high
risk; fund research on prevention and treatment for teens; and

improve reporting requirements and data collection for substance related accidents and mortality.

Only by effectively preventing and treating substance use disorders in the teen population can policymakers prevent many of the health and social consequences and their enormous costs that fall to government. In fact, preventing teen substance use and treating teen addiction present one of the few opportunities where both goals of protecting the public health and closing severe budgetary shortfalls can be addressed simultaneously.

Educators and Community Organizations

Next to the home, school is the place where teens spend the most time. Schools and communities in which teens reside can reinforce the health message—educating parents, students and community members that teen substance use is a preventable public health problem and addiction is a treatable disease. Schools and community partners can look for signs of trouble and get help for those students who need it. They can implement comprehensive and age-, gender-and culturally appropriate prevention programs and put in place fair and consistent substance use policies that connect teens with needed health services.

The Media

Understanding the extent to which media messages can result in unhealthy behavior among teens, media organizations have an obligation to help promote healthy, rather than destructive, youth behavior. They can do this by finding creative yet profitable ways to craft messages that discourage adolescent substance use, eliminating marketing efforts to adolescents that make addictive substances appear attractive, and using new technology to counteract pro-substance use media and advertising messages.

Researchers

Increasing our understanding of the causes and consequences of teen substance use and developing and evaluating innovative approaches to address this health issue are of critical importance. Researchers can add to this knowledge in many ways, including developing and conducting studies on the effectiveness of promising prevention programs, early interventions and treatments tailored to high school-age teens, exploring best practices for implementation and finding a cure for addiction.

Teens

Teens have a personal stake and responsibility in assuring their own health and future opportunities. They can do this by equipping themselves with accurate information about the causes, effects and consequences of substance use and about the nature of addiction; by encouraging their friends and peers to be healthy and safe; and by intervening early with friends in need of help.

Endnotes

1. Estimated numbers are based on Census population estimates.
2. Used in the past 30 days.
3. Meet clinical criteria for nicotine dependence or alcohol or other drug abuse or dependence; also referred to in this report as addiction.
4. Among all high school students, 11.9 percent have a substance use disorder.
5. Twenty-nine percent of students nationwide and 47 percent of students in the nation's 50 largest cities drop out of school.
6. The Youth Risk Behavior Survey puts this percentage at 20.2, but does not provide trend data on this measure or a measure of current prescription drug misuse.
7. Ages 12–19.
8. Past year.
9. Students ages 18 and younger.
10. Those who report having been victims of such behavior at school in the past six months in 2005.
11. See Chapter VII.
12. In this report, we have used the general term addiction interchangeably with substance use disorders, defined as those who meet clinical criteria for nicotine dependence or alcohol o other drug abuse or addiction.
13. As with other health research, the research on the neurological effects of addictive substances on the adolescent brain primari has been conducted on animals.
14. See Appendix A for an overview of the key components of the study. Appendices B through D present the survey instruments and frequency data for parents, students and schoo personnel, respectively, and Appendix E presents the names an affiliations of the key informants interviewed for this study
15. Risky substance use is defined for the purpose of these analyses as: current smokers of any age, underage drinkers, adults who engaged in binge drinking one or more times in th past 30 days, adult drinkers who exceed the U.S. Department of Agriculture (USDA) guidelines of no more than one drink per day for women or two drinks per day for men, current users of any illicit drug and/or current misusers of any controlled prescription drug. Among children exposed to adult risky substance users, 31.7 percent are exposed to current smokers, 25.7 percent are exposed to excessive and/or binge drinkers and 7.6 percent are exposed to current users of other drugs.
16. Including those who meet clinical criteria for past month nicotine dependence (11.1 percent), past year alcohol abuse or dependence (7.3 percent) and/or past year other drug abuse or dependence (2.5 percent).
17. Comparable data on treatment for nicotine dependence are not available.
18. Including formal treatment at hospitals, rehabilitation facilities or mental health centers.
19. More detailed recommendations are provided in Chapter XI.

Critical Thinking

1. This report finds that a significant number of high school students have used addictive substances. To what extent do you believe American culture plays a role in the use adolescent substance use?

2. Provide a discussion of possible prevention measures for teen substance abuse and to what extent you believe they are possible or plausible. What is needed for these prevention measures to be implemented?

Medical Marijuana and the Mind

More Is Known about the Psychiatric Risks than the Benefits

HARVARD MENTAL HEALTH LETTER

The movement to legalize marijuana for medical use in the United States has renewed discussion about how this drug affects the brain, and whether it might be useful in treating psychiatric disorders.

Unfortunately, most of the research on marijuana is based on people who smoked the drug for recreational rather than medical purposes. A review by researchers in Canada (where medical marijuana is legal) identified only 31 studies (23 randomized controlled trials and 8 observational studies) specifically focused on medical benefits of the drug.

A separate review by the American Medical Association (AMA) also concluded that the research base remains sparse. This was one reason that the AMA recently urged the federal government to reconsider its classification of marijuana as a Schedule 1 controlled substance (prohibiting both medical and recreational use), so that researchers could more easily conduct clinical trials.

Consensus exists that marijuana may be helpful in treating certain carefully defined medical conditions. In its comprehensive 1999 review, for example, the Institute of Medicine (IOM) concluded that marijuana may be modestly effective for pain relief (particularly nerve pain), appetite stimulation for people with AIDS wasting syndrome, and control of chemotherapy-related nausea and vomiting.

Given the availability of FDA-approved medications for these conditions, however, the IOM advised that marijuana be considered as a treatment only when patients don't g enough relief from currently available drugs. Addition research since then has confirmed the IOM's core findings a recommendations.

Although anecdotal reports abound, few randomized co trolled studies support the use of medical marijuana for ps chiatric conditions. The meager evidence for benefits must weighed against the much better documented risks, particular for young people who use marijuana.

Challenges in Drug Delivery

Marijuana is derived from the hemp plant, *Cannabis.* Althou marijuana contains more than 400 chemicals, researchers be understand the actions of two: THC (delta-9-tetrahydrocannabino and cannabidiol.

THC is the chemical in marijuana primarily responsible f its effects on the central nervous system. It stimulates cannab noid receptors in the brain, triggering other chemical reactio that underlie marijuana's psychological and physical effects both good and bad.

Less is known about cannabidiol, although the research su gests that it interacts with THC to produce sedation. It m independently have anti-inflammatory, neuroprotective, or an psychotic effects, although the research is too preliminary to applied clinically.

Drug delivery remains a major challenge for medical ma juana. The FDA has approved two pills containing synthe THC. Dronabinol (Marinol) combines synthetic THC w sesame oil. Most of the active ingredient is metabolized d ing digestion, so that only 10% to 20% of the original do reaches the bloodstream. Nabilone (Cesamet) uses a slight different preparation of synthetic THC that is absorbed mo completely into the bloodstream. Among the concerns abo both of these drugs, however, are that they do not work rapid and the amount of medication that reaches the bloodstream v ies from person to person.

Another medication under investigation in the United Sta (and already approved for sale in Canada) combines THC a

---

Key Points

- Medical marijuana may be an option for treating certain conditions, such as nerve pain or chemotherapy-related nausea.
- There is not enough evidence to recommend medical marijuana as a treatment for any psychiatric disorder.
- The psychiatric risks are well documented, and include addiction, anxiety, and psychosis.

nnabidiol. In Canada, it is marketed as Sativex. This drug is metimes referred to as "liquid cannabis" because it is sprayed der the tongue or elsewhere in the mouth, using a small ndheld device. However, it takes time to notice any effects, the drug has to be absorbed through tissues lining the mouth fore it can reach the bloodstream.

Inhalation is the fastest way to deliver THC to the blood-ream, which is why patients may prefer smoking an herbal eparation. But while this method of drug delivery works fast, noking marijuana exposes the lungs to multiple chemicals d poses many of the same respiratory health risks as smok-g cigarettes. Limited research suggests that vaporizers may duce the amount of harmful chemicals delivered to the lungs ring inhalation.

lore Psychiatric Risk than Benefit

rt of the reason marijuana works to relieve pain and quell usea is that, in some people, it reduces anxiety, improves ood, and acts as a sedative. But so far the few studies evaluat-g the use of marijuana as a treatment for psychiatric disorders e inconclusive, partly because this drug may have contradic-ry effects in the brain depending on the dose of the drug and born genetic vulnerability.

Much more is known about the psychiatric risks of mari-ana (whether used for recreational or medical purposes) than benefits.

ddiction

servational studies suggest that one in nine people who nokes marijuana regularly becomes dependent on it. Research th in animals and in people provides evidence that marijuana an addictive substance, especially when used for prolonged riods.

Addiction specialists note with concern that THC concen-tion has been increasing in the herbal form of marijuana. In e United States, THC concentrations in marijuana sold on the eet used to range from 1 to 4% of the total product; by 2003, erage THC concentration had risen to 7%. Similar trends are ported in Europe. This increased potency might also acceler-e development of dependence.

Less conclusive is the notion that marijuana is a "gateway ig" that leads people to experiment with "hard" drugs such cocaine. The research is conflicting.

nxiety

though many recreational users say that smoking marijuana lms them down, for others it has the opposite effect. In fact, e most commonly reported side effects of smoking marijuana intense anxiety and panic attacks. Studies report that about –30% of recreational users experience such problems after noking marijuana. The people most vulnerable are those who ve never used marijuana before.

Dose of THC also matters. At low doses, THC can be sedat-. At higher doses, however, this substance can induce intense sodes of anxiety.

It is not yet known whether marijuana increases the risk of developing a persistent anxiety disorder. Observational stud-ies have produced conflicting findings. Studies of recreational users suggest that many suffer from anxiety, and it is difficult to know what underlies this association. Possibilities include selection bias (e.g., that anxious people are more likely to use marijuana), a rebound phenomenon (e.g., that marijuana smok-ers feel worse when withdrawing from the substance), and other reasons (e.g., genetic vulnerability).

Mood Disorders

Little controlled research has been done about how marijuana use affects patients with bipolar disorder. Many patients with bipolar disorder use marijuana, and the drug appears to induce manic episodes and increases rapid cycling between manic and depressive moods. But it is not yet clear whether people who use marijuana are at increased risk of developing bipolar disorder.

The small amount of research available on depression is also muddied. In line with what studies report about anxiety, many marijuana users describe an improvement in mood. Animal studies have suggested that components of marijuana may have antidepressant effects. Yet several observational studies have suggested that daily marijuana use may, in some users, actually increase symptoms of depression or promote the development of this disorder.

For example, an Australian study that followed the outcomes of 1,601 students found that those who used marijuana at least once a week at ages 14 or 15 were twice as likely to develop depression seven years later as those who never smoked the substance—even after adjusting for other factors. Young women who smoked marijuana daily were five times as likely to develop depression seven years later as their nonsmoking peers. Although such studies do not prove cause and effect, the dose-outcomes relationship is particularly worrisome.

Psychosis

Marijuana exacerbates psychotic symptoms and worsens out-comes in patients already diagnosed with schizophrenia or other psychotic disorders. Several large observational studies also strongly suggest that using marijuana—particularly in the early teenage years—can increase risk of developing psychosis.

An often-cited study of more than 50,000 young Swedish soldiers, for example, found that those who had smoked mari-juana at least once were more than twice as likely to develop schizophrenia as those who had not smoked marijuana. The heaviest users (who said they had used the drug more than 50 times) were six times as likely to develop schizophrenia as the nonsmokers.

Until recently, the consensus view was that this reflected selection bias: Individuals who were already vulnerable to developing psychosis or in the early stages (the prodrome) might be more likely to smoke marijuana to quell voices and disturbing thoughts. But further analyses of the Swedish study, and other observational studies, have found that marijuana use increases the risk of psychosis, even after adjusting for possible confounding factors.

Although cause and effect are hard to prove, evidence is accumulating that early or heavy marijuana use might not only trigger psychosis in people who are already vulnerable, but might also cause psychosis in some people who might not otherwise have developed it.

Certainly genetic profile mediates the effect of marijuana. People born with a variation of the gene COMT are more vulnerable to developing psychosis, for example. Because there is as yet no reliable way for clinicians to identify vulnerable young people in advance, however, it is safest to restrict use of medical marijuana to adults.

Other Effects

A review of side effects caused by medical marijuana found that most were mild. When compared with controls, people who used medical marijuana were more likely to develop pneumonia and other respiratory problems, and experience vomiting, and diarrhea.

There's no question that recreational use of marijuana produces short-term problems with thinking, working memory, and executive function (the ability to focus and integrate different types of information). Although little research exists on medical marijuana, anecdotal reports indicate that some patients take the drug at night to avoid these types of problems.

The real debate is about whether long-term use of marijuana (either for medical or recreational purposes) produces persistent cognitive problems. Although early studies of recreational users reported such difficulties, the studies had key design problems. Typically, they compared long-term marijuana smokers with people who had never used the drug, for example, without controlling for baseline characteristics (such as education or cognitive functioning) that might determine who continues smoke the drug and who might be most at risk for thinking a memory problems later on.

Recent studies suggest that although overall cognitive abili remains intact, long-term use of marijuana may cause subtle lasting impairments in executive function. There is no conse sus, however, about whether this affects real-world functionin

Additional research, focused on the benefits and cons quences of medical marijuana use for specific disorders, m help to clarify some issues. In the meantime, there is n enough evidence to recommend marijuana as a medical trea ment for any psychiatric disorder.

References

Crippa JA, et al. "Cannabis and Anxiety: A Critical Review of the Evidence," *Human Psychopharmacology* (Oct. 2009): Vol. 24, No. 7, pp. 515–23.

Grinspoon L, et al. *Marijuana: The Forbidden Medicine* (Yale University, 1997).

Iversen LL. *The Science of Marijuana, Second Edition* (Oxford University Press, 2008).

Wang T, et al. "Adverse Effects of Medical Cannabinoids: A Systematic Review," *Canadian Medical Association Journal* (June 17, 2008): Vol. 178, No. 13, pp. 1669–78.

Critical Thinking

1. Fifteen states all permit the use of medical marijuana. Why have these states chosen to allow marijuana for pain relief?

2. Provide a discussion of the primary issues inherent in states' legalization of marijuana.

Scripps Research Team Finds Stress Hormone Key to Alcohol Dependence

The Findings Suggest Development of Drug Treatment for Substance Abuse

M. ROBERTO

La Jolla, CA—January 25, 2010—A team of scientists from The Scripps Research Institute has found that a specific stress hormone, the corticotropin-releasing factor (CRF), is key to the development and maintenance of alcohol dependence in animal models. Chemically blocking the stress factor also blocked the signs and symptoms of addiction, suggesting a potentially promising area for future drug development.

The article, the culmination of more than six years of research, will appear in an upcoming print edition of the journal *Biological Psychiatry.*

"I'm excited about this study," said Associate Professor Marisa Roberto, who led the research. "It represents an important step in understanding how the brain changes when it moves from a normal to an alcohol-dependent state."

The new study not only confirms the central role of CRF in alcohol addiction using a variety of different methods but also shows that in rats the hormone can be blocked on a long-term basis to alleviate the symptoms of alcohol dependence.

Previous research had implicated CRF in alcohol dependence, but had shown the effectiveness of blocking CRF only in acute single doses of an antagonist (a substance that interferes the physiological action of another). The current study used three different types of CRF antagonists, all of which showed an anti-alcohol effect via the CRF system. In addition, the chronic administration of the antagonist for 23 days blocked the increased drinking associated with alcohol dependence.

Out of Control

Alcoholism, a chronic disease characterized by compulsive use of alcohol and loss of control over alcohol intake, is devastating both to individuals and their families and to society in general. About a third of the approximately 40,000 traffic fatalities every year involve drunk drivers, and direct and indirect public health costs are estimated to be in the hundreds of billions of dollars yearly.

"Research to understand alcoholism is important for society," said Roberto, a 2010 recipient of the prestigious Presidential Early Career Award for Scientists and Engineers. "Our study explored what we call in the field 'the dark side' of alcohol addiction. That's the compulsion to drink, not because it is pleasurable—which has been the focus of much previous research—but because it relieves the anxiety generated by abstinence and the stressful effects of withdrawal."

CRF is a natural substance involved in the body's stress response. Originally found only in the area of the brain known as the hypothalamus, it has now been localized in other brain regions, including the pituitary, where it stimulates the secretion of corticotropin and other biologically active substances, and the amygdala, an area that has been implicated in the elevated anxiety, withdrawal, and excessive drinking associated with alcohol dependence.

To confirm the role of CRF in the central amygdala for alcohol dependence, the research team used a multidisciplinary approach that included electrophysiological methods not previously applied to this problem.

The results from these cellular studies showed that CRF increased the strength of inhibitory synapses (junctions between two nerve cells) in neurons in a manner similar to alcohol. This change occurred through the increased release of the neurotransmitter GABA, which plays an important role in regulating neuronal excitability.

Blocking the Stress Response

Next, the team explored if the effects of CRF could be blocked through the administration of CRF antagonists. To do this, the scientists tested three different CRF1 antagonists (called antalarmin, NIH-3, and R121919) against alcohol in brain slices and injected R121919 for 23-days into the brains of rats that were exposed to conditions that would normally produce a dependence on alcohol.

Remarkably, the behavior of the "alcohol-dependent" rats receiving one of the CRF antagonists (R121919) mimicked their non-addicted ("naive") counterparts. Instead of seeking out large amounts of alcohol like untreated alcohol-dependent rats, both the treated rats and their non-addicted brethren self-administered alcohol in only moderate amounts.

"This critical observation suggests that increased activation of CRF systems mediates the excessive drinking associated with development of dependence," said Roberto. "In other words, blocking CRF with prolonged CRF1 antagonist administration may prevent excessive alcohol consumption under a variety of behavioral and physiological conditions."

Importantly, in the study, the rats did not exhibit tolerance to the suppressive effects of R121919 on alcohol drinking. In fact, they may have become even more sensitive to its effects over time—a good sign for the efficacy of this type of compound as it might be used repeatedly in a clinical setting.

The scientists' cellular studies also supported the promising effects of CRF1 antagonists. All of the CRF antagonists decreased basal GABAergic responses and abolished alcohol effects. Alcohol-dependent rats exhibited heightened sensitivity to CRF and the CRF1 antagonists on GABA release in the central amygdala region of the brain. CRF1 antagonist administration into the central amygdala reversed dependence-related elevations in extracellular GABA and blocked alcohol-induced increases in extracellular GABA in both dependent and naive rats. The levels of CRF and CRF1 mRNA in the central amygdala of dependent rats were also elevated.

Roberto notes that another intriguing aspect of the work is that it provides a possible physiological link between stress-related behaviors, emotional disorders (i.e. stress disorders, anxiety, depression), and the development of alcohol dependence.

In addition to Roberto, the paper, "CRF-induced Amygdala GABA Release Plays a Key Role in Alcohol Dependence," was co-authored by Maureen T. Cruz, Nicholas W. Gilpin, Valentina Sabino, Paul Schweitzer, Michal Bajo, Pietro Cottone, Samuel G. Madamba, David G. Stouffer, Eric P. Zorrilla, George F. Koob, George R. Siggins, and Loren H. Parsons, all of Scripps Research. For more information, see *Biological Psychiatry* www.ncbi.nlm.nih.gov/pubmed/20060104?log$=activity

This research was supported by the National Institutes of Health's National Institute on Alcohol Abuse and Alcoholism (NIAAA) and National Institute on Drug Abuse (NIDA) as well as the Pearson Center for Alcoholism and Addiction Research and the Harold L. Dorris Neurological Research Institute, both at Scripps Research.

About the Scripps Research Institute

The Scripps Research Institute is one of the world's largest independent, non-profit biomedical research organizations, at the forefront of basic biomedical science that seeks to comprehend the most fundamental processes of life. Scripps Research is internationally recognized for its discoveries in immunology, molecular and cellular biology, chemistry, neurosciences, autoimmune, cardiovascular, and infectious diseases, and synthetic vaccine development. Established in its current configuration in 1961, it employs approximately 3,000 scientists, postdoctoral fellows, scientific and other technicians, doctoral degree graduate students, and administrative and technical support personnel. Scripps Research is headquartered in La Jolla, California. It also includes Scripps Florida, whose researchers focus on basic biomedical science, drug discovery, and technology development. Scripps Florida is located in Jupiter, Florida.

Critical Thinking

1. Could this hormone be used to replace current alcohol-addiction treatments such as antabuse, etc.? Why?

2. What are the ethical considerations with this treatment?

The Genetics of Alcohol and Other Drug Dependence

DANIELLE M. DICK AND ARPANA AGRAWAL

This article explores the hypothesis that certain genetic factors increase a person's risk of both alcohol abuse and dependence and other drug abuse and dependence. first reviews the evidence suggesting that certain genetic ctors contribute to the development of alcohol and other drug AOD) use disorders, as well as to the development of a variety forms of externalizing psychopathology—that is, psychiatric sorders characterized by disinhibited behavior, such as antiso-al personality disorder, attention deficit/hyperactivity disorder, d conduct disorder. After summarizing the difficulties associated ith, and recent progress made in, the identification of specific nes associated with AOD dependence, the article then dis-sses evidence that implicates several genes in a person's risk r dependence on both alcohol and illicit drugs.

Genetic Epidemiology of AOD Dependence

lcohol dependence frequently co-occurs with dependence illicit drugs (Hasin et al. 2007). Both alcohol use disorders e., alcohol abuse and alcohol dependence) and drug use dis-ders (drug abuse and drug dependence) are influenced by veral factors. For example, family, twin, and adoption studies ve convincingly demonstrated that genes contribute to the evelopment of alcohol dependence, with heritability estimates nging from 50 to 60 percent for both men and women (McGue)99). Dependence on illicit drugs only more recently has been vestigated in twin samples, but several studies now suggest at illicit drug abuse and dependence also are under signifi-nt genetic influence. In these studies of adult samples, heri-bility estimates ranged from 45 to 79 percent (for reviews, e Agrawal and Lynskey 2006; etc. Kendler et al. 2003a; suang et al. 2001).

Twin studies also can be used to assess the extent to which e *co-occurrence* of disorders is influenced by genetic and/ environmental factors. Thus, a finding that the correlation tween alcohol dependence in twin 1 and drug dependence twin 2 is higher for identical (i.e., monozygotic) twins, who

share 100 percent of their genes, than for fraternal (i.e., dizygotic) twins, who share on average only 50 percent of their genes, indicates that shared genes influence the risk of both alcohol and drug dependence. The twin studies conducted to date sup-port the role of such shared genetic factors. For example, in the largest twin study of the factors underlying psychiatric disorders, Kendler and colleagues (2003b) analyzed data from the Virginia Twin Registry and found that a common genetic factor contributed to the total variance in alcohol dependence, illicit drug abuse and dependence, conduct disorder, and adult antisocial behavior. This pattern also has been identified in sev-eral other independent twin studies (Krueger et al. 2002; Young et al. 2000). Taken together, these findings suggest that a sig-nificant portion of the genetic influence on alcohol dependence and drug dependence is through a general predisposition toward externalizing disorders, which may manifest in different ways (e.g., different forms of AOD dependence and/or antisocial behavior) (see Figure). However, some evidence also suggests that disorder-specific genetic influences contribute to AOD dependence (Kendler et al. 2003b). These specific influences likely reflect the actions of genes that are involved in the metab-olism of individual drugs.

The idea that alcohol and drug dependence share a genetic liability with each other, as well as with other forms of exter-nalizing psychopathology, is further supported by electrophysi-ological studies recording the brain's electrical activity. These studies, which are conducted using electrodes placed on the person's scalp, provide a noninvasive, sensitive method of mea-suring brain function in humans. They generate a predictable pattern in the height (i.e., amplitude) and rate (i.e., frequency) of brain waves that can show characteristic abnormalities in people with certain types of brain dysfunction. For example, electrophysiological abnormalities have been observed in people with a variety of externalizing disorders as well as in unaffected children of these people. These findings suggest that electro-physiological measurements can be used as markers of a genetic vulnerability to externalizing disorders.

One commonly measured electrophysiological characteristic is the so-called P3 component of an event-related potential—that is, a spike in brain activity that occurs about 300 milliseconds after a person is exposed to a sudden stimulus (e.g., a sound or light). Researchers have observed that the amplitude of the P3 component is reduced in alcohol-dependent people and their children, suggesting that this abnormality is a marker for a genetic predisposition to alcohol dependence (Porjesz et al. 1995). However, the abnormal P3 response is not specific to alcohol dependence but appears to be associated with a variety of disinhibitory disorders, including other forms of drug dependence, childhood externalizing disorders, and adult antisocial personality disorder, again suggesting a shared underlying predisposition to multiple forms of AOD dependence and other externalizing problems (Hicks et al. 2007).[1]

Interestingly, electrophysiological abnormalities are most pronounced in alcohol-dependent people who also have a diagnosis of illicit drug abuse or dependence (Malone et al. 2001). This observation is consistent with data from twin and family studies suggesting that co-morbid dependence on alcohol and another drug represents a more severe disorder with higher heritability than dependence on one drug alone (Johnson et al. 1996; Pickens et al. 1995). This conclusion also appears to be supported by new studies exploring the roles of specific genes, which are discussed later in this article.

Identifying Specific Genes Related to AOD Dependence

With robust evidence indicating that genes influence both alcohol dependence and dependence on illicit drugs, efforts now are underway to identify specific genes involved in the development of these disorders. This identification, however, is complicated by many factors. For example, numerous genes are thought to contribute to a person's susceptibility to alcohol and/or drug dependence, and affected people may carry different combinations of those genes. Additionally, environmental influences have an impact on substance use, as does gene–environment interaction (Heath et al. 2002). Finally, the manifestation of AOD dependence varies greatly among affected people, for example, with respect to age of onset of problems, types of symptoms exhibited (i.e., symptomatic profile), substance use history, and presence of co-morbid disorders.

Despite the complications mentioned above, the rapid growth in research technologies for gene identification in recent years has led to a concomitant increase in exciting results. After suffering many disappointments in early attempts to identify genes involved in complex behavioral outcomes (i.e., phenotypes), researchers now are frequently succeeding in identifying genes that help determine a variety of clinical phenotypes. These advances have been made possible by several factors. First, advances in technologies to identify a person's genetic makeup (i.e., genotyping technology) have dramatically lowered the cost of genotyping, allowing for high-throughput analyses of the entire genome. Second, the completion of several large-scale research endeavors, such as the Human Genome Project, the International HapMap Project,[2] and other government and privately funded efforts,

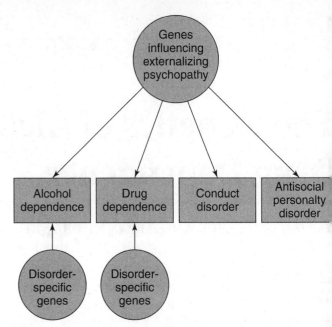

Figure Schematic representation of a model to illustrate the influence of genetic factors on the development of alcohol dependence, dependence on other drugs, and other externalizing disorders (e.g., conduct disorder or antisocial personality disorder). Some of the proposed genetic factors are thought to have a general influence on all types of externalizing conditions, whereas others are thought to have a disorder-specific influence.

have made a wealth of information on variations in the human genome publicly available. Third, these developments have been complemented by advances in the statistical analysis of genetic data.

Several large collaborative projects that strive to identify genes involved in AOD dependence currently are underway. The first large-scale project aimed at identifying genes contributing to alcohol dependence was the National Institute of Alcohol Abuse and Alcoholism (NIAAA)-sponsored Collaborative Study on the Genetics of Alcoholism (COGA), which was initiated in 1989. This study, which involves collaboration of investigators at several sites in the United States, examine families with several alcohol-dependent members who were recruited from treatment centers across the United States. The study has been joined by several other gene identification studies focusing on families affected with alcohol dependence, including the following:

- A sample of Southwestern American Indians (Long et al. 1998);
- The Irish Affected Sib Pair Study of Alcohol Dependence (Prescott et al. 2005a);
- A population of Mission Indians (Ehlers et al. 2004);
- A sample of densely affected families collected in the Pittsburgh area (Hill et al. 2004); and
- An ongoing data collection from alcohol-dependent individuals in Australia.

Importantly, most of these projects include comprehensive psychiatric interviews that focus not only on alcohol use and alcohol use disorders but which also allow researchers to collect formation about other drug use and dependence. This comprehensive approach permits researchers to address questions out the nature of genetic influences on AOD dependence, as scussed below.

More recently, additional studies have been initiated that ecifically seek to identify genes contributing to various forms illicit drug dependence as well as general drug use problms (for more information, see www.nida.nih.gov/about/ ganization/Genetics/consortium/index.html). Through these mbined approaches, researchers should be able to identify th genes with drug-specific effects and genes with more neral effects on drug use. The following sections focus on sevral groups of genes that have been identified by these research forts and which have been implicated in affecting risk for pendence on both alcohol and illicit drugs.

enes Encoding Proteins Involved Alcohol Metabolism

ne genes that have been associated with alcohol dependnce most consistently are those encoding the enzymes that etabolize alcohol (chemically known as ethanol). The main thway of alcohol metabolism involves two steps. In the first ep, ethanol is converted into the toxic intermediate acetalhyde; this step is mediated by the alcohol dehydrogenase DH) enzymes. In a second step, the acetaldehyde is further oken down into acetate and water by the actions of aldehyde hydrogenase (ALDH) enzymes. The genes that encode the DH and ALDH enzymes exist in several variants (i.e., alleles) at are characterized by variations (i.e., polymorphisms) in the quence of the DNA building blocks. One important group of DH enzymes are the ADH class I isozymes ADH1A, ADH1B, d ADH1C. For both the genes encoding ADH1B and those coding ADH1C, several alleles resulting in altered proteins ve been identified, and the proteins encoded by some of these leles exhibit particularly high enzymatic activity in laborary experiments (i.e., in vitro) (Edenberg 2007). This suggests at in people carrying these alleles, ethanol is more rapidly nverted to acetaldehyde.[3] Several studies have reported lower equencies of both the *ADH1B*2* and *ADH1C*1* alleles, which code some of the more active proteins, among alcoholics an among non-alcoholics in a variety of East Asian populans (e.g., Shen et al. 1997) and, more recently, in European pulations (Neumark et al. 1998; Whitfield et al. 1998).

In addition, genome-wide screens to identify genes linked alcoholism and alcohol-related traits have been conducted three independent samples consisting largely of people of uropean descent—the COGA study (Saccone et al. 2000), the sh Affected Sib Pair Study of Alcohol Dependence (Prescott al. 2005*a*), and an Australian sample (Birley et al. 2005). ese studies have found evidence that a region on chromome 4 containing the ADH gene cluster shows linkage to the enotypes studied. This cluster contains, in addition to the nes encoding ADH class I isozymes, the genes *ADH4, ADH5,* DH6, and *ADH7*, which encode other ADH enzymes. Polyorphisms exist for each of these genes, some of which also ve been associated with alcohol dependence (Edenberg et al. 06; Luo et al. 2006*a,b;* Prescott et al. 2005*b*).

Interestingly, the effects of these genes do not appear to be limited to alcohol dependence. One study compared the frequency of alleles that differed in only one DNA building block (i.e., single nucleotide polymorphisms [SNPs]) throughout the genome between people with histories of illicit drug use and/or dependence and unrelated control participants. This study detected a significant difference for a SNP located near the ADH gene cluster (Uhl et al. 2001). More recent evidence suggests that genetic variants in the *ADH1A, ADH1B, ADH1C, ADH5, ADH6,* and *ADH7* genes are associated with illicit drug dependence and that this association is not purely attributable to co-morbid alcohol dependence (Luo et al. 2007). The mechanism by which these genes may affect risk for illicit drug dependence is not entirely clear. However, other observations[4] also indicate that enzymes involved in alcohol metabolism may contribute to illicit drug dependence via pathways that currently are unknown but independent of alcohol metabolism (Luo et al. 2007).

Genes Encoding Proteins Involved in Neurotransmission

AODs exert their behavioral effects in part by altering the transmission of signals among nerve cells (i.e., neurons) in the brain. This transmission is mediated by chemical messengers (i.e., neurotransmitters) that are released by the signal-emitting neuron and bind to specific proteins (i.e., receptors) on the signal-receiving neuron. AODs influence the activities of several neurotransmitter systems, including those involving the neurotransmitters γ-aminobutyric acid (GABA), dopamine, and acetylcholine, as well as naturally produced compounds that structurally resemble opioids and cannabinoids. Accordingly, certain genes encoding components of these neurotransmitter systems may contribute to the risk of both alcohol dependence and illicit drug dependence.

Genes Encoding the GABA_A Receptor

GABA is the major inhibitory neurotransmitter in the human central nervous system—that is, it affects neurons in a way that reduces their activity. Several lines of evidence suggest that GABA is involved in many of the behavioral effects of alcohol, including motor incoordination, anxiety reduction (i.e., anxiolysis), sedation, withdrawal signs, and preference for alcohol (Grobin et al. 1998). GABA interacts with several receptors, and much of the research on alcohol's interactions with the GABA system has focused on the GABA_A receptor. This receptor also is the site of action for several medications that frequently are misused and have high addictive potential, such as benzodiazepines, barbiturates, opiates, α-hydroxybutyrates, and other sedative–hypnotic compounds. Accordingly, this receptor likely is involved in dependence on these drugs as well (Orser 2006).

The GABA_A receptor is composed of five subunits that are encoded by numerous genes, most of which are located in clusters. Thus, chromosome 4 contains a cluster comprising the genes *GABRA2, GABRA4, GABRB1,* and *GABRG1;* chromosome 5 contains *GABRA1, GABRA6, GABRB2,* and *GABRG2;* and chromosome 15 contains *GABRA5, GABRB3,* and *GABRG3* (see www.ncbi.nlm.nih.gov/sites/entrez?db=gene).

Interest in the GABA$_A$ receptor genes on chromosome 4 grew when this region consistently was identified in genome-wide scans looking for linkage with alcohol dependence (Long et al. 1998; Williams et al. 1999). Subsequently, COGA investigators systematically evaluated short DNA segments of known location (i.e., genetic markers) that were situated in the GABA$_A$ receptor gene cluster on chromosome 4. These studies found that a significant association existed between multiple SNPs in the *GABRA2* gene and alcohol dependence (Edenberg et al. 2004). This association has been replicated in multiple independent samples (Covault et al. 2004; Fehr et al. 2006; Lappalainen et al. 2005; Soyka 2007). In addition, the same SNPs in the *GABRA2* gene have been shown to be associated with drug dependence in both adults and adolescents (Dick et al. 2006*a*), as well as with the use of multiple drugs in another independent sample (Drgon et al. 2006).

Variations in the *GABRA2* gene are associated not only with AOD dependence but also with certain electrophysiological characteristics (i.e., endophenotypes) in the COGA sample (Edenberg et al. 2004). As reviewed above, these electrophysiological characteristics are not unique to alcohol dependence but also are found in individuals with other forms of externalizing psychopathology. This association supports the hypothesis that the *GABRA2* gene generally is involved in AOD use and/or externalizing problems. Interestingly, subsequent analyses investigating the role of *GABRA2* in drug dependence (Agrawal et al. 2006) found that the association with *GABRA2* was strongest in people with co-morbid AOD dependence, with no evidence of association in people who were only alcohol dependent. This observation supports the assertion that co-morbid AOD dependence may represent a more severe, genetically influenced form of the disorder.

Several other GABA$_A$ receptor genes have yielded more modest evidence of association with different aspects of AOD dependence. Thus, *GABRB3* (Noble et al. 1998) and *GABRG3* (Dick et al. 2004) are modestly associated with alcohol dependence, *GABRA1* (Dick et al. 2006*b*) is associated with alcohol-related phenotypes (e.g., history of alcohol-induced blackouts and age at first drunkenness), and *GABRG2* (Loh et al. 2007) is associated with aspects of drug dependence. These findings await confirmation in independent samples.

Genes Involved in the Cholinergic System

The cholinergic system includes neurons that either release the neurotransmitter acetylcholine or respond to it. Acetylcholine generally has excitatory effects in the human central nervous system—that is, it affects neurons in a way that enhances their activity. It is thought to be involved in such processes as arousal, reward, learning, and short-term memory. One of the receptors through which acetylcholine acts is encoded by a gene called *CHRM2*. In the COGA sample, linkage was observed between a region on chromosome 7 that contains the *CHRM2* gene and alcohol dependence, and subsequent experiments confirmed that an association existed between alcohol dependence and the *CHRM2* gene (Wang et al. 2004). This association has been replicated in a large independent study (Luo et al. 2005) that also found evidence that the gene was associated with drug dependence.

As with the *GABRA2* gene described above, the association between *CHRM2* and alcohol dependence in the COGA sample was strongest in people who had co-morbid AOD dependence (Dick et al. 2007). Additional analyses in the COGA sample have suggested that *CHRM2* is associated with a general increased risk of externalizing disorders, including symptoms of alcohol dependence and drug dependence (Dick et al. 2008). This potential role of *CHRM2* in contributing to the general liability of AOD use and externalizing disorders is further supported by findings that *CHRM2*, like *GABRA2*, also is associated with certain electrophysiological endophenotypes (Jones et al. 2004).

Genes Involved in the Endogenous Opioid System

Endogenous opioids are small molecules naturally produced in the body that have similar effects as the opiates (e.g., morphine and heroin) and which, among other functions, modulate the actions of other neurotransmitters. The endogenous opioid system has been implicated in contributing to the reinforcing effects of several drugs of abuse, including alcohol, opiates, and cocaine. This is supported by the finding that the medication naltrexone, which prevents the normal action of endogenous opioids (i.e., is an opioid antagonist), is useful in the treatment of alcohol dependence and can reduce the number of drinking days, amount of alcohol consumed, and risk of relapse.

Research on the role of the endogenous opioids in AOD dependence has centered mainly on a gene called *OPRM1*, which encodes one type of opioid receptor (i.e., the μ-opioid receptor), although the results so far have been equivocal. This gene contains a polymorphism resulting in a different protein product (i.e., a non-synonymous polymorphism) that in one study was found to bind one of the endogenous opioids (i.e., β-endorphin) three times as strongly as the main variant of the gene (Bond et al. 1998); other studies, however, could not confirm this finding (Befort et al. 2001; Beyer et al. 2004).

Laboratory studies have suggested that *OPRM1* is associated with sensitivity to the effects of alcohol (Ray and Hutchison 2004). In addition, several studies have reported evidence of an association between *OPRM1* and drug dependence (e.g., Bart et al. 2005). Other studies, however, have failed to find such an association (e.g., Bergen et al. 1997), and a combined analysis of several studies (i.e., a meta-analysis) concluded that no association exists between the most commonly studied *OPRM1* polymorphism and drug dependence (Arias et al. 2006). However, this finding does not preclude the possibility that other genetic variants in *OPRM1* and/or other genes related to the endogenous opioid system are involved in risk for drug dependence. For example, a recent study determining the genotypes of multiple genetic variants across the gene uncovered evidence of association with *OPRM1* and AOD dependence (Zhang et al. 2006).

Researchers also have investigated genetic variations in other opioid receptors and other components of the endogenous opioid system; however, the results have been mixed. One study

Zhang et al. 2007) found modest support that the genes *OPRK1* and *OPRD1*—which encode the κ- and δ-opioid receptors, respectively—are associated with some aspects of drug dependence. Other researchers (Xuei et al. 2007) reported evidence that the genes *PDYN, PENK,* and *POMC*—which encode small molecules (i.e., peptides) that also bind to opioid receptors—may be associated with various aspects of drug dependence.

Genes Involved in the Endogenous Cannabinoid System

Endogenous cannabinoids are compounds naturally produced in the body that have a similar structure to the psychoactive compounds found in the cannabis plant and which bind cannabinoid receptors. The endogenous cannabinoid system is thought to regulate brain circuits using the neurotransmitter dopamine, which likely helps mediate the rewarding experiences associated with addictive substances. The main cannabinoid receptor in the brain is called CB1 and is encoded by the *CNR1* gene, which is located on chromosome 6. This gene is an excellent candidate gene for being associated with AOD dependence because the receptor encoded by this gene is crucial for generating the rewarding effects of the compound responsible for the psychoactive effects associated with cannabis use (i.e., Δ9-tetrahydrocannabinol). However, the findings regarding the association between *CNR1* and AOD dependence to date have been equivocal, with some studies producing positive results (e.g., Zhang et al. 2004) and others producing negative results (e.g., Herman et al. 2006). Most recently, Hopfer and colleagues (2006) found that a SNP in the *CNR1* gene was associated with cannabis dependence symptoms. Moreover, this SNP was part of several sets of multiple alleles that are transmitted jointly (i.e., haplotypes), some of which are associated with developing fewer dependence symptoms, whereas others are associated with an increased risk for cannabis dependence. Finally, a recent case–control study found that multiple genetic variants in *CNR1* were significantly associated with alcohol dependence and/or drug dependence (Zuo et al. 2007).

Conclusions

For both alcohol dependence and drug dependence, considerable evidence suggests that genetic factors influence the risk of these disorders, with heritability estimates of 50 percent and higher. Moreover, twin studies and studies of electrophysiological characteristics indicate that the risk of developing AOD dependence, as well as other disinhibitory disorders (e.g., antisocial behavior), is determined at least in part by shared genetic factors. These observations suggest that some of a person's liability for AOD dependence will result from a general externalizing factor and some will result from genetic factors that are more disorder specific.

Several genes have been identified that confer risk to AOD dependence. Some of these genes—such as *GABRA2* and *CHRM2*—apparently act through a general externalizing phenotype. For other genes that appear to confer risk of AOD dependence—such as genes involved in alcohol metabolism and in the endogenous opioid and cannabinoid systems—however, the pathways through which they affect risk remain to be elucidated. Most of the genes reviewed in this article originally were found to be associated with alcohol dependence and only subsequently was their association with risk for dependence on other illicit drugs discovered as well. Furthermore, studies that primarily aim to identify genes involved in dependence on certain types of drugs may identify different variants affecting risk, underscoring the challenge of understanding genetic susceptibility to different classes of drugs.

This review does not exhaustively cover all genes that to date have been implicated in alcohol and illicit drug dependence. For example, several genes encoding receptors for the neurotransmitter dopamine have been suggested to determine at least in part a person's susceptibility to various forms of drug dependence. In particular, the *DRD2* gene has been associated with alcohol dependence (Blum et al. 1990) and, more broadly, with various forms of addiction (Blum et al. 1996). This association remains controversial, however, and more recent studies suggest that the observed association actually may not involve variants in the *DRD2* gene but variants in a neighboring gene called *ANKK1* (Dick et al. 2007b). Studies to identify candidate genes that influence dependence on illicit drugs, but not on alcohol, are particularly challenging because of the high co-morbidity between alcohol dependence and dependence on illicit drugs. Therefore, meaningful studies require large sample sizes to include enough drug-dependent people with no prior history of alcohol dependence.

The increasingly rapid pace of genetic discovery also has resulted in the identification of several genes encoding other types of proteins that appear to be associated with alcohol use and/or dependence. These include, for example, two genes encoding taste receptors (i.e., the *TAS2R16* gene [Hinrichs et al. 2006] and the *TAS2R38* gene [Wang et al. 2007]) and a human gene labeled *ZNF699* (Riley et al. 2006) that is related to a gene previously identified in the fruit fly *Drosophila* as contributing to the development of tolerance to alcohol in the flies. Future research will be necessary to elucidate the pathways by which these genes influence alcohol dependence and/or whether they are more broadly involved in other forms of drug dependence.

Notes

1. Abnormalities in the P3 response also have been associated with risk for other psychiatric disorders, such as schizophrenia (van der Stelt et al. 2004).

2. The International HapMap Project is a multicountry effort to identify and catalog genetic similarities and differences in human beings by comparing the genetic sequences of different individuals in order to identify chromosomal regions where genetic variants are shared. Using the information obtained in the HapMap Project, researchers will be able to find genes that affect health, disease, and individual responses to medications and environmental factors.

3. Rapid acetaldehyde production can lead to acetaldehyde accumulation in the body, which results in highly unpleasant effects, such as nausea, flushing, and rapid heartbeat, that may deter people from drinking more alcohol.

4. For example, the medication disulfiram, which inhibits another enzyme involved in alcohol metabolism called aldehyde dehydrogenase 2 (ALDH2) and is used for treatment of alcoholism, has demonstrated a treatment effect in cocaine dependence (Luo et al. 2007).

5. The SNP was not located in one of those gene regions that encode the actual receptor (i.e., in an exon) but in a region that is part of the gene but is eliminated during the process of converting the genetic information into a protein product (i.e., in an intron).

Critical Thinking

1. Why are electrophysiological abnormalities most pronounced in alcohol-dependent people who also have a diagnosis of illicit drug abuse or dependence?

2. What are risk factors for for cannabis dependence? Explain.

DANIELLE M. DICK, PhD, is an assistant professor of psychiat, psychology, and human genetics at the Virginia Institute for Psych atric and Behavioral Genetics, Virginia Commonwealth Universi Richmond, Virginia. **ARPANA AGRAWAL,** PhD, is a research assista professor in the Department of Psychiatry, Washington Universi St. Louis, Missouri.

Acknowledgments—Danielle M. Dick is supported by NIAAA gra AA–15416 and Arpana Agrawal is supported by National Institu on Drug Abuse (NIDA) grant DA–023668. The COGA project supported by grant U10–AA–08401 from NIAAA and NIDA.

Understanding Recreational Ecstasy Use in the United States: A Qualitative Inquiry

Masuma Bahora, Claire Sterk, and Kirk W. Elifson

Introduction

Ecstasy and its users began receiving media attention in the United States in the mid-1990s. During the 1970s and 1980s was used in some psychotherapy as a means to assist people cope with past traumatic past experiences (Beck & Rosenbaum, 1994; Millman & Beeder, 1994). The increase in the use ecstasy among young adults in the 1990s triggered attention and a renewed interest among policymakers, service providers, researchers, and the general public (Beck & Rosenbaum, 1994). By the year 2003, in the United States ecstasy became Schedule I drug under the Controlled Substance Act (Drug Enforcement Administration, 2003).

During the 1980s, at least a decade earlier than in the United States, ecstasy use already was being noticed in other parts of the world, most notably in the United Kingdom and Australia. Its use frequently was associated with raves (Diemel & Blanken, 1999; Forsyth, Barnard, & McKeganey, 1997; Hammersley, Ditton, Smith, & Short, 1999; Hammersley, Khan, & Ditton, 2002; Hitzler, 2002; Measham, Parker, Aldridge, 1998; Schwartz & Miller, 1997; Riley, Gregory, Dingle, & Cadger, 2001; Spruit, 1999). In the 1990s, the rave rage blew over to North America (Gross, Barrett, Shestowsky, Pihl, 2002; Sloan, 2000). Ravers (those attending raves) tended to be young and white, and predominantly from a middle class background in the United States (Johnston, O'Malley, & Bachman, 2001). Subsequent studies among ecstasy users revealed an increased representation of non-white and non-middle class individuals. For example, this trend was reported in the United Kingdom (Measham et al., 1998), the Netherlands (Spruit, 1999), and the United States (Boeri, Sterk, & Elifson, 2004).

To date, ecstasy remains easily available on the drug market in the United States (Byrnes, 2003; Chang, 2001; Schensul, Diamond, Disch, Bermudez, & Eiserman, 2005), which may explain the spread of its use into wider groups and more diverse settings (Boeri, Sterk, & Elifson, 2004; Eiserman, Diamond, & Schensul, 2005). Increasingly, U.S. studies conducted by social science and public health researchers began focusing on the potential negative consequences of ecstasy use, including inquiries with a focus on the need for effective prevention and health education about ecstasy (Baggott, 2002; Carlson et al., 2004; Dew, Elifson, & Sterk, 2006; Gamma, Jerome, Liechti, & Sumnall, 2005; McElrath & McEvoy, 2002; Reid, Elifson, & Sterk, 2007; Riley & Hayward, 2004; Scholey et al., 2004; Theall, Elifson, & Sterk, 2006). Findings from these and other studies reveal that ecstasy is typically viewed as a relatively safe drug with minimal health consequences. In terms of its social consequences, the main risk was being detected as using an illegal substance and subsequent criminal justice involvement. Among those users who did express some awareness or concerns of health risks associated with ecstasy use, their positive use experiences tended to overwrite their worries (Boys et al., 2000; Gamma et al., 2005; Hansen, Maycock, & Lower, 2001; Lenton, Boys, & Norcross, 1997; Shewan, Dalgarno, & Reith, 2000; Topp, Hando, Dillon, Roche, & Solowij, 1999). Ecstasy, despite its illegal nature, was viewed as a substance that did not interfere with leading a normal life in mainstream society. Parker and his colleagues introduced the notion of a possible "normalisation" of ecstasy and other club drugs in the United Kingdom, especially among recreational users (Measham, Newcombe, & Parker, 1994; Parker, 2005; Parker, Williams, & Aldridge, 2002). They defined recreational use as "the occasional use of certain substances in certain settings and in a controlled way" (Parker, 2005, p. 206) with a recognition of such use as "perceived and sometimes tolerated as an embedded social practice" (Duff, 2005, p. 162). The normalisation of club drugs was supported by the reality that young British drug users included "well-adjusted and successful goal-oriented, non-risk taking young persons who see drug taking as part of their repertoire of life" (Parker, 1997, p. 25). Parker and colleagues distinguished five dimensions of normalisation, including access/availability, drug-trying rates, rates of recent/regular drug use, social accommodation of sensible recreational drug use, and cultural acceptance. In this paper, we explore the insider's perspective that of active young adult ecstasy users, on recreational ecstasy use. Their views largely have been ignored in the literature. In addition, we explore their views on the access and availability of ecstasy and the extent to which social circumstances accommodate its use.

Methods
Study Procedures

The data presented in this paper are part of a larger project, Project X, an investigation of the ecstasy scene in Atlanta, Georgia. Between September 2002 and October 2007, we conducted 112 face-to-face open-ended interviews with young adult ecstasy users. During that period, we also tracked possible changes in the local ecstasy scene. The only major shift we noted was an expansion of its use at raves, which made it more widely available. As is common in qualitative studies, we have a convenience sample. Our initial recruitment was based on information from our own previous research, that of other local drug researchers and information from local social and health service providers. Using ethnographic mapping we identified additional locations for recruitment (Boeri et al., 2004; Sterk, Theall, & Elifson, 2006, 2007). We employed targeted sampling (Watters & Biernacki, 1989) and theoretical sampling (Glaser & Strauss, 1967; Strauss & Corbin, 1998).

A team of ethnographers and interviewers, including three white, one African American and one Asian American woman and two African-American and one Hispanic men conducted the recruitment and interviewing. Potential participants were screened in or near the setting where they were recruited such as at coffee shops, bars, clubs, parks, college dorms and off-campus student housing. Passive recruitment, involving the posting of flyers in local music venues and areas with greater concentrations of young adults, was also utilised. Individuals who called the project phone line listed on the flyers were screened over the phone using the same short form recruiters presented. The screening consisted of a number of socio-demographic questions and questions about past and current drug use.

To be eligible for participation in Project X, the participants had to be between 18 and 25 years and be an active ecstasy user, which was defined as having used ecstasy at least four times in the past 90 days prior to the interview. Exclusion criteria included being in drug treatment or any other institutional setting, being unable to conduct the interview in English, and being intoxicated at the time of the interview.

Once a potential respondent was identified as meeting the study's criteria, interviews were scheduled for interested individuals. The interviews were held at mutually agreed upon central locations and included such venues as the project offices, the participant's home, a local restaurant or cafeteria, coffee shop, community centres, and the interviewer's car. The consent procedures, approved by both Georgia State University's and Emory University's Institutional Review Boards, were reviewed and signed prior to the collection of any data. The average length of time to complete the interview was 90 min, with a range from one to 2.5 h. The study participants received US$ 15 (US dollars) compensation for their time.

The in-depth interviews were organised around an intervie guide that listed topics derived from the literature and our ow past research. Among these topics were initial and continue ecstasy use, use patterns, types of users, the impact of set ar setting, ecstasy market characteristics, and perceived soci and health consequences. No direct questions were asked abo defining recreational use or normalisation. The topics listed the interview guide were not addressed in a specific order fall participants. Instead, the participants were allowed to guic the flow of the interview. If a topic did not naturally emerge, t interviewer would probe. Demographic information was co lected using a close-ended format questionnaire.

Data Analysis

The qualitative data analysis was guided by a modifie grounded theory approach (Charmaz, 1983; Glaser & Straus 1967; Sterk, Theall, & Elifson, 2000; Strauss & Corbin, 1998 The open-ended interviews were transcribed and the te imported into the qualitative analysis software MAXqda2. Tl interview transcripts were read and summary memos writte followed by a next reading during which first-level (ope codes were assigned. Inter-coder reliability was established I using multiple coders for the same transcript. The codes we then clustered into categories and descriptive and axial codir notes were included, explaining the decision-making process followed by the team. Inductive and deductive questionir occurred throughout this process to identify similarities ar differences in the data. Subsequently, the categories were clu tered into themes allowing more abstraction and checking negative cases. The salient themes that emerged in the conte of the focus of this paper centered on recreational ecstasy u and normalisation.

Results
Sample Characteristics

Among the 112 study participants a majority were male ((percent), white (54 percent), educated at least at the hig school level (63 percent), and self-identified as middle class higher (64 percent). Their median age was 20.7 years, with tl youngest person being 18 and the oldest 25. When asked abo their relationship status, approximately two-fifths (44 percen indicated that they were not involved in a steady relationshi Almost one-half (49 percent) of the study participants live independently, either by renting or by owning a residence.

When asked about their age of first ecstasy use, the medi was 17 years. The oldest person was 24 when first tryir ecstasy and the youngest was 11. Overall, the study partic pants had been using ecstasy for a median of 2.6 years, wi the longest time of ecstasy use being 11 years and the short less than 1 year but at least 3 months. In terms of their use du ing the past 90 days prior to the interview, the median was days. Four was the fewest number of days of use, which w the minimum requirement for enrollment. One study partic pant reported almost daily use (88 days) and this person was

utlier. Close to three-fourths (73.8 percent) of the study par-
icipants had friends who also used ecstasy. Poly drug use was
ommon (Boeri, Sterk, Bahora, & Elifson, in press).

Recreational Ecstasy Use

When we asked the respondents to elaborate on their drug use
rajectories, many indicated that they viewed the use of ecstasy
s a recreational activity. They did not associate its use with
ymptoms of withdrawal or craving or serious negative health
nd social effects. When exploring dimensions of recreational
se, we learned that it was less about the frequency of use or the
ength of time a person had been using ecstasy. Instead, the rec-
eational nature of ecstasy use was largely captured by a user's
bility to take the drug without interference with their everyday
unctioning in mainstream society. Good grades, employment,
nd healthy relationships were cited as examples of evidence.
A 19-year-old white female explained:

> I do a lot of drugs, but I function well. I do well in school;
> I have healthy relationships. Most of the people that I'm
> around. . .they make good grades, they're good workers.
> They can keep jobs. . .they get along with their parents. If
> you just kind of keep it [ecstasy use] under control, then
> you can still just live your life normally.

Several study participants explained the unique nature of
cstasy, thereby highlighting that its high as well as its coming
own were smooth. Consequently, they experienced less of an
mmediate desire for a next high, which in turn prevented bing-
ng. Instead, some reported taking a booster dose as a means to
rolong the high. Ecstasy was described as a drug with some
uilt-in control mechanism. However, some action on the part
f the user remained necessary; for example, by only using
cstasy in certain settings or with certain people. A 19-year-old
white college student discussed his approach to delineate his
aily activities from his ecstasy use.

> I don't go out to get blazed every day of the week or
> get so screwed up on ecstasy everyday of the week that
> [I] don't know what's going on. . .I keep myself, for the
> majority, sober during the week. . .Any day that the world
> kind of slows down is a day that I can take to myself and
> have a good time for me. But as long as the world's, you
> know, moving about its business during the week, I want
> to make sure I can still be there too. I don't want to get
> to the point where I'm. . .so screwed up that I'm behind
> everybody else.

Others explained that by using ecstasy at set-aside times,
uch as weekend, holidays, or special occasions, contributed to
remaining enjoyable. They were unsupportive of an ecstasy
abit that involved daily use. Among them were those who pre-
erred no or limited use during the week or when working. They
xplained that the weekend and other times off from school or
ork were most carefree, therefore the best for an enjoyable
cstasy high. A 20-year-old female, who frequently used with
er boyfriend, remarked:

> I go to school at night and I work in the mornings. . .he
> goes to work at night and he goes to school in the day. So
> it's kind of weird, like. . .that's kind of why we do it on
> special occasions like Fridays or like, Saturdays. Because
> we really, like, are so busy during the week [and] we just,
> basically, have our own time on the weekends.

Those who did report daily ecstasy use in the past 90 days
tended to be a minority. In addition, they often also used other
drugs such as heroin, cocaine or methamphetamine. Ecstasy
was a drug they added to an already established drug repertoire.
Compared with the effects, including the coming down and
longing for the other drugs, ecstasy was perceived as harmless
which in turn was associated with recreational.

The study participants referred to ecstasy as a means to relax
and unwind independent of their frequency of use. A 19-year-
old student athlete discussed this as follows:

> . . .if I want to get crazy pretty much ecstasy is one of
> my only options. . .I mean I'm not that crazy of a person.
> I don't have, like, a record or anything. But its [ecstasy's]
> something that I like to take. It's still enjoyable to
> me. . .It's something that I can take off my shoes and
> relax and enjoy others' company and have a good time.

One of the unique features mentioned by almost all study
participants was that one of the effects of ecstasy use was an
ability to easily connect to others. Some added it that it allowed
them to be more open and less shy or withdrawn. Those who
tended to use alone were an exception. Their reflections
revealed that ecstasy allowed them to relax and be in touch
with themselves. A number of them also indicated that ecstasy
served as a form of self-medication similar to the prescribed
medications they had for diagnosed mental health problems.
One woman began using ecstasy immediately after having had
a miscarriage and she continued to use it when feeling down
because it helped her so well that first time.

Some study participants expressed concerns about persons
who used ecstasy alone, commenting that solitary use was
'depressing' and a sign of a problematic and unregulated habit.
A main component of the recreational use in the company of
friends as that they would keep "each other in check." Some
referred to ecstasy as solidifying their friendship. A 21-year-old
white male explained:

> . . .it's different when you're with people you know
> because. . .like rolling with a group of your friends
> already enhances that friendship so much. Because
> you've got those memories of what was, you know,
> until you roll the next time, the happiest moment in your
> life and you're with these people. . .So it really, really
> strengthens the bond you have with your friends to roll
> with them. You've got a lot of memories there.

A young female elaborated on this thought comparing her
ecstasy-using friends to family. She also explained that the
connection established between friends while using ecstasy
remained long after the high was over.

I think that relationship[s] you create with people around ecstasy are very, very influential or significant because it is so emotional. And I think it's hard to let go of people that you've met...because there's so much emotional background between two people when you share an experience on ecstasy.

Ecstasy Use and Mainstream Lives: Normalisation

As ecstasy use extended beyond raves and ravers, it became more widely available. According to a number of study participants, the increased availability or wider access allowed them to obtain the drug from a person they knew. In addition, we learned that the expansion of settings and the diversification of ecstasy users were viewed by many as a sign of normalisation. They explained that it made it more difficult to pinpoint or stereotype ecstasy users.

Availability and Accessibility of Ecstasy

None of the study participants indicated experiencing trouble obtaining ecstasy. The task of obtaining ecstasy was described as "effortless" or "like buying a bag of potato chips." Few worried about being detected as engaged in an illegal behavior when procuring ecstasy. Some declared it easier than being an under-aged person buying alcohol. The reality appeared to be that someone in the network of friends had ecstasy or that the group easily could get it through a dealer. Those dealers, whose market mainly was limited to raves in the early days, now could be found at local clubs or bars or at their private residence. One young male user described his experiences at a local club:

...there's always three of four people that as soon as I walk in I'm, like, alright, and I just walk around the outside of, like, around the inside of the club. And I always find it. It's easy. Fifteen minutes and [if] you can't find pills at the Globe, there's a problem. You're not looking.

A common theme among the study participants was the emerging popularity of ecstasy and the inability to "pigeonhole [ecstasy] into one specific demographic or another." A 24-year-old African-American male comments on this shift:

Well for one—more and more people are knowing about ecstasy because it's more common now, you know. And now since like everybody is doing it...it's kind of like almost getting like marijuana...cause so many have accepted it...Cause before it was kind of like, you know, I don't want to be stereotypical but it's like...you know only white people do this drug. I don't know if it was cause maybe they heard about it first, or maybe it happened in a certain, you know, area first and then it finally got around to this community or that community...but next thing you know, you're like in the club [and] everybody doing it.

This user, like others, held the view that the more aware individuals became about ecstasy, the more commonplace its use became in different contexts.

Social Accommodation of Recreational Ecstasy Use

The belief that ecstasy was analogous to other known substances perceived as harmless contributed to the reduced risk that the study participants associated with ecstasy use. Those who differentiated between soft and hard drugs, frequently placed ecstasy in the 'soft drug' category, alongside cigarettes, cannabis, alcohol, and LSD. A 21-year-old African American male explained why he ranked ecstasy directly above cannabis in relative harm, but beneath LSD, speed, crack, heroin and cocaine:

Everybody takes ecstasy...and I haven't seen anyone die, fall out or whatever. So it's just like marijuana. It hit the scene and it ain't killing people so.

The majority of participants also asserted that it was nearly impossible to become addicted to or dependent on ecstasy. Typically, they based this belief on their own experiences as well as those experiences of their peers. Further justification was provided by the lack of experiencing withdrawal symptoms or craving. A substantial number of the study participants moreover believed that their ability to "take it or leave it" at will was indicative of ecstasy's inability to be addictive. A 21-year-old male explained, "I know that for me to survive every day I don't have to do ecstasy...because it's a choice. I want to do it. Not because I feel like I have to do it." Other study participants, as a result of their experimentation with other drugs, came to the same conclusion about ecstasy's addictiveness. Referencing her experiences of addiction with methamphetamine, this 21-year-old said:

I don't think it's addictive because I feel like I've experienced addiction with meth and that's a different kind of thing. It just kind of stops you from doing the things you want to do...Like with ecstasy when you come down, you're like, 'Wow that was really fun, that was really special, I'd like to do that again.' And when you come off of speed you're like, 'Yo, we need to get more high, we need to go buy anther bag.' so it's kind of debilitating and I don't think ecstasy really does you like that.

Few study participants considered ecstasy to be an addictive substance, indicating that it might create some mental dependence. Nevertheless, they went on to explain that ecstasy itself had limited addictive properties but that a person with limited willpower maybe could develop a habit.

Perception of Risk Regarding Recreational Ecstasy Use

When reflecting upon possible negative effects of ecstasy, some study participants recalled having heard or read about some long-term side effects associated with extended ecstasy use. However, none of them knew a person who had experienced dramatic or abnormal side effects. Negative reports were regarded skeptically and categorised as hearsay. A 20-year-old female who had been using ecstasy for approximately 2 years, replied:

I've watched, like, Dateline, not too long ago. And it they said—people really don't know, you know, like, really about it and never study, like, the long—term effects on it. Like, as far as, deaths, I never knew anybody who died of ecstasy. Or, you know, like OD'd, I never knew anybody like that. I heard of a girl. . .she didn't know that she was even taking it. So she was freaking out. . .that's the only thing. That's the only one, you know, the only person that I heard of, like, freaking out. Other than that, the people I do it with and other people I have done it with over the years and it's like, no, they haven't told me of had any bad effects. As far as, like, I haven't heard, they haven't told me anything.

This respondent, like many others, was cautious to embrace the validity of circulating information on ecstasy, relying on personal accounts of consequences. A doubtful 20-year-old male explained "I am starting to hear more about the news about ecstasy and the effect that is has on people. And then I m starting to see my friends. . .and its not happening to them, ut it is happening to the people on the news." Having sought variety of sources including internet chat rooms, telecast eports, and print media, users frequently referenced the ambiuity in reports on effects of ecstasy, confirming their general istrust of the media. Whether commenting that 'people don't ally know about it' or that researchers had not studied longrm effects of the drug, they concluded that available knowldge was inconclusive at best. A 24-year-old male discussed is suspicion of the information about ecstasy's effect on the ody, presented on television:

. . .supposedly it like puts holes in your brain and does something to your spinal cord and stuff. . .I mean, I watch like a lot of Dateline, and you know they did something on Oprah about it. Or like in the paper, you know, they're always trying to do something to scare, you know? They're trying to show stuff to scare you to leave it alone.

The majority of study participants perceived any experienced egative side effects of ecstasy use to be minor and of little conern. Their main worry tended to be the potential of dehydration. his, however, was easily addressed by assuring the sufficient take of fluids. Others described having experienced a temorary loss of perfect vision or hearing but, at the same time xplained that this was because they truly become "emerged in e high." Few study participants who began using in the raves ays mentioned that ecstasy has become "safer," noting that they ave not heard recently of ecstasy being cut with heroin. Overall, ttle distinction was made between possible short or long-term ffects of ecstasy use. In general the notion seemed to be that ny short-term negative effects were minimal and that long-term ffects were a public health scare tactic to keep people away om the drug. The general consensus appeared to be that any egative effects were overwritten by positive use experiences.

Discussion

'he aim of this paper is to examine the meaning and culture f recreational ecstasy use among a sample of young ecstasy

users in Atlanta, Georgia. In doing so, we sought to explore findings in the context of the 'normalisation' thesis, focusing on the social and contextual factors, as well as the influence of knowledge about possible consequences of ecstasy use, that contribute to users' perceptions of risk. This study gives further evidence to studies noting that the meaning of recreational drug use, namely ecstasy use, for adolescents and young adults has and is changing. In exploring how this process of normalisation is constructed in the lives of young adults, we hope to further consider the implication these data have on current treatment and policy models.

The majority of study participants viewed themselves as recreational ecstasy users, identifying their ability to maintain their daily activities, and function in mainstream society (Beck & Rosenbaum, 1994; Solowij, Hall, & Lee, 1992). By prioritising their responsibilities including employment, education, and family relationships, participants appeared to frame their consumption of ecstasy around these activities and believed their drug use to be another activity that fit into their leisure or recreational time. Accordingly, they did not identify with drug users who are often typified as reckless, irresponsible, or unable to negotiate their existence in mainstream society (Shildrick, 2002; Shiner & Newburn, 1997). Instead, participants' experiences were mirrored in the literature focusing on ecstasy, demonstrating its users to be conscientious and controlled in their patterns of use (Baggott, 2002; Gamble & George, 1997; Hansen et al., 2001; Panagopolous & Ricciardelli, 2005; van de Wijngaart et al., 1999). These findings present an overall cohesive picture of purposeful and conscientious consumption of ecstasy among young adults, providing corroborating evidence to studies proposing the emergence of a new type of drug user who is 'well-adjusted, responsible, and outgoing adolescent or young adult who uses drugs recreationally, very deliberately, and very strategically' (Duff, 2005; Parker, 1997,p. 25). In this study, we suggest that users' generally minimal level of concern appeared to stem partly from their perceptions of ecstasy's prevalence in their immediate and larger social networks, as well as easy accessibility, confirming aspects of Parker's normalisation thesis (Parker, 2005). Their repeated exposure and contact with individuals who used ecstasy served, in essence, to accommodate ecstasy's recreational use, and desensitise participants to the possibilities of ecstasy's negative consequences. Given the social nature of ecstasy consumption, further research needs to clarify the role peer networks can play in intervention and recovery services. Contributing to users' perception of ecstasy's risk was their mistrust of a great deal of mass media's messages about ecstasy's adverse effects, a trend that is confirmed in available literature (Eiserman et al., 2005; McElrath & McEvoy, 2002). Participants believed ecstasy unlikely to cause such long-term effects as brain damage or death, despite research linking ecstasy to hyperthermia, dehydration, depression, and impaired cognitive functioning (Hegadoren, Baker, & Bourin, 1999; Parrott, 2002; Parrott, Sisk, & Turner, 2000). Of information that was widely circulated, study participants categorised these accounts as rumors, thereby disparaging their credibility and accuracy. Given these findings, it is unsurprising that these young ecstasy users remained undeterred in their substance-using pattern, and believed ecstasy to be generally safe.

It can be argued that in a 'normalised drug culture', the actual risk of harm increases due to the presence of ill-informed, inexperienced users who are not able to easily access the knowledge informally held within a more entrenched illicit drug culture (Baxter, Bacon, Houseman, & Van Beek, 1994; Henderson, 1993; Masterson, 1993; Merchant & MacDonald, 1994). This research, combined with our own findings, alludes to the saliency of providing accurate and detailed information, specifically addressing acute adverse risks but also strategies to reduce negative experiences and moderate harmful patterns of drug use. By placing emphasis on a user's self-awareness in the myriad of settings of their consumption patterns, we provide tools to young adults weighing benefits against potential dangers (Parker & Egginton, 2002).

The limitations of this study need to be acknowledged. First, though this sample may be representative of young adult ecstasy users in the Atlanta area, we are unable to generalise our findings to wider populations in other cities and countries. The specific impact of drug legislation and law enforcement, as well as trends in drug availability may vary significantly across localities. Second, the cross-sectional design of this study limited our ability to draw causal conclusions between participants' beliefs and attitudes regarding ecstasy use and their changes in behavior, as well as perceptions of availability and risk. Finally, it is important to note that findings from this study are based upon self-reported data, which may be subject to recall and social desirability bias. Although a 90-day time frame was used to minimise recall bias, participants may have altered responses in attempts to create rapport with interviewers or out of fear in reporting illegal activities.

Despite these limitations, findings from the current study as well as previous work point to the need of re-examining current drug-intervention and education models and the theories that drive these policies for young adults. These policies should strive to consider accounts of youth and young adults' drug using experiences and the culture that encompasses it. With only their input can prevention and intervention strategies be better informed and equipped to reduce the harms associated with their drug use. Further, considering that in some cases users were not only aware of the risk involved in taking ecstasy, but also willing to forego the risk to participate in the drug-using behavior, services designed for young adults and adolescents, alike, should consider the willingness of these youth to accept such risks. In criminalising their drug using behaviors, and concentrating efforts on cessation, we neglect to engage a vast number of young ecstasy users who perceive their behavior as sensible, safe, and acceptable.

Acknowledgments

This research was supported by NIDA grant R01 DA014232 and the Emory Center for AIDS Research. The views presented in this paper are those of the authors and do not represent those of the funding agencies. The authors thank Johanna Boers and Miriam Boeri for their contributions to the research and the participants who made this study possible.

References

Baggott, M. J. (2002). Preventing problems in ecstasy users; reduce use to reduce harm. *Journal of Psychoactive Drugs, 34*(2), 145–162.

Baxter, T., Bacon, P., Houseman, M., & Van Beek, I. (1994). Targeting psychostimulant drug users—the rave safe project. *Paper presented at the 1994 Autumn School of Studies on Alcohol and Drugs.* Melbourne, St. Vincents Hospital.

Beck, J., & Rosenbaum, M. (1994). *Pursuit of ecstasy: The MDMA experience.* Albany, NY: State University of New York Press.

Boeri, M., Sterk, C., Bahora, M. & Elifson, K. (in press). Poly-drug use among ecstasy users: Separate, synergistic, and indiscriminate patterns. *Journal of Drug Issues.*

Boeri, M., Sterk, C., & Elifson, K. (2004). Rolling beyond raves: Ecstasy use outside the rave setting. *Journal of Drug Issues, 34*(4), 831–860.

Boys, A., Fountain, J., Marsden, J., Griffiths, P., Stillwell, G., & Strang, J. (2000). *Drugs decisions: A qualitative study of young people.* London: Health Education Authority.

Byrnes, J. (2003). Changing view on the nature and prevention of adolescent risk taking. In D. Romer (Ed.), *Reducing adolescent risk: Toward an integrated approach.* Thousand Oaks: Sage.

Carlson, R., McCaughan, J., Falck, R., Wang, J., Siegal, H., & Daniulaityte, R. (2004). Perceived adverse consequences associated with MDMA/Ecstasy use among young polydrug users in Ohio: Implications for intervention. *International Journal of Drug Policy, 15*(4), 265–274.

Chang, L. (2001). Neuroimaging studies in chronic effects of MDMA/Ecstasy use. In *NIDA Scientific Conference on MDMA/Ecstasy: Advances, challenges, and future directions* National Institute on Drug Abuse. Bethesda, MD, July.

Charmaz, K. (1983). The grounded theory method: An explication and interpretation. In R. M. Emerson (Ed.), *Contemporary field research: A collection of readings.* Prospect Heights, IL: Waveland Press.

Dew, B., Elifson, K., & Sterk, C. (2006). Treatment implications for young adult users of MDMA. *Journal of Addictions and Offender Counseling, 26*(2), 84–98.

Diemel, S., & Blanken, P. (1999). Tracking new trends in drug use. *Journal of Drug Issues, 29*(3), 529–548.

Duff, C. (2005). Party drugs and party people. *International Journal of Drug Policy, 16*(3), 161–170.

Eiserman, J., Diamond, S., & Schensul, J. (2005). Rollin' on E: A qualitative analysis of ecstasy use among inner city adolescents and young adults. *Journal of Ethnicity in Substance Abuse, 4*(2), 9–38.

Forsyth, A., Barnard, M., & McKeganey, N. (1997). Musical preference as an indicator of adolescent drug use. *Addiction, 92*(10), 1317.

Gamble, L., & George, M. (1997). 'Really useful knowledge': The boundaries, customs, and folklore governing recreational drug use in a sample of young people. In P. Erickson, D. Riley, Y. Cheung, & P. O'Hare (Eds.), *Harm reduction: A new direction for drug policies and programs.* Toronto: University of Toronto Press.

Gamma, A., Jerome, L., Liechti, M., & Sumnall, H. (2005). Is ecstasy perceived to be safe? A critical survey. *Drug and Alcohol Dependence, 77*(2), 185–193.

Glaser, B., & Strauss, A. (1967). *The discovery of grounded theory.* New York: Free Press.

ross, S., Barrett, S., Shestowsky, J., & Pihl, R. (2002). Ecstasy and drug consumption patterns: A Canadian rave population study. *Canadian Journal of Psychiatry, 47*(6), 546–551.

ammersley, R., Ditton, J., Smith, I., & Short, E. (1999). Patterns of ecstasy use by drug users. *British Journal of Criminology, 39*(4), 625–647.

ammersley, R., Khan, F., & Ditton, J. (2002). *Ecstasy and the rise of the chemical generation.* New York: Routledge.

ansen, D., Maycock, B., & Lower, T. (2001). 'Weddings, parties, anything. . .', a qualitative analysis of ecstasy use in Perth, Western Australia. *International Journal of Drug Policy, 12*(2), 181–199.

egadoren, K., Baker, G., & Bourin, M. (1999). 3, 4-Methylenedioxy analogues of amphetamine: Defining the risks to humans. *Neuroscience and Biobehavioral Reviews, 23*(4), 539–553.

enderson, S. (1993). Fun, fashion, & fission. *International Journal of Drug Policy, 4,* 122–129.

itzler, R. (2002). Pill kick: The pursuit of "ecstasy" at techno-events. *Journal of Drug Issues, 32*(2), 459–466.

ohnston, L., O'Malley, P., & Bachman, J. (2001). *Monitoring the future National results on adolescent drug use: Overview of key findings.* Bethesda, MD: National Institute on Drug Abuse.

enton, S., Boys, A., & Norcross, K. (1997). Raves, drugs and experience: Drug use by a sample of people who attend raves in Western Australia. *Addiction, 92*(10), 1327–1337.

asterson, A. (1993). Digital Hippies. *Revelation,* (December/January), 20–27.

cElrath, K., & McEvoy, K. (2002). Negative experiences on ecstasy: The role of drug, set, and setting. *Journal of Psychoactive Drugs, 34*(2), 199–207.

easham, F., Newcombe, R., & Parker, H. (1994). The normalization of recreational drug use amongst young people in North-West England. *British Journal of Sociology, 45*(2), 287–312.

easham, F., Parker, H., & Aldridge, J. (1998). The teenage transition: From adolescent recreational drug use to the young adult dance culture in Britain in the mid-1990s. *Journal of Drug Issues, 28*(1), 9–32.

erchant, J., & MacDonald, R. (1994). Youth & the rave culture, ecstasy & health. *Youth and Policy, 45,* 16–38.

illman, R., & Beeder, A. (1994). The new psychedelic culture: LSD, ecstasy, "rave" parties and the Grateful Dead. *Psychiatric Annals, 24*(3), 148.

anagopolous, I., & Ricciardelli, L. (2005). Harm reduction and decision making among recreational ecstasy users. *International Journal of Drug Policy, 16*(1), 54–64.

arker, H. (1997). Adolescent drug pathways in the 1990s. In J. Braggins (Ed.), *Tackling drugs together: One year on.* London: Institute for the Study and Treatment of Delinquency.

arker, H. (2005). Normalization as a barometer: Recreational drug use and the consumption of leisure by younger Britons. *Addiction Research and Theory, 13*(3), 205–215.

arker, H., & Egginton, R. (2002). Adolescent recreational alcohol and drugs careers gone wrong: Developing a strategy for reducing risks and harms. *International Journal of Drug Policy, 13,* 419–432.

arker, H., Williams, L., & Aldridge, J. (2002). The Normalization of 'sensible' recreational drug use: Further evidence from the North West England longitudinal study. *Sociology, 36*(4), 941–964.

arrott, A. (2002). Recreational Ecstasy/MDMA, the serotonin syndrome, and serotonergic neurotoxicity. *Pharmacology, Biochemistry, and Behavior, 71*(4), 837–844.

Parrott, A., Sisk, E., & Turner, J. (2000). Psychobiological problems in heavy ecstasy (MDMA) polydrug users. *Drug and Alcohol Dependence, 60*(1), 105–110.

Reid, L., Elifson, K., & Sterk, C. (2007). Ecstasy and gateway drugs: Initiating the use of ecstasy and other drugs. *Annals of Epidemiology, 17*(1), 74–80.

Riley, S., & Hayward, E. (2004). Patterns, trends, and meanings of drug use by dance-drug users in Edinburgh, Scotland. Drugs, Education. *Prevention and Policy, 11*(3), 243–262.

Riley, S., James, C., Gregory, D., Dingle, H., & Cadger, M. (2001). Patterns of recreational drug use at dance events in Edinburgh, Scotland. *Addiction, 96*(7), 1035–1048.

Schensul, J., Diamond, S., Disch, W., Bermudez, R., & Eiserman, J. (2005). The diffusion of ecstasy through urban youth networks. *Journal of Ethnicity in Substance Abuse, 4*(2), 39–71.

Scholey, A., Parrott, A., Buchanan, T., Hefferman, T., Ling, J., & Rodgers, J. (2004). Increased intensity of ecstasy and polydrug usage in the more experienced recreational Ecstasy/MDMA users: A WWW study. *Addictive Behaviors, 29*(4), 743–752.

Schwartz, R., & Miller, N. (1997). MDMA (Ecstasy) and the rave. *American Academy of Pediatrics, 100*(4), 705–708.

Shewan, D., Dalgarno, P., & Reith, G. (2000). Perceived risk and risk reduction among ecstasy users: The role of drug, set, and setting. *International Journal of Drug Policy, 10*(6), 431–453.

Shildrick, T. (2002). Young people, illicit drug use, and the question of normalization. *Journal of Youth Studies, 5*(1), 35–50.

Shiner, M., & Newburn, T. (1997). Definitely, maybe not: The normalization of recreational drug use amongst young people. *Sociology, 31*(3), 1–19.

Sloan, J. (2000). It's all the rave: Flower power meets technoculture. *American Criminal Justice Society Today, 29*(1), 3–6.

Solowij, N., Hall, W., & Lee, N. (1992). Recreational MDMA use in Sydney: A Profile of ecstasy users and their experiences with the drug. *British Journal of Addiction, 87*(8), 1161–1172.

Spruit, I. P. (1999). Ecstasy use and policy responses in the Netherlands. *Journal of Drug Issues, 29*(3), 653–677.

Sterk, C., Theall, K., & Elifson, K. (2000). Women and drug treatment experiences: A generational comparison of mothers and daughters. *Journal of Drug Issues, 30*(4), 839–861.

Sterk, C., Theall, K., & Elifson, K. (2006). Young adult ecstasy use patterns: Quantities and combinations. *Journal of Drug Issues, 36*(1), 201–228.

Sterk, C., Theall, K., & Elifson, K. (2007). Individual action and community context: The health intervention project. *American Journal of Preventative Medicine, 32*(6), 177.

Strauss, A., & Corbin, J. (1998). *Basics of qualitative research: Techniques and procedures for developing grounded theory.* Thousand Oaks: Sage.

Theall, K., Elifson, K., & Sterk, C. (2006). Sex, touch, and HIV risk among ecstasy users. *AIDS and Behavior, 10*(2), 169–178.

Topp, L., Hando, J., Dillon, P., Roche, A., & Solowij, N. (1999). Ecstasy use in Australia: Patterns of use and associated harms. *Drug and Alcohol Dependence, 55*(1–2), 105–115.

van de Wijngaart, G., Braam, R., de Bruin, D., Fris, M., Maalaste, N., & Verbraeck, H. (1999). Ecstasy use at large-scale dance events in the Netherlands. *Journal of Drug Issues, 29,* 679–701.

Watters, J., & Biernacki, P. (1989). Targeted Sampling: Options for the study of hidden populations. *Social Problems, 36*(4), 416.

Critical Thinking

1. What is meant by normalization, and what role does it play in recreational ecstasy use? Provide an example of normalization.

2. Given what we know about the perceptions of ecstasy use among users, how should we approach prevention of ecstasy use?

MASUMA BAHORA *Emory University, Rollins School of Public Health, Department of Behavioral Sciences and Health Education, 1518 Clifton Road N.E., Atlanta, GA 30322, USA.* **CLAIRE E. STERK** *Georgia State University, Department of Sociology, Atlanta, GA, USA. and Corresponding author. Tel.: +1 404 727 9124; fax: +1 404 727 1369. E-mail address: csterk@emory.edu (C.E. Sterk).* **KIRK W. ELIFSON** *Emory University, Rollins School of Public Health, Department of Behavioral Sciences and Health Education, 1518 Clifton Road N.E., Atlanta, GA 30322, USA and Georgia State University, Department of Sociology, Atlanta, GA, USA.*

Examination of Over-the-Counter Drug Misuse among Youth[1]

ERIN J. FARLEY AND DANIEL J. O'CONNELL

Introduction

Potential harm from the intentional misuse of over-the-counter (OTC) medicines among youth has become an area of increased concern among medical practitioners and researchers (Bryner et al. 2006; Lessenger et al. 2008; Substance Abuse and Mental Health Services Administration (SAMHSA) 2006). Although the likelihood of death from overdose is rare, research has revealed an increase in dextromethorphan (a key ingredient in numerous cough and cold medicines) abuse cases reported to poison control centers (Bryner et al. 2006). Equally important is the suspicion that OTC use may be a stepping stone to other forms of drug misuse and abuse.

While OTC misuse has garnered increased media coverage, it has not yet attracted an equivalent interest among researchers. Further, it is possible that research to date has inappropriately specified the relationship between OTC and other drug misuse. Extant research has examined the relationship between OTC misuse and illicit drug use by utilizing a single construct, limiting the ability to completely flesh out the dimensions of this relationship between drug use. One area that needs further attention is if and how OTC misuse among youth is associated with other types of drug use. By combining all categories of drugs under a single construct, the nuances of how particular drugs relate to OTC use is diminished. This paper examines the current state of knowledge on OTC misuse by examining the prevalence of OTC misuse and its relationship with other types of drug use among a specific cohort to expand the current understanding of the problem.

Prevalence of OTC Misuse

OTC cough and cold medicines (e.g., Coricidin and Nyquil) can be easily purchased from pharmacies and drug stores. Adolescents typically ingest OTC medicines for the ingredient dextromethorphan (DXM). DXM is a synthetic drug related to opiates, which has the ability to produce effects similar to psychotropic drugs (Bobo et al. 2004; SAMHSA 2006). These effects include sensory enhancement, perceptual distortion, and hallucinations. DXM can be found in as many as 140 different cold and cough medications (Bobo et al. 2004; SAMHSA 2008). Misuse of these types of OTC drugs often involve youth seeking inexpensive and easily accessible substitute for other drugs that are more difficult to obtain.

Misuse of OTC drugs, especially in combination with other types of drugs, can lead to a variety of serious health problems, including confusion, blurred vision, slurred speech, loss of coordination, paranoia, high blood pressure, loss of consciousness, irregular heartbeat, seizure, panic attacks, brain damage, coma, and possibly death (Bobo et al. 2004; Food and Drug Administration 2005). Yet, there is a growing concern that youth who intentionally misuse OTC drugs misperceive that they are safe because these types of drugs are legal and prevalent (Johnston et al. 2006). If this misperception is contributing to the misuse of OTC drugs, the consequences can be serious. On the other hand, this same misperception also points towards potentially efficacious prevention programs focused on educating youth to the harm posed by these drugs.

Prevalence by Age

The abuse or misuse of OTC drugs appears to be mostly a problem among younger persons. A Drug Abuse Warning Network (DAWN) report revealed that 12,584 emergency department visits were associated with DXM use in 2004 (SAMHSA 2006). Among these, 44% (5,581) were associated with the nonmedical use of DXM products among patients aged 12 to 20. Findings from this report highlight that negative consequences associated with OTC misuse are more likely to occur among youth and young adults. For example, the rate of visits to the emergency department resulting from nonmedical use of DXM was 7.1 per 100,000 youths ages 12 to 20. For older age groups the rate was 2.6 visits or fewer per 100,000 (Bobo and Fulton 2004). In addition, a recent National Survey on Drug Use and Health (NSDUH) report highlighted OTC misuse as a significant problem among youth and young adults (SAMHSA 2008). According to this report, respondents age 12 to 17 years were more likely than those age 18 to 25 years to report past year misuse of OTCs (SAMHSA 2008).

One signal that OTC misuse is becoming of greater concern among researchers is the addition of an OTC measure ("to get high") by both the Monitoring the Future and the National Drug Use and Health in 2006 into their annual surveys. The 2007 Monitoring the Future (MTF) survey revealed that 4% of eighth graders, 5% of tenth graders and 6% of twelfth graders report past year use of OTCs to get high (Johnston et al., 2008). For eighth graders in particular, self-report misuse of OTCs was lower than past year marijuana (10%), inhalant (8%), and alcohol (32%) use. However, OTC misuse was higher than past year hallucinogen (2%), ecstasy (2%), Oxycontin (2%), Vicodin (3%), Ritalin (2%), and tranquilizer (2%) use.

Prevalence by Gender, Race, and Ethnicity

Extant research reveals significant gender differences in OTC misuse. A 2008 NSDUH report found an interaction of age and gender on self-report OTC misuse. While females age 12 to 17 years were more likely than males in the same age group to report past year OTC misuse, males age 18 to 25 years were more likely to report past year OTC misuse in comparison to females in the same age group (SAMSHA 2008). Other research has found significant gender differences in OTC misuse. For instance, both Steinman's (2006) analysis of 39,345 high school students from Ohio and Ford's (2009) examination of the 2006 National Survey on Drug Use and Health data (ages 12 to 17) revealed significant gender differences with females more likely to report OTC misuse than males (Ford 2009; Steinman 2006).

Research on racial and ethnic differences in OTC misuse is less clear. While Steinman's (2006) findings revealed Native Americans were more likely to report misuse, followed by white, "other/mixed," Hispanic, Asian, and African-American, the national survey conducted by SAMHSA (2008) revealed whites were more likely to report OTC misuse, followed by Hispanic and African-American. Misuse by Native Americans may be an additional area of concern, but the extant data indicate that whites and females are particularly at risk.

OTC Misuse Association with Prescription and Illicit Drugs

While the existing literature of OTC misuse is scant, there are key observations to be noted from research on the nonmedical use of prescription drugs (NMUPDs). Prior research on the NMUPDs has repeatedly highlighted the strong relationship between illicit prescription drug use and cigarette, alcohol, marijuana, and other drug use (Boyd et al. 2006; McCabe et al. 2004; McCabe et al. 2005; Simoni-Wastila et al. 2004). These findings suggest that nonmedical users of prescription drugs may not be a qualitatively different category of drug users, but are in fact part of well-established group of poly-drug users. It is unclear from available research whether the relationship between OTC and street drugs is the same as prescribed drugs.

Current research suggests there is reason to be concerne about the phenomena of youth mixing cough and col medicines with other types of drugs. A 2006 DAWN repo revealed that among those emergency department visits tha involved DXM, 13% of 12 to 17 year old visits and 36% c 18 to 20 year old visits involved combinations of DXM an alcohol. In addition, Steinman's (2006) research on OTC mi use in Ohio high schools revealed OTC misuse was associate with alcohol, cigarette, marijuana, and other illicit drug us (e.g., cocaine, LSD, and ecstasy). Research by Ford (2009 also found a significant relationship between OTC misus and binge drinking, marijuana use, prescription drug use, an other illicit drug use. Steinman (2006) emphasized the stron association between OTC misuse with alcohol and other illic drugs suggesting that OTC misuse is not a "gateway" dru but only one of a number of substance utilized by adolescent

OTC as the Gateway?

The gateway drug concept suggests that there are lower tiere drugs that open the way towards other drugs, and that drug us itself is responsible for opening the gate (Kandel 1975; Kand et al. 1975; Kandel et al. 2002). Other studies have attempte to refute this concept, suggesting that more serious drug use may in fact use harder drugs prior to drugs like marijuan (Mackesy-Amiti et al. 1997). Early teen drug use may large be dictated by what drugs are available to adolescents, as we as a desire to alter one's consciousness. Access to most drug however, is not evenly distributed. Marijuana use by olde youth may provide access to a small group of marijuana user while another group might have access to prescription drug and another, access to drugs like cocaine. Unlike these oth substances, almost all youth have access to OTC drugs.

While it has been shown empirically that "drug users us drugs," that is, using any substance increases the probabili of using any other substance, this pattern may not be exclu sively based on availability. In our modern consumer cultur adolescents are faced with multiple choices, and increasingl the type of drug is one of them. Recognizing that the choice c drug is related to both availability and preference, it is impo tant to understand the pattern of correlation between differe drugs. Just as there are more choices in terms of which drug there are also more choices regarding where to obtain drug Those involved in traditional street drugs like marijuana an ecstasy are getting drugs from those who sell them, nece sitating some link to a criminal element. Those using OT drugs and prescription drugs can sidestep this path, which ha important considerations for prevention policy.

The Current Study

This study intends to tease out the relationship between OT misuse and the use of different types of drugs. Previo analyses have tended to lump "other illegal drugs" togeth in one category. If early teen usage is related to drug choic and availability, combining drugs may mask relationships th xist among individual drugs. The current study utilized a large enough sample to examine drugs both individually and in groups, and attempted to investigate which drugs are associated with OTC use.

The objective of the current study is twofold: First, the prevalence of OTC misuse among a sample of eighth grade public school students is examined, including gender and race differences in OTC misuse; Second, the relationship between OTC misuse and other substance use is examined to identify patterns of use, with a specific focus on whether estimating the effects of other illegal drugs individually provides more insight than using a single construct.

Methods

Data for the current study are from the 2005 Delaware School Survey. Data was collected by The Center for Drug and Alcohol Studies (CDAS) at the University of Delaware. CDAS has conducted an annual survey of eighth grade public school students since 1995 (the annual survey also measures fifth and eleventh graders). In order to ensure confidentiality and foster honesty, survey administrators are University personnel and not teachers. Passive parental and active student consent is solicited before administrating the survey. The purpose of the survey is to track prevalence rates of drug use among Delaware public school students.

A single question, "how often do you use OTC drugs (cough & cold meds, Nyquil) to get high?" measured eighth grade self-reports of OTC misuse. Response options included "never," "before, but not in past year," "a few times in past year," "once or twice a month," "once or twice a week," and "almost everyday." This measure was recoded into a dichotomous variable (0 = not in past year, 1 = in past year).

Other substance questions included past year cigarette, alcohol, and marijuana use. Binge drinking was also measured and defined as three drinks at a time in the last two weeks. Other drug use (with the intent of getting high) questions included: uppers (speed, meth, crank, diet pills), sedatives (tranquilizers, barbiturates, Xanax), heroin, inhalants, ecstasy, hallucinogens, pain relievers, stimulants (Ritalin, Adderall, Cylert etc.), albuterol, and crack/cocaine. All drug measures were recoded into dichotomous variables (0 = not in past year, 1 = in past year).

First, univariate and bivariate analyses were utilized to examine the prevalence of OTC use and the relationship with other substances; second a series of logistic regressions were used to demonstrate the difference between using a single construct "other illicit drug use" differs from utilizing each drug measure individually.

Results

A total of 7,815 eighth graders completed the 2005 survey (50% female and 50% male). The racial and ethnic distribution of students sampled consisted of 53% (3,975) white, 28% (2,065) black, 8% (632) Puerto Rican or Mexican, 2.6% (198) Asian, 1.9% (142) American Indian/Native Alaskan,

and 6.8% (509) "Other." With Steinman's (2006) findings that Native Americans reported the highest levels of OTC misuse, we conducted a crosstabulation as an initial examination into racial variation. While American Indians/Native Alaskans represented only 2.5% of the students reporting OTC misuse in the past year, this represented 13% of American Indians/Native Alaskans students, this being the highest rate of use in comparison to the other racial categories. This finding lends support to Steinman's (2006) findings. Due to small cell counts the race categories for Puerto Rican, Mexican, Asian, American Indian/Native Alaskan and "other" were collapsed into one encompassing "other" category. Subsequent crosstabulation analysis revealed no significant variation between White, Black and "other" students. As a result, the race variable was collapsed into white and nonwhite (0 = white, 1 = non-white) for use in the multivariate models.

The past year OTC misuse prevalence in eighth grade Delaware sample was 10% (n = 704). Table 1 displays the breakdown of student self-reports: 86% of eighth graders reported never misusing OTCs, 9% report past year use, and 4% report misusing OTC in the past month.

Table 2 demonstrates a significant difference between male and female past year misuse of OTC drugs but no significant difference between white and nonwhite students.

Crosstabulations of OTC and other drugs are presented in Table 3. The percent of people using OTC drugs is given for those who used and did not use each substance in the past year. For example, the first substance column alcohol is interpreted

Table 1 Eighth Grade Self-Reports of OTC Abuse to Get High

	Percentage
Never	86%
Before, but not in past year	5%
Few times in past year	5%
Once or twice a month	3%
Once or twice a week	1%
Almost everyday	0%*

*Note: Less than one-half of one percent.

Table 2 Crosstabulation of OTC Abuse by Gender and Race

	Past Year OTC Abuse
Gender*	
Male	8%
Female	12%
Race	
White	10%
NonWhite	10%

*Note: Significant at the .001 level.

as 5.6% of those who did not use alcohol in the past year used OTC drugs, while 15.1% of those who did use alcohol used OTC drugs. The distribution is not uniform across drug types. There is a clear distribution of the type of adolescents most likely to be misusing OTC drugs. There appear to be four steps in the distribution in Table 3. First, youth who do not report using a given substance remain below 10% across all substances. Second, those youth who used alcohol and marijuana used OTC drugs at the lowest rate among users, hovering between 15% and 22% (Binge drinkers). Third, those using the more traditional street drugs such as ecstasy, hallucinogens, inhalants, heroin and cocaine formed a middle tier, reporting OTC use on the 25% to 30% range. Fourth and final, there is a group of persons using prescription drugs who are more likely to use OTC drugs as well. Those youths who used sedatives, amphetamines, pain relievers and stimulants were substantially more likely to use OTC drugs, with all categories reporting over 40% OTC users and 56% of those who use pain relievers using OTC drugs as well. In order to further investigate how these relationships function, we next employed regression techniques to control for the effect of other drugs.

The multivariate analyses begin in Table 4, with findings from the initial logistic regression (Model 1). This model tested the traditional means of measuring the effects of other illicit drugs by utilizing a single construct. Of the 7 variables, three did not reach significance (nonwhite, past year binge drinking and past year marijuana use). The odds of females misusing OTC drugs are 1.6 times greater (OR = 1.603, p = .000) than their male counterparts, holding all other variables constant. The odds of past year cigarette users misusing OTC drugs is 1.4 times greater (OR = 1.385, p =.011) than nonusers. The odds of past year alcohol users misusing OTC drugs is 1.8 times greater (OR = 1.779, p =.000) than nonusers. Using the single construct other illicit drugs category produced the largest effect, returning an odds ratio of 7.7 (OR = 7.685, p = .000) indicating that youth who reported using any of the other drugs reported in Table 3 increased the odds of using OTC drugs in the past year by 7.7 times.

The suggestion is that combining all other drugs into one construct misses variation among individual drugs. In order to tease out this concept, a logistic regression analysis examining the effect of other illicit drugs measured individually is presented as Model 2 in Tables 4A (Model 1)and 4B (Model 2). When compared to Model 1, there are no major differences

Table 3 Percent of OTC Use or Nonuse of Other Substances

	Did Not Use Drug	Used Drug
Alcohol	5.6%	15.1%
Binge Drink	8.1%	22%
Marijuana	7.8%	17.3%
Ecstasy	9.3%	31.0%
Hallucinogen	9.2%	31.0%
Sedatives	9.0%	48.3%
Albuterol	7.8%	28.2%
Amphetamines	8.9%	44.0%
Inhalants	8.3%	35.2%
Pain Relievers	7.1%	56.2%
Ritalin	8.8%	45.8%
Heroin	9.4%	25.4%
Crack/Cocaine	9.1%	32.5%

Table 4A Reduced Logistic Regression Preducting Past Year OTC Misuse (Model 1

	B	S.E.	Wald	Sig.	OR	95% CI
Constant	−.316	.108	1122.595	.000	.027	
Female	.472	.092	26.451	.000	1.603	1.339, 1.918
NonWhite	.085	.091	.806	.354	1.088	.910, 1.301
Past Year Cigarette Use	.325	.128	6.446	.011	1.385	1.077, 1.780
Past Year Alcohol Use	.576	.108	28.653	.000	1.779	1.441, 2.197
Binge Drinking	.180	.132	1.859	.173	.197	.924, 1.549
Past Year Marijuana Use	−.144	.129	1.259	.262	.866	.673, 1.114
Other Illegal Drug Use	2.039	.094	469.024	.000	7.685	6.390, 9.243
Past Year Ecstasy	-	-	-	-	-	-
Past Year Hallucinogens	-	-	-	-	-	-
Past Year Albuterol	-	-	-	-	-	-
Past Year Sedatives	-	-	-	-	-	-
Past Year Amphetamines	-	-	-	-	-	-
Past Year Inhalants	-	-	-	-	-	-
Past Year Pain Relievers	-	-	-	-	-	-
Past Year Ritalin	-	-	-	-	-	-
Past Year Heroin	-	-	-	-	-	-
Past Year Crack/Cocaine	-	-	-	-	-	-

in the effects of the lower tiered drugs on OTC misuse, when other variables were accounted for. The exceptions to this are the smokeable substances, cigarettes and marijuana, both of which lose significance in Model 2.

The odds of females misusing OTC drugs remained approximately 1.5 times greater (OR = 1.497, p = .000) than their male counterparts, holding all other variables constant. Modest effects were again found for cigarettes smokers (OR = 1.333, p < .05) and alcohol users (OR = 1.766, p = .000). The largest effects, however, were among users of pain relievers. The odds of students who reported past year use of illicit pain relievers reporting OTC drug misuse were over 9 times more likely than those who did not report pain reliever use (OR = 9.920, p = .000). Similarly, albuterol (or other asthma medicine) misusers were 4 times more likely to report OTC misuse in comparison to nonusers (OR = 4.071, p = .000). In addition, inhalant misusers were approximately twice as likely to report OTC misuse (OR = 2.302, p = .000). Similar effects were found for cocaine use (OR = 2.560, p < .01), and Ritalin use to get high (OR = 1.964, p < .01). Finally, heroin use significantly declined among those students who reported past year OTC drug misuse (OR = .321, p < .05).

Discussion and Conclusion

This study questioned whether combining all drugs into one construct is an appropriate measure in the current drug environment in which youth have more choices in terms of type of drug and routes of acquiring the drugs. While the current study replicates the findings of prior research indicating that OTC use is correlated with other drug use, the study demonstrated that this relationship is by no means uniform, and that combining drugs other than marijuana and alcohol into a single "other drug" construct misses the nuanced variation between drugs.

The objective of this study was to examine the relationship between past year OTC misuse and other drug types including other illicit drugs and the NMUPDs. Bivariate analyses revealed that nonmedical users of prescription drugs were more likely to use OTC drugs, and users of drugs like alcohol and marijuana were least likely to misuse OTC drugs. Our full model (Tables 4A and 4B) revealed that modeling drugs individually and allowing them to essentially "fight it out" in a regression analysis showed that past year nonmedical use of pain relievers and albuterol were by far the strongest predictors of OTC misuse.

Unlike Steinman's (2006) findings which led him to explore answers to the question of why is OTC misuse associated with more serious drug use, our findings lead us to ask the question, why is OTC misuse significantly associated with the NMUPDs? The significant association between OTC misuse and the NMUPDs (i.e., pain relievers, albuterol, and Ritalin) may be due to the similar accessibility or mode of acquisition for the two types of drugs. For example, both OTC drugs and prescription drugs may be easily accessible from friends at school, at home in the medicine cabinet, or, in the case of OTC drugs, from their local drug store. Acquiring OTC or prescription drugs does not require contact with a traditional

Table 4B Full Logistic Regression Predicting Past Year OTC Misuse (Model 2)

	B	S.E.	Wald	Sig.	OR	95% CI
Constant	−3.502	.110	1008.918	.000	.030	
Female	.403	.098	16.794	.000	1.497	1.234, 1.816
NonWhite	.141	.098	2.058	.151	1.151	.959, 1.395
Past Year Cigarette Use	.297	.141	4.139	.042	1.333	1.011, 1.757
Past Year Alcohol Use	.569	.113	25.248	.000	1.766	1.415, 2.205
Binge Drinking	.154	.150	1.059	.303	1.167	.870, 1.565
Past Year Marijuana Use	−.107	.141	.573	.449	.899	.682, 1.185
Other Illegal Drug Use	-	-	-	-	-	-
Past Year Ecstasy	−.307	.396	.600	.439	.736	.338, 1.600
Past Year Hallucinogens	−.533	.365	1.916	.166	.587	.276, 1.248
Past Year Albuterol	1.404	.122	132.464	.000	4.071	3.205, 5.170
Past Year Sedatives	.290	.320	.821	.365	1.336	.714, 2.499
Past Year Amphetamines	.138	.311	.197	.657	1.148	.624, 2.113
Past Year Inhalants	.834	.172	23.449	.000	2.302	1.643, 3.227
Past Year Pain Relievers	2.295	.148	239.336	.000	9.920	7.418, 13.267
Past Year Ritalin	.675	.244	7.662	.006	1.964	1.218, 3.169
Past Year Heroin	−1.137	.536	4.505	.034	.321	.112, .917
Past Year Crack/Cocaine	.940	.344	7.487	.006	2.560	1.306, 5.019

drug dealer which some students do not have access to and others might find discomforting.

The widespread and growing prevalence of OTC misuse is partially facilitated by its easy accessibility and the perception that OTC drugs are not as harmful as more traditional drugs. The relationship between these OTC and NMUPD may be due to the misperception that OTC and prescription drugs are safer than other types of drugs.

One relationship which appears counterintuitive to the finding that OTC use is more prominently associated with the NMUPD is the significant relationship between OTC misuse and crack/cocaine use. Not only did crack/cocaine use have a larger effect on OTC misuse than cigarette use, alcohol use, inhalant use, and illicit Ritalin use, crack/cocaine use is also a notable step into more serious types of drug use. One possible explanation is that crack/cocaine users often use some type of depressant to "take the edge off." It may thus be that some youth who are using crack/cocaine are also using OTC drugs to ease the "crash" from crack/cocaine. Further research is needed to explore the dimensions of this relationship.

What appears to emerge from this study is that misusers of OTC drugs are more likely to be using pills (sedatives, stimulants, pain relievers) and asthma drugs to get high than they are the traditional marijuana, cocaine, and hallucinogens of earlier eras (See Table 2). MTF data have already shown the new drug users are more likely to initiate use through prescription drugs rather than marijuana (Mackesy-Amiti et al. 1997). That finding, coupled with those above lead us to question whether there may be a shift in adolescent drug use on the horizon or even occurring currently.

A general awareness about the misuse potential of OTC drugs among adolescents already exists. This awareness can be seen in the recent movement to place OTC drugs behind cashier counters and also limiting the number of OTC drugs an individual can buy at one time. The findings from this analysis help to further our understanding of OTC misuse among youth.

Research limitations need to be acknowledged. The data utilized for the current analysis was cross-sectional data and limits our ability to examine directionality of drug misuse. The sample was drawn from a single state, thus limiting its generalizability. In addition, no survey data is available for students who were absent the day the survey was administered. Further, the OTC measure utilized represented one general question about OTC drug misuse instead of a list of OTC drugs by type. This general OTC measure limits our ability to interpret differences in misuse by type of OTC drug.

Based on the findings from this study, the authors emphasize continued education for adolescents on the dangers of misusing OTC drugs. Combating misuse should involve educating parents about the dangers of the drugs in their house and the potential for misuse, especially among youth who may not already be known for misusing or abusing drugs. OTC drug use occurs among inexperienced drug users and traditional signs of drug use among youth may not be successful in identifying youth who are abusing OTC drugs.

References

Bobo, William V. and Robert B. Fulton. 2004. "Commentary on: Severe Manifestations of Coricidin Intoxication." *American Journal of Emergency Medicine* 22: 624–625.

Boyd, Carol J., Sean E. McCabe, and Christian J. Teter. 2006. "Medical and Nonmedical Use of Prescription Pain Medication by Youth in a Detroit-Area Public School District." *Drug and Alcohol Dependence* 81: 37–45.

Bryner, Jodi K., Uerica K. Wang, Jenny W. Hui, Merlin Bedodo, Conan MacDougall, and Ilene B. Anderson. 2006. "Dextromethorphan Abuse in Adolescence: An Increasing Trend 1999–2004." *Archives of Pediatrics & Adolescent Medicine* 160:1217–1222.

Food and Drug Administration. 2005. "FDA Warns Against Abuse of Dextromethorphan (DXM). (Talk Paper T05–23). Rockville, MD: National Press Office. (Also available at http://www.fda/gov/bbs/topics/answers/2005/ans01360.html.)

Ford, Jason A. 2009. "Misuse of Over-the-Counter Cough or Cold Medications Among Adolescents: Prevalence and Correlates in a National Sample." *Journal of Adolescent Health* 44: 505–507.

Johnston, Lloyd D., Patrick M. O'Malley, Jerald G. Bachman, and John E. Schulenberg. 2006. National press release, Teen drug use continues down in 2006, particularly among older teens; but use of prescription-type drugs remains high. University of Michigan News Service, Ann Arbor.

Johnston, Lloyd D., Patrick M. O'Malley, Jerald G. Bachman, and John E. Schulenberg. 2008. "Monitoring the Future National Results on Adolescent Drug Use, Overview of Key Findings, 2007." (*NIH Publication No. 08-6418*). Bethesda, MD: National Institution on Drug Use.

Kandel, Denise and Richard Faust. 1975. "Sequence and Stages in Patterns of Adolescent Drug Use." *Archives of General Psychiatry* 32: 923–932.

Kandel, Denise. 1975. "Stages in Adolescent Involvement in Drug Use." *Science* 190: 912–914.

Kandel, D. and K. Yamaguchi. 2002. "Stages of Drug Involvement in the US Population." Pp. 65–89 in *Stages and Pathways of Drug Involvement: Examining the Gateway Hypothesis,* edited by Denise B. Kandel. New York, Cambridge University Press.

Lessenger, James E. and Steven D. Feinberg. 2008. "Abuse of Prescription and Over-the-Counter Medications." *Journal of the American Board of Family Medicine* 21: 45–54.

Mackesy-Amiti, Mary Ellen, Michael Fendrich, and Paul J. Goldstein. 1997. "Sequence of Drug Use Among Serious Drug Users: Typical vs Atypical Progression." *Drug and Alcohol Dependence* 45: 185–96.

McCabe, Sean E., Carol J. Boyd, and Christian J. Teter. 2005. "Illicit Use of Opioid Analgesics by High School Seniors." *Journal of Substance Abuse Treatment* 28: 225–230.

McCabe, Sean E., Christian J. Teter, and Carol J. Boyd. 2004. "The Use, Misuse, and Diversion of Prescription Stimulants Among Middle and High School Students." *Substance Use and Misuse* 39: 1095–1116.

Steinman, Kenneth J. 2006. "High School Students' Misuse of Over-The-Counter Drugs: A Population-Based Survey in an Urban Area." *Journal of Adolescent Health* 38: 445–447.

Substance Abuse and Mental Health Services Administration (SAMHSA). 2006. The New Dawn Report: Emergency

Department visits Involving Dextromethorphan. Office of Applied Studies. Rockville, MD.

ubstance Abuse and Mental Health Services Administration (SAMHSA). 2008. "The NSDUH Report: Misuse of Over-the-Counter Cough and Cold Medications among Persons Aged 12 to 25." Office of Applied Studies. Rockville, MD.

imoni-Wastila, Linda, Grant Ritter, and Gail Strickler. 2004. "Gender and Other Factors Associated with Nonmedical use of Abusable Prescription Drugs." *Substance Use and Misuse* 39: 1–23.

Note

1. Original study supported by Delaware Health and Human Services, Division of Substance Abuse and Mental Health, through the Substance Abuse Prevention and Treatment Block Grant from the Substance Abuse and Mental Health Services Administration (SAMHSA), U.S. Department of Health and Human Services. Support for this study also received from The Delaware Legislature through the Delaware Health Fund.

Critical Thinking

1. Discuss the factors that contribute to the prevalence of over-the-counter drug misuse by teens.

2. Are their gender differences in misuse of over-the-counter misuse of drugs? If so, why do you think this is? If not, why not?

A Framework to Examine Gateway Relations in Drug Use: An Application of Latent Transition Analysis

Mildred M. Maldonado-Molina and Stephanie T. Lanza

Introduction

Despite slight decreases in alcohol and tobacco use in recent years, alcohol and tobacco use continues to be a significant public health concern among adolescents (Johnston, O'Malley, Bachman, & Schulenberg, 2009). According to the Monitoring the Future Study, 58.3% of tenth graders have tried alcohol, 31.7% have tried tobacco, and 29.9% have tried marijuana (Johnston et al., 2009). Similarly, according to the Youth Behavior Risk Survey, 74.7% of high school students have ever tried alcohol, 48.8% have tried cigarettes, and 36.9% marijuana (Eaton et al., 2008). Literature concerning the etiology of drug use among youth suggests that legal drugs (e.g., alcohol and tobacco) serve as gateway drugs for illicit drug use. The gateway hypothesis of drug use has been defined as the notion of a progressive and hierarchical sequence of stages of drug use, suggesting an ordered progression of drug use involvement (Kandel, 1975; Kandel, 2002; Kandel, Yamaguchi, & Cousino Klein, 2006). According to this hypothesis, drug use involvement can be described by a sequence depicting the order by which adolescents try drugs; and the most common sequence starts with legal drugs (either alcohol or cigarettes), which are believed to increase the risk for trying illegal and harder drugs, such as marijuana, cocaine, and heroin.

Kandel provided the first attempt to systematically review what was known about the gateway hypothesis (Kandel, 2002). Specifically, Kandel and Jessor (2002) used three interrelated propositions to summarize current knowledge on the gateway hypothesis (Kandel & Jessor, 2002). First, the sequencing proposition suggests that drug use involvement includes "trying different classes or categories of drugs in an ordered fashion" (Kandel & Jessor, 2002, p. 365). Empirical evidence suggests that the drug use sequence typically starts with alcohol or cigarettes, followed by drunkenness, marijuana, and harder drugs (Collins, 2002; Fergusson, Boden, & Horwood, 2006; Hawkins, Hill, Guo, & Battin-Pearson, 2002; Kandel, 2002; Kandel & Yamaguchi, 2002). Second, the association proposition suggests that the "use of certain drugs is associated with increased risk for other more advanced drugs" (p. 366). Etiological, prevention and intervention studies have provided strong support for this proposition; therefore, many prevention efforts have targeted the reduction of initiation of gateway drugs based on the association proposition by arguing that preventing initiation of legal drugs reduces the likelihood of initiation of other illegal drugs (Botvin, Griffin, Diaz, & Ifil-Williams, 2001; Bretteville-Jensen, Melberg, & Jones, 2008; Cleveland & Wiebe, 2008; Degenhardt et al., 2009; Fergusson, et al., 2006; Lessem et al., 2006; Martin, 2003; Rebelion & Van Gundy, 2006; Wagner & Anthony, 2001).

A gap in the literature is that although the term gateway hypothesis is well known, there is no widespread agreement about exactly how to operationalize the gateway hypothesis applied to the study of drug use involvement among adolescents. In the current study, we integrate the frameworks of Kandel and Jessor (2002) and Collins (2002) to provide an operational definition of the gateway hypothesis that will allow the examination of whether or not a gateway relation exists between two drugs using empirical data. We develop this framework with the aim of describing a set of conditions to guide the evaluation of whether a drug serves as a gateway for another drug. In sum, the present study will (1) propose an operational definition of the gateway hypothesis for the progression of drug use, and (2) demonstrate its use in a longitudinal study of adolescent drug use onset using latent transition analysis.

An Operationalization of the Gateway Hypothesis

Kandel and Jessor (2002) provided a schema for organizing the literature on the gateway hypothesis. In the current study, we integrate the first two propositions suggested by Kandel & Jessor (2002) (i.e., sequencing and association proposition) with the methodological operationalization of the gateway hypothesis as outlined by Collins (2002). Collins (2002) called for an explicit probability-based definition of the gateway hypothesis using latent transition analysis to estimate the relevant probabilities. She argued that there is a gateway relation between drug A and drug B if:

1. There is a clear order whereby drug A is tried before drug B.
2. The probability of trying drug B is greater for those who have tried drug A when compared to those who have not tried drug A.

The first condition established an order in which the drugs are ied, an important, but not sufficient condition for a gateway rela- on between two drugs. The second condition tested whether use f one drug is associated with increased risk for use of the other rug. According to this definition, both of these conditions must be et in order for a gateway relation to exist between drugs.

In the current study, we propose an operational definition of the ateway hypothesis that like Collins (2002) is probability-based, nd focuses on the risk for using drug B at a later time (conditional n use of a gateway drug at an earlier time). There is *no gateway elation* if: drug A precedes the use of drug B, but use of drug A at n earlier time does not increase the risk for use of drug B at a later me (i.e., odds equal to 1). To evaluate whether one drug increases e risk for another drug, we use latent transition analysis (LTA) to longitudinal model of drug use in order to estimate the odds of sing drug B after having tried drug A. In the next section of this anuscript, we (a) describe LTA (as a statistical tool to test gate- ay relations) and (b) introduce three empirical demonstrations for sting the gateway relations using a national sample data of ado- scents from a longitudinal study. In the first example, we test for gateway relation between cigarettes and marijuana; the second sts for a gateway relation between alcohol and marijuana; and the ird tests for a gateway relation between alcohol and cigarettes.

Methods

Participants

o illustrate how to test for gateway relations using longitudinal ata, we used data from the National Longitudinal Study of Ado- scent Health (Add Health; Harris, 2009). We used data from one hort of adolescents in tenth (*n* = 2019) grade who were first terviewed between April and December 1995; and the same abjects were interviewed again between April and August 1996. e included data from wave 1 and wave 2 because it captures the

adolescence developmental period in which the initiation of drugs typically occurs; recent data from Add Health included measures among young adults. For the current study, adolescents were age 15.7 years old (*sd* = .46) at wave 1 (53.7% females and 46.3% males). Youth were predominantly White (72.2%); and other eth- nic groups were also included (16.8% African American/Black and 13.6% self-identified as Latino/Hispanic ethnic background).

Measures

To measure an individual's level of drug use, five items were used at each wave. Table 1 reports the frequency distribution and percent- age of drug use at each time. Responses on these items were coded "never used" and used "once or more." Three items were used to measure alcohol and drunkenness at each time. Alcohol use was assessed with one item: During the past 12 months, on how many days did you drink alcohol? Drunkenness were measured with two additional items: Over the past 12 months, on how many days did you drink five or more drinks in a row? and Over the past 12 months, on how many days have you gotten drunk or 'very, very high' on alcohol? One item was used to measure cigarette smoking at each wave: During the past 30 days, on how many days did you smoke cigarettes? One item was used to measure marijuana at each wave: During the past 30 days, how many times did you use marijuana? In the Add Health study, the time frame for reporting cigarette and marijuana use was the last 30 days, whereas alcohol and drunken- ness were assessed during the last 12 months. The use of other illicit drugs (i.e., recent use of cocaine) was not included because of very low sample size (*n* = 24 at time 1 and *n* = 18 at time 2).

Analytical Strategy

To evaluate whether a gateway relation existed between two drugs, three analytical steps were followed:

1. Fit a latent transition model.

Table 1 Frequency Distribution of Recent Drug Use of Each Categorized tem at Each Time of Measurement, *n* = 2019

em		Time I		Time 2	
		N	%	N	%
lcohol[1]	Yes	1090	53.99	917	45.42
	No	923	45.72	844	41.82
	Missing	6	0.30	258	12.78
igarettes[2]	Yes	597	29.57	622	30.81
	No	1409	20.26	1150	56.96
	Missing	13	0.64	247	12.24
+ Drinks[1]	Yes	643	31.85	574	28.43
	No	1371	67.90	1193	59.09
	Missing	5	0.25	252	12.48
runk[1]	Yes	693	34.32	589	29.17
	No	1323	65.53	1179	58.40
	Missing	3	0.15	251	12.43
arijuana[2]	Yes	321	15.90	262	12.98
	No	1654	81.92	1477	73.16
	Missing	44	2.18	280	13.87

ast 12 months,
ast 30 days

2. Identify population at risk.
3. Calculate the odds ratio *(OR)* to evaluate gateway relations.

This procedure was followed to examine the gateway relation in both directions, that is, drug A to drug B and then drug B to drug A. We describe each step below. All models were fit using proc latent transition analysis (LTA) (Lanza, Lemmon, Schafer, & Collins, 2008), available for download at http://methodology.psu.edu.

Step 1: Fit a Latent Transition Model

LTA provides a way of testing for the probability-based definitions of the gateway relations discussed in the previous section. LTA, an extension of latent class analysis to longitudinal data, takes a categorical approach to the latent variable (in this case drug use behaviors), and expresses change in the form of transition probabilities (Collins & Lanza, 2010; Collins & Wugalter, 1992; Lanza, et al., 2008). LTA is an ideal framework for examining the gateway hypothesis because it accommodates for examining measurement error in drug use behavior items, and it provides a means of estimating and testing stage-sequential models with longitudinal data. The model has been used extensively to estimate stage-sequential models of drug use behavior over time (e.g., Collins, 2002; Guo, Collins, Hill, & Hawkins, 2000; Maldonado-Molina et al., 2007; Patrick et al., 2009).

First, to identify a model that best represented the heterogeneity in patterns of drug use, we relied on several model fit information criteria (i.e., Bayesian Information Criteria (Raftery, 1986) and Aikaike Information Criterion (Akaike, 1973). Based on these criteria, we compared several competing models (from two to eight stages of drug use). Second, to interpret each drug-use stage in the selected model, we first examined the probability of responding "yes" (or "no") to each item conditional on latent stage membership. These parameters are important because they are used to determine which stages of drug use are characterized by a high probability of endorsing each drug item, and form the basis on which stages of drug use are labeled. For instance, a stage characterized by low probability of responding "yes" to the alcohol and drunkenness items but high probability of responding "yes" to cigarette and marijuana items could be labeled the "cigarette and marijuana stage." Third, we examined the probability of membership in each drug use stage. For instance, we estimated the probability of membership in the "no use" stage, and compared it with the probability of membership in the "alcohol only" stage or the "alcohol, cigarettes, and marijuana" stage. These parameters are very important when testing for gateway relations because they reflect the prevalence of each drug in combination with other drugs. In addition, based on these stage prevalences, the overall probability of using a particular drug can be calculated by including drug-use stages that include that drug. Also of importance in a study of gateway relations is any drug use stages that do not emerge in the LTA model. For instance, we would not expect to see a stage characterized by marijuana use but not use of one or more legal substances (e.g., alcohol and cigarettes). Finally, we examined the probability of drug-use stage membership at time 2 conditional on stage membership at time 1. These parameters are a key component when testing for gateway relations between drugs because they reflect initiation of drug use over time conditional to prior drug use. For instance, for two times of measurement, a transition probability might represent the probability of membership in the "alcohol and cigarettes" stage at time 2 conditional on

membership in the "alcohol only" stage at time 1, revealing important information about sequencing of the drug use and providing essential elements for estimating *OR*.

Step 2: Identify Population at Risk

To define the population at risk for initiating drug B, we estimated the proportion of the population that have not used drug B at time 1. For instance, to estimate whether a gateway relation exists between cigarettes and marijuana, we first identified the population of those who are not using marijuana at time 1. These individuals may or may not report cigarette use at time 1; of interest is the increased risk for later marijuana use that cigarette use poses.

Among the population at risk (e.g., individuals who are not reporting drug B at time 1), we estimated the following four probabilities:

1. Probability of using drug B at time 2 conditional on having used drug A at time 1 (quantity *a*)
2. Probability *of not* using drug B at time 2 conditional on having used drug A at time 1 (*b*)
3. Probability of using drug B at time 2 conditional on *not* having used drug A at time 1 (*c*)
4. Probability *of not* using drug B at time 2 conditional on *not* having used drug A at time 1 (*d*)

These estimates correspond to the 2 × 2 table presented below.

Step 3: Test for Gateway Relations Using Longitudinal Data

To examine whether drug A serves as a gateway for drug B, we used longitudinal data to estimate the risk of using drug B at time 2, a later time conditional on having used drug A at an earlier time (e.g., time 1), where *OR* is equal to the odds ratio is equal 1, there is no gateway relation because there is no increased risk of using drug B at time 2 conditional on having used drug A at time 1 (*OR = l*). There is a gateway relation if the odds ratio is greater than 1, indicating that there is increased risk of using drug B at time 2 conditional on having used drug A at time 1.

In order to conduct hypothesis testing, we estimated an LTA (as identified in step 1), then generated 1000 bootstrap samples, estimated the LTA model for each dataset and combined estimates from these bootstrap samples (see Appendix A). Therefore, uncertainty in the estimates is reflected by combining results across 1000 generated datasets. Bootstrap is an appropriate method because the tests of gateway hypotheses require creating linear combinations of LTA parameter estimates. Because we do not have standard errors of these newly-created parameters, we need to use the bootstrap or a related procedure in order to conduct significance tests based on these linear combinations. Estimates to calculate gateway relations represent the combined estimates from 1000 bootstrap samples (see Appendix A for an illustration).

Probabilities to Identify Population at Risk

		Drug B at Time 2	
		Yes	No
Drug A at Time 1	Yes	*a*	*b*
	No	*c*	*d*

Results

Stages of Drug Use: Results from a Latent Transition Analysis Model

In step one of our analyses we found that a model with seven stages of drug use best represented the heterogeneity in patterns of drug use among adolescents. A 7-class model ($G^2 = 380.12$, $df = 940$) provided the lowest *AIC*, and one of the lowest *BIC*'s (*AIC* = 546.12, *BIC* = 1011.78) when compared with several competing models (see Table 2). Model selection indices suggested that the optimal model has between five stages (no use, A, C, AD, and ACDM) and seven stages. Upon careful consideration of these models, the seven-stage model was selected because it was more precise in depicting stages of drug use, including two additional stages (CM and ACD). Specifically, the five-stage model included: no use, A, C, AD, and ACDM; the six-stage model included: five stages described above + ACD; and the seven-stage model included: six stages + CM. These stages are consistent with the

literature and indicate that a group of adolescents try marijuana without the recent use of alcohol (i.e., CM), and there is a group of adolescents who engage in alcohol and smoking behaviors without the use of marijuana (i.e., ACD stage).

The probability of responding "yes" to each item conditional on membership in a drug use stage is shown in Table 3. Note that high (over .7) probabilities are shown in bold to facilitate interpretation. The prevalence at Time 1 and Time 2 for each drug use stage is also reported in Table 3. For instance, at Time 1, approximately half of adolescents belong to the "No use" stage of recent drug use (44.9%), followed by "Alcohol Only" and "Alcohol, Cigarettes, Drunkenness, and Marijuana" users (15.8% and 14.7%, respectively), "Alcohol and Drunkenness" (11.3%), "Alcohol, Cigarettes, and Drunkenness" users (6.5%), "Cigarettes only" users (5.1%) and "Cigarettes and Marijuana" (1.8%) users.

Table 4 reports the prevalence in a drug use stage at Time 2 conditional on membership at Time 1 behavior (i.e., transition probabilities). For instance, 78.9% of adolescents were in the "No use" stage at Time 2 conditional on membership in the same drug use stage at Time 1. Similarly, among "Alcohol Only" users at Time 1, 43% remained in this stage one year later (time 2), while 14.3% experienced drunkenness, and 12.8% experienced drunkenness and smoking behaviors. Among "Cigarettes only" users at Time 1, 16.3% advanced to experienced drunkenness, and 14.0% belong to the advanced stage of drug use (describing alcohol, smoking, drunkenness, and marijuana behaviors).

Table 2   Model Selection for Competing Models

Number of Classes	G^2	df	BIC	AIC
2	1431.68	1010	1530.62	1457.68
3	1011.88	1000	1186.91	1057.88
4	620.11	988	886.47	690.11
5	499.99	974	**872.90**	597.99
6	419.82	958	914.49	549.82
7	380.12	940	1011.78	**546.12**
8	346.58	920	1130.44	552.58

Example 1: Gateway Relation between Cigarettes and Marijuana

To estimate whether cigarettes serve as a gateway drug for marijuana, we calculated the population at risk (i.e., individuals who did not report marijuana use at time 1). We combined estimates using the bootstrap method, and result indicated that 79.2% of adolescents did not report marijuana use at time 1 (average of

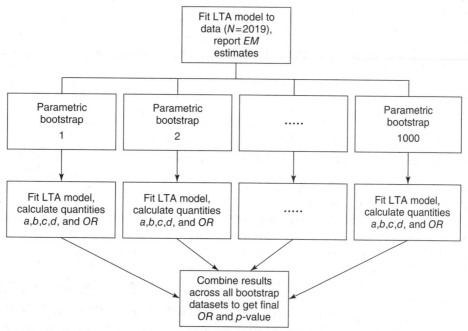

Appendix A.   Steps to test for gateway relations using bootstrap datasets

Table 3 Item Response Probability of a "Yes" Conditional on Status Membership for Each Drug Use Item and Time 1 and 2 Prevalence in Stages of Drug Use

| Stage | Item-response probability | | | | | Prevalence | |
| | | | | | | Time 1 | Time 2 |
	Alcohol	Cigarette	Drink	Drunk	Marijuana	%	%
No	0.078	0.012	0.000	0.000	0.007	.449	.430
A	**1.00**	0.085	0.211	0.235	0.054	.158	.121
C	0.281	**1.00**	0.000	0.000	0.000	.051	.084
AD	1.00	0.153	**0.901**	**0.981**	0.178	.113	.105
CM	0.381	**0.835**	0.000	0.000	**1.00**	.018	.031
ACD	**1.00**	**0.999**	**0.865**	**0.827**	0.000	.065	.087
ACDM	**1.00**	**0.908**	**0.914**	**0.964**	**0.730**	.147	.141

No = No use; A = Alcohol only; C = Cigarettes only; AD = Alcohol and Drunkenness; CM = Cigarettes and Marijuana; ACD = Alcohol, Cigarettes, and Drunkenness; ACDM = Alcohol, Cigarettes, Drunkenness, and Marijuana. Estimates (.000) were estimated to be zero; no parameters were fixed. Estimates in bold represent high probability of endorsing the item. Parameters were constrained to be equal across time.

Table 4 Transition Probabilities: Probability of Membership in Each Stage of Drug Use at Time 2 Conditional on Drug Use Membership at Time 1

| | Time 2 stage | | | | | | |
Time 1 stage	No	A	C	AD	CM	ACD	ACDM
No	.789	.077	.038	.046	.003	.028	.018
A	.204	.430	.053	.143	.042	.128	—
C	.163	—	.475	—	.059	.163	.140
AD	.154	124	.066	.412	.034	.070	.141
CM	.188	.004	.180	.120	.196	.130	.183
ACD	.100	—	.200	—	—	.556	.143
ACDM	.057	.032	.075	.087	.091	—	.659

—indicates that this conditional probability was estimated to zero (within rounding). No probabilities were fixed. No = No use; A = Alcohol only; C = Cigarettes only; AD = Alcohol and Drunkenness; CM = Cigarettes and Marijuana; ACD = Alcohol, Cigarettes, and Drunkenness; ACDM = Alcohol, Cigarettes, Drunkenness, and Marijuana.

membership in stages of drug use that did not include marijuana; i.e.. No, A, C, AD, and ACD stages). Next, we calculated four quantities (see Table 5, Panel A). To calculate quantity *a* (e.g. cigarettes users at time 1 and marijuana users at time 2), we calculated the proportion of adolescents who were in stages involving cigarettes use (i.e., C and ACD) and who transition to stages, including marijuana use (i.e., CM or ACDM). To calculate quantity *b* (the proportion of adolescents who were cigarettes users at time 1 and who were *not* exposed to marijuana at time 2), we estimated the proportion of adolescents who were in the C and ACD stages at time 1 and in the No use, A, C, AD, or ACD stage at time 2. To calculate quantity c (adolescents *not* exposed to cigarettes a time 1 but were exposed to marijuana at time 2), we estimated the proportion of adolescents who were in the No use, A, and AD stages and transition to the CM or ACDM stages at time 2. Finally, to calculate quantity *d* (adolescents *not* exposed to cigarettes at time 1 and *not* exposed to marijuana at time 2), we estimated the proportion of those who were in the No, A, and AD stages at time 1 and who were in the No, A, C, AD, or ACD stage at time 2 (see Appendix B for an illustration on how these four quantities were estimated). Results indicate that a gateway relation might exist ($OR = 1.91$; $p = .07$), indicating a trend of increased risk of recent

marijuana use (drug B) at time 2 among adolescents who reporte cigarette use (drug A) at time 1, compared to those who did no report cigarette use at time 1.

To evaluate the role of marijuana as a gateway drug for ciga rettes, we calculated the population at risk (those who reporte not using cigarettes at time 1; 89.9%); however, there was not stage of drug use that included marijuana at time 1 without th use of cigarettes. For instance, two stages of drug use include marijuana users (i.e., CM and ACDM); however, there was n "Marijuana only" or "Alcohol and Marijuana" stage to calcula the prevalence of those exposed to marijuana at time 1 (amon the population at risk; non-smokers at time 1). Therefore, th odds of recent cigarette use at time 2 conditional on time 1 mar juana use were not estimable because among the population risk the probability of using cigarettes at time 2 conditional having used marijuana at time 1 was zero.

Example 2: Gateway Relation between Alcohol and Marijuana

To estimate the role of alcohol as a gateway drug for marijuan we identified the population at risk (i.e., the proportion of th population who were not using marijuana at time 1) (79.2%) an

Table 5 Gateway Relations between (A) Cigarettes and Marijuana, (B) Alcohol and Marijuana, and (C) Alcohol and Cigarettes

Panel A: Cigarettes and Marijuana

		Marijuana use at time 2		
		Yes	No	
Cigarettes at time 1	Yes	0.025	0.125	OR = 1.91
	No	0.061	0.581	

Increased risk: Among population at risk (those who were not marijuana users at time 1), the risk for using marijuana at time 2 was 1.91 times higher among those exposed to cigarettes at time 1 (.168) when compared to the unexposed population (.095).

Panel B: Alcohol and Marijuana

		Marijuana use at time 2		
		Yes	No	
Alcohol at time 1	Yes	0.033	0.182	OR = 1.75
	No	0.054	0.524	

Increased risk: Among population at risk (those who were not marijuana users at time 1). the risk for using marijuana at time 2 was 1.75 times higher among those exposed to alcohol (. 152) at time 1 when compared to the unexposed population (.10).

		Alcohol use at time 2		
		Yes	No	
Marijuana at time 1	Yes	0.014	0.058	OR = 0.58
	No	0.236	0.557	

Not increased risk: Among population at risk (those who were not alcohol users at time 1). the risk for using alcohol at time 2 was higher among non-marijuana users (.30) when compared with marijuana users at time 1 (.20).

Panel C: Alcohol and Smoking

		Smoking at time 2		
		Yes	No	
Alcohol at time 1	Yes	0.100	0.145	OR = 1.22
	No	0.229	0.421	

Not increased risk: Among population at risk (those who were not cigarette users at time 1), the risk for using cigarettes at time 2 was higher among alcohol users (.40) when compared with non-alcohol users at time 1 (.37).

		Alcohol use at time 2		
		Yes	No	
Smoking at time 1	Yes	0.034	0.176	OR = 0.41
	No	0.209	0.443	

Not increased risk: Among population at risk (those who were not alcohol users at time 1), the risk for using alcohol at time 2 was higher among non-smokers (.33) when compared with smokers at time 1 (.16).

When calculated the four quantities needed for the odds ratio (see Table 5, Panel B). The odds ratio of recent marijuana use at time 2 conditional on time 1 recent alcohol use was 1.75, suggesting that there is increased risk of recent marijuana use (drug B) by time 2 conditional on having recently used alcohol (drug A) at time 1 (p = .04). Therefore, we found evidence that alcohol serves as a gateway drug for marijuana.

To estimate the role of marijuana as a gateway drug for alcohol, we estimated the population at risk (i.e., the proportion of the population who were not using alcohol at time 1, 86.4%), and then calculated four quantities (see Table 5, Panel B). Results indicated that the risk for using alcohol at time 2 was higher among the unexposed population (.29) when compared to the exposed population (.20), suggesting that a higher proportion of the population at risk who were not exposed to marijuana were alcohol users at time 2.

Therefore, results indicate that marijuana did not serve as a gateway drug for alcohol because it was not associated with increased risk of recent alcohol use (drug B) by time 2 conditional on having recently used marijuana (drug A) at time 1 (see Appendix C for an illustration on how these quantities were estimated).

Example 3: Gateway Relation between Alcohol and Cigarettes

Results indicated that a gateway relation exist between alcohol and cigarettes because use of alcohol at time 1 was associated with increased risk for cigarette use at time 2 (OR = 1.24; p = .002). Therefore, we found support that recent use of alcohol serve as a gateway drug for recent cigarette use. We also tested the role of cigarettes as a gateway drug for alcohol and results suggest

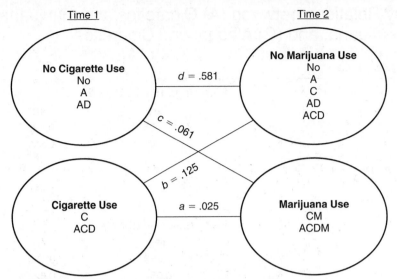

Appendix B. Gateway relation between cigarettes and marijuana

a = Exposed lo cigarettes at time 1 and exposed to marijuana at time 2; b = Exposed to cigarettes at time 1 and *not* exposed to marijuana at time 2; c = *Not* exposed to cigarettes to time 1
and exposed to marijuana at time 2; d = *Not* exposed to cigarettes at time 1 and *not* exposed
to marijuana at time 2.

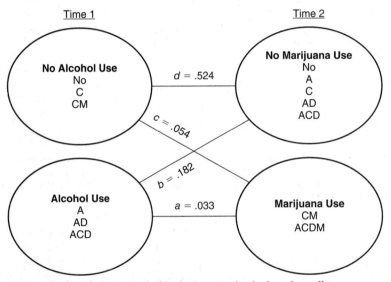

Appendix C. Gateway relation between alcohol and marijuana

Figure C1. Alcohol as a gateway for marijuana use

a = Exposed to alcohol at time 1 and exposed to marijuana at time 2; b = Exposed to alcohol
at time 1 and *not* exposed to marijuana at time 2; c = *Not* exposed to alcohol to time 1 and
exposed to marijuana at time 2; d = *Not* exposed to alcohol at time 1 and *not* exposed to
marijuana at time 2.

that a gateway relation does not exist between use of cigarettes time 1 and alcohol use at time 2, because the risk for alcohol use at time 2 was higher among the unexposed population (i.e., not cigarettes users, .325) when compared with the exposed (i.e., cigarette users, .163) population (see Appendix D for an illustration). Therefore, there is no evidence for increased risk for alcohol use at time 2 conditional on having used cigarettes at time 1.

Discussion

This study extends current literature on the gateway hypothesis by proposing a framework for examining the gateway hypothesis of drug use among adolescents. The present study integrated conce tual and methodological approaches to the study of the gatew hypothesis, as outlined by Kandel and Jessor (2002) and Colli (2002), and proposed an operational definition to test the ga way hypothesis. We proposed to test gateway relations by usi longitudinal data to estimate the odds of using a drug at a la time conditional on use of the gateway drug at an earlier time. T framework was illustrated by examining whether a gateway re tion exists between:

1. Cigarettes and marijuana
2. Alcohol and marijuana
3. Alcohol and cigarettes

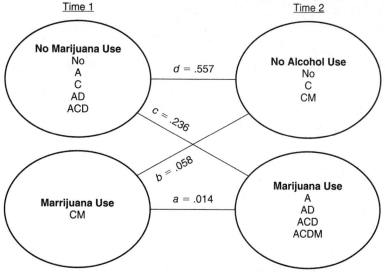

Figure C2.   Marijuana as a gateway for marijuana use

a = Exposed to marijuana at time 1 and exposed to alcohol at time 2; b = Exposed to marijuana at time 1 and *not* exposed to alcohol at time 2; c = *Not* exposed to marijuana to time 1 and exposed to alcohol at time 2; d = *Not* exposed to marijuana at time 1 and *not* exposed to alcohol at time 2.

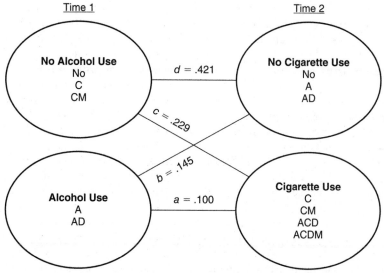

Appendix D.   Gateway relation between alcohol and cigarettes

Figure D1.   Alcohol as a gateway for cigarettes use

a = Exposed to alcohol at time 1 and exposed to cigarettes at time 2; b = Exposed to alcohol at time 1 and not exposed to cigarettes at time 2; c = *Not* exposed to alcohol to time 1 and exposed to cigarettes at time 2; d = *Not* exposed to alcohol at time 1 and *not* exposed to cigarettes at time 2.

Results indicated that both alcohol and cigarettes served as a gateway drug for marijuana, and alcohol also served as a gateway for cigarettes.

Previous studies examining the gateway hypothesis have reported inconsistent findings, mostly as the result of differences in the conceptualizations and operationalizations of the hypothesis (Kandel, 2002). Most of the work on the gateway hypothesis, including work from Kandel and colleagues, has been based on an approach that reflects a hierarchical and unidimensional order of use (Kandel, 2002). One limitation of these cross-sectional studies is that it prevents the examination of the temporal order by which drugs are initiated. Therefore, to evaluate gateway relations, the current study used longitudinal data to examine patterns of drug use among youth. By using longitudinal data, this study described the prospective nature of drug use involvement among adolescents by modeling the etiology of behavior as a series of stages of drug use. The current project also expanded the probability-based definition first proposed by Collins (2002) to guide the investigation of whether a gateway relation exists between drugs. Using the proposed framework for testing the gateway hypothesis can shed light on the strength of the association between gateway drugs.

The current study is consistent with previous studies that applied LTA to examine transitions in substance use behavior using data from the Add Health Study (e.g., Collins, 2002; Hyatt

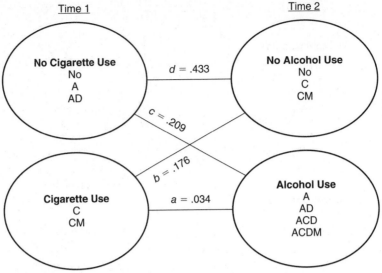

Figure D2. Cigarettes as a gateway for alcohol use

a = Exposed to cigarettes at time 1 and exposed to alcohol at time 2; b = Exposed to cigarettes at time 1 and not exposed to alcohol at time 2; c = *Not* exposed to cigarettes to time 1 and exposed to alcohol at time 2; d = *Not* exposed to cigarettes at time 1 and *not* exposed to alcohol at time 2.

& Collins, 2000; Lanza & Collins, 2002); however, none of these studies has evaluated a recent substance use model. For instance, Lanza and Collins (2002) reported eight stages of lifetime drug use onset among adolescents. Hyatt and Collins (2002) and Collins (2002) also applied latent transition analysis to examine risk and protective factors associated with onset of substance use, and they also reported eight stages describing a lifetime model of drug use. The current study identified seven of these eight stages of drug use, with the exception of a stage describing recent use of alcohol and cigarettes without engaging in drunkenness behaviors. This may be expected due to the focus on recent use as opposed to lifetime use. As a result, the current study represents an application of LTA using a national representative study to examine patterns of recent substance use among adolescents.

The current study also used repeated assessments of recent use of each drug when examining the gateway hypothesis. Each item assessed whether adolescents had recently use each drug, including alcohol, cigarettes, drunkenness, and marijuana. An alternative approach would be to examine whether the dosage by which a drug is tried at time 1 is associated with increased risk for trying another drug. A model examining youth's engagement with large quantities of a drug and experiencing abuse and/or dependence would shed light on whether a large dose of one drug, as opposed to simply trying a drug, serves a gateway role for another drug.

By using the proposed operational definition of gateway relations, researchers can examine the relation between drug dose and other risk factors associated with adolescent problem behaviors. Indeed, the definitions of the gateway relations outlined in the current study can be applied to the study of association of any events, particularly to examine whether one event is a risk factor for a subsequent event. Using such a framework can extend the current definition of gateway relations beyond the examination of the gateway hypothesis of drug use among youth. It is also important to acknowledge that, in addition to dosage, the sampling of times of measurement (temporal design of the study) can influence the interpretation of gateway relations. This is an important consideration when drawing conclusions about the gateway hypothesis because the duration between observations will influence whether researchers can observe the transitions between initiations of each drug in a sequence. In the current study, the was a one-year period between measurements. It is possible that the spacing between observations was too far apart, and therefore, potential gateway relations between drugs might have been overlooked. For instance, if the initiation of two drugs occurs very close in time (e.g., initiation of alcohol and cigarettes both occur within the same month) and the study design measures transition between drugs that occur over the course of a year, then the study risks overlooking the ordered sequence by which these drugs are initiated. On the other hand, if the spacing between observations was too close together (e.g. monthly measurements when transitions tend to occur much less frequently), then researchers risk overlooking important gateway relations. The significant gateway relations that were identified, however, suggest that the temporal design was reasonable for studying drug use behavior in this population.

Several limitations of the current study are worth noting. First, this study only included one cohort of middle adolescents of the National Longitudinal Study of Adolescents Health. Future studies should examine patterns of drug use involvement among youth in other stages of development, particularly early adolescence when initiation of drug use is most problematic (Brown, Miller, & Clayton, 2004; Griflin, Botvin, Epstein, Doyle, & Diaz, 2000; Henry, Slater, & Oetting, 2005; Tucker, Ellickson, Orlando, Martino, & Klein, 2005). It is possible that different gateway relations hold in younger and older cohorts. For instance, we examined patterns of drug use behaviors among ninth and eleventh grade cohorts of Add Health and found a similar structure of recent drug use. Such results would suggest prevention programs that could be targeted differentially to adolescents, depending on both their age and their level of drug use at the time of intervention. Another limitation of the current study is that, although it uses a national representative dataset, this dataset was collected in 1995-1996. Therefore rrent patterns of drug use involvement might differ from those of decade ago, as the availability of drugs changes with restrictive licies, and with more aggressive efforts to limit youth's access illegal drugs, and the availability of new drugs in the market. ture studies should compare how stages of recent drug use (from rrent and previous studies) compare to more contemporary data. e current study provides a set of guidelines that will permit such comparison. Importantly, the current study did not examine differential gateway relations by moderators such as gender or race/ hnic group. Such analyses are an important area of future study.

Despite its limitations, the current study extended the literature the gateway hypothesis by proposing a general probability-based mework for evaluating and testing the gateway hypothesis of ug use among adolescents. Future research is merited to exame factors that moderate gateway relations in this population and evaluate gateway relations among other combinations of drugs d in other populations. The proposed guidelines for examining the teway hypothesis provide a general framework for testing gateway ations between drugs to better inform the prevention of advancevent in drug use among adolescents.

cknowledgments

is study was funded by grants from the National Institute on lcohol Abuse and Alcoholism (AA-017480) and the National stitute on Drug Abuse (DA 10075 and DA 02303). The authors ank Dr. Linda M. Collins, Professor of Human Development d Family Studies, Professor of Statistics, and Director of The ethodology Center at The Pennsylvania State University for r contribution in the early stages of conception and design of is project. This manuscript also benefited from discussions with lleagues at the Methodology Center, The Pennsylvania State niversity.

eferences

kaike, H. 1973 Information theory and an extension of the maximum likelihood principle. In B. N. Petrov & F. Csaki (Eds.), *Second International Symposium on Information Theory* (pp. 267–281). Budapest: Akademiai Kaido.

otvin, G. J., Griffin, K. W., Diaz, T., & Ifil-Williams, M. 2001 Drug abuse prevention among minority adolescents: Post-test and one-year follow-up of school-based preventive intervention. *Prevention Science, 2*(1), 1–13.

etteville-Jensen, A. L., Melberg, H. O., & Jones, A. M. 2008 Sequential patterns of drug use initiation—Can we believe in the gateway theory? *B E Journal of Economic Analysis & Policy, 8*(2), 1-30.

own, T. L., Miller, J. D., & Clayton, R. R. 2004 The generalizeability of substance use predictors across racial groups. *Journal of Early Adolescence, 24,* 274–302.

eveland, H. H., & Wiebe, R. P. 2008 Understanding the association between adolescent marijuana use and later serious drug use:

Gateway effect or developmental trajectory? *Development and Psychopathology, 20,* 615–632.

Collins, L. M. 2002 Using latent transition analysis to examine the gateway hypothesis. In D. B. Kandel (Ed.), *Stages and pathways of drug involvement: examining the gateway hypothesis* (pp. 254–269). Cambridge: University Press.

Collins, L. M., & Lanza, S. T. 2010 *Latent class and latent transition analysis for the social, behavioral, and health sciences.* New York: Wiley.

Collins, L. M., & Wugalter, S. E. 1992 Latent class models for stage-sequential dynamic latent-variables. *Multivariate Behavioral Research, 27*(1), 131–157.

Degenhardt, L., Chiu, W. T., Conway, K., Dierker, L., Glantz, M., Kalaydjian, A., Merikangas, K., Sampson, N., Swendsen, J., Kessler, R.C. 2009 Does the 'gateway' matter? Associations between the order of drug use initiation and the development of drug dependence in the National Comorbidity Study Replication. *Psychological Medicine, 39*(1), 157–167. doi: 10.1017/s0033291708003425

Eaton, D. K., Kann, L., Kinchen, S., Shanklin, S., Ross, J., Hawkins, J., Harris, W.A., Lowry, R., McManus, T., Chyen, D., Lim, C., Brener, N.D., Wechsler, H. 2008 Youth risk behavior surveillance United States, 2007. *Morbidity and Mortality Weekly Report, 57*(SS-4).

Fergusson, D. M., Boden, J. M., & Horwood, L. J. 2006 Cannabis use and other illicit dris use: Testing the cannabis gateway hypothesis. *Addiction, 101*(4), 556–569.

Griffin, K. W., Botvin, G. J., Epstein, J. A., Doyle, M. M., & Diaz, T. 2000 Psychosocial and behavioral factors in early adolescence as predictors of heavy drinking among high school seniors. *Journal of Studies on Alcohol, 61*(4), 603–606.

Guo, J., Collins, L. M., Hill, K. G., & Hawkins, J. D. 2000 Developmental pathways to alcohol abuse and dependence in young adulthood. *Journal of Studies on Alcohol, 61,* 799–808.

Harris, K. M. 2009 The National Longitudinal Study of Adolescent Health (Add Heath), Waves I & II, 1994-1996; Wave III. 2001–2001; Wave IV, 2007–2009. Chapel Hill, NC: Carolina Population Center. University of North Carolina at Chapel Hill.

Hawkins, J. D., Hill, K. G., Guo, J., & Battin-Pearson, S. R. 2002 Substance use norms and transitions in substance use: Implications for the gateway hypothesis. In D. B. Kandel (Ed.), *Stages and pathways of drug involvement: Examining the gateway hypothesis* (pp. 42–64). Cambridge: University Press.

Henry, K. L., Slater, M. D., & Oetting, E. R. 2005 Alcohol use in early adolescence: The effect of changes in risk taking, perceived harm and friends' alcohol use. *Journal of Studies on Alcohol, 66*(2), 275-283.

Hyatt, S. L., & Collins, L. M. 2000 Using latent transition analysis to examine the relationship between parental permissiveness and the onset of substance use. In J. Rose, L. Chassin, C. Presson & S. Sherman (Eds.), *Multivariate applications in substance use research: New methods for new questions* (pp. 259–288). Hillsdale, NJ: Earlbaum.

Johnston, L. D., O'Malley, P., Bachman, J. G., & Schulenberg, J. 2009 Monitoring the Future national results on adolescent drug use: Overview of key findings, 2008. Bethesda, MD: National Institute on Drug Abuse.

Kandel, D. B. 1975 Stages in adolescent involvement in drug use. *Science, 190*(4217), 912–914.

Kandel, D. B. 2002 *Stages and pathways of drug involvement: Examining the gateway hypothesis.* Cambridge: University Press.

Kandel, D. B., & Jessor, R. 2002 The gateway hypothesis revisited. In D. B. Kandel (Ed.), *Stages and pathways of drug involvement: Examining the gateway hypothesis* (pp. 365–372). Cambridge: University Press.

Kandel, D. B., & Yamaguchi, K. 2002 Stages of drug involvement in the U.S. population. In D. B. Kandel (Ed.), *Stages and pathways of drug involvement: Examining the gateway hypothesis* (pp. 65–89). Cambridge: University Press.

Kandel, D. B., Yamaguchi, K., & Cousino Klein, L. 2006 Testing the gateway hypothesis. *Addiction, 101,* 470–476.

Lanza, S. T., & Collins, L. M. 2002 Pubertal timing and the onset of substance use in females during early adolescence. *Prevention Science, 3*(1), 69–82.

Lanza, S. T., Lemmon, D. R., Schafer, J. L., & Collins, L. M. 2008 PROC LCA & PROC LTA User's Guide, Version 1.1.5 beta *The Methodology Center:* The Pennsylvania State University.

Lessem, J. M., Hopfer, C. J., Haberstick, B. C., Timberlake, D., Ehringer, M. A., Smolen, A., Hewitt, J.K. 2006 Relationship between adolescent marijuana use and young adult illicit drug use. *Behavior Genetics, 36*(4), 498–506.

Maldonado-Molina, M., Collins, L. M., Lanza, S. T., Prado, G., Ramirez, R., & Canino, G. 2007 Patterns of substance use onset among Hispanics in Puerto Rico and the United States. *Addictive Behaviors, 32,* 2434–2437.

Martin, K. R. 2003 Youths' opportunities to experiment influence later use of illegal drugs. *NIDA Notes, 17,* 8–10.

Patrick, M., Collins, L. M., Smith, E. A., Caldwell, L., Flisher, A., & Wegner, L. 2009 A prospective longitudinal model of substance use onset among South African adolescents. *Substance Use and Misuse, 44*(5), 647–662.

Raftery, A. E. 1986 A note on Bayes factors for log-linear contingency table models with vague prior information. *Journal of the Royal Statistical Society. Series B (Methodological), 48*(2), 249–250.

Rebellon, C. J., & Van Gundy, K. 2006 Can social psychology delinquency theory explain the link between marijuana and other illicit drug use? A longitudinal analysis of the gateway hypothesis. *Journal of Drug Issues, 36*(3), 515–539.

Tucker, J. S., Ellickson, P. L., Orlando, M., Martino, S. C., & Klein, D. J. 2005 Substance use trajectories from early adolescence to emerging adulthood: A comparison of smoking, binge drinking and marijuana use. *Journal of Drug Issues, 35*(2), 307–331.

Wagner, F. A., & Anthony, J. C. 2001 Into the world of illegal drug use: Exposure opportunity and other mechanisms linking the us of alcohol, tobacco, marijuana, and cocaine. *American Journal of Epidemiology, 155*(10), 918–925.

Critical Thinking

1. The authors use a clear operational definition for gateway drug use. Could this same definition be applied to behaviors other than drug use? Provide an example.

2. What are the arguments that do not favor the gateway drug theory? In other words, what problems do you see in the logic of this study, if any?

DR. MILDRED M. MALDONADO-MOLINA is Assistant Professor the Department of Epidemiology and Health Policy Research a the Institute for Child Health Policy at the University of Florid Her research focuses on health disparities of alcohol and substan use, delinquency behaviors, and effects of public policies to redu disparities in alcohol-related consequences. **DR. STEPHANIE LANZA** is Scientific Director of The Methodology Center at Pe State. She currently leads a research team focused on advanci latent class analysis and related methods. Her latest book, w Linda Collins, PhD, is *Latent Class and Latent Transition Analys With Applications in the Social, Behavioral, and Health Scienc* (2010) Wiley.

From *The Journal of Drug Issues*, vol. 40, no. 4. October 2010, pp. 901–924. Copyright © 2010 by the College of Criminology and Criminal Justice, Florida State University. Reprinted by permission via the Copyright Clearance Center.

Social Estrangement: Factors Associated with Alcohol or Drug Dependency among Homeless, Street-Involved Young Adults

Anna J. Thompson et al.

Introduction

Substance abuse is highly prevalent among homeless young people. Estimates from empirical studies suggest that 39% to 70% of homeless youth abuse drugs or alcohol (Chen, Thrane, Whitbeck, & Johnson, 2006; Martijn & Sharpe, 2006). In nationally representative samples, marijuana is the most frequently used drug by homeless youth (Haley, Roy, Leclerc, Boudreau, & Boivin, 2004; Thompson, 2004), and its use has been reported as two to three times higher than among other young adults. Rates of cocaine use are four to five times higher and amphetamine use is three to four times higher among homeless adolescents compared to housed peers (Greene & Ringwalt, 1997). Whitbeck and colleagues (2004) compared a non-probability sample of homeless youth with a nationally representative sample of same-aged housed youth. They found that the prevalence of homeless youth meeting criteria for drug abuse was more than 10 times greater for males and 7 times greater for females than housed youth (Whitbeck, Chen, Hoyt, Tyler, & Johnson, 2004). Other research has shown varying rates of alcohol and drug abuse and dependency among this youth population. For example, Kipke and colleagues reported that 71% of their sample of homeless youth met criteria for alcohol and/or illicit drug use disorder (Kipke, Montgomery, Simon, & Iverson, 1997), while Mundy and colleagues found that 48% of homeless youth met DSM-IV criteria for alcohol abuse or dependence and 39% met criteria for drug abuse or dependence (Mundy, Robertson, Robertson, & Greenblatt, 1990). Substance abuse and dependency also appeared to increase the longer these young people remained homeless (Johnson, Whitbeck, & Hoyt, 2005; Rew, Taylor-Seehafer, & Fitzgerald, 2001), with drug overdose being highly prevalent as well (Sibthorpe, Drinkwater, Gardner, & Bammer, 1995).

Although society regards drug and alcohol use as the primary hindrance to homeless individual's successful transition off the street, homeless young people view drug and alcohol use as a valuable coping strategy. These young adults have more favorable attitudes toward drugs than their non-homeless peers (Fors & Rojek, 1991), and describe drug use as a common and useful approach to numbing the daily experiences of life on the street. Using drugs is perceived as a strategy to alleviate the stress of street life and the negative emotional effects of traumatic experiences. With housing that often includes sleeping in public places, homeless youth report using drugs and alcohol as a way to keep warm and suppress hunger (Ayerst, 1999). Some drugs are used to help them stay awake for extended periods in an effort to lessen the chances of victimization (Ayerst, 1999; Fest, 2003). Drugs also provide a means of escape from the physical and emotional pain associated with estrangement from social norms and resources (Zlotnick, Tam, & Robertson, 2003).

Recently, research on homeless adults has employed a conceptual framework of "societal estrangement" to understand individual characteristics, family systems, and societal influences pivotal in the progressive accumulation of challenges experienced by homeless individuals (Grigsby, Baumann, Gregorich, & Roberts-Gray, 1990; Piliavin, Sosin, Westerfelt, & Matsueda, 1993). Noting that sustained homelessness reflects greater estrangement from societal institutions, Piliavin and colleagues developed a conceptual model that features four sources or domains of estrangement, including: (a) institutional/societal disaffiliation, (b) human capital, (c) identification with homeless culture, and (d) psychological dysfunction (Piliavin et al., 1993; Sosin & Bruni, 2000). Others have drawn upon this conceptualization to further develop the framework (Zlotnick et al., 2003) and examined the four domains of estrangement among runaway/homeless youth (Thompson & Pollio, 2006). These four domains will provide an organizing structure for examining societal estrangement as experienced by young homeless people and their alcohol and/or drug dependency.

Disaffiliation is defined as detachment from social institutions through weakening of associative bonds and relationships, social isolation, and unstable social networks (Castel, 2000). It is often measured in research studies in terms of lack of support from family/friends and limited utilization of formal services and providers (Zlotnick et al., 2003). Bahr theorized that disaffiliation may result from a person's voluntary withdrawal from their community, whereby they choose a deviant role (Bahr, 1973; Bahr & Caplow, 1973). Thus, drug addiction may lead to societal estrangement and disaffiliation from institutions and relationships. Vulnerable groups, such as homeless young people, exhibit disaffiliation through poor school performance or academic failure, conflict with the law, or isolation from supportive, pro-social relationships (Malloy, Christ, & Hohloch, 1990). These young people often report that their initial runaway episode (an experience that is truly disaffiliating from family) was perpetrated by stressful events in the home, such as family conflict, maltreatment by parents or other family members, and/or parental substance abuse (Rew, Fouladi, & Yockey, 2002; Thompson, 2004). Parental substance abuse has been shown to be a common experience among homeless young people. For example, one study found that 55% of homeless youth came from families where the father abused substances and 46% had mothers who abused substances (Ginzler, Cochran, Domenech-Rodriguez, Cauce, & Whitbeck, 2003). Growing up in these families may increase the child's risk of substance abuse and precocious departure from parental homes. Thus, those who have greater disaffiliation from family and friends, use substances, and have little contact with needed services are more likely to remain homeless and isolated from society (Piliavin et al., 1993).

Human capital reflects individual's skills and knowledge that produce goods and services (Bullock, Stallybrass, & Trombley, 1988; Shinn et al., 2007). Often defined as the ability to create personal, social, and economic assets, human capital has historically been measured by educational level, literacy and income (Shinn et al., 2007). Among homeless young people who lack occupational proficiency, developing the street smarts necessary to locate resources and adapt to the street economy are skills needed to survive (Lankenau, Clatts, Welle, Goldsamt, & Gwadz, 2005). Although some survival strategies may be antisocial in nature, such as drug trafficking or property crime, nontraditional resources are often essential for support and subsistence among homeless individuals who lack parental or familial assistance (Bender, Thompson, McManus, Lantry, & Flynn, 2007). Research suggests that adolescent's perceptions of peer's acceptance and the profitability of illicit drug dealing shapes their view of using and selling drugs (Johnson, Wish, Schmeidler, & Huizinga, 1991). Alienation from conventional sources of income generation and the belief that selling drugs is a viable means to make money are important reasons for choosing illegal activities to create human capital (Little & Steinberg, 2006). In addition, homeless adolescents who derive income from drug dealing typically live in contexts characterized by high physical and social disorder, low parental interaction or monitoring, and high levels of peer deviance (Kidd, 2003). Research shows that high-frequency drug users who are immersed with life on the streets are also heavily involved in property crimes and drug trafficking (Farabee, Shen, Hser, Grella, & Anglin, 2001). Therefore, given that successful drug dealing requires time and a certain degree of planning, homeless youth with little parental monitoring or supervision would have greater opportunity to participate in illicit drug sales (Little & Steinberg, 2006).

Identification with homeless culture suggests that homelessness is a type of cultural experience that is unique to this specific group of individuals. The greater the length of time away from family, the more likely they are to find similarly-situated peers and become drawn into street culture (Fest, 2003). Although no research to date identifies the trajectory or the length of time away from home required to acculturate to the homeless lifestyle, anecdotal evidence suggests youth who spend more than 30 days away from home are likely to shift in this direction (Fest, 2003). Additional indicators of acculturation may include survival strategies, such as engaging in survival sex for drugs, food, or shelter (Dembo, Pacheco, Schmeidler, Fisher, & Cooper, 1997; Whitbeck & Simons, 1990). Young people who become entrenched in street life through involvement in activities associated with surviving on the street become alienated from traditional community structures (Fest, 2003; Tyler & Johnson, 2006). They assimilate to a street economy where delinquent and/or criminal behaviors become common (Piliavin, Wright, & Mare, 1996). Status offenses such as dropping out of school may lead to more serious offenses of violent crime and theft as a means of survival (Lindsey, Kurtz, Jarvis, Williams, & Nackerud, 2000; Mallett, Rosenthal, Myers, Milburn, & Rotheram-Borus, 2004). Acculturation to the streets and street economy progresses with the length of exposure to homelessness and other homeless peers (Auerswald & Eyre, 2002; Gaetz, 2004; Kidd, 2003; Kipke, Unger, O'Connor, Palmer, & LaFrance, 1997).

Research has suggested that similarly-situated, homeless peers provide an important learning environment for initiating drug use and provide opportunities and reinforcement for drug-using behaviors (Kipke et al., 1997). Affiliation with deviant peers is the strongest factor associated with substance abuse disorders (Johnson et al., 2005), as the street lifestyle encourages and rewards substance use (Tyler & Johnson, 2006). One study found that marijuana use rose from 24% in the month before running away to 39% after leaving home and that hallucinogen use increased from 5% to 11% after leaving home (Kipke et al., 1997). This is likely due to youth coming in contact with increased access to drugs and alcohol, seeking out drug-using friends after initiating drug use, and embedding themselves in social networks that reinforce drug-related choices, attitudes, and behaviors (Baron, 1999). Substance use becomes a central theme around which to organize activities and becomes a normative behavior. As the lure of drugs and alcohol becomes a strategy to fend off the myriad of detrimental experiences of street-involved young people (McMorris, Tyler, Whitbeck, & Hoyt, 2002), the result is further societal estrangement.

Psychological dysfunction is disproportionately high among homeless youth, particularly depression, suicidal thoughts and attempts (Mallett et al., 2004; Stewart et al., 2004). The process of running away, being kicked out of parental homes, or abandoned by families can be expected to induce complex and troubling emotional and behavioral responses. Previous research suggests that many homeless adolescents display depressive symptoms (Whitbeck, Hoyt, & Bao, 2000), have few adaptive skills for coping with stress (Dalton & Pakenham, 2002), experience suicidal ideation and behaviors (Noell & Ochs, 2001) and exhibit various trauma symptoms (Thompson, McManus, & Voss, 2006).

Research generally supports the relationship between the risk of mental health disorders and co-morbid substance abuse (Kilpatrick et al., 2003). Psychiatric disorders frequently seen in conjunction with substance abuse include mood, conduct, and anxiety disorders. One study found that over half of homeless youth respondents exhibited symptoms of clinical depression, had thoughts of suicide, and had an alcohol or drug disorder (Unger, Kipke, Simon ontgomery, & Johnson, 1997); another study reported that of the omeless youth who met lifetime diagnostic criteria for at least e substance abuse disorder, more than 90% met criteria for a ental disorder (Johnson et al., 2005).

Although the relationships between substance use and each the domains of societal estrangement have been studied sepa-ely among homeless populations, little research has been nducted to elucidate how the four theoretical domains might edict homeless youths' alcohol and drug dependency. Thus, s exploratory study is aimed to measure and analyze the four mains of estrangement (i.e., disaffiliation, human capital, entification with homeless culture, and psychological dysfunc-on), and to understand how these domains predict alcohol and ug dependency among a group of highly vulnerable young ople. A descriptive correlational design was used to address o research questions: (1) What are the differences between meless young people who are alcohol or drug dependent and ose who are not? (2) Which domains of estrangement sig-ficantly predict alcohol or drug dependency among homeless, eet-involved young adults?

Method

etting

rticipants were recruited from among homeless youth receiving rvices from a community drop-in center located in Central Texas m September 2006 to May 2007. The drop-in center, typical of ers across the country, provides outreach and support services to meless/runaway youth ranging in age from 16 to 23 years. The nter provides a safe environment for young people during the day d offers case management services, hygiene supplies, laundry cilities, food, clothing, education/GED preparation, educational oups, transportation services, medical care, immunizations, HIV unseling and testing, and pregnancy testing. As drop-in centers e one of the most common sources of services accessed by street uth (Taylor-Seehafer, 2004), this service agency provided the ost likely source for homeless young adults assembling in one cation.

ample

uth recruited for participation in the study included those iden-ed by drop-in center staff as being 18 to 23 years of age and own to use alcohol and/or drugs. Case managers approached uth who, from their experience working with the individual, t inclusion criteria. As a standard practice by the drop-in center, uth who enter the facility are subjectively evaluated for intoxica-n or being under the influence of drugs. Those who come to the op-in center in this condition are asked to leave until they are ber and no longer high. Thus, case managers made the deter-nation whether a particular individual was eligible for recruit-nt into the study based on their knowledge of that person and ir current level of sobriety. For those who did meet the inclusion teria, each had the study described to them and were invited to eak with research assistants. Young people who agreed to learn re about the research study were taken to a private room at the op-in center where the study was fully explained and consent rms for participation were signed. The explanation included

information about who was conducting the study, the voluntary nature of participation, the confidentiality of the data collected, and the option of stopping the interview at any time. Youth were informed that the interview would require approximately one hour and that they would receive $10 for their participation. After providing informed consent, eligible youth completed self-report questionnaires that addressed issues of societal estrangement and substance dependency. Questionnaires were read to each partici-pant to control for literacy problems often found among this youth population.

One hundred eighty-five youth, ranging in age from 18 to 23 years (mean = 20.8, $SD \pm 1.6$), agreed to participate. Partici-pants were predominantly White/not Latino ($n = 125$, 67.6%), with the remainder identifying themselves as Black/not Latino ($N = 3$, 1.6%), Latino ($n = 8$, 4.3%), American Indian ($n = 4$, 2.2%) or other/mixed ethnicity ($n = 44$, 23.8%). Most reported living "on the streets" or outdoors ($n = 102$, 55.1%) and "panhandled" ($n = 138$, 74.6%) or performed temporary work ($n = 98$. 53.0%) to earn money. Less than half had graduated from high school ($n = 86$, 46.5%) and most had been arrested at least once during their lifetime ($n = 167$, 90.3%).

The majority of these young people reported drinking alcohol ($N = 149$, 80.6%) and 61% ($n = 113$) were identified as alcohol dependent. Of the 84.9% ($n = 157$) who reported using drugs, more than half (54.6%, $n = 101$) were drug dependent. Although youth reported using a wide variety of substances, the predominant drug of choice was marijuana (71.9%, $n = 133$) or heroin/morphine/opi-ates (13.5%, $n = 25$).

Measures

The dependent variable for the current study was alcohol and drug dependency and was measured by the Mini International Neuro-psychiatric Interview (MINI). The MINI is a widely-used, brief, structured diagnostic interview developed by psychiatrists in the United States and Europe for assessing DSM-IV psychiatric disor-ders (Lecrubier et al., 1997; Sheehan et al., 1998). With an admin-istration time of approximately 15 to 20 minutes for the full MINI, this structured psychiatric interview allows screening for substance abuse and dependency and Axis I psychiatric disorders. For this study, only the alcohol (8 items) and drug (10 items) dependency modules were administered. Alcohol and drug dependency were each coded as yes = 1 or no = 0. Drug dependency was based on the drug the individual self-identified as the one they used most frequently. Cronbach's alpha for the alcohol dependency items in this sample was moderately high ($alpha = .78$), as was the alpha for drug dependency ($alpha = .73$).

Variables that measured basic demographics and the four domains of estrangement were collected through a combination of researcher-generated questions and standardized instruments. Demographic variables included gender (1 = male, 2 = female), ethnicity (minority = 1, white = 2), and age.

Disaffiliation was measured by the following variables: (1) respondent primarily lived on the street, including public places such as parks and abandoned buildings (1 = yes, 0 = no), (2) carried a weapon as a means of keeping themselves safe (yes = 1, no = 0), (3) total number of arrests for violent offenses, (4) parental assis-tance and support in the previous six months (1 = almost never to 4 = a lot of the time), (5) number of days parent used alcohol in the 30 days before the youth left home, and (6) number of days parent used marijuana in the 30 days before the youth left home.

Human capital variables included single-items querying how the youth obtained money, such as (1) panhandling, (2) working full-time, (3) working part-time or doing temporary work, (4) selling drugs or making money from other illegal activities, (5) selling blood/plasma, and (6) other street friends or family friends giving the respondent money (all coded yes = 1, no = 0).

Culture of homelessness variables included: (1) the number of drugs the respondent used during the past 6 months, (2) marijuana identified as the drug used most frequently, (3) heroin/opiates identified as the drug used most frequently, (4) methamphetamines identified as the drug used most frequently, (5) the number of days in the past month that street friends drank alcohol, (6) length of time the youth spent engaged in street life each day (coded very little = 1, to most all day = 4), and (7) the Future Time Perspective Scale (FTP) (Heimberg, 1963; Mahon & Yarcheski, 1994). The FTP Scale is a 25-item 7-point summated rating scale that defines future time perspective as the degree to which an individual views the future as predictable, structured, and controllable. Higher scores indicate an extended and hopeful perspective regarding the future with a positive view of successful attainment of goals and dreams (Heimberg, 1963). In studies with other homeless youth, Rew and colleagues (Rew, Fouladi, Land, & Wong, 2007) reported strong reliability with alpha = .90 for females and .89 for males. For this sample, the Cronbach alpha = .70

Psychological dysfunction was measured by assessing positive affect. This six-item scale was adapted from the K6 scale (Kessler et al., 2002) that was developed to evaluate psychological distress. Questions were revised, as requested by the drop-in center, to query positive mood rather than distress. This revision aimed to diminish the likelihood of participants experiencing psychological distress due to negatively-worded questions related to their mental health. The revised questions included: "During the past month,. . . . I felt tranquil, serene, and calm," "I felt hopeful," "I felt relaxed and not easily agitated," "I felt cheerful, like nothing could get me down," "I felt everything was easy and effortless," and "I felt valued." Reliability was calculated for the revised items with fairly strong results (alpha = .84).

Data Analysis

To answer the research questions, the sample was divided into two subgroups: alcohol dependent/not dependent and drug dependent/not dependent. To determine the differences between homeless youth who were identified as alcohol or drug dependent compared to those who were not, t-tests and chi square analyses were conducted. Bivariate relationships were established between each societal estrangement domain (disaffiliation, human capital, culture of homelessness, psychological dysfunction) and the dichotomous alcohol or drug dependency outcome variables. As none of the demographic variables were significantly related to alcohol or drug dependency, they were not included as control variables in subsequent analyses. All variables in each estrangement domain that were statistically significant at the .05 level in the bivariate analyses were entered into multivariate logistic regression models. Separate logistic regression models were calculated for alcohol and drug dependency to examine the effect of indicators of the four estrangement domains on the likelihood of youth being dependent on alcohol or not and dependent on drugs or not.

Results
Group Differences
Alcohol Dependent vs. Non-Dependent

Results of the chi-square and t-tests indicated some significa differences between homeless young people who were alcoh dependent and those who were not (See Table 1). Among disaffil ation variables, significantly more alcohol dependent young adu reported living on the street ($x^2 = 89.73$, $p \leq .01$) and carrying weapon to keep themselves safe ($x^2 = 8.89$, $p \leq .001$) than you adults who were not alcohol dependent. Dependent youth report their parents drank more often ($x^2 = -1.79$, $p \leq .05$), but smoke marijuana less often ($x^2 = 1.35$, $p \leq .05$) than did the parents their non-dependent counterparts.

Regarding sources of income as indicators of human capit engaging in panhandling was reported more often as a means of ma ing money among alcohol dependent youth ($x^2 = 7.98$, $p \leq .001$), b fewer alcohol dependent youth reported selling their blood or plasn for money compared to non-dependent youth ($x^2 = 9.59$, $p \leq .00$) Significantly more alcohol dependent young adults reported se ing drugs ($x^2 = .64$, $p \leq .05$) than did those who were not alcoh dependent.

Among indicators of immersion in the homeless culture, alc hol dependent young people reported using a greater numb of drugs ($x^2 = -3.38$, $p \leq .01$), used marijuana more frequent ($x^2 = 4.38$, $p \leq .01$), and had friends who drank alcohol more da each month ($x^2 = -3.79$, $p \leq .001$) than did those not depende on alcohol. In addition, alcohol dependent youth spent the majo ity of their time hanging out on the street ($x^2 = 1.77$, $p \leq .05$) a had lower scores on the scale measuring perspectives of the futu ($x^2 = 3.2$, $p \leq .001$) than their non-dependent counterparts. How ever, the indicator of psychological dysfunction, positive affe was not significantly different between these groups.

Alcohol Dependent
vs. Non-Dependent

Similar to results of alcohol dependency, Table 2 shows biva ate analyses of disaffiliation variables that indicated significan more drug-dependent young adults carded a weapon for safe ($x^2 = 7.81$, $p \leq .01$). These drug dependent youth also reported ha ing a greater number of violent offense charges ($x^2 = -2.10$, $p \leq .0$ and used marijuana more days each month ($x^2 = 1.35$, $p \leq .05$) tha did their non-dependent counterparts.

Indicators of human capital showed that drug dependent you people were significantly more likely than non-dependent you to sell drugs ($x^2 = 7.19$, $p \leq .001$) or get money from frien ($x^2 = 4.0$, $p \leq .05$), while more non-dependent youth report working full time than did their drug dependent counterpa ($x^2 = 3.80$, $p \leq .05$).

In terms of the culture of homelessness domain, drug-depende young adults used a greater number of drugs ($x^2 = -2.34$, $p \leq .0$ used less marijuana ($x^2 = 6.25$, $p \leq .01$), but used more hero morphine/opiates ($x^2 = 16.32$, $p \leq .001$) than did non-depende young adults. As with alcohol dependent youth, drug depe dent youth scored lower on the Future Time Perspective sca ($x^2 = 89.73$, $p \leq .01$) than those not drug dependent. Fewer dru dependent youth reported working full time ($x^2 = 3.80$, $p \leq .0$ but reported dealing drugs as a source of income than did no dependent youth ($x^2 = 7.19$, $p \leq .001$). According to the indicator

Table 1 Social Estrangement Differences between Alcohol Dependent/ Non-Dependent Homeless Youth

Characteristics	Dependent	Not Dependent	
	N (%) Mean ± SD	N (%) Mean ± SD	t/x^2
Disaffiliation			
Primarily live on street	72 (62.7)	30 (19.6)	9.73**
Carry a weapon	81 (43.8)	36 (19.4)	8.89**
Total violent offenses	.44 ± 1.7	.37 ± 1.1	−.34
No parental assistance	50 (27.0)	23 (12.4)	4.03
Parent alcohol use	14.6 ± 14.1	11.0 ± 12.5	−1.7*
Parent marijuana use	7.4 ± 12.1	9.9 ± 13.3	1.35*
Ever arrested	103 (55.7)	64 (34.6)	.26
Ever juvenile detention	45 (24.3)	38 (20.5)	2.98
Ever in jail	47 (25.4)	51 (27.6)	.88
Human capital			
Panhandling	93 (84.9)	46 (54.1)	7.98***
Work full time	33 (34.8)	24 (22.2)	.35
Temporary work	63 (61.1)	37 (38.9)	.34
Dealing drugs	41 (38.5)	22 (24.5)	.64*
Selling blood/plasma	4 (9.8)	12 (6.2)	9.59***
Friends give money	58 (56.2)	34 (35.8)	.30
Homeless culture			
# drugs used	5.1 ± 2.5	3.9 ± 2.2	−3.38**
Use Marijuana	75 (81.2)	58 (51.8)	4.38*
Use Heroin/opiates	19 (15.3)	6 (9.7)	2.71
Use Methamphetamines	5 (3.7)	1 (2.3)	1.29
#days friends drank/month	26.6 ± 8.1	20.9 ± 12.2	−3.7***
Spent most of day on street	52 (47.6)	26 (30.4)	1.77*
Future Time Perspective	86.7 ± 18.9	95.7 ± 17.3	3.2**
Psychological dysfunction			
Positive affect score	19.8 ± 6.2	20.8 ± 6.9	.93

*p ≤ .05, **p ≤ .01, *** p ≤ .001

Table 2 Social Estrangement Differences between Drug Dependent/ Non-Dependent Homeless Youth

Characteristics	Dependent	Not Dependent	
	N (%) Mean ± SD	N (%) Mean ± SD	t/x^2
Disaffiliation			
Primarily live on street	61 (55.8)	41 (46.2)	2.97
Carry a weapon	73 (39.5)	44 (23.8)	7.81**
Total violent offenses	.61 ± 1.9	.17 ± .56	−2.1*
No parental assistance	38 (20.5)	35 (18.9)	3.11
Parent alcohol use	12.3 ± 13.6	14.3 ± 13.5	1.0
Parent marijuana use	9.92 ± 13.7	6.59 ± 11.0	−1.8*
Ever arrested	94 (50.8)	73 (39.5)	1.98
Ever juvenile detention	47 (25.4)	36 (19.5)	.25
Ever in jail	80 (43.2)	58 (31.4)	2.50
Human capital			
Panhandling	76 (41.1)	63 (34.1)	.01
Work full time	25 (13.5)	32 (17.3)	3.80*

(continued)

Table 2 Social Estrangement Differences between Drug Dependent/
Non-Dependent Homeless Youth *(continued*

Characteristics	Dependent	Not Dependent	
Temporary work	60 (32.4)	40 (21.6)	2.56
Dealing drugs	43 (23.2)	20 (10.8)	7.19***
Selling blood/plasma	6 (3.2)	10 (5.4)	2.06
Friends give money	57 (30.8)	35 (18.9)	4.0*
Homeless culture			
# drugs used	5.0 ± 2.3	4.2 ± 2.6	−2.34*
Use Marijuana	65 (35.1)	68 (36.8)	6.25**
Use Heroin/opiates	23 (12.4)	2 (1.1)	16.32***
Use Methamphetamines	5 (2.7)	1 (.5)	2.07
# days friends drank/month	25.2 ± 9.6	23.8 ± 10.7	−.93
Spent most of day on street	42 (22.7)	36 (19.5)	.03
Future Time Perspective	87.9 ± 18.5	92.9 ± 18.7	1.76*
Psychological dysfunction			
Positive affect score	19.4 ± 6.3	21.1 ± 6.7	1.78*

* $p \le .05$, ** $p < .01$. *** $p \le .001$

psychological dysfunction, drug dependent young people scored significantly lower on positive mood ($x^2 = 1.78$, $p \le .05$) than their non-dependent counterparts.

Predictors of Alcohol Dependence

Table 3 displays the odds ratios for reporting alcohol dependency or no dependency according to indicators of the four estrangement domains. For the disaffiliation domain, the odds of alcohol dependency were higher for those who carried a weapon to ensure their safety ($OR = 2.58$) and whose parents used less marijuana in the month before the youth left home ($OR = .96$). The only significant predictor of the human capital domain indicated that the likelihood of alcohol dependency decreased for those who reported selling their blood or plasma for money ($OR = .08$). Indicators of the culture of homelessness domain showed that the greater number of drugs used ($OR = 1.24$), spending more time each day on the street with other homeless youth ($OR = 3.68$), and having more friends who drank alcohol ($OR = 1.05$) significantly increased the likelihood of alcohol dependency. However, for every unit increase in the scale measuring future plans and dreams, youth had a 5% reduction in the odds of alcohol dependence ($OR = .95$). The final estrangement domain, psychological dysfunction, was not a significant predictor of alcohol dependence (model $x^2 = 63.47$ ($df = 13$), $p < .001$).

Predictors of Drug Dependence

As shown in Table 4, indicators of disaffiliation revealed that the odds of being drug dependent increased for those who carried a weapon ($OR = 2.52$). The only human capital domain variable that significantly predicted drug dependency was measured by youth who reported they received money from friends

and increased the likelihood of drug dependency ($OR = 1.93$ Indicators of the culture of homelessness domain showed th for every unit increase in use of heroin/opiates, these you adults were 38 times more likely to meet criteria for drug depe dency ($OR = 38.37$). The psychological dysfunction doma did not change the odds of drug dependence (model $x^2 = 42.8$ ($df = 10$), $p < .001$).

Discussion

Results of this study confirm previous findings that a large percen age of homeless youth not only use substances, but are depende on them as well (Chen et al., 2006; Martijn & Sharpe, 2006). this sample, the vast majority reported high levels of alcohol a drug use, with more than half being identified as dependent. Pol substance use was also highly prevalent, consistent with prev ous reports of the normative nature of this behavior among th young adult population (Peterson, Baer, Wells, Ginzler, & Ga rett, 2006). Previous studies have suggested that these you people typically use the substances most readily available the region of the country in which they travel (McManus Thompson, in press). Nearly 75% of youth reported their drug choice was marijuana while smaller percentages preferred heroi methamphetamines, or other hard drugs. The popularity of mar juana has been cited in previous studies of homeless youth (Haley al., 2004), and consistently reported as being nearly universal amo this population of young adults.

Alcohol Dependency

Findings suggested several differences between those who report alcohol dependence and those who did not. Among alcohol depe dent homeless young adults, disaffiliation appeared greater as th carried weapons, lived predominately on the street, and reporte

Table 3 Logistic Regression to Predict Alcohol Dependency by Domains of Estrangement

Estrangement domains/variables	B (SE)	OR	95% C.I.
Disaffiliation			
Primarily live on street	.43 (.45)	1.53	.35-3.6
Carry weapon	.95 (.44)	2.58*	1.1-6.1
# days parent alcohol use	.03 (.02)	1.03	.99-1.1
# days parent marijuana use	−.03 (.02)	.96*	.93-99
Human capital			
Panhandling	.03 (.51)	1.03	.38-2.8
Dealing drugs	−.31 (.47)	.65	.26-1.64
Selling blood/plasma	−2.5 (.78)	.08**	.02-.37
Homeless culture			
# drugs used	.22 (.10)	1.24*	1.0-1.5
Use Marijuana	−.47 (.48)	.63	.34-1.6
# days friends drank	.05 (.02)	1.05*	1.0-1.1
Spent most of day on street	1.3 (.57)	3.68*	1.2-11.2
Future Time Perspective	−.05 (.01)	.95**	.93-99
Psychological dysfunction			
Positive affect score	.001 (.03)	1.00	.94-1.07
Model x^2	63.47 (df = 13), $p \le .001$		

$*p \le .05,$ $**p \le .01$

Table 4 Logistic Regression to Predict Drug Dependency by Domains of Estrangement

Estrangement domains/variables	B (SE)	OR	95% C.I.
Disaffiliation			
Total violent offenses	.36 (.26)	1.44	.85-2.4
Carry weapon	.93 (.39)	2.52*	1.2-5.5
# days parent marijuana use	.02 (.02)	1.02	.99-1.0
Human capital			
Dealing drugs	.24 (.43)	1.27	.54-2.9
Money from friends	.66 (.40)	1.93*	.88-4.2
Homeless culture			
# drugs used	.04 (.08)	1.04	.89-1.2
Use Marijuana	.38 (.51)	1.47	.54-4.0
Use Heroin/opiates	3.65 (1.16)	38.37**	30.9-75.6
Future Time Perspective	−.02 (.01)	.98	.96-1.0
Psychological dysfunction			
Positive affect score	−.03 (.03)	0.97	.91-104
Model x^2	42.80 (df = 10), $p \le .001$		

$*p \le .05,$ $**p \le .01$

their parents drank more alcohol (but used less marijuana) than young adults who were not alcohol dependent. Although those who were alcohol dependent used few harder drugs than marijuana, they reported using a greater variety of drugs than did those who were not alcohol dependent. It is likely that the prominence of alcohol use in their daily lives is encouraged by other street peers who also abuse alcohol. Among this sample, street friends appeared to drink nearly every day and they spent most of each day hanging out with other street-involved young people. Not surprisingly, those who were not alcohol dependent were more likely than those who were dependent to earn most of their money from selling their blood or plasma, presumably because their blood was "clean," while alcohol dependent young adults depended on dealing drugs or panhandling to earn money. This combination of characteristics suggests that those dependent on alcohol have truly disaffiliated themselves from parents and other societal institutions, such as regular employment and education, to become entrenched in street culture.

Findings suggest varying support for the predictive power of the four estrangement domains. Specifically, youth's disaffiliation from societal norms as indicated by carrying a weapon, predicted dependency. However, parents' marijuana use predicted non-dependence on alcohol. In this group of homeless young people, many had left parental homes years earlier. Thus, they had been living on the streets for extended periods of time and parental substance use had little effect on their own use or dependency. Carrying a weapon suggests societal disaffiliation that goes beyond merely living on the streets, but engaging in activities required to remain safe while living rough.

Although dealing drugs and panhandling were human capital indicators related to alcohol dependency, only selling one's blood or plasma for money predicted not being dependent on alcohol. However, indicators of homeless cultural identity were highly predictive of alcohol dependency as homeless young adults appeared to be greatly influenced by street peers, as evidenced by the increased time they spent on the street each day, their poly-substance use, having street friends who drank alcohol nearly every day, and perceiving few hopes and dreams for their future.

This combination of predictors suggests that alcohol dependent young people may find it more difficult to live with others in traditional settings. They prefer living outdoors or in public spaces, but recognize the safety issues involved in living on the street and carry weapons in order to keep themselves and their belongings safe. The combination of alcohol abuse as a social activity and the need for safety often results in groups of homeless young people clustering together in loose associations in order to diminish victimization and provide emotional support to one another (Bender et al., 2007). A lack of hope and motivation concerning leaving the streets also leads homeless youth to form ties with similarly situated others and develop loose connections aimed at improving their survival strategies (Raleigh-DuRoff, 2004). They construct quasi-families that provide emotional and financial support, as well as safety (Bender et al., 2007). Although mutually supportive, these "family units" may further entrench these young people in the street economy and culture (Thompson, Kim, Flynn, & Kim, 2007; Unger et al., 1998). Abusing alcohol, then, becomes a common and normative daily activity that provides not only respite from the daily stress of living on the street, but is an activity around which social and emotionally supportive interactions occur.

Drug Dependency

Similar to alcohol dependent youth, differences between those who were dependent on drugs and those who were not were noted. Those identified as drug dependent were more likely to report carrying a weapon, experiencing more violent offender charges, and engaging in drug distribution. These dependent young people more frequently listed their drug of choice as heroin or other opiates; whereas, rates of marijuana use were less among these young adults. Not surprisingly, a greater proportion of drug-dependent youth admitted to dealing or selling drugs as a way to earn money.

Nearly all of the respondents in this sample had been arrested, spent some time in jail and/or had been admitted to juvenile detention facilities. Past research suggests this population is heavily involved in criminal/illegal activity and these activities are influenced by various factors related to peer involvement and the street economy (Baron, 2003). Many of these young adults reported carrying a weapon to keep safe. As the street lifestyle is overwhelmingly dominated by criminal behaviors and substance abuse, being under the influence while committing a crime appears likely for those heavily involved in this subculture (Baron, 1997).

Predictors of drug dependency highlighted issues of the combination of drug and street culture. Specifically, carrying a weapon, relying on other street friends for money, and using 'hard' drugs increased the likelihood of drug dependency. Previous research has suggested that economically disadvantaged groups are also socially isolated, which may create an atmosphere of constant physical threat and victimization (Baron, 1997). These living conditions, compounded with the need for monetary and material resources, may lead to criminal and violent activities (Baron, 2003). Young homeless males who engage in this high-risk lifestyle are more likely to become involved in violent altercations due to their association with other homeless males who are involved in violent or criminal behaviors (Gaetz, 2004). As a drug dependent lifestyle requires continuous infusions of money, heavy involvement in property crime and drug distribution are common.

Peer influences also play a major role in youths' immersion; the street environment and peers have been identified as one of the most important risk factors for use of illegal drugs (Inciardi & Surratt, 1998). Homeless young people often seek out similarly situated peers who provide opportunities and reinforcement for drug-using attitudes and behavior (Johnson et al., 2005), even drawing upon one another for money and other material support. In this study, features of the homeless subculture, especially regarding extensive use of hard drugs such as heroin, methamphetamines, or other opiates was associated with drug dependency. Previous research indicates that the homeless experience itself encourages the use of hard-core illegal drugs (Baron, 1999; Bender et al., 2007). Street involvement provides opportunities to sample various substances, especially as young adults travel from one region of the country to the other and become increasingly isolated from conventional society.

In general, factors that predicted alcohol and drug dependence were dissimilar. Overall, the conceptual variables measuring the domains of estrangement predicted more of the variance in alcohol dependence than drug-dependence with the largest group of predictors in the culture of homelessness domain. This is likely due to these young adults' extensive experience in street-involved activities and entrenchment in the homeless lifestyle. As Auerswald and Eyre (2002) have shown, becoming acculturated to the street economy, drugs, and the homeless lifestyle contribute to survival in the harsh environment. Therefore, results support the notion that being engaged in activities that center on the homeless lifestyle is highly associated with other behaviors common to street living, such as alcohol and drug abuse.

Limitations

It is important to consider methodological limitations of this study when interpreting the results. First, the study included a convenience sample of youth accessing drop-in services. This service historically frequented by various subgroups of homeless and traveling young people, including those who do not utilize other homeless services. Although, the characteristics of the young people in this study appear similar to other studies of street-involved youth (Bousman et al., 2005; Rew, 2002), future research would be needed to determine whether this sample of street-involved homeless youth have comparable experiences to those accessing services in other areas of the country.

In addition, caseworkers at the drop-in center did not collect information on the number of individuals who refused to participate. Although this creates difficulty in assessing possible selection bias, the caseworkers only sought participation from youth they knew used substances and were not currently intoxicated or under the influence of drugs. As caseworkers were very familiar with the participants due to their frequent utilization of drop-in services, the caseworker's reported that few youth who were approached refused to participate. This level of participation by the young people increases the likelihood that this sample characterizes the youth population sought for this study.

The present study also relied on retrospective self-reports for data collection. While some concern for youth diminishing their reports of alcohol and drug misuse exists, interviewers found them remarkably forthcoming and open in discussions of their use, similar to others who note that self-reports of drug use are reasonably valid (Babor, Stephens, & Marlatt, 1987). Although these self-reports are uncorroborated by external sources, interviewers found youth willing, even anxious, to describe their drug/alcohol use behaviors beyond the quantitative data reported here. The qualitative responses of these youth are described in a separate publication. Other studies have noted similar accuracy and willingness to disclose risky behaviors among this population (Anglin, Hser, & Chou, 1993), further supporting the findings associated with youth reports in this study.

Finally, the cross-sectional design of this study precludes drawing causal inferences concerning the conceptual domains of societal estrangement and substance dependency. Although bivariate analysis confirm the usefulness of the societal estrangement domains related to alcohol and drug dependency, there is a potential for bidirectional associations and time ordering cannot be determined. To address this limitation, multivariate logistic regression models were utilized to increase the ability to control alternative hypotheses and the credibility of inferences drawn from these data. These findings point to the need for further research that incorporates use of longitudinal or other time-series designs to examine societal estrangement predictors of substance dependency over time.

Conclusions

While recognizing the limitations of this study, findings confirm the magnitude of alcohol/drug dependence among homeless young adults and demonstrate the societal estrangement domains related substance dependence. Results highlight the need for agencies providing care to these youth to assess alcohol and drug use and develop referral mechanisms and brief interventions that target alcohol/drug issues. Service providers that identify, understand, and facilitate social processes that result in reduced harm without judgment or condemnation will likely find greater success in assisting these young people. Conveying genuine concern, while recognizing their unique perspectives, lifestyles and culture is more likely to help youth find solutions to their concerns and difficulties than prescriptive approaches.

Note

1. This research was supported with funding and administration from the Center for Social Work Research at the University of Texas at Austin School of Social Work and the National Institute on Drug Abuse (5K01-DA015671).

References

Anglin, D. M., Hser, Y., & Chou, C. 1993 Reliability and validity of retrospective behavioral self-report by narcotics addicts. *Evaluation Review, 17,* 91–108.

Auerswald, C. L., & Eyre, S. L. 2002 Youth homelessness in San Francisco: A life cycle approach. *Social Science & Medicine, 54*(10), 1497–1512.

Ayerst, S. L. 1999 Depression and stress in street youth. *Adolescence, 34*(135), 567–575.

Babor, T. F., Stephens, R. S., & Marlatt, G. A. 1987 Verbal report methods in clinical research on alcoholism: Response bias and its minimization. *Journal of Studies on Alcohol, 48*(5), 410–424.

Bahr, H. M., & Caplow, T. 1973 *Old men drunk and sober.* New York: New York University Press.

Bahr, J. 1973 *Skid Row: An introduction to disaffiliation.* New York: Oxford University Press.

Baron, S. W. 1997 Risky lifestyles and the link between offending and victimization. *Studies on Crime & Crime Prevention, 6*(1), 53–71.

Baron, S. W. 1999 Street youths and substance use: The role of background, street lifestyle, and economic factors. *Youth & Society, 31*(1), 3–26.

Baron, S. W. 2003 Street youth violence and victimization. *Trauma Violence Abuse, 4*(1), 22–44.

Bender, K., Thompson, S. J., McManus, H. H., Lantry, J., & Flynn, P. M. 2007 Capacity for survival: Exploring strengths of homeless street youth. *Child and Youth Care Forum, 36,* 25–42.

Bousman, C. A., Blumberg, E. J., Shillington, A. M., Hovell, M. F., Ji, M., Lehman, S., & Clapp, J. 2005 Predictors of substance use among homeless youth in San Diego. *Addictive Behaviors, 30*(6), 1100–1110.

Bullock, A., Stallybrass, O., & Trombley, S. (Eds.) 1988 *The Fontana dictionary of modern thought, 2nd Ed.* London: Fontana.

Castel, R. 2000 The roads to disaffiliation: Insecure work and vulnerable relationships. *International Journal of Urban and Regional Research, 24*(3), 519–535.

Chen, X., Thrane, L., Whitbeck, L. B., & Johnson, K. 2006 Mental disorders, comorbidity, and post-runaway arrests among homeless and runaway adolescents. *Journal of Research on Adolescence, 16*(3), 379–402.

Dalton, M. M., & Pakenham, K. I. 2002 Adjustment of homeless adolescents to a crisis shelter: Application of a stress and coping model. *Journal of Youth & Adolescence, 31*(1), 79–85.

Dembo, R., Pacheco, K., Schmeidler, J., Fisher, L., & Cooper, S. 1997 Drug use and delinquent behavior among high risk youths. *Journal of Child and Adolescent Substance Abuse, 6*(2), 1–25.

Farabee, D., Shen, H., Hser, Y. I., Grella, C. E., & Anglin, M. D. 2001 The effect of drug treatment on criminal behavior among adolescents in DATOS-A. *Journal of Adolescent Research, 16*(6), 679–690.

Fest, J. 2003 Understanding street culture: A prevention perspective. *School Nurse News, 20*(2), 16–18.

Fors, S. W., & Rojek, D. G. 1991 A comparison of drug involvement between runaways and school youths. *Journal of Drug Education, 21*(1), 13–25.

Gaetz, S. 2004 Safe streets for whom? Homeless youth, social exclusion, and criminal victimization. *Canadian Journal of Criminology and Criminal Justice, 46*(4), 423–455.

Ginzler, J. A., Cochran, B. N., Domenech-Rodriguez, M., Cauce, A. M., & Whitbeck, L. B. 2003 Sequential progression of substance use among homeless youth: an empirical investigation of the gateway theory. *Substance Use & Misuse., 38*(3–6), 725–758.

Greene, J. M., & Ringwalt, C. L. 1997 Substance use among runaway and homeless youth in three national samples. *American Journal of Public Health, 87*(2), 229–236.

Grigsby, C., Baumann, D., Gregorich, S. E., & Roberts-Gray, C. 1990 Dissaffiliation to entrenchment: A model for understanding homelessness. *Journal of Social Issues, 46*(4), 141–157.

Haley, N., Roy, E., Leclerc, P., Boudreau, J. F., & Boivin, J. F. 2004 Characteristics of adolescent street youth with a history of pregnancy. *Journal of Pediatric and Adolescent Gynecology, 17*(5), 313–320.

Heimberg, L. K. 1963 *The measurement of future time perspective.* Unpublished Doctoral Dissertation, Vanderbilt University, Nashville.

Inciardi, J. A., & Surratt, H. L. 1998 Children in the streets of Brazil: Drug use, crime, violence, and HIV risks. *Substance Use & Misuse, 33*(7), 1461–1480.

Johnson, B. D., Wish, E., Schmeidler, J., & Huizinga, D. 1991 Concentration of delinquent offending: Serious drug involvement and high delinquency rates. *Journal of Drug Issues, 21*, 205–229.

Johnson, K. D., Whitbeck, L. B., & Hoyt, D. R. 2005 Substance abuse disorders among homeless and runaway adolescents. *Journal of Drug Issues, 35*(4), 799–816.

Kessler, R. C., Andrews, G., Colpe, L. J., Hiripi, E., Mroczek, D. K., Normand, S. L. T., Walters, E. E., & Zaslavsky, A. M. 2002 Short screening scales to monitor population prevalences and trends in non-specific psychological distress. *Psychological Medicine, 32*, 959–979.

Kidd, S. A. 2003 Street Youth: Coping and interventions. *Child & Adolescent Social Work Journal, 20*(4), 235–261.

Kilpatrick, D. G., Ruggiero, K. J., Acierno, R., Saunders, B. E., Resnick, H. S., & Best, C. L. 2003 Violence and risk of PTSD, major depression, substance abuse/dependence, and comorbidity: Results from the National Survey of Adolescents. *Journal of Consulting And Clinical Psychology, 71*(4), 692–700.

Kipke, M. D., Montgomery, S. B., Simon, T. R., & Iverson, E. F. 1997 Substance abuse disorders among runaway and homeless youth. *Substance Use & Misuse, 32*(7–8), 969–986.

Kipke, M. D., Unger, J. B., O'Connor, S., Palmer, R. F., & LaFrance, S. 1997 Street youth, their peer group affiliation and differences according to residential status, subsistence patterns, and use of services. *Adolescence, 32*(127), 655–669.

Lankenau, S. E., Clatts, M. C., Welle, D., Goldsamt, L. A., & Gwadz, M. V. 2005 Street careers: Homelessness, drug use, and sex work among young men who have sex with men (YMSM). *International Journal of Drug Policy, 16*(1), 10–18.

Lecrubier, Y., Sheehan, D., Weiller, E., Amorim, P., Bonora, I., Sheehan, K., Janavs, J., & Dunbar, G. 1997 The MINI International Neuropsychiatric Interview-A short diagnostic structured interview: Reliability and validity according to the CIDI. *European Psychiatry, 12,* 224–231.

Lindsey, E. W., Kurtz, D., Jarvis, S., Williams, B., & Nackerud, L. 2000 How runaway and homeless youth navigate troubled waters: Personal strengths and resources. *Child & Adolescent Social Work Journal, 17*(2), 115–140.

Little, M., & Steinberg, L. 2006 Psychosocial correlates of adolescent drug dealing in the inner city: Potential roles of opportunity, conventional commitments, and maturity. *Journal of Research Crime and Delinquency, 43*(4), 357–386.

Mahon, N. E., & Yarcheski, T. J. 1994 Future time perspective and positive health practices in adolescents. *Perceptual and Motor Skills, 79*, 395–398.

Mallett, S., Rosenthal, D., Myers, P., Milburn, N., & Rotheram-Borus, M. J. 2004 Practising homelessness: A typology approach to young people's daily routines. *Journal of Adolescence, 27*(3) 337–349.

Malloy, C., Christ, M. A., & Hohloch, F. J. 1990 The homeless: Social isolates. *Journal of Community Health Nursing, 7*(1), 25–36.

Martijn, C., & Sharpe, L. 2006 Pathways to youth homelessness. *Social Science & Medicine, 62*(1), 1–12.

McManus, H. H., & Thompson, S. J. in press Trauma among unaccompanied homeless youth: The integration of street culture into a model of intervention. *Journal of Aggression, Maltreatment, and Trauma.*

McMorris, B. J., Tyler, K. A., Whitbeck, L. B., & Hoyt, D. R. 2002 Familial and "on-the-street" risk factors associated with alcohol use among homeless and runaway adolescents. *Journal of Studies on Alcohol, 63*(1), 34–43.

Mundy, P., Robertson, M., Robertson, J., & Greenblatt, M. 1990 The prevalence of psychotic symptoms in homeless adolescents. *Journal of the American Academy of Child and Adolescent Psychiatry, 29*(5), 724–731.

Noell, J. W., & Ochs, L. M. 2001 Relationship of sexual orientation to substance use, suicidal ideation, suicide attempts, and other factors in a population of homeless adolescents. *Journal of Adolescent Health., 29*(1), 31–36.

Peterson, P. L., Baer, J. S., Wells, E. A., Ginzler, J. A., & Garrett, S. B. 2006 Short-term effects of a brief motivational intervention to reduce alcohol and drug risk among homeless adolescents. *Psychology of Addictive Behaviors, 20*(3), 254–264.

Piliavin, I., Sosin, M. R., Westerfelt, A. H., & Matsueda, R. L. 1993 The duration of homelessness careers: An exploratory study. *Social Service Review, Dec.* vol. 67.4, pp. 576–598.

Piliavin, I., Wright, B. R., & Mare, R. D. 1996 Exists from and returns to homelessness. *Social Service Review, Mar.* 32–57.

Raleigh-DuRoff, C. 2004 Factors that influence homeless adolescents to leave or stay living on the street. *Child & Adolescent Social Work Journal 21*(6), 561–571.

Rew, L. 2002 Characteristics and health care needs of homeless adolescents. *Nursing Clinics of North America, 37*(3), 423–431.

Rew, L., Fouladi, R.T., Land, L., & Wong, Y. J. 2007 Outcomes of a brief sexual health intervention for homeless youth. *Journal of Health Psychology, 12*(5), 818–832.

Rew, L., Fouladi, R. T., & Yockey, R. D. 2002 Sexual health practices of homeless youth. *Journal of Nursing Scholarship, 34*(2), 139–145.

Rew, L., Taylor-Seehafer, M., & Fitzgerald, M. 2001 Sexual abuse, alcohol and other drug use, and suicidal behaviors in homeless adolescents. *Issues in Comprehensive Pediatric Nursing, 24*(4) 225–240.

Sheehan, D. V., Lecrubier, Y., Sheehan, K. H., Amorim, P., Janavs, J., Weiller, E., Hergueta, T., Baker, R., & Dunbar, G. C. 1998 The Mini-International Neuropsychiatric Interview (M.I.N.I.): The development and validation of a structured diagnostic psychiatric interview for DSM-IV and ICD-10. *Journal of Clinical Psychiatry, 59*(Suppl 20), 22–33.

Shinn, M., Gottlieb, J., Wett, J. L., Bahl, A., Cohen, A., & Baron Ellis, D. 2007 Predictors of homelessness among older adults in New York City: Disability, economic, human and social capital and stressful events. *Journal of Health Psychology, 12*(5), 696–708.

Sibthorpe, B., Drinkwater, J., Gardner, K., & Bammer, G. 1995 Drug use, binge drinking and attempted suicide among homeless and potentially homeless youth. *Australian & New Zealand Journal of Psychiatry, 29*(2), 248–256.

Sosin, M. R., & Bruni, M. 2000 Personal and situational perspectives on rejection of a homeless and substance abuse program: An exploratory study. *Social Work Research, 24*(1), 16–27.

Stewart, A. J., Steiman, M., Cauce, A. M., Cochran, B. N., Whitbeck, L. B., & Hoyt, D. R. 2004 Victimization and post-traumatic stress disorder among homeless adolescents. *Journal of the American Academy of Child and Adolescent Psychiatry, 43*(3), 325–331.

Taylor-Seehafer, M. 2004 Positive youth development: Reducing the health risks of homeless youth. *The American Journal of Maternal/Child Nursing, 29*(1), 36–40.

Thompson, S. J. 2004 Risk/protective factors associated with substance use among runaway/homeless youth utilizing emergency shelter services nationwide. *Substance Abuse, 25*(3), 13–26.

Thompson, S. J., Kim, J., Flynn, P., & Kim, H. 2007 Peer relationships: Comparison of homeless youth in the U.S. and South Korea. *International Social Work, 50*(6), pp. 783–795.

Thompson, S. J., McManus, H. H., & Voss, T. 2006 PTSD and substance abuse among youth who are homeless: Treatment issues and implications. *Brief Treatment and Crisis Intervention, 6*(4), 1–12.

Thompson, S. J., & Pollio, D. 2006 Identifying the role of disaffiliation, psychological dysfunction, identification of runaway culture, and human capital in the runaway history of adolescents. *Social Work Research, 30*(4), 245–251.

Tyler, K. A., & Johnson, K. A. 2006 Pathways in and out of substance use among homeless-emerging adults. *Journal of Adolescent Research, 21*(2), 133–157.

Unger, J. B., Kipke, M. D., Simon, T. R., Montgomery, S. B., & Johnson, C. J. 1997 Homeless youths and young adults in Los Angeles: Prevalence of mental health problems and the relationship between mental health and substance abuse disorders. *American Journal of Community Psychology, 25*(3), 371–394.

Unger, J. B., Simon, T. R., Newman, T. L., Montgomery, S. B., Kipke, M. D., & Albornoz, M. 1998 Early adolescent street youth: An overlooked population with unique problems and service needs. *Journal of Early Adolescence, 18*(4), 325–348.

Whitbeck, L. B., Chen, X., Hoyt, D. R., Tyler, K. A., & Johnson, K. D. 2004 Mental disorder, subsistence strategies, and victimization among gay, lesbian, and bisexual homeless and runaway adolescents. *Journal of Sex Research, 41*(4), 329–342.

Whitbeck, L. B., Hoyt, D. R., & Bao, W.N. 2000 Depressive symptoms and co-occurring depressive symptoms, substance abuse, and conduct problems among runaway and homeless adolescents. *Child Development, 71*(3), 721–732.

Whitbeck, L. B., & Simons, R. L. 1990 Life on the streets. The victimization of runaway and homeless adolescents. *Youth & Society, 22*(1), 108–125.

Zlotnick, C., Tam, T., & Robertson, M. J. 2003 Disaffiliation, substance use, and exiting homelessness. *Substance Use & Misuse, 38*(3–6), 577–599.

Critical Thinking

1. How do social isolation and drug use work together?

2. The authors ask, "What are the differences between homeless youth who are drug dependent and those who are not?" Discuss your perspective on what they found.

SANNA J. THOMPSON, PHD, is an Associate Professor at the University of Texas at Austin, School of Social Work. Her area of research focuses on risk factors associated with runaway and homeless youth, most specifically related to substance abuse and trauma. She also has conducted research of family-based interventions that aim to increase engagement and retention of families and adolescents in treatment. **LYNN REW, EDD,** is the Denton and Louise Cooley and Family Centennial Professor in Nursing at the University of Texas at Austin, School of Nursing. She has conducted extensive research with high-risk children and adolescents, including a longitudinal study of health-risk behaviors in youth and sexual health practices of homeless adolescents. **AMANDA BARCZYK, MSW,** is a social work doctoral student at The University of Texas in Austin. She received her Masters of Social Work at the University of Pennsylvania in 2006. Her research focus encompasses issues of mental health policy, with concentration on issues of stigma. **PEPPER MCCOY, MSW,** is a doctoral student at the University of Texas at Austin, School of Social Work. She received her Masters of Social Work at University of Houston in 2006. Her research interests focus on adolescent suicide, poverty and child witnesses of domestic violence. **ADA MI-SEDHI** was an undergraduate research assistant at the University of Texas at Austin, School of Social Work and received her Bachelors of Social Work in 2008. She plans to pursue a dual degree Masters in Social Work and Public Health.

From *The Journal of Drug Issues*, Fall 2009, pp. 905–929. Copyright © 2009 by the College of Criminology and Criminal Justice, Florida State University. Reprinted by permission via the Copyright Clearance Center

UNIT 3

The Major Drugs of Use and Abuse

Unit Selections

Learning Outcomes

After reading this Unit, you should be able to:

- Discuss the key factors in the debate to legalize marijuana.

- Discuss the dangers and public health challenges created by the new drug, bath salts.

- Discuss the influences that help perpetuate the problem of binge drinking on college campuses.

- Discuss the methods the United States and its allies intend to employ to disrupt heroin production in Afghanistan and Colombia.

- List and discuss the distinct features associated with the spread of methamphetamine use across the United States.

Student Website

www.mhhe.com/cls

Internet References

The American Journal of Psychiatry
   http://ajp.psychiatryonline.org/cgi/content/abstract/155/8/1016
Multidisciplinary Association for Psychedelic Studies (MAPS)
   www.maps.org
National Institute on Drug Abuse
   www.drugabuse.gov
Office of Applied Studies
   www.oas.samhsa.gov
QuitNet
   www.quitnet.org
Streetdrugs.org
   www.streetdrugs.org

The following articles discuss those drugs that have evolved historically to become the most popular drugs of choice. Although pharmacological modifications emerge periodically to enhance or alter the effects produced by certain drugs or the manner in which various drugs are used, basic pharmacological properties of the drugs remain unchanged. Crack is still cocaine, ice is still methamphetamine, and black tar is still heroin. In addition, all tobacco products supply the drug nicotine, coffee and a plethora of energy drinks provide caffeine, and alcoholic beverages provide the drug ethyl alcohol. All these drugs influence the way we act, think, and feel about ourselves and the world around us. They also produce markedly different effects within the body and within the mind.

To understand why certain drugs remain popular over time, and why new drugs become popular, one must be knowledgeable about the effects produced by individual drugs. Why people use drugs is a bigger question than why people use tobacco. However, understanding why certain people use tobacco, or cocaine, or marijuana, or alcohol is one way to construct a framework from which to tackle the larger question of why people use drugs in general. One of the most complex relationships is the one between Americans and their use of alcohol. More than 76 million Americans have experienced alcoholism in their families.

The most recent surveys of alcohol use estimate that 127 million Americans currently use alcohol. The use of alcohol is a powerful influence that serves to shape our national consciousness about drugs. The relationship between the use of alcohol and tobacco and alcohol and illicit drugs provides long-standing statistical relationships. The majority of Americans, however, believe that alcohol is used responsibly by most people who use it, even though approximately 10 percent of users are believed to be suffering from various stages of alcoholism.

Understanding why people initially turn to the nonmedical use of drugs is a huge question that is debated and discussed in a voluminous body of literature. One important reason why the major drugs of use and abuse, such as alcohol, nicotine, cocaine, heroin, marijuana, amphetamines, and a variety of prescription, designer, over-the-counter, and herbal drugs, retain their popularity is because they produce certain physical and psychological effects that humans crave. They temporarily restrain our inhibitions; reduce our fears; alleviate mental and physical suffering; produce energy, confidence, and exhilaration; and allow us to relax. Tired, take a pill; have a headache, take a pill; need to lose weight, take a pill; need to increase athletic performance, the options seem almost limitless. There is a drug for everything. Some drugs even, albeit artificially, suggest a greater capacity to transcend, redefine, and seek out new levels of consciousness. And they do it upon demand. People initially use a specific drug, or class of drugs, to obtain the desirable effects historically associated with the use of that drug.

Heroin and opiate-related drugs such as Oxycontin and Vicodin produce, in most people, a euphoric, dreamy state of well-being. The abuse of these prescription painkillers is one of the fastest growing (and alarming) drug trends. Methamphetamine and related stimulant drugs produce euphoria, energy,

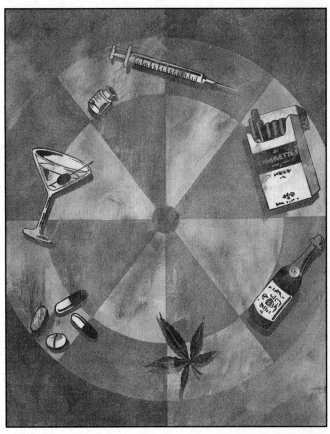

© Lisa Zador/Getty Images

confidence, and exhilaration. Alcohol produces a loss of inhibitions and a state of well-being. Nicotine and marijuana typically serve as relaxants. Ecstasy and other "club drugs" produce stimulant as well as relaxant effects. Various over-the-counter and herbal drugs attempt to replicate the effects of more potent and often prohibited or prescribed drugs. Although effects and side effects may vary from user to user, a general pattern of effects is predictable from most major drugs of use and their analogs. Varying the dosage and altering the manner of ingestion is one way to alter the drug's effects. Some drugs, such as LSD and certain types of designer drugs, produce effects on the user that are less predictable and more sensitive to variations in dosage level and to the user's physical and psychological makeup.

Although all major drugs of use and abuse have specific reinforcing properties perpetuating their continued use, they also produce undesirable side effects that regular drug users attempt to mitigate. Most often, users attempt to mitigate these effects with the use of other drugs. Cocaine, methamphetamine, heroin, and alcohol have long been used to mitigate each other's side effects. A good example is the classic "speedball" of heroin and cocaine. When they are combined, cocaine accelerates and intensifies the euphoric state of the heroin, while the heroin softens the comedown from cocaine. Add to this the almost limitless combinations of prescription drugs, mixed and traded at "pharming" parties, and an entirely new dimension for altering drugs' physiological effects emerges. Additionally, other powerful influences on drug taking, such as advertising for alcohol, tobacco, and certain prescription drugs, significantly impact the public's drug-related consciousness. The alcohol industry, for example, dissects numerous layers of society to specifically market alcoholic beverages to subpopulations of Americans, including youth. The same influences exist with tobacco advertising.

What is the message in Philip Morris's advertisements about i‌ attempts to mitigate smoking by youth? Approximately 500,00‌ Americans die each year from tobacco-related illness. Add t‌ the mix advertising by prescription-drug companies for inn‌ merable human maladies and one soon realizes the enormit‌ of the association between business and drug taking. Subse‌ quently, any discussion of major drugs could begin and en‌ with alcohol, tobacco, and prescription drugs.

Marijuana and Medical Marijuana

John Birchard

Marijuana, whose botanical name is cannabis, has been used by humans for thousands of years. It was classified as an illegal drug by many countries in the 20th century. But over the past two decades, there has been a growing movement to legalize it, primarily for medical purposes.

Medical marijuana use has surged in the 15 states and the District of Columbia that allow its use. But states and cities are also wrestling with the question of what medical marijuana is, or should be.

The Montana House of Representatives voted in February 2011 to repeal the state's six-year-old medical marijuana law. The 63-to-37 vote, largely along party lines in the Republican-controlled chamber, pushed Montana to the front lines of a national debate about social policy, economics and health regarding medical marijuana use

Montana's House speaker, Mike Milburn, a Republican and sponsor of the repeal bill, who said he thought that the arguments about medical use had been a pretext for encouraging recreational use and creating a path to full legalization. He said he feared gang drug wars in Montana's cities and debilitation of its youth. If the legislation is passed by the Montana Senate, it would face an uncertain fate on the desk of Gov. Brian Schweitzer, a Democrat, who has said he believes the laws need to be tightened, but he has not taken a position on repeal.

New Mexico's Republican governor, Susana Martinez, has also expressed interest in repeal in 2011. Colorado was formulating some of the most detailed rules in the nation for growing and selling. Lawmakers in New Jersey have jousted with the governor over regulation.

In November 2010, Californians defeated Proposition 19, a ballot measure that would have legalized possession and growing of marijuana outright, and taxed and regulated its use. California already reduced its penalty for possession, putting those caught with small amounts of the drug on the same level as those caught speeding on the freeway.

Advocates for Proposition 19 had said that if legalized California could raise $1.4 billion in taxes and save precious law enforcement and prison resources. Attorney General Eric Holder had insisted that the federal government would continue to enforce its laws against marijuana in California even if they conflict with state law.

Currently 15 states allow the use of marijuana for pain relief, nausea and loss of appetite by people with AIDS, cancer and other debilitating diseases. Those laws, however, are at odds with federal law. The federal government continues to oppose any decriminalization of the drug. And while the Obama administration has signaled some leeway when it comes to medical marijuana, raids on dispensaries and growers by law enforcement agencies are still common—even in California, where the industry effectively began in 1996, with the passage of the landmark Proposition 215, which legalized medical marijuana.

Rules vary widely in the states that permit medical marijuana. Some states require sellers to prove nonprofit status—often as a collective or cooperative—and all states require that patients have a recommendation from a physician. But even those in favor of medical marijuana believe that the system is ripe for abuse or even unintentional lawbreaking.

Although party line positions defined the issue in Montana, with Republicans mostly lined up in favor of restriction or repeal, there is widespread agreement among legislators and residents that medical marijuana has become something very different than it was originally envisioned to be.

Sixty-two percent of voters approved the use of medical marijuana in a Montana referendum in 2004. But the real explosion of growth came only in 2010, after the federal Department of Justice said in late 2009 that medical marijuana would not be a law enforcement priority. Since then, the numbers of patients have quadrupled to more than 27,000—in a state of only about 975,000 people—and millions of dollars have been invested in businesses that grow or supply the product.

With a growing number of Americans favoring legalization—a Gallup poll released in October 2010 found a record 46 percent approving of legalization—perhaps no ballot measure in the country was more closely watched than Proposition 19 in California.

The California ballot measure would have allowed anyone over 21 to buy, possess, use or cultivate marijuana. It would have barred personal possession of more than one ounce as well as smoking the drug in public or around minors.

Some civil rights activists favored the legalization of the drug on the grounds that marijuana arrests are wildly disproportionate in their racial impact and adversely affect minorities.

But the measure was strongly opposed by law enforcement, which said it would actually end up costing the state in increased public health and safety expenses.

As more and more states allow medical use of the drug, marijuana's supporters are pushing hard to burnish the image of marijuana by franchising dispensaries and building brands; establishing consulting, lobbying and law firms; setting up trade shows and a seminar circuit; and constructing a range of other marijuana-related businesses.

In July 2010, the Department of Veterans Affairs announced that it will formally allow patients treated at its hospitals and clinics to use medical marijuana in states where it is legal, a policy clarification that veterans had sought for several years.

The department directive resolves the conflict in veterans facilities between federal law, which outlaws marijuana, and the 14 states that allow medicinal use of the drug, effectively deferring to the states.

Marijuana is the only major drug for which the federal government controls the only legal research supply and for which the government requires a special scientific review. The University of Mississippi has the nation's only federally approved marijuana plantation. If researchers wish to investigate marijuana, they must apply to the National Institute on Drug Abuse to use the Mississippi marijuana and must get approvals from a special Public Health Service panel, the Drug Enforcement Administration and the Food and Drug Administration.

Critical Thinking

1. Fifteen states allow the use of medical marijuana. Why have these states chosen to allow marijuana for pain relief?

2. Provide a discussion of the primary issues inherent in states' legalization of marijuana.

Officials Fear Bath Salts Becoming the Next Big Drug Menace

SHEILA BYRD

Fulton, Miss.-When Neil Brown got high on bath salts, he took his skinning knife and slit his face and stomach repeatedly. Brown survived, but authorities say others haven't been so lucky after snorting, injecting or smoking powders with such innocuous-sounding names as Ivory Snow, Red Dove and Vanilla Sky.

Law enforcement agents and poison control centers say the bath salts, with their complex chemical names, are an emerging menace in several U.S. states where authorities talk of banning their sale. Some say their effects can be as powerful as those of methamphetamine.

From the Deep South to California, emergency calls are being reported over exposure to the stimulants the powders often contain: mephedrone and methylenedioxypyrovalerone, also known as MDPV.

Sold under such names as Ivory Wave, Bliss, White Lightning and Hurricane Charlie, the chemicals can cause hallucinations, paranoia, a rapid heart rate and suicidal thoughts, authorities say. In addition to bath salts, the chemicals can be found in plant foods that are sold legally at convenience stores and on the Internet. However, they aren't necessarily being used for the purposes on the label.

Mississippi lawmakers this week began considering a proposal to ban the sale of the powders, and a similar measure is being sought in Kentucky. In Louisiana, the bath salts were outlawed by an emergency order after the state's poison center received more than 125 calls in the last three months of 2010 involving exposure to the chemicals.

In Brown's case, he said he had tried every drug from heroin to crack and was so shaken by terrifying hallucinations that he wrote to one Mississippi paper urging people to stay away from the bath salts.

"I couldn't tell you why I did it," Brown said, pointing to his scars. "The psychological effects are still there."

While Brown survived, sheriff's authorities in one Mississippi county say they believe one woman overdosed on bath salts there. In southern Louisiana, the family of a 21-year-old man says he cut his throat and ended his life with a gunshot. Authorities are investigating whether a man charged with capital murder in the December death of a Tippah County, Miss., sheriff's deputy was under the influence of the bath salts.

The stimulants are not regulated by the Drug Enforcement Administration, but are facing federal scrutiny. Law officers say some of the substances are being shipped from Europe, but origins are still unclear.

Gary Boggs, an executive assistant at the DEA, said there is a lengthy process to restrict these types of designer chemicals, including reviewing the abuse data. But it's a process that can take years.

Mark Ryan, director of Louisiana's poison control center, said he thinks state bans on the chemicals can be effective. He said calls about the salts have dropped sharply since Louisiana banned their sale in January.

Ryan said cathinone, the parent substance of the drugs, comes from a plant grown in Africa and is regulated. He said that MDPV and mephedrone are made in a lab and that they are not regulated because they are not marketed for human consumption. The stimulants affect neurotransmitters in the brain, he said.

The drugs cause "intense cravings," he said. "They'll binge on it three or four days before they show up in an ER. Even though it's a horrible trip, they want to do it again and again."

Ryan said at least 25 states have received calls about exposure, including Nevada and California. He said Louisiana leads with the greatest number of cases at 165, or 48 percent of the U.S. total, followed by Florida with at least 38 calls to its poison center.

Rick Gellar, medical director for the California Poison Control System, said the first call about the substances came in Oct. 5, and a handful of calls have followed since. But he warned: "The only way this won't become a problem in California is if federal regulatory agencies get ahead of the curve. This is a brand-new thing."

In the Midwest, the Missouri Poison Center at Cardinal Glennon Children's Medical Center in St. Louis received at least 12 calls in the first two weeks of January about teenagers and young adults abusing such chemicals, said Julie Weber, the center's director. The center received eight calls about the powders all of last year.

Richard Sanders, a general practitioner working in Covington, La., said his son, Dickie, snorted some of the bath salts and endured three days of intermittent delirium. Dickie Sanders cut his throat but missed major arteries. As he continued to have visions, his physician father tried to calm him. But the elder Sanders said that as he slept, his son went into another room and shot himself.

"If you could see the contortions on his face. It just made him crazy," Sanders said. He added that the coroner's office confirmed that the chemicals were detected in his son's blood and urine.

Sanders warns that the bath salts are far more dangerous than some of their names imply.

"I think everybody is taking this extremely lightly. As much as we outlawed it in Louisiana, all these kids cross over to Mississippi and buy whatever they want," he said.

A small packet of the chemicals typically costs as little as $20.

In northern Mississippi's Itawamba County, Sheriff Chris Dickinson said his office has handled about 30 encounters with bath-salts users in the past two months alone. He said the problem grew last year in his rural area after a Mississippi law began restricting the sale of pseudoephedrine, a key ingredient in making methamphetamine.

Dickinson said most of the bath-salts users there have been meth addicts and can be dangerous when using them.

"We had a deputy injured a week ago. They were fighting with a guy who thought they were two devils. That's what makes this drug so dangerous," he said.

But Dickinson said the chemicals are legal, leaving him no choice but to slap users just with a charge of disorderly conduct, a misdemeanor.

Kentucky state lawmaker John Tilley said he's moving to block the drug's sale there, preparing a bill for consideration when his legislature convenes shortly. Angry that the powder can be bought legally, he said: "If my 12-year-old can go in a store and buy it, that concerns me."

Critical Thinking

1. Describe what "bath salts" is and in what ways it is dangerous.
2. Given what we know about bath salts, propose a public health plan to address the increase in their use.

Binge Drinking and Its Consequences Up Among American College Students

MADELINE ELLIS

Scott Krueger, a freshman student at Massachusetts Institute of Technology (MIT), likely bore dreams of achieving academic glory and a long life of happiness and success. But those dreams were cut short when, in 1997, he died of alcohol poisoning with his blood–alcohol level at five times the drunken driving standards in that state. His fraternity brothers reported that he had multiple drinks within a short period of time—he was binge drinking.

However, Scott isn't the only college student who has met his demise through industrial-strength guzzling. In 1995, 318 people, ages 15–24, died from alcohol poisoning alone, many of them after a night binge at college. At the University of Virginia, a tradition called "Fourth-year Fifth," which has seniors drinking a fifth of hard liquor at the final game of the football season, has killed 18 students since 1990. The long-term risks of college drinking practices are just as sobering. As many as 300,000 of today's students will eventually die of alcohol-related causes such as drunk driving accidents, cirrhosis of the liver, heart disease, and various cancers.

But apparently the countless tragedies and alarming statistics have done nothing to curtail the habit. In fact, according to a new study from the U.S. National Institute on Alcohol Abuse and Alcoholism, binge drinking among American college students is on the rise; as is its consequences. From 1999 to 2005, the percentage of students aged 18 to 24 who said they had binged on alcohol in the last month rose from 41.7 percent to nearly 45 percent; drunk driving proportions among this group increased from 26.5 percent to almost 29 percent and the number of drinking-related deaths went from 1,440 in 1998 to 1,825 in 2005, an increase of 3 percent. But the greatest increase was seen in death from unintentional poisoning, which nearly tripled between 1998 and 2005.

But alcohol misuse among college students doesn't just affect the individual drinker; there are often consequences for other students, faculty members, the college, and the community as a whole. Consider these statistics:

- More than 696,000 students between the ages of 18 and 24 are assaulted by another student who has been drinking.

- More than 97,000 students between the ages of 18 and 24 are victims of alcohol-related sexual assault or date rape.
- 400,000 students between the ages of 18 and 24 had unprotected sex and more than 100,000 students between the ages of 18 and 24 report having been too intoxicated to know if they consented to having sex.
- About 11 percent of college student drinkers report that they have damaged property while under the influence of alcohol.
- More than 25 percent of administrators from schools with relatively low drinking levels and over 50 percent from schools with high drinking levels say their campuses have a "moderate" or "major" problem with alcohol-related property damage.

But many experts say the problem often begins before college. Recently, a study presented at the 2009 meeting of the Society for Prevention Research in Washington, D.C. revealed that the earlier alcohol is introduced to a child, the greater the likelihood that he or she will binge drink in college. Moreover, "the greater number of drinks that a parent set as a limit for the teens, the more often they drank and got drunk in college," said researcher Caitlin Abar of the Prevention Research and Methodology Center at Pennsylvania State University. On the other hand, whether the parents themselves drank appeared to have little effect on predicting their child's behaviors toward teen alcohol use.

In 31 states, parents can legally serve alcohol to their underage children. And though U.S. teenagers drink less often than adults, they tend to drink more at a time—five drinks in a sitting, on average—according to lead researcher Ralph Hingson, director of the institute's division of epidemiology and prevention research. "We as a society have a collective responsibility to try and change this culture of drinking at colleges and among young people," he said.

A growing number of colleges and universities are addressing campus drinking problems by providing prevention education; expanding counseling services; and offering more alternatives, such as alcohol-free parties. Hingson said that a number of these interventions have been shown to work, but that some colleges are not implementing them. "The challenge for us is to make sure colleges understand what things are working," he said. "We have to get them to expand screening and interventions to reach wider populations of students and work with communities."

Hingson says efforts similar to those used to reduce smoking are needed to deal with the drinking problem among our youth. "We as a society have a collective responsibility to try and change this culture of drinking at colleges and among young people." Dr. David L. Katz, director of the Prevention Research Center at Yale University School of Medicine, says for that to happen, society needs to take drinking among college students more seriously and the practice needs to be discouraged by those whose opinions matter the most—friends in their own peer group. "Options for bad judgment available to a college student are determined by society, and ours is decidedly ambivalent about alcohol," Katz said. "Drinking to excess is often given favorable treatment in the media, and in social groups."

At the same time, all of us must encourage college students to take personal responsibility for making healthy choices with the only lives they will ever have. Drinking to excess doesn't need to be a rite of passage and driving under the influence isn't a requirement for graduation.

Critical Thinking

1. Do wider social views toward college drinking influence it? Why?

2. What could colleges do to prevent students binge drinking?

From *Health News*, June 16, 2009. Copyright © 2009 by Health News. Reprinted by permission.

Public Lands: Cartels Turn U.S. Forests into Marijuana Plantations Creating Toxic Mess

PHIL TAYLOR

Empty turtle shells, decaying skunk carcasses and a set of deer antlers lay strewn about an empty campsite in California's Sierra National Forest.

The butchered animals, as well as several five-pound pro-ane canisters, camp stoves, and heaps of trash, were all that emained of the 69 marijuana plantations recently uncovered in resno County as part of operation "Save our Sierras."

The massive operation that began in February has already eized about 318,000 marijuana plants worth an estimated $1.1 illion, officials announced last week. In addition to 82 arrests, ie multijurisdictional federal, state, and local operation netted 2 pounds of processed marijuana, more than $40,000 in cash, 5 weapons and three vehicles.

"Mexican drug trafficking organizations have been operat-ig on public lands to cultivate marijuana, with serious con-equences for the environment and public safety," said Gil erlikowske, chief of the White House's Office of National rug Control Policy at a briefing on the investigation.

Subjects arrested were booked on charges of cultivation of arijuana, possession for sale, possession of a firearm during ommission of a felony, and conspiracy.

The drug plantations are as much an environmental menace s they are a public safety threat.

Growers in Fresno County used a cocktail of pesticides nd fertilizers many times stronger than what is used on esidential lawns to cultivate their crop. "This stuff leaches ut pretty quickly," said Shane Krogen, executive director f the High Sierra Volunteer Trail Crew in charge of helping lear the land of chemicals and trash so it can begin its slow estoration.

While the chemical pesticides kill insects and other organ-sms directly, fertilizer runoff contaminates local waterways nd aids in the growth of algae and weeds. The vegetation turn impedes water flows that are critical to frogs, toads, nd salamanders in the Kings and San Joaquin rivers, Kro-en said.

Northward-Shifting Operations

The Sierra operations are the latest in a growing number of illegal plantations run by foreign suppliers who have moved north of the U.S.–Mexico border where they are closer to U.S. drug markets. Of the 82 individuals arrested in the "Save our Sierras" sting, all but two were Mexican or some other foreign nationality.

Bankrolled by sophisticated drug cartels, suppliers are side-stepping border patrols to grow in relative obscurity on Forest Service, Bureau of Land Management and National Park Ser-vice lands across the West and even into the Southeast.

"It's easier to cross the border to grow marijuana on public lands than to grow it in Mexico and smuggle it across," Krogen said.

Earlier this month, $2.5 million worth of marijuana was seized from a sophisticated pot-growing operation in the moun-tains near Colorado's Cheesman Reservoir in the Pike National Forest. In early June, hikers in a remote area of southwest Idaho stumbled upon a marijuana crop that netted 12,545 marijuana plants with an estimated street value of $6.3 million.

"There is a growing issue of marijuana cultivation on public lands in the U.S., especially in California and Oregon, and it appears they have discovered southwestern Idaho," said BLM special agent in charge Loren Good.

Temperate climates on the West Coast have nurtured what has become a booming marijuana market. The number of mari-juana plants confiscated by Forest Service officials has risen by an average of 51 percent in each of the past four years, reaching a high of 3.3 million plants in 2008.

The number of plants seized in California national forests alone has risen steadily from 569,000 in 2003 to 2.4 million in 2008.

"It's definitely a trend," said Keith McGrath, a law enforce-ment officer in BLM's Idaho office who was part of last month's raid in a far-flung desert canyon.

"We're seeing a shift to more organized grows and larger grows," McGrath said. "They're being set up and run through the cartels, and it's becoming a big chunk of our work load."

Strengthening Law Enforcement

Federal agencies are responding by beefing up law enforcement patrols and investing in technologies like helicopter surveillance and unmanned aerial drones to track down marijuana growers operating in California's lush woodlands.

Forest Service law enforcement staff was doubled from 14 to 28 agents in California between 2007 and 2008, said spokesman John Heil, resulting in the eradication of 3.1 million marijuana plants in the last fiscal year.

Congress is responding too, with a recent $3 million supplemental appropriation secured by Sen. Dianne Feinstein (D-Calif.) that allowed the Park Service to add 25 new law enforcement officers to its Pacific Region parks, said Ron Sundergill, regional director for the Washington, D.C.-based National Parks Conservation Association.

Sundergill applauded the land management agencies for increasing the pressure on illegal growers but said he fears such efforts are depleting agencies' already-thin budgets for things like interpretive services and ranger tours.

"Our parks shouldn't have to spend their limited resources fighting drug cartels when those resources could instead be used to educate and inspire our children—the future stewards of our national parks," Sundergill said.

More money is likely to be provided if Congress approves Interior's fiscal 2010 budget later this year. Feinstein, who chairs the subcommittee in charge of Interior Spending, said she was concerned over the increasing threat of drug cartels on public lands and would look to increase resources for enforcement.

Meanwhile, agency officials say they will remain vigilant in seeking out marijuana growers, even as they venture deeper into the nation's public lands network.

"As more pressure happens in California, they're going to start looking at Oregon, Nevada, and Idaho," said Krogen, of the High Sierra Volunteer Trail Crew. "Then they'll start looking at the Southeast too, closer to distribution."

Critical Thinking

1. How would you go about deterring the cartels from using public lands as their personal marijuana plantations?

2. Can you think of other ways in which we are affected by this type of behavior?

Pseudoephedrine Smurfing Fuels Surge in Large-Scale Methamphetamine Production in California

Situation Report

Preface

This Situation Report is in response to a request from the Office of National Drug Control Policy for information regarding pseudoephedrine smurfing in California. The National Drug Intelligence Center collected and analyzed data and reporting from 2007 through May 2009 related to methamphetamine production and pseudoephedrine smurfing. This report draws upon data from the National Seizure System (NSS) as well as information obtained through interviews with federal, state, and local law enforcement officers.

Executive Summary

Pseudoephedrine smurfing* has become increasingly organized and widespread in California, particularly since 2007, fueling an increase in the number of large-scale methamphetamine laboratories in the state.[1] Among the increased number of large-scale laboratories are those operated by Mexican criminal groups that have relocated to California from Mexico since 2007. Mexican criminal groups and some independent operators are increasingly acquiring bulk quantities of pseudoephedrine through smurfing. Despite strong efforts by law enforcement to curtail smurfing, there is no indication that this practice will decline in the near term. In fact, pseudoephedrine acquired through smurfing in California in 2009 was sent in bulk to methamphetamine producers in Mexico, an indication that some criminal groups in Mexico still find it easier to acquire pseudoephedrine through smurfing in California than from other sources.

Discussion

Pseudoephedrine smurfing increased significantly in California in 2008 and early 2009. The incidence of individuals and criminal groups organizing pseudoephedrine smurfing operations that supply pseudoephedrine to California-based methamphetamine producers has increased throughout California. These smurfing operations began to gain prominence in late 2007, when pseudoephedrine availability and methamphetamine production decreased in Mexico. For instance, in October 2007, a Fresno County investigation revealed that a couple had been conducting daily precursor chemical smurfing operations, soliciting homeless individuals to travel from store to store to purchase pseudoephedrine. In exchange, the couple paid each person approximately $30 and sometimes gave the individuals alcohol. Evidence seized from the couple's vehicle included packages of pseudoephedrine, pharmacy listings torn from an area telephone directory, and several cellular telephones. Similar smurfing operations increased in 2008 and have continued at high levels in 2009. In fact, law enforcement officials in 21 large California cities report that pseudoephedrine smurfing increased in their areas in 2008 and 2009.

Methamphetamine production in California-based superlabs[†] has increased since 2007 because of pseudoephedrine supplied to producers through organized smurfing. Large-scale methamphetamine production by Mexican criminal groups increased in California in 2008 and early 2009 as many methamphetamine producers in Mexico relocated to California, most likely because pseudoephedrine had become more available to some producers through smurfing in California than it was in Mexico. The rise in large-scale methamphetamine production is evidenced by increased methamphetamine superlab and dumpsite seizures. NSS data indicate that the number of superlabs seized in California increased from 10 in 2007 to 15 in 2008. Moreover, the proportion of larger superlabs (those capable of producing 20 or more pounds of methamphetamine) increased during that period from 2 of 10 superlabs in 2007 to 5 of 15 in 2008. Keeping pace with 2008 seizures, 7 superlab seizures were reported to NSS for California in 2009 (through May 26), 5 of them capable of producing 20 or more pounds of methamphetamine.

---

*Smurfing is a method used by some methamphetamine and precursor chemical traffickers to acquire large quantities of pseudoephedrine. Individuals purchase pseudoephedrine in quantities at or below legal thresholds from multiple retail locations. Traffickers often enlist the assistance of several associates in smurfing operations to increase the speed with which chemicals are acquired.

---

† Superlabs are laboratories capable of producing 10 or more pounds of methamphetamine in a single production cycle.

According to Central Valley California High Intensity Drug Trafficking Area reporting, the superlabs operating in that area—the primary large-scale methamphetamine production area in the United States—are producing methamphetamine with pseudoephedrine acquired primarily through California-based smurfing operations. In fact, the Fresno and Stanislaus/San Joaquin Methamphetamine Task Forces report that officers at laboratory sites commonly find evidence of large-scale and organized smurfing, including pseudoephedrine product price lists, store receipts, coupons for pseudoephedrine products, pseudoephedrine product packaging, paper shredders, gallon-size freezer bags, and 5-gallon plastic buckets filled with various commercial brands of pseudoephedrine tablets.[2] In addition, officers frequently discover trash bags full of pseudoephedrine blister packs and empty bags containing residue from pseudoephedrine tablets at laboratory dump-sites in their area, which is a further evidence of large-scale pseudoephedrine smurfing. By 2009, California pseudoephedrine smurfing had increased to the extent that some Los Angeles area smurfers were not only supplying pseudoephedrine for large-scale production in California but also supplying pseudoephedrine to methamphetamine producers in Mexico.[3]

Intelligence Gaps

The actual number of methamphetamine superlabs operating California is unknown and may be much higher than the laborato seizure number—which has increased—suggests. Law enforce ment reporting indicates that superlabs are becoming more dif cult to detect, not because there are fewer laboratories, but becau laboratory operators have adapted to law enforcement pressure a improved their laboratory concealment methods by operating remote areas.[6] As a result, there may be significantly more larg scale production at undetected superlabs than the laboratory se zure data indicate.

Outlook

The number of superlabs in California will remain rel tively high in the near term as criminal groups ar individuals supply laboratory operators with bulk pse doephedrine acquired through smurfing. There is no inc cation that pseudoephedrine smurfing will decline in the near ter Smurfing is widespread, well organized, and increasing througho California. The continued ban on pseudoephedrine imports in Mexico will most likely limit the availability of the chemical

---

Methamphetamine Production in Mexico

Ephedrine and pseudoephedrine import restrictions in Mexico resulted in decreased Mexican methamphetamine production in 2007.[4] In 2005, the government of Mexico (GOM) began implementing progressively increasing restrictions on the importation of ephedrine and pseudoephedrine and other chemicals used for methamphetamine production. In fact, in 2007, the GOM announced a prohibition on ephedrine and pseudoephedrine imports into Mexico for 2008 and a ban on the use of both chemicals in Mexico by 2009.[5] Pseudoephedrine import restrictions resulted in a significant decrease in methamphetamine production in Mexico in 2007, as evidenced by a reduced flow of the drug from Mexico into the United States. NSS data show a sharp decrease in the amount of methamphetamine seized at or between ports of entry (POEs) along the Southwest Border from 2005 (1,950.26 kg) and 2006 (1,882.01 kg) to 2007 (only 1,046.47 kg)—a 44 percent decrease from 2006 to 2007. NSS data show that the amount of methamphetamine seized at or between POEs along the Southwest Border remained well below 2006 levels in 2008 (1,255.52 kg). The amount of methamphetamine seized at or between POEs along the Southwest Border appears to be trending upward in 2009. As of May 26, 2009, 1,001.29 kilograms of methamphetamine had been seized, possibly suggesting some resurgence of methamphetamine production in Mexico.

Sources

Federal

Executive Office of the President
  Office of National Drug Control Policy
    High Intensity Drug Trafficking Areas
      California Border Alliance Group
      Central Valley California
        Fresno Methamphetamine Task Force
        Stanislaus, San Joaquin Methamphetamine Task Force
      Los Angeles
        Los Angeles County Regional Criminal Information Clearinghouse
      Northern California
U.S. Department of Justice
  Bureau of Justice Assistance
    Western States Information Network
  Drug Enforcement Administration
    El Paso Intelligence Center
    National Seizure System

State and Local

California
  Alameda County Drug Task Force
  Bay Methamphetamine Task Force
  Los Angeles Police Department
  Merced Sheriff's Department
  Sacramento Police Department
  San Diego Law Enforcement Coordination Center

Article 21. Pseudoephedrine Smurfing Fuels Surge in Large-Scale Methamphetamine Production in California

at country, thereby limiting any incentive for Mexican metham-
hetamine producers to move their operations back to Mexico. In
ct, evidence of California smurfers supplying pseudoephedrine
methamphetamine producers in Mexico in 2009 illustrates the
ontinued difficulty that producers in that country are experiencing
acquiring the chemical.

ndnotes

1. Central Valley California High Intensity Drug Trafficking Area.
2. Fresno Methamphetamine Task Force, Stanislaus, San Joaquin
   Methamphetamine Task Force.

3. Phone interviews with Los Angeles Police Department,
   June 4, 2009.
4. NDIC *National Methamphetamine Threat Assessment* 2009,
   December 2008, Product Number 2008-Q0317-006.
5. United Nations reporting.
6. Fresno Methamphetamine Task Force, Stanislaus, San Joaquin
   Methamphetamine Task Force.

Critical Thinking

1. How does smurfing impact legal sales of OTC medications?
2. What can be done to eradicate smurfing?

om *Situation Report*, United States Department of Justice, June 2009.

UNIT 4

Other Trends in Drug Use

Unit Selections

Learning Outcomes

After reading this Unit, you should be able to:

- Explain why some drug-related trends are more specific to certain subpopulations of Americans than others.

- Describe the significance of socioeconomic status in influencing drug trends.

- Determine the influences that have contributed to the dramatic spread of prescription drug abuse in the United States.

- Determine what roles advertising and the media play in influencing drug use.

- Explain the factors that cause drug-related trends to change.

Student Website

www.mhhe.com/cls

Internet References

Drug Story.org
www.drugstory.org/drug_stats/druguse_stats.asp

Marijuana as a Medicine
http://mojo.calyx.net/~olsen

Monitoring the Future
www.monitoringthefuture.org

Prescription Drug Abuse
www.prescription-drug-abuse.org

Prescriptions Drug Use and Abuse
www.fda.gov/fdac/features/2001/501_drug.htm

SAMHSA
www.drugabusestatistics.samhsa.gov/trends.htm

United States Drug Trends
www.usdrugtrends.com

Rarely do drug-related patterns and trends lend themselves to precise definition. Identification, measurement, and prediction of the consequence of these trends is an inexact science, to say the least. It is, nevertheless, a very important process. One of the most valuable uses of drug-related trend analysis is the identification of subpopulations whose vulnerability to certain drug phenomena is greater than that of the wider population. These identifications may forewarn of the implications for the general population. Trend analysis may produce specific information that may otherwise be lost or obscured by general statistical indications. For example, tobacco is probably the most prominent of gateway drugs, with repeated findings pointing to the correlation between the initial use of tobacco and the use of other drugs.

The analysis of specific trends related to drug use is very important, as it provides a threshold from which educators, health-care professionals, parents, and policymakers may respond to significant drug-related health threats and issues. Over 20 million Americans report the use of illegal drugs. The current rate of illicit drug use is similar to the rates of the past three years. Marijuana remains as the most commonly used illicit drug with more than 14 million current users.

Historically, popular depressant and stimulant drugs—such as alcohol, tobacco, heroin, and cocaine—produce statistics that identify the most visible and sometimes the most constant use patterns. Other drugs such as marijuana, LSD, ecstasy, and other "club drugs" often produce patterns widely interpreted to be associated with cultural phenomena such as youth attitudes, popular music trends, and political climate.

Two other continuing trends are those that involve the abuse of prescription drugs and those that involve the use of methamphetamine. Americans are abusing prescription drugs more than ever before with the most frequently mentioned offenders being oxycodone and hydrocodone. Currently, more than 5 million persons use prescription pain relievers for nonmedical reasons. Of those who used pain relievers for nonmedical reasons, 56 percent obtained them for free from a friend or relative. As more and more drugs get prescribed within the population, a steady trend, more and more drugs become easily accessible. The National Institute of Drug Abuse reports that 20 percent of the U.S. population over 12 has used prescription drugs for nonmedical reasons. Currently, prescription drug abuse among youth ranks second behind only marijuana. The good news is that drug use by youth has declined or leveled in several important categories such as those associated with marijuana, alcohol, and methamphetamine. And although methamphetamine use is down, it is reported by local and state officials in the West and Midwest as the number one illegal-drug problem.

Although the federal government has modified its survey methods to more accurately identify the number of meth users, many worry that the meth problem is still understated and greatly outweighs those problems associated with other illegal drugs in the West, Southwest, and Midwest. Information concerning drug-use patterns and trends obtained from a number of different investigative methods is available from a variety of sources. On the national level, the more prominent sources are the Substance Abuse and Mental Health Services Administration, the National Institute on Drug Abuse, the Drug Abuse Warning Network, the national Centers for Disease Control, the Justice Department, the Office of National Drug Control Policy, the surgeon general, and the DEA. On the state level, various justice departments, including attorney generals'

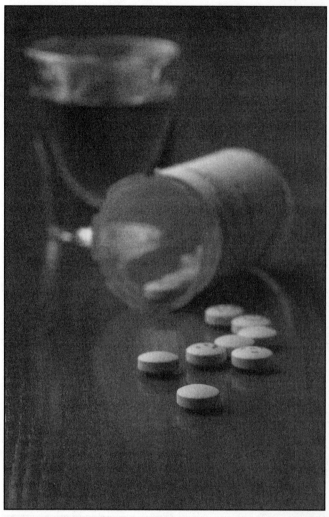

© Ingram Publishing

offices, the courts, state departments of social services, state universities and colleges, and public health offices maintain data and conduct research. On local levels, criminal justice agencies, social service departments, public hospitals, and health departments provide information. On a private level, various research institutes and universities, professional organizations such as the American Medical Association and the American Cancer Society, hospitals, and treatment centers, as well as private corporations, are tracking drug-related trends. Surveys abound with no apparent lack of available data. As a result, the need for examination of research methods and findings for reliability and accuracy is self-evident. The articles in this unit provide information about some drug-related trends occurring within certain subpopulations of Americans. While reading the articles, it is interesting to consider how the trends and patterns described are dispersed through various subpopulations of Americans and specific geographical areas. Additionally, much information about drugs and drug trends can be located quickly by referring to the list of websites in the front section of this book.

Adolescent Painkiller Use May Increase Risk of Addiction, Heroin Use

ALCOHOLISM & DRUG ABUSE

Prescription opiate abuse is not only increasing among adolescents, but it predisposes them to becoming addicted as adults, according to animal research published earlier this month. Furthermore, clinicians report that prescription opiates are now a "gateway" drug that leads to heroin, with adolescent units, typically devoted to alcohol and marijuana, now treating more and more patients for opiate addiction.

"We're terrified," said Mary Jeanne Kreek, MD, professor and head of laboratory at the Laboratory of the Biology of Addictive Diseases at The Rockefeller University in New York City. "We don't know where prescription opiate illicit use is going to go, and we don't know how many will become addicted." Kreek, who with lead author Yong Zhang, PhD, and others conducted the study comparing the effects of oxycodone on adolescent and adult mice, spoke to *ADAW* last week about the effects of prescription opiates on the developing brain.

Adolescents may start using prescription opiates for the same reasons they start using any drug of abuse, said Kreek: risk-taking, impulsivity, and peer pressure. But that initial use could progress to addiction, because of the drug's effects on the dopamine system, she said. With heroin, as many as one in three who ever use it become addicted. In addition, once tried even once, opiates can be alluring to adolescents. "Opiates have what a lot of young people are looking for today—an escape from life's problems," she said.

The Mouse Study

The mouse study found that the lowest dose of oxydocone led to increased dopamine levels in adolescent mice, but not in adult mice. When the adolescent mice were re-exposed to oxycodone as adults, they had higher levels of dopamine than adults who were exposed to the same amount but had not been exposed as adolescents.

In addition, the adolescent mice self-administered smaller amounts of oxycodone, and less frequently, than adult mice did.

These findings suggest that adolescent mice are more sensitive to the oxycodone. Kreek hypothesized that this is because of the state of the adolescent brain, which has rapidly increasing dopamine receptors.

The number of dopamine receptors in the mouse bra increases exponentially from birth to early adolescence, a remain at a plateau at mid-adolescence (the equivalent age 13 to 16 years) and then begin to decline until adulthoo It is this rapid development of dopamine receptors which mig be the key to adolescent sensitivity to drugs.

Epidemiological studies have already proven that the earli adolescents initiate use of alcohol or cigarettes, the great the likelihood that they will be dependent as adults. When u is initiated as adults, the chance of subsequent dependen plummets.

"Adolescence is when we are forming our memories, o cues, and learning," said Kreek. "You don't want to batter a bra that's learning, and I look at drug abuse as battering a brain."

Gateway to Heroin

Kreek's study suggests that human adolescents are more se sitive to prescription opiates, said Joseph Frascella, Ph director of the division of clinical neuroscience at the Natior Institute on Drug Abuse (NIDA), which funded the stud "We know that the earlier kids get involved in drugs, the mo likely they are to have careers in drugs," Frascella told *ADAW*

"In a sense this is a gateway theory at work—if you sta with one drug, does it lead you down the path to anothe like heroin," said Frascella. "I really don't think we know t answer to this yet. It could be that the kids who are willing do these heavy drugs have some kind of brain vulnerability."

But even if science is still studying the reasons behi adolescent use of opiates, treatment providers see the effec In Buffalo, N.Y., providers are reporting increased numbers young people coming in with prescription opiate dependen and with heroin addiction. "When we opened in 1990, the thr major gateway drugs were marijuana, alcohol, and nicotine said Dick Gallagher, executive director of Alcohol and Dr Dependency Services, Inc., a 210-bed treatment facility f adolescents and young adults. "Now, there are four gatewa drugs, and one is prescription opiates," he said.

Buffalo is a case in point because heroin is less expensi than prescription opiates there, because both are popular amo ung people there, and because the treatment system is coping th so much opiate dependency among adolescents, according treatment providers.

"Ten years ago we would see five people a month in trou- e with prescription opiates," said Robert B. Whitney, M.D., ending physician in the division of chemical dependency Erie County Medical Center in Buffalo, where there are 0 out-patient slots and 400 beds for addiction treatment. ow we see more than five a day."

And prescription opiates are a gateway for heroin use, hitney told *ADAW*. "There's a limit to how much Oxycontin hydrocodone they can get just to maintain themselves," said. "They find that with heroin, they may get better anagement of their withdrawal."

Whitney described a typical pathway to heroin, with prescrip- n drugs as the gateway. The user starts with oral opiates, moving crushing and snorting them, to snorting heroin. These people y "at least I'm not using a needle," said Whitney. However, entually many find that snorting the heroin gets too expen- ve or they can't maintain their addiction, and they move to travenous use.

"There's a pattern of kids that have utilized the painkillers, d want to go on to the next level," Gallagher said. Heroin is less pensive than prescription opiates, and it's accessible, he said.

he Adolescent and Pain

hat if an adolescent takes a prescription opiate for pain— es the Kreek study imply that this adolescent will be at eater risk for later addiction? "That's an excellent question," d NIDA's Frascella. "The data seem to suggest that if you ke a medication for pain, there's a different response than if u take it just to get high."

Kreek agreed. "We do know that persons in severe pain have lifferent neurobiological substrate," she said.

However, Kreek warned that opiates are overprescribed for ute pain. "I'm not talking about cancer and chronic pain," e said. But it's not necessary for someone to get two weeks' pply of painkillers when they only need 48 hours' worth, she

said. "We can talk to the patient in two days and see if we've misjudged," she said. "But in general you can step down to a much lighter drug."

And Whitney in Buffalo related a story of a patient who three years ago at the age of 15 was in a car accident and went home from the hospital with a legitimate prescription for hydroco- done. "Within a month she was taking not only what they gave her but what she could get from her friends," he said. This girl— initially a patient in his hospital due to a car accident—became his patient due to heroin addiction.

"For sure prescription opiates are a gateway drug," said Whitney. "They're getting the heroin problem into a population that we did not see using opiates at all before." This population of young people requires long-term treatment.

Gallagher agreed, saying that for the adolescents, treatment for opiate addiction must be go on for months. "Don't think you can treat these kids in 28 days unless you have intensive support after," he said.

The Kreek study of mice lends credence to what the treat- ment providers are reporting. "If you want to make the jump to humans—which we shouldn't do, but we do—our findings sug- gest that recovery [from opiate addiction] is very slow," Kreek told *ADAW*, adding that the findings also show chemically that adolescent brains do have special vulnerabilities to opiates.

Resources

"Behavioral and Neurochemical Changes Induced by Oxycodone Differ Between Adolescent and Adult Mice" is published in the current issue of *Neuropsychopharmacology*. For the full text, go to http://www.nature.com/npp/journal/vaop/ncurrent/full/ npp2008134a.html.

Critical Thinking

1. Adolescents are more susceptible to addiction while abusing prescription drugs. What are the reasons for this, and why is it important in relation to age and drug abuse?

2. How can parents address this?

Extreme Barbarism, a Death Cult, and Holy Warriors in Mexico: Societal Warfare South of the Border?

ROBERT J. BUNKER AND JOHN P. SULLIVAN

This short essay is about impression—gut feelings combined with a certain amount of analytical skill—about recent trends taking place in Mexico concerning the ongoing criminal insurgencies being waged by the various warring cartels, gangs, and mercenary organizations that have metastasized throughout that nation (and in many other regions as well). The authors spent over eight hours sequestered together about a month ago on a five-hundred mile 'there and back again road trip' to attend a training conference as instructors for the Kern County Chiefs of Police. Our talks centered on Mexican Drug Cartels, 3rd Generation Gangs, 3rd Phase Cartels, Criminal Insurgency Theory, and a host of related topics most folks just don't normally discuss in polite company. In the car, and at the conference, we were bombarded by Sullivan's never ending twitter and social networking news feeds—in Spanish and English—linked to the criminal violence in Mexico. If Dante had been our contemporary, we fear, he could just have easily taken a stroll through some of the cities and towns of Mexico using those news feeds and substituting the imagery for the circles of hell he described in his early 14th century work the *Divine Comedy*.

The hours of conversation about the conflicts in Mexico, bolstered by the news feeds and even the Q&A from the training time provided to the Kern Chiefs, provided us both with much to reflect upon. Additionally, both authors are currently co-writing three essays for a follow-on project to the earlier *Narcos Over the Border* (Routledge) book, the work that zenpundit.com found as ". . . one of the more disturbing academic works recently published in the national security field, not excluding even those monographs dealing with Islamist terrorism and Pakistan," concerning Mexico's immense problems.[1] If this were not enough, as part of our ongoing collaboration, the authors have been trying to determin[e] what to make of Hazen's June 2010 *International Revie[w] of the Red Cross* paper "Understanding gangs as arme[d] groups."[2] Her conclusions just don't correlate with th[e] empirical evidence stemming from the cartel and gan[g] related incidents regularly occurring in Mexico. Th[is] work suggests to us that American street gang researc[h]ers, whose work Hazen utilized as the basis of her anal[y]sis, are totally insulated from the reality of the conflic[t] in Mexico—just as are many members of the Americ[an] public and their elected officials. For good or for ba[d] we are not so well insulated, having tracked what h[as] been taking place in that country for some years no[w]. The ongoing review (for the purposes of identifying ca[r]tel tattoos, cult icons, and instances of ritual killing) [of] the images of the tortured and broken bodies—some [no] longer recognizable as once ever being human beings-continually haunts us both.

Our impression is that what is now taking place [in] Mexico has for some time gone way beyond secular a[nd] criminal (economic) activities as defined by tradition[al] organized crime studies.[3] In fact, the intensity of chan[ge] may indeed be increasing. Not only have *de facto poli[ti]cal* elements come to the fore—*i.e.,* when a cartel tak[es] over an entire city or town, they have no choice but [to] take over political functions formerly administered [by] the local government—but social (*narcocultura*) a[nd] religious/spiritual (*narcocultos*) characteristics are n[ow] making themselves more pronounced. What we are like[ly] witnessing is Mexican society starting to not only unra[vel] but to go to war with itself. The bonds and relationshi[ps] that hold that society together are fraying, unravelin[g] and, in some instances, the polarity is reversing itself wi[th] trust being replaced by mistrust and suspicion. Traditio[nal] Mexican values and competing criminal value systems a[re] ngaged in a brutal contest over the 'hearts, minds, and ouls' of its citizens in a street-by-street, block-by-block, nd city-by-city war over the future social and political rganization of Mexico. Environmental modification is king place in some urban centers and rural outposts as eviant norms replace traditional ones and the younger eneration fully accepts a criminal value system as their aseline of behavior because they have known no other. he continuing incidents of ever increasing barbarism— ome would call this a manifestation of evil even if secu- rly motivated—and the growing popularity of a death ult are but two examples of this clash of values. Addi- onally, the early rise of what appears to be cartel holy arriors may now also be taking place. While extreme arbarism, death cults, and possibly now holy warriors und in the Mexican cartel wars are still somewhat the xception rather than the rule, each of these trends is xtremely alarming, and will be touched upon in turn.

Extreme Barbarism

he 8 March 2011 video highlighted under the article Narco Execution Videos and its Effects on the Popula- on in General" is about as bad as it gets:

> This video surfaced today on the narco blogs, its content is extremely violent. It is unknown exactly when it was filmed, nor where it took place.
>
> The film lasts seven minutes, in which a group of masked men in military style clothing have hung a man by his feet. This person was clearly still alive when the assailants castrated him. Music can be heard playing in the background as one of the men step in and strategically peels back the face and skin of the victim before decapitating him. After it is over, the people standing around joke and laugh while they take cell pictures of this gruesome act. The video ends with the body being hacked up into pieces, and put into black plastic trash bags.[4]

Torture-killings have been part and parcel of the drug ars in Mexico but the level of brutality now appears ery much to be in a sustained pattern. Since that video as aired, a number of other heinous acts have been hronicled in these additionally selected *Borderland Beat* ttp://www.borderlandbeat.com/) postings. Just a few xamples from early April quickly portray the horrors king place in Mexico on an increasingly common basis:

- 5 April 2011: Several narco blogs have recently released a video showing a young blond haired woman decapitating a man whose head and hands are bound with what appears to be duct tape. It is unknown where and when the 14-minute video was made. During the video you can hear unidentified

men advise the woman on how to perform the beheading, as well as their concerns that the event be documented properly on video. As the woman continues severing the victim's head with a machete, you can hear an unidentified man refer to her as "La Guera Loca" (the crazy blond), while another man says "This is what happens to those who help the Zetas." After the woman finishes the decapitation and briefly poses with the head as a trophy, others begin to dismember the victim's body and skin the face and skull.

- 7 April 2011: Two men were recently found brutally murdered and posed in front of a shop in the Guadalupe neighborhood of Tepic, Nayarit. According to preliminary reports, the men were both skinned alive before their hearts were removed. At this time, neither man has been identified. *Note:* This is somewhat reminiscent of an alleged Los Zetas incident that took place earlier—". . . a June 6, 2010, torture/mass murder where six victims were found in a Cancun cave with their hearts cut out and 'Z' carved in their abdomens. . . ."[5]

- 8 April 2011: Wednesday afternoon, 42-year-old Roberto Abarca Serna, a Social Science professor at the University Autonomous of Guerrero and the founder of Carrizo Theater Company, was kidnapped outside his home in Acapulco by a group of armed gunmen. The kidnappers called Abarco Serna's wife and demanded a $40,000 pesos [*US dollar equivalent not specified*] ransom for his release. When his wife, Citlalli Delgado Galdino, took the money to her husband's kidnappers, she too was taken by force. The kidnappers tied Ms Delgado to a chair and forced her to watch as they beheaded her husband.

- 11 April 2011: Army troops found 16 more bodies in the mass graves outside the northern city of San Fernando, raising the total number of bodies discovered to 88, the Mexican Defense Secretariat said. *Note: These mass graves, and others like them in Northern Mexico, are now yielding hundreds of bodies of innocent victims likely killed by Los Zetas enforcers, the majority of which were Central Americans riding buses up North as they attempted to migrate to the US.*

This list could go on and on with dozens of similar incidents chronicled over the last month—the majority of them only reported in the Mexican press and never trans- lated into English—with many times that number never even reported because of the impunity provided to those who commit such heinous acts. It is said that less than 2%

of those who engage in criminal acts in Mexico are ever convicted and sentenced for their crimes.[6] The incidents of maiming, torture, and brutality are simply not subsiding in Mexico and anyone who says otherwise is not actually monitoring the violence that is taking place on a daily basis. It is of little wonder that many towns in Northern Mexico have been depopulated, with businesses and residences burned down and others boarded up and abandoned by their owners. While this is getting little traction in the US press, Mexico is starting to see internally displaced populations related to narco and criminal violence now estimated to be in excess of 200,000 individuals.[7]

A Death Cult

Increasingly, stories and reports are being written on *Santa Muerte*—the Death Saint—indigenous to Mexico though also now found in the United States and in Central America. This unsanctioned quasi-Catholic saint has in the past been worshiped as a 'grim reaper' type figure by marginal elements—peasants, the urban poor, and criminals—in Mexican society. Offerings of flowers, fruits, corn, beer, and other commodities, along with petitions for good health, luck with love, and even coming into wealth have been made at *Santa Muerte* altars. Often, the images of Jesus, the Virgin, and the saints of last resort (such as Judas Tadeo) would be found together with images of the death saint. Rainbow colors and lighter candle shades (representative of more benign candle magic spells) had dominated in the past though a harsher gray area element had always existed that focused on cursing others, defending against spells, and protecting oneself from being arrested or being sentenced to prison. Many times the images of other unsanctioned saints, such as *Jesus Malverde* and *Juan Soldado,* are also found in tandem with that of *Santa Muerte* in the possession of the harsher gray area worshipers who engage in criminal activities.

While this saint has been around for over five decades, a narco-criminal variant has since emerged that has elevated *Santa Muerte* into a dark and vengeful deity in her own right. This variant of *Santa Muerte* has nothing even remotely to do with Catholicism and is rapidly gaining adherents. The total number of *Santa Muerte* worshipers is somewhere in the low millions with the actual breakdown along the continuum of belief—traditional, gray area, and the darker narco-criminal variant—unknown. An educated guess would be that the traditional and gray area believers still dominate but as *narcocultura* spreads, especially amongst the young in Mexico, more worshipers will continue to gravitate to the harsher aspects of the faith.

What is known is that the darker variant of *Santa Muerte* is by no means benign and that simple commodities are unacceptable as offerings. Dark altars laden with weapons, money, narcotics, and sometimes stained with blood have been identified. The stakes have been raised now that petitions to cause agonizing death to one's enemies and bless cartel operatives before battle are being made, in essence providing them spiritual armor against other criminal forces and Mexican authorities. Human body parts and bowls of blood left at *Santa Muerte* altars, both public and private, are becoming more common as are actual human sacrifices and the ritualized dismemberment of the dead. Examples of what appear to be death cult sacrifices, rituals, and activities include:

- The stacking of headless bodies and the staged placement of body parts. One grisly incident photo shows a skinned skull resting on severed arms with the victim's male genitalia held in the palm of one of their hands.
- Decapitated heads left at the tombs of deceased drug lords—implicated as *Santa Muerte* worshipers—as sacrificial offerings.
- Decapitated heads offered directly to *Santa Muerte* by her worshipers.
- Victims killed at *Santa Muerte* altars/shrines.
- The ritual burning of decapitated heads as offerings.
- The removal of the hearts of victims.
- The skinning of victims while alive.
- The likely desecration of shrines belonging to more benign Saints.
- The use of black candle magic to request that the deity kill one's enemies.
- The threatening of a kidnap victim at a *Santa Muerte* altar with divine wrath if they failed to cooperate with their captors.
- The alleged smoking of a victim's ashes mixed with cocaine in a 'smoking death' ritual.[8]

The authors are well aware of the old 'Satanic panic' scare of much of the 1980s and how, for a time, Satanists and their covens were thought to be lurking near practically every preschool in the US so our intent is not to overplay the threat posed by the narco-criminal variant of *Santa Muerte.*[9] On the other hand, organized cartel groups such as *Los Zetas,* and members of independent kidnap kill teams, such as the one that engaged in the Chandler Arizona beheading in late 2010, have increasingly become followers of this dark and vengeful deity. Tattoos of *Santa Muerte* have been found on their operatives, altars and other icons have been found in their possession, and the members have been tied to death cult sacrifices and rituals. Even *Santa Muerte* high priest David Romo has been linked to a *Los Zetas* kidnapping cell and related criminal activities.[10] Additionally, quite a few incidents are known only to Mexican and US law enforcement and have not been widely reported in the press or have been filed as news stories that have been quickly forgotten. Example of the latter are the April 2011 *Santa Muerte* worshipers linked to killings in Chicago—some of the victims had their throats cut while bound—and the January 2010 human sacrifice that took place in Ciudad Juarez.[11]

To suggest that at least a thousand heavily armed and increasingly fanatical *Santa Muerte* followers of the narco-criminal variant, with blood on their hands, and at times on their altars, now exist simply cannot be disputed. That would mean that only 1-in-13 to 1-in-15 of the estimated 13,000 to 15,000 *Los Zetas* hard-core operatives—less than 10% of them—have become death cult followers; a ridiculously low estimate given what we know of *Los Zetas* training and indoctrination profiles.[12]

Holy Warriors

La Familia Michoacana (LFM), one of the dominant cartels in Mexico with thousands of members, is an evangelical-criminal organization based on a bizarre fusion of Christian teachings, the writings of John Eldredge (*Wild at Heart* et al.), and the teachings of the original La Familia leadership. Catechisms and doctrine have been produced by "El Más Loco" (The Craziest One) and others. They help to facilitate the indoctrination of new recruits and guide them through the stages of spiritual passage as they advance within the ranks of the cartel. Symbolism and icons utilized by cartel members include crucifixes, rosaries, the LFM tattoo, and related *narcocultra* adornments. Many of the brothers and sisters who belong to the cartel are considered 'saved souls' salvaged from the streets and from drug and alcohol rehabilitation centers and, once indoctrinated as true believers, can be considered adherents of a militarized form of pseudo-Christianity. Past allegations of cartel ties to the New Jerusalem Movement in Mexico and related apocalyptic beliefs have been made concerning LFM.[13]

La Familia has thus always been a cult based organization and steeped in notions of 'Divine Justice'. In September 2006, LFM threw five severed heads onto the *Sol y Sombra* nightclub floor with the accompanying narco-banner (*narcomanta*) "The family doesn't kill for money. It doesn't kill for women. It doesn't kill innocent people, only those who deserve to die. Know that this is divine justice."[14] In January 2010, the group was accused of sewing a victim's face onto a soccer ball though it just as likely could have been the work of an allied cartel with

a pronounced sense of sick humor.[15] Still, the ritualized violence which forms the basis of control through fear exercised by this cartel even runs though basic aspects of its enforcer training:

In mid-2010 Miguel "El Tyson" Ortiz Miranda, a captured La Familia activist, described the training of the organization's potential hit men. He said that a group of 40 are taken to Jesús del Monte, a mountainous zone, and are directed to pursue, shoot, and cook 15 victims. This exercise tests whether recruits can conquer their fear and overcome the sight of their quarries' blood.[16]

Additionally, dismembered bodies with LFM carved into them and dumped onto the streets is a not-uncommon occurrence in Michoacana and other cartel controlled territories. The beating of sinners with barbed wire wrapped boards and whips—their backs flayed and bloodied—has also been reported. In fact, LFM has imposed its own criminal-spiritual based law in its territories—essentially a pseudo-Christian equivalent to Sharia Law found in Islamist lands that has meted out harsh punishments to teenagers wearing sagging pants, hairnets, and who have engaged in other undesirable activities. Furthermore, Catholic priests who challenge LFM dictates have been subjected to death threats.

La Familia Michoacana has been taking a pounding of late with much of its senior leadership now killed or captured. The targeting of this cartel has become a Mexican Government priority since it is considered every bit as dangerous as *Los Zetas* cartel. Many media commentators, and even some researchers, have suggested that the cartel is on the verge of disintegration. Indeed, LFM called for a truce with the Mexican Government and finally disbanded in January 2011 by means of their own pronouncement via numerous *narcomantas*. Still, at the legacy middle management and lower levels, the former LFM cadre remain relatively unscathed and still exert much control over Michocana and the other former territories.

This crisis of leadership in LFM, however, has recently resulted in a new cartel appearing in Michoacana. The new cartel—*Los Caballeros Templarios* (Knights Templar)—appeared in March 2011 and proclaimed itself the successor to LFM by means of over thirty *narcomantas*.[17] In truth, it is unknown if the entire cadre of the cartel itself has morphed into *Los Caballeros Templarios* or if only a large splinter faction of *La Familia* has decided to establish this new organization. What is clear is the name and iconitry behind this new cartel directly invokes Christian Medieval symbolism pertaining to God's holy warriors. This is highly significant and elevates the central cartel tenet of 'Divine Justice' to an even more pronounced level than that initially promoted by LFM. The Knights Templar (aka Knighthood of the Temple of Solomon) a military-religious order, were the Papacy's mid-12th to late-13th century shock troops in the Holy Land and were known not only for their piety but for their bloodlust in battle against the infidel.

Los Caballeros Templarios, so the rhetoric goes, would thus represent a 21st century criminal-military-religious order that views itself as the protectors of the people of Michoacana. While many consider such rhetoric nothing more than a sham, enough true believers have already been indoctrinated to require that we take the rise of such a cult-like order as a very serious development. The English translation of the narcobanners proclaiming the rise of this cartel is as follows:

> To the society of Michoacan we inform you that from today we will be working here on the altruistic activities that were previously performed by the Familia Michoacana, we will be at the service of Michoacan society to attend to any situation which threatens the safety of the Michoacanos.
>
> Our commitment to society will be: to safeguard order; avoid robberies, kidnappings, extortion; and to shield the state from possible rival intrusions.
>
> Sincerely, The Knights Templar[18]

Numerous text only based *narcomantas* tied to and set next to victims murdered by this cartel—hanging from bridges and trees, placed in chairs, and dumped on the street—have already turned up over the last few months. Iconitry is also already appearing for this new cartel that includes the *Templarios* name with a shield with a red cross, a white battle flag with a white cross, and an armored knight holding a sword. To date, no *Templarios* tattoos specifically relating to cartel members have been identified on corpses or on former LFM members that have been captured in news or in blog photos, however, that too will come if this new cartel survives into the future.

Conclusions

Whether we are now catching glimpses of societal warfare actually breaking out south of the US–Mexican border, *i.e.,* between traditional Mexican society and that of criminal insurgents, we will leave the reader to consider. What we wish to do here is identify three major concerns, derived from very dark forms of spirituality, that pertain to the incidents of extreme barbarism, the rise of a death cult, and the emergence of holy warriors in Mexico that are deeply troubling to us:

- The continuing forms of extreme barbarism evident in the torture and killings of cartel and gang victims in Mexico is creating a growing cadre of hardened killers; some of whom are still in their childhoods. While most of these killings are secular

in nature, the very participation in such acts of barbarism will forever change a person. This goes beyond 'the dark stain left on the soul' religious arguments which may have their own merits to focus on the fact that a growing number of cartel and gang enforcers in Mexico are actively engaging in, and becoming accustomed to, sociopathic behaviors reminiscent of serial killers. Skinning people, cutting out their hearts, castrating them or cutting off their breasts, throwing them in a vat of acid, or setting them on fire *while they are alive* is incrementally becoming more accepted in *narcocultura* as a means of settling scores and doing away with ones' enemies. What this will eventually mean for Mexican society is unknown but the value system of these hardened killers, and what spirituality they may eventually gravitate to, will directly be in conflict with anything resembling Mexican civil society.

- There are documented incidents of ritual killing, human sacrifice, and petitions for divine intervention (such as death magic) in Mexico tied to the narco-criminal version of *Santa Muerte.* The removal of hearts, the offering of a human heads, the leaving of the dead as offerings at public shrines, the ritual burning of heads, and altars found with bowls of blood in them suggest *Santa Muerte* has indeed become an increasingly powerful deity in her own right to those that worship her. The call for Holy War by *Santa Muerte* high priest David Romo, linked to *Los Zetas,* as a result of the wholesale destruction of *Santa Muerte* temples by the Mexican government in Northern Mexico is also alarming as is *Los Zeta* cartel's increasing embrace of the death saint as their spiritual patron and divine benefactor. What the future holds for this death cult is unknown, but it is not good for Mexico, and the massive growth of its narco-criminal variant suggests many new worshippers are now praying at her dark altars.

- A self-sacrifice component of the holy warrior archetype may be emerging as the ideology of the new *Los Caballeros Templarios* cartel evolves. While we never thought we would consider this as a potential in Mexico, the possibility of future *Templarios* suicide (martyrdom) operations—likely based on active-aggressor assaults to kill high value targets such as Mexican governmental officials responsible for targeting this cartel—has to now be at least contemplated. Human sacrifice to God in this instance, unlike that of the emerging death cult in Mexico, is derived from ones' own spilling of blood as a martyr and not the spilling of your victim's blood. Since car bomb use in Mexico has been relatively restrained to date, no expectation currently exists that *Templarios* martyrdom operations will employ VBIEDs in the near term, but such operations could conceivably at some point come to pass.

The Thirty Years' War in Europe (1618–1648) was nown for its sheer brutality and in many ways repre- nted a conflict between the old Medieval order and mething entirely new. Heinous and barbaric acts and ass depopulation ensued due to a conflict that took on ligious overtones. We now wonder what historians will meday say about the Narco-Criminal Wars in Mexico 006–?) and those social and political forms that emerge om the ashes of a broadening conflict now taking place uth of our border. While that which is taking place in exico is nowhere near the horrors of the Thirty Years' ar, a death toll of 40,000 is fast approaching and new rms of dark spirituality are now being injected into hat heretofore has been considered only criminal, hence cular, insurgencies taking place. Mexico's new 'narco- lture' as embodied in *narcocorridos* (songs glorifying rcotraffickers) and the saints of the new cults or 'narco- ligions' have profound potentials for the soul and social bric of a nation.[19]

lotes

1. "Book Review: Narcos Over the Border by Robert J. Bunker (Ed.)" *zenpundit.com*. 5 April 2011. http://zenpundit .com/?p=3870.

2. Her conclusions are that "Some gangs–the institutionalized and very violent–may in fact share characteristics with insurgencies, and thus the conflict lens and armed group framework might apply. But very few gangs reach this level, suggesting that such an approach is neither appropriate nor useful for understanding the thousands of gangs that exist in communities across the globe" (p. 386). Jennifer M. Hazen, "Understanding gangs as armed groups." *International Review of the Red Cross*. Vol. 92, No. 878. June 2010: 369–386. While these conclusions are indicative of the basic 'American street gang' derived from studies conducted by Thrasher, Klein, Maxson, and others they have nothing to do with the reality of armed gangs that operate in Mexico, Central America, Colombia, Brazil, Sierra Leone, and increasingly in many other regions of the Globe.

3. Both authors have numerous *Small Wars Journal* publications on what is taking place in Mexico. These include: "The Mexican Cartel Debate: As Viewed Through Five Divergent Fields of Security Studies," "Criminal Insurgencies in Mexico: Web and Social Media Resources," and "Criminal Insurgency in the Americas."

4. See http://www.borderlandbeat.com/2011/03/narco-execution -videos-and-its-effects.html.

5. John P. Sullivan and Samuel Logan, "Los Zetas: Massacres, Assassinations and Infantry Tactics." *Homeland1.com*. 24 November 2010. http://www.homeland1.com/domestic -international-terrorism/articles/913612-Los-Zetas-Massacres -Assassinations-and-Infantry-Tactics/.

6. The original report is in Spanish and was published in *Milenio*. See *Borderland Beat*, "Study: 98.5% of Crimes Go Unpunished in Mexico." Saturday, 13 November 2010. http://www. borderlandbeat.com/2010/11/study-985-of-crimes-go -unpunished-in.html.

7. Associated Press, "Mexico Drug War Displaces 230,000 and Half Find Refuge in the U.S., Says Report." *Fox News*. 25 March 2011. http://latino.foxnews.com/latino/news/2011/03/25 /report-mexico-drug-war-displaces-230000-half-refuge/.

8. Our analysis is based on Pamela L. Bunker, Lisa J. Campbell, and Robert J. Bunker, "Torture, beheadings, and narcocultos." *Small Wars & Insurgencies*. Vol. 21., No.1. March 2010: 165-169; *Noticieros Televisa*, "Identifican cabeza 'ofrendada' en tumba de 'El Barbas'." 18 January 2010. http://www2.esmas.com/noticierostelevisa/mexico /estados/130952/identifican-cabeza-abandonada-tumba-el -barbas; and on other English and Spanish sources including some incident photos and altar images. Useful background resources were Tony M. Kail, *Magico-Religious Groups and Ritualistic Activities: A Guide for First Responders*. Boca Raton, FL: CRC Press, 2008 and Tony Kail, *Santa Muerte: Mexico's Mysterious Saint of Death*. La Vergne, TN: Fringe Research Press, 2010.

9. For information on the 'Satanic panic' scare see some of the works highlighted in Robert J. Bunker and Pamela L. Bunker, *Subject Bibliography: Beheadings & Ritualized Murders*. FBI Academy Library, Quantico, VA: August 2007. http:// fbilibrary.fbiacademy.edu/bibliographies /beheadings&ritualmurders.htm.

10. Claudia Bolaños, "Detienen a líder de Iglesia de la Santa Muerte." *El Universal*. 4 Martes 2011. http://www.eluniversal. com.mx/notas/734953.html.

11. Frank Main and Kim Janssen, "Sources: Two charged in double murder suspected in 10 other killings." Chicago *Sun-Times*. 2 April 2011. http://www.suntimes.com/4054640-417/sources -two-charged-in-double-murder-suspected-in-10-other-killings. html; and *El Diario*, "Atribuyen crimen de menor a promesas hechas a Santa Muerte." 10 January 2011. http://www.diario .com.mx/notas.php?f=2011/01/10&id=1cc7002c4dd7445755dc fbe8662e081a.

12. Alfredo Corchado, "Drug cartels taking over government roles in parts of Mexico." *The Dallas Morning News*. 30 April 2011. http://www.dallasnews.com/news/state/headlines/20110430-drug -cartels-taking-over-government-roles-in-parts-of-mexico.ece.

13. George W. Grayson, "E-Notes: La Familia: Another Mexican Deadly Syndicate." Foreign Policy Research Institute. February 2009. http://www.fpri.org/enotes/200901.grayson.lafamilia. html.

14. Samuel Logan and John P. Sullivan, "Mexican Crime 'Family' is Cloaked in 'Divine Justice'." *Mexidata.info*. Monday, August 24, 2009. http://mexidata.info/id2378.html.

15. Associated Press, "Drug cartel stitches victim's face on soccer ball." *Msnbc.com*. 8 January 2010. http://www .msnbc.msn.com/id/34774234/ns/world_news-americas/t /drug-cartel-stitches-victims-face-soccer-ball/.

16. George W. Grayson, *La Familia Drug Cartel*. Carlisle, PA: Strategic Studies Institute, US Army War College, December 2010: 47.

17. Hannah Stone, "New Cartel Announces Takeover from Familia Michoacana." *In Sight.* Monday, 14 March 2011. http://www.insightcrime.org/insight-latest-news/item/671-new-cartel-announces-take-over-from-familia-michoacana.

18. Ibid.

19. We are not the only concerned observers. See Alma Guillermoprieto, "Days of the Dead: The new narcocultura," *The New Yorker,* 10 November 2008 for an excellent analysis by an eminent Mexican journalist of these potentials at http://newyorker.com/reporting/2008/11/10/08111fact_guillermprie

DR. ROBERT J. BUNKER AND JOHN P. SULLIVAN are frequent contributors to *Small Wars Journal.* This commentary, "Extreme Barbarism, a Death Cult, and Holy Warriors in Mexico: Societal Warfare South of the Border?" was first published in *Small Wars Journal* May 22, 2011, and reposted per a Creative Commons authorization

College Students' Cheap Fix
Increasing Number Using ADHD Drug to Stay Alert

Trina Jones, Katie Berger, and Alexandra Schwappach

By her sophomore year of college, Kaley, a Washington State University student, routinely popped the prescription drug Adderall to help her study.

The 20-year-old has never had a prescription for the stimulant, but she found it easy to obtain it from friends. She first swallowed pills, then began "railing," or snorting, it at parties. Kaley, one of several students who agreed to speak on condition that their last names not be printed, used Adderall to stay up for days at a time studying for exams or finishing her homework. At parties, she could drink more alcohol without feeling intoxicated.

Last year, while cramming for a midterm, she stayed up all night, fueled by the drug.

"I ended up being in a complete daze for my midterm, and turned it in half-blank, crying," Kaley said. "Then I slept for two days."

National studies show that as many as 1 in 4 students in a college setting may have abused Adderall, and two surveys are under way at WSU to examine student use. College students are twice as likely to use the drug nonmedically as their peers who aren't in college, according to a report this year from the U.S. Department of Health and Human Services.

For students seeking a quick, cheap fix—pills cost about $3 to $5, though the price spikes during final exams—the stimulant allows them to be more productive and focused during late-night cram sessions.

The way students are taking the drug poses additional concerns. Studies show that up to 40 percent of students are snorting the drug, increasing the rate of absorption and the risk, said Patricia Maarhuis, prevention coordinator for WSU's Alcohol, Drug Counseling, Assessment and Prevention Services.

Adderall has also emerged on the party scene, where the stimulant lets students stay awake, even after a night of heavy drinking.

"In a full blackout normally they would be down, out for the count, passed out—but they're up, they're walking, they're talking, they're even a little jittery," Maarhuis said. "But they have absolutely no recall the next day. They might even drive or walk around, but they are indeed in a full blackout. They just haven't lost consciousness."

The drug's legitimate pharmaceutical uses include treatment of attention-deficit hyperactivity disorder and narcolepsy. But experts say Adderall is surprisingly simple to obtain, and its side effects are not well-known by casual users, including potentially severe health risks such as cardiac problems, psychosis, and weight loss.

"It's a careful balance," said Kevin Conway, deputy director at the National Institute on Drug Abuse in Bethesda, Md. "We want to make sure people who need it get it. We are concerned because there is a high rate of misuse of a serious drug."

Handing It Out 'Like Gum'

When Matthew, a 22-year-old WSU student, wanted a prescription for Adderall, he turned to a sympathetic doctor.

"I know I don't have (ADHD), but Adderall helps me a lot with school, so I got the prescription so I wouldn't have the hassle of finding it," Matthew said. "I was written a prescription for 60 pills, which is a lot, so I would save a stash for myself and then give some to my friends."

Access is fairly easy. Many students know friends or family members with a prescription, according to several students interviewed. Others say it's simple enough to look up ADHD symptoms, then describe them to a physician.

"(Students) will hand it out like gum," Maarhuis said.

Adderall's popularity is spread through social media tools such as Facebook and Twitter.

More than a dozen students at WSU have joined Facebook groups praising Adderall. On Twitter, posts on Adderall roll in by the minute, typically praising but occasionally cursing the drug.

"Gonna party up all night with alcohol and Adderall!!" a sample Tweet from Tacoma reads.

But students are doing more online than just talking about it. A Google search for "buy Adderall" results in more than 900,000 hits. Internet sales of medical drugs by illegitimate and often off-shore "pharmacies" may reach $75 billion a year by 2010, according to a 2008 study from the University of Maryland.

Maarhuis predicts more and more students will buy Adderall online, posing another concern.

"The real stuff is bad enough," she said. "God knows what you're getting from these sites, and what it's being cut with."

Traditionally, alcohol has been the No. 1 substance abused on college campuses. Marijuana has ranked second, and substances like cocaine come in at a distant third. In the past 10 years, the use of Adderall and other cognitive stimulants has shot up, outpacing cocaine and almost reaching marijuana levels, Maarhuis said.

Adderall poses a significant risk of psychological addiction, which leads to people using the drug compulsively, regardless of negative effects, said Rebecca Craft, a WSU biopsychology professor. Alice Young, a psychology professor at Texas Tech University who specializes in psychopharmacology, said that the drug may temporarily help a student study and remember, but recall may suffer if the student stops taking it.

"My main concern is not the single use," Young said. "It's the beginning to think you have to use to get the edge."

Officer Matthew Kuhrt, a drug recognition expert for the WSU Police Department, confirmed that "prescription medicine is becoming more and more of a problem." The WSU Police Department has had three cases involving Adderall this year. In 2008, the school revoked the recognition of the Alpha Kappa Lambda fraternity after drug detectives found evidence of cocaine, marijuana, and "significant quantities of Ritalin and Adderall."

Washington State Attorney General Rob McKenna is working on several programs to combat Adderall abuse in the state. He wants to reach students before they make bad drug decisions, not after, he said.

"The solution lies in education and outreach, not law enforcement," McKenna said.

Long-Term Effects Not Known

Even critics of Adderall acknowledge that the drug benefits some people.

Brian, 24, a 2009 WSU graduate, is one. He began taking Adderall after being diagnosed with attention-deficit disorder at age 7, but stopped when he was in high school because he thought it was unnecessary.

"I started taking it again in college," Brian said. "I'm sure wouldn't have graduated on time without it."

On the other side, WSU student Nicholas Cone stoppe using his legal prescription of Adderall because he said he di not like the crash he experienced after taking it.

"The focus I had for about four hours wasn't worth feelin sick when it was over," said Cone, a senior economics major.

The biggest concern may be the lack of knowledge abou Adderall's effects on the body, experts say. Adderall has bee on the market for less than 10 years, and long-term studies hav not been completed, nor have studies on Adderall's interaction with other drugs, Maarhuis said.

Others see cognitive stimulants as a step toward the future With care, they could be used to help professionals maintai focus, according to a December 2008 article in the scienc journal Nature.

Drugs like Adderall eventually may be recommended fc jobs that require alertness and focus, such as pilots or eme gency room doctors, according to interviews with experts.

While the best option may be well-rested surgeons, i today's society the choice may be between an Adderall-takin doctor and a sleep-deprived one, Craft said.

Craft said she believes the use of Adderrall to be risin among professors and researchers, although she hasn't see it at WSU. As people age, they cannot perform on the sam schedule they could when they were younger, but some peopl cannot handle this, so they take a drug, she said.

Professionals like Maarhuis, Young, and Craft worry about culture of expectations beyond human limits and risky medica tion for everyone who cannot perform as expected.

"It's a real reflection of this cascading shift toward highe and higher production," Craft said. "I'd rather be a little le productive."

Critical Thinking

1. What are the reasons for the persistent trends of college students to abusing Adderall?

2. How does this trend impact learning?

3. What can be done do change it?

Methadone Rises as a Painkiller with Big Risks

ERIK ECKHOLM AND OLGA PIERCE

Suffering from excruciating spinal deterioration, Robby Garvin, 24, of South Carolina, tried many painkillers before his doctor prescribed methadone in June 2006, just before Mr. Garvin and his friend Joey Sutton set off for a weekend at an amusement park.

On Saturday night Mr. Garvin called his mother to say, "Mama, this is the first time I have been pain free, this medicine just might really help me." The next day, though, he felt bad. As directed, he took two more tablets and then he lay down for a nap. It was after 2 P.M. that Joey said he heard a strange sound that must have been Robby's last breath.

Methadone, once used mainly in addiction treatment centers to replace heroin, is today being given out by family doctors, osteopaths and nurse practitioners for throbbing backs, joint injuries and a host of other severe pains.

A synthetic form of opium, it is cheap and long lasting, a powerful pain reliever that has helped millions. But because it is also abused by thrill seekers and badly prescribed by doctors unfamiliar with its risks, methadone is now the fastest growing cause of narcotic deaths. It is implicated in more than twice as many deaths as heroin, and is rivaling or surpassing the tolls of painkillers like OxyContin and Vicodin.

"This is a wonderful medicine used appropriately, but an unforgiving medicine used inappropriately," said Dr. Howard A. Heit, a pain specialist at Georgetown University. "Many legitimate patients, following the direction of the doctor, have run into trouble with methadone, including death."

Federal regulators acknowledge that they were slow to recognize the dangers of newly widespread methadone prescribing and to confront physician ignorance about the drug. They blame "imperfect" systems for monitoring such problems.

In fact, a dangerously high dosage recommendation remained in the Food and Drug Administration-approved package insert until late 2006. The agency has adjusted the label and is now considering requiring doctors to take special classes on prescribing narcotics.

Between 1999 and 2005, deaths that had methadone listed as a contributor increased nearly fivefold, to 4,462, a number that federal statisticians say is understated since states do not always specify the drugs in overdoses. Florida alone, which keeps detailed data, listed methadone as a cause in 785 deaths

in 2007, up from 367 in 2003. In most cases it was mixed with other drugs like sedatives that increased the risks.

The rise of methadone is in part because of a major change in medical attitudes in the 1990s, as doctors accepted that debilitating pain was often undertreated. Insurance plans embraced methadone as a generic, cheaper alternative to other long-lasting painkillers like OxyContin, and many doctors switched to prescribing it because it seemed less controversial and perhaps less prone to abuse than OxyContin.

From 1998 to 2006, the number of methadone prescriptions increased by 700 percent, according to Drug Enforcement Administration figures, flooding parts of the country where it had rarely been seen.

But too few doctors, experts say, understand how slowly methadone is metabolized and how greatly patients differ in their responses. Some prescribe too much too fast, allowing methadone to build to dangerous levels; some fail to warn patients of the potential dangers of mixing methadone with alcohol or sedatives, or do not keep in contact during the perilous initial week on the drug. And some patients do not follow the doctor's orders.

"Those problems were not soon recognized," said Dr. Bob Rappaport, a division director at the Food and Drug Administration. He added: "Methadone is an extremely difficult drug to use, even for specialists. People were using it rather blithely for several years."

Dr. James Finch, an addiction specialist in Durham, N.C., said, "In the clinical and regulatory communities, everyone is trying to run and catch up with and deal with the causes of methadone overdoses."

This year the federal government started sponsoring voluntary classes that teach doctors the elaborate precautions they should take with methadone, like inching upward from low starting doses and screening patients for addictive behavior. (While Robby Garvin's doctor could argue that the dosage he was taking was reasonable—one to two 10-mg tablets, three times a day—and he was cleared by his state medical board, many specialists would have started him on a lower dose.)

In what critics call a stunning oversight, the F.D.A.-approved package insert for methadone for decades recommended starting doses for pain at up to 80 mg per day. "This could unequivocally cause death in patients who have not recently been using narcotics," said Dr. Robert G. Newman, former president of Beth Israel Medical Center in New York and an expert in addiction.

The F.D.A. says that in the absence of reports of problems by doctors or surveillance systems, "we would have no reason to suspect that the dosing regimen" might need to be adjusted.

In November 2006, after reports of overdoses and deaths among pain patients multiplied and The Charleston Gazette reported on the dangerous package instructions, the F.D.A. cut the recommended starting limit to no more than 30 mg per day. "As soon as we became aware of deaths due to misprescribing for pain patients, we began the process of instituting label changes," Dr. Rappaport said.

Methadone, which is made by Roxane Laboratories Inc. of Columbus, Ohio, and Covidien-Mallinckrodt Pharmaceuticals of Hazelwood, Mo., creates dependency and is sometimes sought by abusers who say they experience a special buzz when mixing it with Xanax.

While the greatest numbers of methadone-related deaths have occurred among the middle-aged, the fastest growth—an elevenfold jump between 1999 and 2005, to 615—occurred among those age 14 to 24, which experts say may be mainly a result of pill abuse.

Pain experts say the country is seeing a reprise of the abuse and tragedies that followed the introduction of OxyContin, a time-release form of oxycodone that was heavily marketed in the late 1990s. It became a factor in hundreds of deaths and a focus of law enforcement.

OxyContin is still widely prescribed, but a survey of Medicare plans in 2008, by the research firm Avalere Health LLC, found that many did not even include OxyContin on the list of reimbursable drugs. Critics like Dr. June Dahl, professor of pharmacology at the University of Wisconsin, fault the insurance companies for favoring methadone simply because of its monetary cost. "I don't think a drug that requires such a level of sophistication to use is what I'd call cheap, because of the risks," Dr. Dahl added.

Yet for the right patients, methadone can be a godsend. Alexandra Sherman, a patient of Dr. Heit's at his Fairfax, Va., clinic, suffered for years from hip and shoulder pain that "felt like somebody stabbing me with a knife," she said. Pain began to rule and ruin her days.

Dr. Heit gave her OxyContin and later, because it seemed to work better and because of the expense, switched her to methadone. Her insurance at one point covered only $500 in prescriptions, which paid for just one month's worth of OxyContin, compared with methadone's cost of $35 a month.

Methadone "has given me my life back," Ms. Sherman said.

But Dr. Heit did not just throw drugs at her problem. He told her that she would also have to try physical therapy as well. They signed a contract listing mutual obligations—she would follow directions, he would be on call. He starts patients at low doses, makes them bring in their pill bottles so he can count how many are left, and may give urine tests to deter mixing drugs.

Some doctors, like Dr. Theodore Parran of Case Weste Reserve University, also require methadone patients to gi them the names of relatives or friends they can call from tim to time.

But not all doctors have taken such precautions. Tony Davi a contractor in Victorville, Calif., had just turned 38 in 200 when, after years of migraines and back pain, he saw a ne pain doctor in his Kaiser Foundation Health Plan. The do tor, who had already given him the sedative Xanax, prescribe methadone because of his continued pain.

The second day on the two medications, Mr. Davis sai "I'm feeling really weird,' " recalled his wife, Pebbles Davi The two lay down for a nap and when she woke up, her hu band was dead.

Ms. Davis recalled that the coroner had told her, "Give the medicines he was on, his brain forgot to tell his heart beat and his lungs to pump." The case went to an arbitrate who ruled that although Mr. Davis had overused his drugs the past, the doctor had failed to warn him about the new ris of starting methadone together with Xanax and that the ca was substandard. Ms. Davis was awarded more than $500,00 "I never had any idea of the risk nor did my husband," she sai

Another source of danger has been the conversion table that doctors use when switching patients from one opioid another—telling, for example, how many milligrams of meth done would be equivalent to the level of morphine a patient ha been taking. These charts, until recently, indicated dangerous high doses for methadone. Newer ones suggest lower leve but many experts say these may be useless because methador affects patients so variably.

Now, as the government is making new efforts to teac methadone's challenges, some officials and doctors wou go further, requiring prescribers to take a course before usir methadone.

But many physicians and patient groups are wary of ar steps that would slow access to pain treatments.

As early as 2003, alarmed by the rise in methadone-relate deaths, the Substance Abuse and Mental Health Servic Administration made an urgent call for more systematic ar detailed state and national reporting about opioid deaths— call that still goes unanswered.

Misuse by abusers was first seen as the problem, but no said Dr. H. Westley Clark, director of the Center for Substanc Abuse Treatment of SAMHSA, "We know that a significa share of the methadone deaths involve doctors making wel intended prescriptions."

A majority of victims also used large quantities of alcohol benzodiazepine sedatives but few would have died without opioid as the primary culprit. "You can take a lot of benzod azepines without dying," said Dr. Charles E. Inturrisi of Wei Cornell Medical Center, who said they strengthen the depre sive effect of methadone.

Some doctors prescribe to patients who may be expecte to court danger, like Anna Nicole Smith, who died from drug cocktail including the sedative chloral hydrate and thre benzodiazepines.

Last February, Margaret Moore, 54, who lived alone in South Pasadena, Fla., with a history of alcoholism, depression and chronic back pain from a car accident, was found dead at home. Her doctor had prescribed methadone and valium and, he told investigators, warned her to stop drinking.

Her body was surrounded by empty vodka bottles and a host of pills including bottles of methadone tablets and sedatives. Her death was declared an accident from methadone toxicity.

Since April, SAMHSA has sponsored nine voluntary training courses on the safe prescribing of opioids, and many more are planned, though they will only reach a fraction of prescribers. The agency is also contracting with the American Society of Addiction Medicine to set up a mentoring program, through which prescribing physicians can receive expert advice. The state of Utah has a plan to educate every doctor and pain patient in the state about safe use of methadone and other opioids.

Nancy Garvin, Robby's mother, is one of many relatives of victims who, in the absence of a national registry, have started educational and pressure groups to fight bad prescribing and misuse of the drug.

Still, the death rate appears to be rising, raising the question of what more may be necessary, in law enforcement and in doctor training.

"Methadone can be important for patients when other drugs don't work," said Dr. Inturrisi, "but unless the doctor has the training and resources to manage the patient properly, he's going to get in trouble at a rate that's unacceptable."

This article has been revised to reflect the following correction:

Correction: August 24, 2008

An article last Sunday about concerns over the expanding prescription use of methadone for various injuries erroneously included a drug among those that killed the television personality Anna Nicole Smith in 2007. The medical examiner ruled that she had died as a result of an accidental overdose of the sedative chloral hydrate and three benzodiazepines. The drug cocktail did not include methadone, though traces were found in her system.

Critical Thinking

1. What, traditionally, has methadone been used for in the United States?

2. What type of drug pharmacologically is methadone?

3. How much did prescriptions for methadone increase between 1998–2006?

UNIT 5

Measuring the Social Costs of Drugs

Unit Selections

Learning Outcomes

After reading this Unit, you should be able to:

- Identify where one looks to identify the social costs associated with drug abuse.

- Understand the effects of drug addiction on newborn children.

- Explain how the spread of OxyContin use in the United States has impacted the country.

- Reveal the subpopulations of Americans where fetal alcohol syndrome manifests itself differently and why.

- Explain what you believe is the greatest drug-related threat currently facing the United States.

Student Website
www.mhhe.com/cls

Internet References

BMJ.com a Publishing Group
http://bmj.bmjjournals.com/cgi/content/abridged/326/7383/242/a
Drug Enforcement Administration
www.usdoj.gov/dea
Drug Policy Alliance
www.drugpolicy.org/database/index.html
Drug Use Cost to the Economy
www.ccm-drugtest.com/ntl_effcts1.htm
European Monitoring Center for Drugs and Addiction
www.emcdda.europa.eu/html.cfm/index1357EN.html
National Drug Control Policy
www.ncjrs.org/ondcppubs/publications/policy/ndcs00/chap2_10.html
The November Coalition
www.november.org
TRAC DEA Site
http://trac.syr.edu/tracdea/index.html
United Nations Chronicle—Online Edition
www.un.org/Pubs/chronicle/1998/issue2/0298p7.html

The most devastating effect of drug abuse in America is the magnitude with which it affects the way we live. Much of its influence is not measurable. What is the cost of a son or daughter lost, a parent imprisoned, a life lived in a constant state of fear?

The emotional costs alone are incomprehensible. The social legacy of this country's drug crisis could easily be the subject of his entire book. The purpose here, however, can only be a cursory portrayal of drugs' tremendous costs. More than one U.S. president has stated that drug use threatens our national security and personal well-being. The financial costs of maintaining the federal apparatus devoted to drug interdiction, enforcement, and treatment are staggering. Although yearly expenditures vary due to changes in political influence, strategy, and tactics, examples of the tremendous effects of drugs on government and the economy abound. The federal budget for drug control exceeds 14 billion and includes almost $1.5 billion dedicated to drug fighting in Mexico and Central America under the Merida Initiative. Mexican criminal syndicates and paramilitaries who control trafficking across the U.S. southern border threaten the virtual sovereignty of the Mexican government. Many argue that the situation in Mexico is as dangerous to the United States as the current situation in Afghanistan.

Since 9/11, the restructuring of federal, state, and local law enforcement apparatus in response to terrorism has significantly influenced the nature and extent of drug trafficking in the United States. Huge transnational investigative, intelligence, and enforcement coalitions have formed between the United States and its allies in the war against terrorism. One significant impact of these coalitions has been a tightening of border access and a decreased availability of international trafficking routes. Although drugs are believed to still pour in from Mexico, drug shortages, increased street prices, and a decrease in purity are occurring. Powder heroin is not widely available in the West, and many major U.S. cities are reporting major street declines in the availability of cocaine.

Still, drugs exist, in association with terrorism, as the business of the criminal justice system. Approximately 80 percent of the people behind bars in the country had a problem with drugs or alcohol prior to their incarceration—more of its citizens than almost any other comparable society, and the financial costs are staggering. Doing drugs and serving time produces an inescapable nexus, and it doesn't end with prison. Almost 29 percent of persons on supervised parole or probation abuse drugs. Some argue that these numbers represent the fact that Americans have come to rely on the criminal justice system in an unprecedented way to solve problems of drug abuse. Regardless of the way one chooses to view various relationships, the resulting picture is numbing.

In addition to the highly visible criminal justice-related costs, numerous other institutions are affected. Housing, welfare, education, and health care provide excellent examples of critical institutions struggling to overcome the strain of drug-related impacts. In addition, annual loss of productivity in the workplace exceeds well over a $160 billion per year. Alcoholism alone causes 500 million lost workdays each year. Add to this demographic shifts caused by people fleeing drug-impacted

© Stockbyte/Getty Images

neighborhoods, schools, and businesses, and one soon realizes that there is no victimless public or private institution. Last year, almost 4 million Americans received some kind of treatment related to the abuse of alcohol or other drugs. Almost 23 million Americans need treatment for an illicit drug or alcohol problem. Fetal Alcohol Syndrome is the leading cause of mental retardation in the United States, and still, survey data continue to report that over 11 percent of pregnant women drink alcohol. Add to this injured, drug-related accident and crime victims, along with demands produced by a growing population of intravenous drug users infected with AIDS, and a frighteningly-overwhelmed health-care system comes to the fore. Health-care costs from drug-related ills are staggering. Drug abuse continues to cost the economy more than $13 billion annually in health-care costs alone. Approximately 71 million Americans over 12 are current users of a tobacco product.

It should be emphasized that the social costs exacted by drug use infiltrate every aspect of public and private life. The implications for thousands of families struggling with the adverse effects of drug-related woes may prove the greatest and most tragic of social costs. Children who lack emotional support, self-esteem, role models, a safe and secure environment, economic opportunity, and an education because of a parent on drugs suggest costs that are difficult to comprehend or measure. In some jurisdictions in California and Oregon, as many as 50 percent of child welfare placements are precipitated by methamphetamine abuse.

When reading Unit 5 of this book, consider the diversity of costs associated with the abuse of both legal and illegal drugs. As you read the following articles, consider the historical progressions of social costs produced by drug abuse over the past century. How are the problems of the past replicating themselves and how have science, medicine, and social policy changed in an attempt to mitigate these impacts? Ample evidence informs us that there is no single approach to mitigate the diverse nature of drug-related social impacts. Further, some of the most astounding scientific discoveries about how addiction develops remain mysterious when compared to the reality of the lives of millions who find drugs an end in themselves. Some have argued that the roots of drug-related problems today seem even more elusive, complicated, and desperate. Good progress has been made in treating drug addiction, but only moderate progress has been made in preventing it in the first place. What are the disproportionate ways in which some populations of Americans are harmed by drugs? Are there epidemics within epidemics? How is drug abuse expressed within different populations of Americans? How do the implications for Native American families and culture differ from those for other racial and ethnic groups? What are the reasons for these disparities and how should they be addressed?

The Problem with Drinking

Cheryl Harris Sharman

Efraím was already drunk when he left the wedding at 2 A.M. It had been a "nice wedding," which in Costa Rica means only hard liquor was served. The 21-year-old headed to a local bar for a "sarpe," or nightcap, with some friends. At 5 A.M., one of them finally sent him home in a taxi. Shivering and wrapped in towels, he sat on the carpet near the toilet and threw up.

Hours passed before his father found him in the same spot around 6 in the evening and rushed him to the hospital. The nightmare finally ended after an emergency room doctor injected him with medication for alcohol poisoning.

Tadeo, a young Costa Rican, went to the beach with three friends for a few laughs and a lot of drinks. After eight beers each, they drove home on the dark highway. A truck sped by, its rear lights obscuring the curve ahead. Their car skidded off the road and into a tree. Pinned in the wreckage, Tadeo broke three ribs, fractured his skull, fell unconscious, and remained in a coma for a week.

In Costa Rica, as in most Latin American countries, social gatherings more often than not include alcohol. Weddings and funerals, births and baptisms rely at least in part on drinks to ease grieving or encourage celebration. Aside from special occasions, many homes keep well-stocked bars that facilitate impromptu gatherings.

The drive home, particularly in the half-year-long rainy season, can entail a mix of alcohol and slick, winding roads, with potentially catastrophic results. But no one abstains for this reason. Statistics reflect the outcome: 13 percent of emergency room consultations in 1987 and 33 percent of auto fatalities in 2003 were alcohol related. Yet only 5 percent of Costa Ricans are alcohol dependent.

"The biggest misconception people have is that the problem of alcohol is alcohol dependence, or alcoholism," says Maristela Monteiro, regional advisor on alcohol and substance abuse at the Pan American Health Organization (PAHO). "In terms of society, most public health problems come from acute intoxication."

Medical research shows that long-term alcohol abuse causes liver diseases such as cirrhosis and hepatitis, as well as memory loss, ulcers, anemia, impaired blood clotting, impaired sexual performance, malnutrition, depression, cancer and even brain damage. But from a public health perspective, alcohol's greatest impact comes from occasional high-risk drinking by normally light to moderate drinkers.

"Homicides, traffic accidents, suicides, violent behavior, domestic violence, child abuse or mistreatment, neglect— these are from heavy drinking occasions, but most of these people are not alcohol dependent," says Monteiro.

Studies in the United States show that alcohol is a factor in 25 percent of deaths among people aged 15 to 29. Its direct costs to the U.S. health care system add up to some $19 billion a year, and for the economy as a whole, some $148 billion. As a risk factor for the global burden of illness, alcohol rivals tobacco: It is ranked number five among risks to health worldwide (tobacco is number four), and number one in all but two countries—Canada and the United States—in the Americas.

The most effective policies prevent intoxication by reducing the amount of alcohol people drink.

Experts note that alcohol takes a disproportionate toll on the poor, despite the fact that alcohol consumption tends to increase with educational levels and development. Poor people spend a greater proportion of their income on alcohol, and when drinking problems occur, they have less access to services, may lose their jobs, and bring major hardship on their families.

For all these reasons, many public health experts believe that alcohol policy should be a top priority in every country of the Americas.

Costa Rica is one of many countries that have instituted programs to reduce the toll of alcohol using a variety of measures: taxes and licensing, restrictions on advertising, minimum-age laws, and controls on the hours of operation and location of outlets that sell alcohol.

In addition, Costa Rican law bans alcohol consumption in most public buildings, at sporting events, in the workplace, in parks or on the street, within 100 meters of churches, and on public transportation.

"It is important to use various measures to be effective," says Julio Bejarano, head of research at the Instituto sobre Alcoholismo y Farmacodependencia (IAFA) in San José.

Programs like Costa Rica's are the outcome of a 30-year trend toward viewing alcohol less as an individual malady and more as a problem of public health. The shift began with the 1975 publication of *Alcohol Control Policies in Public Health Perspective* by the Finnish Foundation for Alcohol Studies. Since then, new definitions of alcohol use and abuse have emerged, including classifications for levels of drinking according to their risks to health.

According to the emerging consensus, people with what the U.S. health sector calls "alcoholism" and what the World Health Organization (WHO) calls "alcohol dependence" need to seek treatment. But those engaged in occasional overuse that causes mental or physical health problems—"alcohol abuse" in the United States and "harmful use" disorder for WHO—should be made aware of its impact on their health and urged to reduce their consumption before they become alcohol dependent. A third WHO category, "hazardous use," implies high-risk consumption, or what is sometimes referred to as "binge drinking." "You never had a car accident," Monteiro explains, "but you drink too much and drive." This is a large group of people who also need to cut back.

But the bottom line, says Monteiro, is that good public health policies must aim at preventing intoxication. And the best way to do this is by reducing consumption.

"What has been proven over and over in developed countries and more and more in developing countries, is that we need to reduce the overall consumption of the population," she says.

Monteiro says that experience shows that the most effective way of reducing overall consumption is by increasing prices and taxes on alcohol and restricting availability—that is, where it can be sold, to whom, how much, at what times and on which days.

"Once you reduce the hours of sale, for example, you also control the amount of alcohol people can access and drink. You reduce homicides, accidents, violence—many of the acute consequences decrease significantly. There are several examples—for a long time in Europe, the U.S., and Canada, and now in Latin America and elsewhere—that show that closing bars earlier reduces both accidents and violence."

A 2003 book, *Alcohol: No Ordinary Commodity*, published by Oxford and WHO, reviewed three decades of research and concluded that reducing consumption is key. Their top-10 list of specific measures includes minimum-age laws, government monopolies, restrictions on outlets and hours of sale, taxes, drunk-driving counter-measures and brief interventions for hazardous drinkers.

Limiting Access

Raising the minimum age for purchasing alcohol has long been one of the most effective means of reducing access.

Only a handful of countries have emulated the U.S. minimum age of 21, but this has proven to be an effective policy. When all 50 U.S. states raised their minimum age from 18 to 21, the country as a whole saw a 19 percent net decrease in fatalities among young drivers. The National Highway Traffic Safety Administration estimates that raising the minimum age has saved 17,359 lives since 1975.

Government monopolies on alcohol have also proven effective, but these are increasingly unpopular. Until 1968, Finland prohibited the sale of beer anywhere but in government-owned outlets. In 1968, the country began to allow grocery stores to sell beer, and alcohol consumption climbed by 46 percent overall (increasing particularly among 13- to 17-year-olds). Government monopolies today oversee production, sales or distribution (but not all three) in parts of the United States, Canada, Russia, India, southern Africa and Costa Rica. In Scandinavia, multinational companies have waged legal battles invoking international trade rules to break up longstanding government monopolies on alcohol, increasingly limiting their ability to restrict consumption.

Short of holding monopolies, governments can control where, when and to whom alcohol is sold, restricting the density of outlets through limited licensing and restricted hours of sale. They can also restrict the availability of high- and medium-strength alcoholic beverages. Before 1965, Swedish grocery stores could not sell beer with more than 3.5 percent alcohol. When 4.5 percent beer became legally available in grocery stores, total alcohol consumption increased nearly 15 percent. Twelve years later, Sweden returned to the 3.5 percent limit, and consumption dropped again by the same amount.

Hours of sales are equally important. When Norway closed bars on Saturdays, researchers noted that those most affected by the restricted access were also those deemed likely to engage in domestic violence or disruptive intoxication. An Australian Aboriginal community, Tennant Creek, closed bars on Thursdays and noted that fewer women required hospital attention for domestic injuries.

In Latin America and the Caribbean, Colombia provides one of the leading success stories of limiting alcohol consumption through restricted hours of operation. Rodrigo Guerrero, a physician and public health expert, served as mayor of the second-largest city, Calí, in the mid-1990s and dedicated much of his effort to tackling the city's surging violence problem. He commissioned surveys that found that 40 percent of violence victims and 26 percent of violent death victims in his city were intoxicated. In response, Calí passed a *ley semi seca* ("semi-dry law"), which closed bars and discotheques at 1 A.M. on weekdays and 2 A.M. on Fridays and Saturdays. These and other measures reduced homicides from 80 per 100,000 to 28 per 100,000 in eight years.

Costa Rica also limits hours and days of sale. The law prohibits selling or purchasing alcohol in public places after midnight, the day before and the day after a national election

nd during Holy Week, "the period of highest alcohol con-
umption in Costa Rica," IAFA's Bejarano notes.

Probably the most effective policy to reduce consumption,
owever, is raising taxes on alcoholic beverages. Worldwide,
aising the price of alcohol always reduces consumption.
According to the recent WHO report *Global Status Report:
Alcohol Policy*, the price of beer should always be more than
he price of a soda. And because the harmful effects of alco-
ol use stem from alcohol content, higher-content beverages
hould be taxed at higher rates.

Drinking and Driving

After restricting access, the next most effective policies are
hose aimed at reducing drunk driving. WHO's *Global Status
Report: Alcohol Policy* lists among the most effective coun-
ermeasures sobriety checkpoints, lowered blood-alcohol
mits, license suspension and graduated licensing for novice
rivers. Enforcement is key. Police intervention must be vis-
ole and frequent, and lawbreakers must be punished to the
xtent of the law.

Blood-alcohol limits are a critical part of these efforts.
Very little alcohol impairs motor coordination," explains
Monteiro. "If you drink just over a drink, you are at risk—
ctually, it's less than a drink."

Costa Rica sets the legal blood-alcohol limit for drivers at
.05 percent, although many experts say that problems often
egin at 0.04 percent. Belize, Guatemala, Mexico, Nicara-
ua, Paraguay, Canada and the United States set the limit
t 0.08 percent. These limits are most effective when used
ith checkpoints and random breath testing, according to
esearch.

Other effective measures include screening and "brief
nterventions," prevention tools that have become a corner-
tone of WHO's alcohol policy recommendations. During
outine visits to health facilities or the family doctor, patients
re asked simple questions that screen them for behavioral
isk factors—including alcohol, cigarettes, poor diet, physi-
al inactivity and seatbelt use—and doctors provide brief
ounseling sessions based on the responses.

"This is the epitome of low-technology medicine," says
Thomas Babor, one of the researchers who designed the
Alcohol Use Disorders Identification Test, or AUDIT.

"It's not the kind of thing, like MRIs, that seem to capture
he interest of clinicians. But it probably is of equal impor-
ance, because it provides a way to prevent problems before
hey occur and to minimize problems if they've already started
o develop."

AUDIT has been tested in a variety of countries and has
roven easy to use, inexpensive to implement, and effective
n reducing alcohol consumption at all levels of the popu-
ation. Translated into many languages (including a Span-
sh version available through PAHO), the test and booklet
nclude everything a clinician needs to give the 10-question
est, to score it for one of four levels of risk for alcohol use,

and to talk to patients about cutting back (including scripts
for doctors who are unsure of what to say).

Patients take the test in about one minute, a nurse or recep-
tionist scores it in another minute, and the clinician takes a
few minutes to talk to the patient. Those testing in the first
risk level are cautioned and advised to avoid drinking at least
two days a week. Clinicians tell second-level scorers to minimize the number of drinks per day or week and to cut back on
heavy drinking. Those in the third level receive brief counseling with more tools and goal-setting. Only fourth-level
scorers are referred to an alcohol specialist.

**To reduce drunk driving, lawbreakers must
be prosecuted and punished to the full
extent of the law.**

A 1999 study by Michael Fleming, at the University of
Wisconsin–Madison Medical School, showed that, with a
single counseling session, subjects cut back on their drinking in the first six months and kept it down for four years.
The study also found that every $10,000 invested in interven-
tions saved $43,000 in health costs, with even greater savings
when researchers factored in societal benefits, such as fewer
auto accidents and crimes.

Other policies have been found to be somewhat less effective, but combined with the "top 10," they help minimize the
burden of alcohol. These include having alcohol outlets refuse
to serve intoxicated patrons; training their staff to prevent
and manage aggression; promotion of alcohol-free events;
community mobilization; and public service campaigns in
schools and colleges, on television, and in print, including
warning labels. Bans and restrictions on alcohol advertising
and marketing can help reduce youth exposure to pro-alco-
hol messages. In Latin America, Costa Rica and Guatemala
have completely banned alcohol companies from sponsoring
youth and sporting events, and several other countries forbid
alcohol advertising on Sundays and holidays.

The challenge ahead, says PAHO's Monteiro, is to build
on the work of international alcohol policy experts, using the
available scientific evidence to judge which mix of policies
works best. But she offers a note of caution: "In Europe,
there's almost a reversal of the gains they had before because
of trade agreements. The trade agreements that opened the
markets for equal opportunity for everyone mean that you
cannot have higher taxes or higher prices. You have to allow
advertising for everyone."

She notes that in Sweden, foreign companies have challenged laws forbidding alcohol advertising, arguing that they
give local, better-known products an unfair advantage.

"That is a point that will be critical in the region," says Monteiro, "how to deal with the economic benefits of alcohol in
certain countries while protecting public health and reducing
its social costs."

Moving forward, Monteiro and researchers from 11 countries are embarking on a multicountry study that will show, with precision and hard data, the public health burden of alcohol in the Americas. The study will focus on alcohol use in Belize, Nicaragua, Paraguay and Peru. The results will be added to existing data from Argentina, Brazil, Costa Rica, Mexico, Uruguay, the United States and Canada.

Monteiro believes the new study is particularly timely, as several trends in the region point to a growing alcohol problem. For example, in most countries, women drink more as their educational levels rise. In Costa Rica, the percentage of children 13 to 15 who have tried alcohol rose from 16.3 percent in 1990 to 28.4 percent in 2000. In many countries, pressure from industry has been growing along with the spread of public health measures aimed at reducing alcohol sales.

All these developments call for more research and more action, says Monteiro, because "people not only die from drinking too much; they harm and kill those who don't drink too."

Critical Thinking

1. What can we do differently to address alcohol problems when drinking is almost considered a social must in many countries?

2. Is there a way to balance the economic benefits while protecting public health and reducing the social costs of alcohol?

CHERYL HARRIS SHARMAN is a freelance journalist based in New York City.

Newly Born, and Withdrawing from Painkillers

ABBY GOODNOUGH AND KATIE ZEZIMA

The mother got the call in the middle of the night: her 3-day-old baby was going through opiate withdrawal in a hospital here and had to start taking methadone, a drug best known for treating heroin addiction, to ease his suffering.

The mother had abused prescription painkillers like Oxy-Contin for the first 12 weeks of her pregnancy, buying them on the street in rural northern Maine, and then tried to quit cold turkey—a dangerous course, doctors say, that could have ended in miscarriage. The baby had seizures in utero as a result, and his mother, Tonya, turned to methadone treatment, with daily doses to keep her cravings and withdrawal symptoms at bay.

As prescription drug abuse ravages communities across the country, doctors are confronting an emerging challenge: newborns dependent on painkillers. While methadone may have saved Tonya's pregnancy, her son, Matthew, needed to be painstakingly weaned from it.

Infants like him may cry excessively and have stiff limbs, tremors, diarrhea and other problems that make their first days of life excruciating. Many have to stay in the hospital for weeks while they are weaned off the drugs, taxing neonatal units and driving the cost of their medical care into the tens of thousands of dollars.

Like the cocaine-exposed babies of the 1980s, those born dependent on prescription opiates—narcotics that contain opium or its derivatives—are entering a world in which little is known about the long-term effects on their development. Few doctors are even willing to treat pregnant opiate addicts, and there is no universally accepted standard of care for their babies, partly because of the difficulty of conducting research on pregnant women and newborns.

Those who do treat pregnant addicts face a jarring ethical quandary: they must weigh whether the harm inflicted by exposing a fetus to powerful drugs, albeit under medical supervision, is justifiable.

"I've had pharmacies that have just called back and said: 'This lady's pregnant. Why do you want me to fill this scrip? I can't do that,'" said Dr. Craig Smith, a family practitioner in Bridgton, Me. "But when you stop and think about what actually happens during withdrawal and how violent it can be, that would certainly be not in the baby's best interest."

Still, even doctors who advocate treating pregnant addicts have had moments of doubt.

"At first I was going, 'Gosh, what am I doing?'" said Dr. Thomas Meek, a primary care physician in Auburn, Me. "'Am I really helping these people?'"

There are no national figures that document the extent of the problem, but interviews with doctors, researchers, social workers and women who abused painkillers while pregnant suggest that it has grown rapidly, especially in rural regions, where officials say such abuse is most common.

In Maine, which has been especially plagued by prescription drug abuse, the number of newborns treated or watched for opiate withdrawal, known as neonatal abstinence syndrome, at the state's two largest hospitals climbed to 276 in 2010 from about 70 in 2005. Hospitals in states including Florida and Ohio reported similar increases, and experts said the numbers were probably higher since pregnant women are rarely tested for drug use and many mothers do not admit to abusing opiates.

Tonya, 24, said she was introduced to painkillers like Oxy-Contin, Percocet and Vicodin while working the overnight shift at an industrial bakery an hour from her home. Everyone—including co-workers, the boyfriend she met on the job and their manager—was taking pills, she said.

"It was a lot easier to get through life and have energy," Tonya said at Eastern Maine Medical Center here in January, holding Matthew a month after his birth. He was still being weaned off methadone.

Before she was pregnant, Tonya said, she quickly became addicted, spending all of her money on pills bought on the street. She and her boyfriend, Josh, needed to stave off withdrawal and get through the day, she said.

Now that she is in treatment, Tonya, who like most mothers interviewed for this article did not want her last name used, said her focus was on Matthew. "We put him in this situation," she said, "and we have to help him out of it."

How Little We Know

Rigorous studies on treating infant withdrawal are scarce, and the American Academy of Pediatrics has not published guidelines since 1998.

"It's really remarkable how little we know about the effect of prescription drugs and even nonprescription drugs on the fetus," said Dr. Nora D. Volkow, director of the National Institute for Drug Abuse. "There are real roadblocks in terms of helping us advance the field."

Dr. Mark L. Hudak, a neonatologist in Jacksonville, Fla., is helping to revise the pediatrics academy's guidelines. "There are commonalities, but it's not like you can go to a Website that says, 'This is what should be used by everyone,'" Dr. Hudak said. "No one knows what the best approach is."

Within states, every hospital that delivers babies exposed to painkillers may have its own approach. Eastern Maine treats affected newborns with tiny doses of methadone, while Maine Medical Center in Portland uses morphine combined with phenobarbital, a barbiturate that prevents seizures. Some hospitals are also experimenting with clonidine, a mild sedative that can relieve withdrawal symptoms.

There is growing debate over treatment for pregnant women addicted to prescription drugs, in light of concerns over the effects on their babies. Many are slowly weaned from their dependence with methadone, the standard of care for decades. Methadone, when taken in prescribed doses, keeps a steady amount of opiate in the body, preventing withdrawal and drug cravings that occur when levels dip. But it, too, can be addictive and cause nagging side effects like drowsiness. And for addiction treatment, it can be obtained only at federally licensed clinics where most users have to report for a daily dose.

A growing number of addicts are instead taking buprenorphine, another drug used to treat addiction that some studies suggest staves off drug cravings as effectively as methadone but is less likely to cause withdrawal in newborns. In rural areas of the nation, where methadone clinics are few, buprenorphine is considered a promising alternative because it can be prescribed by primary care doctors and taken at home.

But buprenorphine also appears not to work for some addicts.

Still, a study published in December in The New England Journal of Medicine showed that babies whose mothers had taken buprenorphine required significantly less medication after birth and less time in the hospital than did babies whose mothers were treated with methadone. But researchers cautioned that exposure to buprenorphine in utero can still cause withdrawal symptoms and that further study was needed.

"We don't want it misconstrued that buprenorphine is a miracle drug," said Hendrée E. Jones, a Johns Hopkins University researcher and the study's lead author.

Even less is known about longer-term effects on babies exposed to painkillers, though in a second leg of their study, Dr. Jones and her fellow researchers plan to follow the 131 babies in the cohort until they turn 3.

A recent study by the Centers for Disease Control and Prevention found that babies exposed to opiates in utero, in this case legally prescribed painkillers, had slightly higher rates of birth defects, including congenital heart defects, glaucoma and spina bifida.

Experts say that since many drug users also smoke and abuse alcohol, not to mention that they face extenuating circumstances like poverty, it is difficult to tease out the effect of each substance on their offspring.

"Most of the literature suggests consistently that the drug exposure itself is not the primary concern," said Karol Kaltenbach, a professor at Jefferson Medical College in Philadelphia who studies addiction in pregnant women. "It's the cumulative effect of the drug-using lifestyle—poverty, chaos in the home, domestic violence. All those things affect development."

Not all newborns exposed to opiates have severe enough withdrawal to need medicine; at Maine Medical Center since 2003, about 55 percent of babies exposed to buprenorphine and 80 percent of those exposed to methadone have needed treatment. But it is hard to predict which ones will need it: a newborn whose mother was on a high dose of either drug might need none, while a baby whose mother took a low dose might experience acute withdrawal.

Babies known to have been exposed to drugs are often kept in the hospital for at least five days because withdrawal symptoms usually do not set in immediately. Nurses examine them for a checklist of symptoms every few hours, assigning each baby a score that, if high enough, calls for treatment.

"They don't stop crying, they can't settle down, they don't relax," said Geraldine Tamborelli, nursing director of the birthing unit at Maine Medical Center, which in 2010 diagnosed opiate withdrawal in 121 newborns. "They're struggling in your arms instead of snuggling into you like a baby that is totally fine."

In the neonatal intensive care unit at Eastern Maine, Kendra, 3 days old, was sleeping in a dark, silent room one morning away from the bustle and bright lights that can be especially irritating to babies going through withdrawal. Nurses frequently crept in to observe her, though, and by the afternoon her limbs had stiffened and she was crying excessively and having tremors; it was enough to begin treatment.

"This seems to be ramping up fairly quickly for her," said Dr. Mark Brown, the hospital's chief of pediatrics, "so the decision was to start treatment more quickly."

On the pediatric ward, Matthew started fussing while his mother, Tonya, talked to reporters that afternoon in January; his cry had a strange, reedy pitch that nurses say is common to babies with his condition. The small dose of methadone he had received gave him gas and heartburn, for which he was given two stomach medications. He also was on clonazepam, a muscle relaxant and anti-anxiety drug that helped him metabolize the methadone more slowly.

Tonya said that at first she "didn't believe in" methadone treatment during pregnancy and that doctors had to persuade her that it would not hurt her fetus. She had experienced wrenching withdrawal when she stopped using painkillers after learning she was pregnant, she said, and the doctors had warned her that "when I was feeling that bad, he was feeling 1,000 times worse."

Tonya said that in a previous pregnancy, she quit using drugs altogether and miscarried a month later.

"That was the last thing I wanted to happen this time," she said.

Avoiding Addicts, and Liability

Treating drug-dependent mothers and babies is often lonely work, with little communication among the doctors who take it on. As Dr. Brown said, "My network for people who do this is really very small."

Dr. Mark R. Publicker, an addiction medicine specialist at Mercy Recovery Center in Westbrook, Me., is on a mission to get more of the state's doctors to treat pregnant prescription drug abusers and more hospitals to deliver their babies. Only a handful of doctors here treat pregnant women with buprenorphine, Dr. Publicker said, partly because they fear liability and do not want to deal with addicts.

The fact that most hospitals will not deliver the babies makes doctors even less likely to treat the women.

"It's mostly ignorance," Dr. Publicker said. "It's a concern that it's a risky proposition and that they're going to wind up with an ill baby."

In February, Dr. Smith persuaded Bridgton Hospital, which has only 25 beds, to deliver the babies of women on buprenorphine—a major victory, he said, because until then women in rural southwestern Maine had to drive an hour or more to Maine Medical to deliver.

Courtney, a patient of Dr. Smith's who discovered she was pregnant while in jail for stealing OxyContin from her landlord, said buprenorphine treatment seemed the best of her bleak options.

"I just don't want to mess up," she said.

Tonya, too, said she was determined to make things right for Matthew, who was five weeks old when she took him home to a trailer outside Bangor. He is off the methadone now and appears healthy, but Tonya still has to go to a methadone clinic in Bangor every day for her dose and resist the pressures to return to illicit drug use. Her boyfriend began using opiates as a young teenager, she said, and his father and grandmother abused OxyContin along with him.

"I'm proud that I changed my life," Tonya said. "But at the same time, when you see your child in pain and you know your child is in pain because of a life decision you made, it's the hardest thing in the world."

Critical Thinking

1. What are the physical symptoms newborns exhibit when they are born drug dependent?

2. What are the long-term effects on these drug-addicted newborns?

3. In what areas of the United States are these births most common? Why do you think that is so?

OxyContin Abuse Spreads from Appalachia across United States

BILL ESTEP, DORI HJALMARSON, AND HALIMAH ABDULLAH

Shawn Clusky has seen every side of Kentucky's battle with pain pill addiction over the past 10 years.

Clusky first tried OxyContin at age 17 with his school buddies, shortly after the high-powered narcotic painkiller went on the market. He was an occasional user and seller until about age 21, when he became fully addicted.

When he was 25, he got arrested at a Lexington gas station for selling $15,000 worth of pills. Clusky received probation, but was still using until he was sent to the WestCare rehabilitation center in eastern Kentucky.

He now works there as a counselor.

"A lot of times people believe a drug addict comes from poverty," he said. Not true. "Nine out of 10 of the guys I partied with came from millionaire families; their parents didn't use, they had good families."

Ten years ago, Kentucky learned it had a major drug problem.

OxyContin, a powerful prescription painkiller, was being abused at alarming rates in the Appalachian areas of eastern and southern Kentucky. A decade later, the level of pain pill abuse throughout the state and across the country is at epic levels, officials say.

Despite some successes—including several high-profile drug arrests across the country, increased treatment programs and the adoption of prescription drug monitoring programs in 43 states—the problem is now so entrenched that the cheap flights and van rentals drug traffickers use to travel from Florida to Kentucky and other states to peddle "hillbilly heroin" are nicknamed the "OxyContin Express."

The sheer scope of the problem is a key reason.

Kentucky often ranks at or near the top in U.S. measures of the level of prescription pain pill abuse.

According to a study by the Substance Abuse and Mental Health Services Administration, there was a fourfold increase nationally in treatment admissions for prescription pain pill abuse during the past decade. The increase spans every age, gender, race, ethnicity, education, employment level and region.

The study also shows a tripling of pain pill abuse among patients who needed treatment for dependence on opioids—prescription narcotics.

The rate of overdose-related deaths more than doubled among men and tripled among women in Kentucky from 2000 to 2009, according the state Cabinet for Health and Family Services.

Nearly every family in eastern Kentucky has been touched by prescription-drug addiction and death.

In the late 1990s, it was easier to find OxyContin—pure oxycodone with a time release—in Kentucky. The pill's maker, Purdue Pharma, was selling it "hand over fist" to doctors in eastern Kentucky, rich with coal mine injuries and government health care cards, Clusky said.

Clusky said a high school friend who worked at a pharmacy would steal the pills for his friends, so "It didn't cost any of us anything."

When many of the eastern Kentucky pill sources dried up after law enforcement raids in 2001, Clusky said, the trade moved to Mexico, where oxycodone could be bought for pennies over the counter and sold for as much as $100 a pill in the rural U.S. Clusky began making trips to Nuevo Laredo, driving back home with thousands of pills. By this time, heroin was his drug of choice. He often traveled to larger cities, where heroin could be found more cheaply.

"Five hundred dollars worth of heroin would last me a week. Five hundred dollars worth of oxy would last me one day," Clusky said.

Clusky lived part time in Ohio, sometimes making three doctor-shopping trips a day from Lexington to Dayton. He did a few stints in rehab, at one point trying methadone and Suboxone to treat his opiate addiction. It didn't work.

"I was as useless to society on methadone as I was on heroin," he said.

Nationally, prescription drug abuse has become a front-burner issue. There are more recovery options available now than a decade ago, but many states still don't have enough treatment available for all who need it.

Though Kentucky was no stranger to the abuse of prescription drugs long before federal regulators approved OxyContin in 1996, so many people in rural areas, including Appalachia, started abusing OxyContin in the late 1990s, it earned the nickname "hillbilly heroin."

Many chronic pain sufferers said the drug helped them immensely.

But abusers figured out they could crush a pill and snort or inject it, destroying the time-release function to get a whopping 12 hours' worth of the drug in one rush.

OxyContin quickly became the drug of choice in eastern Kentucky.

"You could leave a bag of cocaine on the street and no one would touch it, but leave one OxyContin in the back of an armored car and they'll blow it up to get at it," U.S. Attorney Joseph Famularo said at the February 2001 news conference announcing the first major roundup involving the drug.

By 2002, a quarter of the overdose deaths in the nation linked to OxyContin were in eastern Kentucky, authorities said.

Police, regulators and elected officials charged that Purdue Pharma, the Connecticut-based maker of OxyContin, marketed the drug too aggressively, feeding an oversupply and diversion into the illicit market.

Purdue Pharma denied that, but the company and three top officials ultimately pleaded guilty in 2007 to misleading the public about the drug's risk of addiction and paid $634.5 million in fines.

Authorities had begun pushing back long before that against growing abuse of OxyContin and other prescription drugs, but addicts and traffickers kept finding ways to get pills.

"Law enforcement adjusts, and the criminals adjust," said Frank Rapier, the head of the Appalachia High Intensity Drug Trafficking Area, which includes 68 counties in Kentucky, Tennessee and West Virginia.

Kentucky Rep. Hal Rogers' voice grows tight with frustration whenever he talks about the prescription drug epidemic that's gripped Appalachia for more than a decade.

"Crook doctors operating these pill mills" in Florida are running rampant and are fueling the flow of illegally obtained prescription drugs to states such as Kentucky, Rogers, the chairman of the House Appropriations Committee, told Attorney General Eric Holder during a recent hearing. "My people are dying."

The White House "has got to act," Rogers said. "We've got more people dying of prescription drug overdoses than car accidents."

The Obama administration counters that it's the first to publicly call the prescription drug abuse problem an epidemic, has stepped up drug arrests and has directed millions in funding to state monitoring programs. The administration says it also has focused efforts on the Appalachia High Intensity Drug Trafficking Area, which includes 68 counties in Kentucky, Tennessee and West Virginia.

In the meantime, Rogers hopes legislation he's co-sponsoring with Rep. Vern Buchanan, a Florida Republican, calling for a tougher federal crackdown on so-called "pill mills"—pain clinics that dispense prescription drugs—will help stem the flow of drugs across state lines.

The measure includes provisions to support state-based prescription drug monitoring programs; to use the money from seized illicit operations for drug treatment; to strengthen prescription standards for certain addictive pain drugs; and to toughen prison terms and fines for pill mill operators.

The bill comes on the heels of Florida Republican Gov. Rick Scott's calls to repeal a monitoring program modeled after Kentucky's and designed to stem interstate prescription drug trafficking—a move lawmakers from Florida and Kentucky and White House officials oppose.

Scott has cited concerns about costs and patient privacy rights. He's turned down a $1 million donation by Purdue Pharma to help pay for a prescription database.

(Estep and Hjalmarson, of the Lexington Herald-Leader, reported from Lexington. Abdullah reported from Washington.)

Critical Thinking

1. What kind of drug is oxycontin? Why is it prescribed?

2. Nationally, how much did oxycontin use increase between 2000–2009?

3. What state ranks at or near the top for prescription painkiller abuse?

From *McClatchy Tribune Information Services*, March 13, 2011. Copyright © 2011 by McClatchy Company–MCT. Reprinted by permission.

Route of Administration for Illicit Prescription Opioids: A Comparison of Rural and Urban Drug Users

April M. YOUNG, JENNIFER R. HAVENS, AND CARL G. LEUKEFELD

Background

There has been a meteoric rise in the rates of illicit prescription opioid use and dependence in the US in recent years.[1, 2] According to the National Survey on Drug Use and Health, prescription opioid nonmedical use has quadrupled in the last 20 years[3] and, among new initiates to illicit drug use, has surpassed marijuana use.[4] Further, it appears that nonmedical prescription opioid use is particularly problematic in rural areas encompassing Appalachian Kentucky, Virginia and West Virginia.[5, 6] The health consequences of nonmedical prescription opioid use can be severe; long-term use can lead to physical dependence and addiction, and, at high-doses, the drugs can cause severe respiratory distress and death.[7] The motives for nonmedical use of prescription drugs are various, but studies have identified one of the most common to be individuals' desire to relieve physical pain.[8] Some evidence suggests that chronic nonmalignant pain may be greater in rural areas of the US,[9] but without further research, proposed links between the rural burden of nonmalignant pain and nonmedical prescription opioid use are largely speculative. The growing burden of nonmedical prescription drug use in America and its unique manifestations in rural areas has warranted more research. For example, differences between characteristics of rural and urban prescription opioid use have been examined using data from signal detection systems,[10] methadone maintenance treatment enrollees,[11] probationers,[12] and drug-related medical examiner cases.[13] However, to our knowledge, there are no reports on rural-urban differences in ways in which individuals are administering prescription opioids.

Route of drug administration has important implications on users' health outcomes, including risk of dependence, susceptibility to infection, and experience of route-specific health complications.[14] Injection drug users, in particular, are at a heightened risk for HIV and hepatitis C infection,[15-18] drug dependence,[19-21] and overdose.[22] Individual-level risk factors related to transitioning to injection drug use (IDU) from other routes of administration include unemployment,[23] insecure income source,[24] homelessness,[23, 25-27] school dropout,[24] and early-onset substance abuse.[28] The extent of individuals' previous substance use[23, 25] and frequency of substance use[26, 27] have also been identified as correlates. A number of social and ecological factors also play a role in drug users' risk for transitioning to injection. Perceived social support or tolerance for injection,[23, 26] social pressure,[29] and geographic proximity to dealers[30] and other IDUs,[31] as well as having friend,[25] sex partner,[23, 32] or family member who engages in IDU, are also associated with transitioning to injection. Drug markets, drug availability,[30, 34] and social norms surrounding typical route of administration, collectively referred to as "site ecology" can also play a role.[27] Temporal trends in transitions to injection sometimes precipitated by changes in drug availability have also been identified.[35, 36] Non-injection routes of administration are typically more expensive in terms of 'bang per buck', thus transitioning to IDU can also entail economic motivation.[35] Previous studies have shown that drug price[30] and cost-effectiveness[27, 29] can play a role in determining patterns in routes of administration as well.

Studies suggest that nonmedical prescription opioid use can involve various routes of administration, the choice of which can be influenced by demographic factors such as gender and age.[37-4] However, the influence of rurality on routes of administration for nonmedical prescription opioid use has not been explored. The purpose of this study was to describe rural-urban differences in route of administration for: buprenorphine, fentanyl, hydrocodone, hydromorphone, methadone, morphine, OxyContin®, and oxycodone.

Methods

A total of 212 participants entered the study in two Kentucky counties, one a non-metropolitan Appalachian county and the other in a metropolitan area of the state's Bluegrass region.[42] The rural county has been designated by the Appalachian Regional Commission as economically depressed.[43] Both counties are predominantly white (97.3% and 77.4%, respectively).[44]

Participants were recruited using snowball sampling, which is most commonly used to access hidden populations such as drug users.[45] In the current study, participants who were initially recruited with flyers or by community key informants who agreed participate in the study were asked to refer additional participants, who in turn were asked to refer additional participants and so on. Participants were eligible if they reported having used any prescription opioid nonmedically in the prior 30 days and OxyContin® at least once in the prior three years (either medically or non-medically). The purposive sampling of OxyContin® users is a product of the purpose of the overall goal of the study, which was to compare outcomes of OxyContin® use among rural and urban drug users.

Data were collected between October 2008 and August 2009. Interviewers were three research assistants who resided in the target communities. After determining eligibility and obtaining informed consent, an interviewer-administered questionnaire was utilized to gather information on socio-demographic, medical, family/social characteristics, and self-reported behaviors. The MINI International Neuropsychiatric Interview, version 5.0[46] was used to measure the following psychiatric disorders: major depressive disorder (MDD), generalized anxiety disorder (GAD), post-traumatic stress disorder (PTSD) and antisocial personality disorder (ASPD). Drug problem severity was examined using a composite score from the Addiction Severity Index (ASI).[47] For the purposes of the current study, participants were also asked to indicate lifetime and recent (past 30 day) use of the following substances for the purposes of getting high: buprenorphine (e.g., Subutex®, Suboxone®), fentanyl patch, hydrocodone (e.g., Norco®, Vicodin®, Lorcet®, Lortab®), hydromorphone (Dilaudid®), methadone tablets, morphine (e.g., MSContin®, Kadian®, Avinza®), OxyContin® (tablets and generic), and other oxycodone (e.g., Tylox®, Percocet®, Percodan®). For each specific drug for which participants reported lifetime use, they were

asked about the frequency of using the following routes of administration: swallowing (including swallowing whole and chewing to swallow), snorting, and injecting. Participants were interviewed in locations such as a library or other public places and were compensated $50 for their time. The study was approved by the University of Kentucky Institutional Review Board.

Analysis

The dependent variable of interest was substance-specific route of administration (i.e. for each substance, there were three dichotomous outcomes defined by lifetime engagement in swallowing, injecting, and/or snorting as a route of administration). Categorical and continuous demographic characteristics of rural and urban drug users were compared using chi-square tests and Mann-Whitney U-tests, respectively. Logistic regression analysis was used to examine differences between rural and urban participants' route of administration, adjusting for age, gender, and race. The statistical software SPSS Version 17.0 (SPSS Inc., Chicago, IL) was used to conduct data analysis.

Results
Description of the Sample

Descriptive characteristics of the sample (n = 212) are displayed in Table 1. Rural drug users comprised 47.6% (n = 101) of the sample. The median age of all participants was 37 years and ranged

Table 1 Comparison of Demographic Characteristics for Rural (n = 101) and Urban (n = 111) Drug Users

Descriptive characteristics	Rural n (%)	Urban n (%)	Total n (%)	P value
Male	57 (58.2)	56 (50.9)	113 (54.3)	0.294
White	96 (95.0)	11 (9.9)	107 (50.5)	**< 0.001**
Age-median (IQR)	33 (27-43)	42 (30-49)	37 (29-47)	**0.004**
Years in county-median (IQR)	31.0 (25-37)	30.5 (16.5-43)	31.0 (23-41)	0.467
Years of formal education-median (IQR)	12.0 (9-12)	12 (12-14)	12.0 (10-12.5)	**< 0.001**
Recent legal income*-median (IQR)	$600 (300-800)	$720.50 (468-1289)	$665 (400-1020)	**0.003**
Employed in Past 30 Days	43 (42.6)	61 (55.0)	104 (49.1)	0.072
Receives Pension for Disability	21 (20.8)	21 (18.9)	42 (19.8)	0.733
Married/Remarried	29 (28.7)	16 (14.4)	45 (21.2)	**0.011**
Non-religious	64 (63.4)	30 (27.0)	94 (44.3)	**< 0.001**
Uninsured	57 (56.4)	68 (61.3)	125 (59.0)	0.488
Has Chronic Medical Problem	57 (56.4)	49 (44.1)	106 (50.0)	0.074
Prescribed Medication for Physical Problem	36 (35.6)	58 (52.3)	94 (44.3)	**0.015**
Ever Treated for Drug/Alcohol Problem	49 (48.5)	48 (43.2)	97 (45.8)	0.442
ASI Composite Drug Use Score-median (IQR)	0.26 (0.14-0.34)	0.08 (0.03-0.17)	0.16 (0.06-0.28)	**< 0.001**

(continued)

Table 1 Comparison of Demographic Characteristics for Rural (n = 101) and Urban (n = 111) Drug Users (Continued)

Descriptive characteristics	Rural n (%)	Urban n (%)	Total n (%)	P value
Psychiatric characteristics				
Major Depressive Disorder	47 (46.5)	28 (25.2)	75 (35.4)	**0.001**
Generalized Anxiety Disorder	41 (40.6)	38 (34.2)	79 (37.3)	0.339
Post-traumatic Stress Disorder	20 (19.8)	13 (11.7)	33 (15.6)	0.105
Anti-social Personality Disorder	32 (31.7)	31 (27.9)	63 (29.7)	0.550

IQR-Interquartile range, ASI-Addiction Severity Index[47]

*Income in past 30 days from employment, unemployment compensation, welfare, pension, benefits, social security, mate, family, friends, or child support

Young et al. Harm Reduction Journal 2010 7:24 doi:10.1186/1477-7517-7-24

from 20 to 69. The majority of participants were men (54%) and 51% were non-Hispanic white. The median number of years of formal education completed was 12. Just under half (49%) had been employed in the past 30 days and 20% were receiving pension for disability. The median monthly legal income was $665 and most participants (59%) did not have health insurance. Just over 21% were married or remarried, 34% were widowed, separated, or divorced, and 45% had never been married. Rural participants were significantly younger, had fewer years of formal education, earned less income than urban participants, and had significantly higher drug problem severity scores on the Addiction Severity Index. Significantly more rural participants were non-Hispanic white, non-religious, and married or remarried than were urban participants.

Approximately half (46%) of participants had ever enrolled in drug or alcohol treatment. Fifty percent of the sample reported that they had a chronic medical problem and 44% were regularly takin[g] prescribed medication for a physical problem. Significantly mor[e] urban participants were regularly taking prescribed medication fo[r] a physical problem than rural participants. Approximately 35% o[f] participants met the DSM-IV criteria for major depressive diso[r]der (MDD), 37% for generalized anxiety disorder (GAD), 16[%] for post-traumatic stress disorder (PTSD), and 30% for anti-soci[al] personality disorder (ASPD). Significantly more rural participan[ts] met criteria for MDD than did urban participants (Table 1).

Drug Use and Route of Administration

Table 2 describes rural and urban nonmedical drug use and th[e] routes of drug administration for each of the drugs. No urban pa[r]ticipants reported lifetime use of buprenorphine or of the fentan[yl]

Table 2 Age-, Gender-, and Race-Adjusted Comparisons for Route of Drug Administration among Rural (n = 101) and Urban (n = 111) Drug Users

	Rural %	Urban %	Adjusted* P-values
Buprenorphine (sublingual tablets)	50.5	0	---
Swallowing	31.7	0	---
Snorting	26.7	0	---
Injecting	3.0	0	---
Fentanyl (patch)	35.6	0	---
Swallowing	25.7	0	---
Snorting	1.0	0	---
Injecting	14.9	0	---
Hydrocodone (tablets)	90.1	91.9	0.408
Swallowing	68.3	91.9	**0.046**
Snorting	74.3	6.3	**< 0.001**
Injecting	0	0	---
Hydromorphone (all formulations)	32.7	4.6	**0.001**
Swallowing	6.9	4.5	0.524
Snorting	5.9	0.9	0.472
Injecting	21.8	0	---
Methadone (tablets)	77.2	3.6	**< 0.001**

(continue[d])

Table 2 Age-, Gender-, and Race-Adjusted Comparisons for Route of Drug Administration among Rural (n = 101) and Urban (n = 111) Drug Users (*Continued*)

	Rural	Urban	Adjusted[*]
Swallowing	27.7	3.6	0.083
Snorting	64.4	0	---
Injecting	1.0	0	---
Morphine (all formulations)	53.5	4.6	**0.007**
Swallowing	14.9	3.6	0.652
Snorting	17.8	0.9	0.547
Injecting	33.7	0	---
OxyContin® (generic/tablets)	86.1	23.6	**0.002**
Swallowing	25.7	22.5	0.442
Snorting	68.3	3.6	**< 0.001**
Injecting	44.6	0	---
Other Oxycodone[**] (tablets)	83.2	50.0	0.374
Swallowing	31.7	47.7	**0.026**
Snorting	68.3	1.8	**< 0.001**
Injecting	3.0	0	---

p-values adjusting for age, race, and gender
Includes, for example, Tylox®, Percocet®, and Percodan®

Young et al. Harm Reduction Journal 2010 **7**:24 doi:10.1186/1477-7517-7-24

patch. Among rural participants, however, 51% reported buprenorphine use and 37% reported fentanyl use, both of which were most commonly administered by swallowing. Interestingly, 15% of rural participants reported injecting fentanyl patch contents. Preferred route of administration varied by substance and by rural/urban status. Among urban participants, swallowing was the most common route of administration across all substances. In age-, race-, and gender-adjusted analyses, urban participants had significantly higher odds of reporting swallowing hydrocodone and oxycodone than did rural participants. Among rural participants, the preferred route of administration varied according to substance. For hydrocodone, methadone, OxyContin®, and oxycodone, snorting was the most frequent route of administration. Significantly more rural participants reported snorting hydrocodone, OxyContin®, and oxycodone than did urban participants, after adjustment for age, race, and gender. For hydromorphone and morphine use among rural drug users, injection was most common. Notably, among rural participants, 67% of hydromorphone users and 63% of morphine users had administered the drugs by injection.

Conclusions

This study offers valuable insight into the intricacies of nonmedical rural opioid use in particular. These findings suggest that alternative routes of administration are common among rural drug users, a phenomenon which is likely related to drug problem severity. This finding has implications for rural substance abuse treatment as well as prevention of transition from oral to other routes of use such as snorting and/or injection. The presence of alternative routes of administration among rural drug users also indicates a need for the implementation of harm reduction interventions within this population.

Competing Interests

This study is funded by Purdue Pharma L.P. Points-of-view and opinions expressed in this article do not necessarily represent those of Purdue Pharma but represent the opinions of the authors.

Authors' Contributions

AY performed the statistical analysis and drafted the manuscript. All authors read and approved the final manuscript.

Acknowledgments

This study is funded by Purdue Pharma L.P.

References

1. Miller N, Greenfeld A: Patient characteristics and risks factors for development of dependence on hydrocodone and oxycodone. *Am J Ther* 2004, 11:26–32.
2. Woolf C, Hashmi M: Use and abuse of opioid analgesics: Potential methods to prevent and deter non-medical consumption of prescription opioids. *Curr Opin Investig Drugs* 2004, 6:61–66.
3. Substance Abuse and Mental Health Services Administration: Nonmedical use of prescription pain relievers. In *The NSDUH Report*. Rockville, MD; Office of Applied Studies; 2004.
4. Substance Abuse and Mental Health Services Administration: *Results from the 2006 National Survey on Drug Use and Health*. Rockville, MD: Office of Applied Studies; 2007.
5. Drug Enforcement Administration. OxyContin®: Pharmaceutical Division: Drug Intelligence Brief. Arlington, VA 2002.

6. Hutchinson A: OxyContin Testimony. *House Committee on Appropriations, Commerce, Justice, State, and Judiciary* 2001.

7. National Institute of Drug Abuse: *Research Report Series: Prescription Drugs Abuse and Addiction (NIH Pub No 05-4881).* Bethesda, MD: National Institute of Drug Abuse; 2005.

8. McCabe SE, Cranford JA, Boyd CJ, Teter CJ: Motives, diversion and routes of administration associated with nonmedical use of prescription opioids. *Addict Behav* 2007, 32(3):562–575.

9. Bouhassira D, Lantéri-Minet M, Attal N, Laurent B, Touboul C: Prevalence of chronic pain with neuropathic characteristics in the general population. *Pain* 2008, 136(3):380–387.

10. Cicero TJ, Surratt H, Inciardi JA, Munoz A: Relationship between therapeutic use and abuse of opioid analgesics in rural, suburban, and urban locations in the United States. *Pharmacoepidemiol Drug Saf* 2007, 16:827–840.

11. Rosenblum A, Parrino M, Schnoll SH, Fong C, Maxwell C, Cleland CM, Magura S, Haddox JD: Prescription opioid abuse among enrollees into methadone maintenance treatment. *Drug Alcohol Depend* 2007, 90:64–71.

12. Havens JR, Oser CB, Leukefeld CG, Webster JM, Martin SS, O'Connell DJ, Surratt HL, Inciardi JA: Differences in prevalence of prescription opiate misuse among rural and urban probationers. *Am J Drug Alcohol Abuse* 2007, 33:309–317.

13. Wunsch MJ, Nakamoto K, Behonick G, Massello W: Opioid deaths in rural Virginia: A description of the high prevalence of accidental fatalities involving prescribed medications. *Am J Addict* 2009, 18:5–14.

14. Strang J, Bearn J, Farrell M, Finch E, Gossop M, Griffiths P, Marsden J, Wolff K: Route of drug use and its implications for drug effect, risk of dependence and health consequences. *Drug Alcohol Rev* 1998, 17:197–211.

15. Xian X, Jun L, Jianling B, Rongbin Y: Epidemiology of hepatitis C virus infection among injection drug users in China: Systematic review and meta-analysis. *Public Health* 2008, 122:990–1003.

16. Chitwood DD, Comerford M, Sanchez JS: Prevalence and risk factors for HIV among sniffers, short-Term Injectors, and long-term injectors of heroin. *J Psychoactive Drugs* 2003, 35:445–453. PubMed Abstract

17. Nelson KE, Galai N, Safaeian M, Strathdee SA, Celentano DD, Vlahov D: Temporal trends in the incidence of human immunodeficiency virus infection and risk behavior among injection drug users in Baltimore, Maryland, 1988–1998. *Am J Epidemiol* 2002, 156:641–653.

18. Alter MJ: Prevention of spread of hepatitis C. *Hepatology* 2002, 36:S93–S98.

19. Gossop M, Griffiths P, Powis B, Strang J: Severity of dependence and route of administration of heroin, cocaine and amphetamines. *Br J Addict* 1992, 87:1527–1536.

20. Gossop M, Griffiths P, Powis B, Strang J: Cocaine: Patterns of use, route of administration, and severity of dependence. *Br J Psychiatry* 1994, 164:660–664.

21. Strang J, Griffiths P, Powis B, Gossop M: Heroin chasers and heroin injectors: Differences observed in a community sample in London, UK. *Am J Addict* 1999, 8:148–160.

22. Gossop M, Griffiths P: Frequency of non-fatal heroin overdose: Survey of heroin users recruited in non-clinical settings. *Br Med J* 1996, 313:402–402.

23. Neaigus A, Miller M, Friedman SR, Hagen DL, Sifaneck SJ, Ildefonso G, des Jarlais DC: Potential risk factors for the transition to injecting among non-injecting heroin users: A comparison of former injectors and never injectors. *Addiction* 2001, 96:847–860.

24. Abelson J, Treloar C, Crawford J, Kippax S, van Beek I, Howard J: Some characteristics of early-onset injection drug users prior to and at the time of their first injection. *Addiction* 2006, 101:548–555.

25. Roy E, Haley N, Leclerc P, Cédras L, Blais L, Boivin JF: Drug injection among street youths in Montreal: Predictors of initiation. *J Urban Health* 2003, 80:92–105.

26. Neaigus A, Gyarmathy A, Miller M, Frajzyngier VM, Friedman SR, des Jarlais DC: Transitions to injecting drug use among noninjecting heroin users. *J Acquir Immune Defic Syndr* 2006, 41(4):493–503.

27. Fischer B, Manzoni P, Rehm JR: Comparing injecting and non-injecting illicit opioid users in a multisite canadian sample (OPICAN Cohort). *Eur Addict Res* 2006, 12:230–239.

28. Fuller CM, Vlahov D, Ompad DC, Shah N, Arrio A, Strathdee SA: High-risk behaviors associated with transition from illicit non-injection to injection drug use among adolescent and young adult drug users: A case-control study. *Drug Alcohol Depend* 2002, 66:189.

29. Bravo MJ, Barrio G, de la Fuente L, Royuela L, Domingo L, Silva T: Reasons for selecting an initial route of heroin administration and for subsequent transitions during a severe HIV epidemic. *Addiction* 2003, 98(6):749–760.

30. Firestone M, Fischer B: A qualitative exploration of prescription opioid injection among street-based drug users in Toronto: Behaviours, preferences and drug availability. *Harm Reduct J* 2008, 5:30. PubMed Abstract

31. Sherman SG, Smith L, Laney G, Strathdee SA: Social influences on the transition to injection drug use among young heroin sniffers: A qualitative analysis. *Int J Drug Policy* 2002, 13:113.

32. Van Ameijden EJ, Van Den Hoek JA, Hartgers C, Coutinho RA: Risk factors for the transition from noninjection to injection drug use and accompanying AIDS risk behavior in a cohort of drug users. *Am J Epidemiol* 1994, 139:1153–1163. PubMed Abstract

33. Strang J, Griffiths P, Gossop M: Heroin in the United Kingdom: Different forms, different origins, and the relationship to different routes of administration. *Drug Alcohol Rev* 1997, 16:329–337.

34. Cicero TJ, Surratt H, Inciardi JA, Munoz A: Relationship between therapeutic use and abuse of opioid analgesics in rural, suburban, and urban locations in the United States. *Pharmacoepidemiol Drug Saf* 2007, 16:827–840.

35. Strang J, Des Jarlais DC, Griffiths P, Gossop M: The study of transitions in the route of drug use: The route from one route to another. *Br J Addict* 1992, 87:473–483.

36. De la Fuente L, Saavedra P, Barrio G, Royuela L, Vicente J: Temporal and geographic variations in the characteristics of heroin seized in Spain and their relation with the route of administration. Spanish Group for the Study of the Purity of Seized Drugs. *Drug Alcohol Depend* 1996, 40:185–194.

37. Hakansson A, Medvedeo A, Andersson M, Berglund M: Buprenorphine misuse among heroin and amphetamine users i malmo, sweden: Purpose of misuse and route of administration *Eur Addict Res* 2007, 13:207–215.

38. Liappas IA, Dimopoulos NP, Mellos E, Gitsa OE, Liappas AI, Rabavilas AD: Oral transmucosal abuse of transdermal fentanyl. *J Psychopharmacol* 2004, 18:277–280.

39. Passik SD, Hays L, Eisner N, Kirsh KL: Psychiatric and pain characteristics of prescription drug abusers entering drug rehabilitation. *J Pain Palliat Car Pharmacother* 2006, 20:5–1

40. Back SE, Payne RA, Waldrop AE, Smith A, Reeves S, Brady KT: Prescription opioid aberrant behaviors: A pilot study of se differences. *Clin J Pain* 2009, 25:477–484.

41. Green TC, Grimes Serrano JM, Licari A, Budman SH, Butler SF: Women who abuse prescription opioids: Findings from the Addiction Severity Index-Multimedia Version® Connect prescription opioid database. *Drug Alcohol Depend* 2009, 103:65–73.

42. United States Department of Agriculture: *2003 Rural-Urban Continuum Codes for Kentucky.* United States Department of Agriculture; 2003. August 18, 2003 edition

43. County Economic Status, Fiscal Year 2010: Appalachian Kentucky [http://www.arc.gov/reports/region_report .asp?FIPS=21999&REPORT_ID=33] *webcite*

44. United States Census Bureau: United States Census 2000. 2000.

45. Barendregt C, Van der Poel A, Van de Mheen D: Tracing selection effects in three non-probability samples. *Eur Addict Res* 2005, 11:124–131.

46. Sheehan DV, Lecrubier Y, Sheehan KH, Amorim P, Janavs J, Weiller E, Hergueta T, Baker R, Dunbar GC: The Mini-International Neuropsychiatric Interview (M.I.N.I.): The development and validation of a structured diagnostic psychiatric interview for DSM-IV and ICD-10. *J Clin Psychiatry* 1998, 59(Suppl):22–33. PubMed Abstract

47. McLellan AT, Kushner H, Metzger D, Peters R, Smith I, Grissom G, Pettinati H, Argeriou M: The Fifth Edition of the Addiction Severity Index. *J Subst Abuse Treat* 1992, 9:199–213.

48. McCabe SE, Boyd CJ, Teter CJ: Subtypes of nonmedical prescription drug misuse. *Drug Alcohol Depend* 2009, 102:63–70.

49. Barrau K, Thirion X, Micallef Jl, Chuniaud-Louche C, Bellemin Ba, San Marco JL: Comparison of methadone and high dosage buprenorphine users in French care centres. *Addiction* 2001, 96:1433–1441.

50. Obadia Y, Perrin V, Feroni I, Vlahov D, Moatti J-P: Injecting misuse of buprenorphine among French drug users. *Addiction* 2001, 96:267–272.

51. Vidal-Trecan Gl, Varescon I, Nabet N, Boissonnas A: Intravenous use of prescribed sublingual buprenorphine tablets by drug users receiving maintenance therapy in France. *Drug Alcohol Depend* 2003, 69:175.

52. Strang J: Abuse of buprenorphine (Temgesic) by snorting. *BMJ (Clin Res Ed)* 1991, 302:969–969.

53. National Drug Intelligence Center: Intelligence Bulletin: Buprenorphine: Potential for Abuse. 2004.

54. Arvanitis ML, Satonik RC: Transdermal fentanyl abuse and misuse. *Am J Emerg Med* 2002, 20:58–59.

55. Martin TL, Woodall KL, McLellan BA: Fentanyl-related deaths in Ontario, Canada: Toxicological findings and circumstances of death in 112 cases (2002–2004). *J Anal Toxicol* 2006, 30:603–610.

56. Woodall KL, Martin TL, McLellan BA: Oral abuse of fentanyl patches (Duragesic®): Seven Case Reports. *J Forensic Sci* 2008, 53:222–225.

57. Streisand JB, Varvel JR, Stanski DR, Le Maire L, Ashburn MA, Hague BI, Tarver SD, Stanley TH: Absorption and bioavailability of oral transmucosal fentanyl citrate. *Anesthesiology* 1991, 75:223–229.

58. Lilleng PK, Mehlum LI, Bachs L, Morild I: Deaths after intravenous misuse of transdermal fentanyl. *J Forensic Sci* 2004, 49:1364–1366.

59. Tharp AM, Winecker RE, Winston DC: Fatal intravenous fentanyl abuse: four cases involving extraction of fentanyl from transdermal patches. *Am J Forensic Med Pathol* 2004, 25:178–181.

60. Kuhlman JJ Jr, McCaulley R, Valouch TJ, Behonick GS: Fentanyl use, misuse, and abuse: A summary of 23 postmortem cases. *J Anal Toxicol* 2003, 27:499–504.

61. Reeves MD, Ginifer CJ: Fatal intravenous misuse of transdermal fentanyl. *Med J Aust* 2002, 177:552–553.

62. Carr BG, Caplan JM, Pryor JP, Branas CC: A meta-analysis of prehospital care times for trauma. *Prehosp Emerg Care* 2006, 10:198–206.

63. MacDonald M, Crofts N, Kaldor J: Transmission of hepatitis C virus: rates, routes, and cofactors. *Epidemiol Rev* 1996, 18:137–148.

64. van den Hoek JA, van Haastrecht HJ, Goudsmit J, de Wolf F, Coutinho RA: Prevalence, incidence, and risk factors of hepatitis C virus infection among drug users in Amsterdam. *J Infect Dis* 1990, 162:823–826. PubMed Abstract

65. Mathers BM, Degenhardt L, Phillips B, Wiessing L, Hickman M, Strathdee SA, Wodak A, Panda S, Tyndall M, Toufik A, Mattick RP: Global epidemiology of injecting drug use and HIV among people who inject drugs: A systematic review. *Lancet* 2008, 372:1733–1745.

66. Aaron S, McMahon JM, Milano D, Torres L, Clatts M, Tortu S, Mildvan D, Simm M: Intranasal transmission of Hepatitis C virus: Virological and clinical evidence. *Clin Infect Dis* 2008, 47:931–934.

67. McMahon JM, Simm M, Milano D, Clatts M: Detection of hepatitis C virus in the nasal secretions of an intranasal drug-user. *Ann Clin Microbiol Antimicrob* 2004, 3:6–6. PubMed Abstract

68. Hall AJ, Logan JE, Toblin RL, Kaplan JA, Kraner JC, Bixler D, Crosby AE, Paulozzi LJ: Patterns of abuse among unintentional pharmaceutical overdose fatalities. *JAMA* 2008, 300(22):2613–20.

69. National Institute of Drug Abuse: InfoFacts: Prescription and over-the-counter medications. [http://www.nida.nih.gov/PDF /Infofacts/PainMed09.pdf] *webcite* Bethesda, MD: National Institute of Drug Abuse; 2009. Accessed October 8, 2010

Critical Thinking

1. Why is route of administration a critical consideration in users' outcomes?

2. Explain why route of administration varied according to rural/urban status of the user.

UNIT 6

Creating and Sustaining Effective Drug Control Policy

Unit Selections

Learning Outcomes

After reading this Unit, you should be able to:

- Explain how drug policy shapes public opinion of drug-related events.

- Explain the roles the media play in shaping drug policy.

- Discuss the problems and issues surrounding the legal use of alcohol different from those surrounding the illegal use of heroin, cocaine, or methamphetamines.

- Describe your opinions on the legalization of medical marijuana, and whether you believe its legalization will result in its being overprescribed.

- Determine to what degree you would argue that the current problems with drug abuse exist because of current drug policies or spite of them.

Student Website

www.mhhe.com/cls

Internet References

Drug Policy Alliance
www.drugpolicy.org

DrugText
www.drugtext.org

Effective Drug Policy: Why Journey's End Is Legalisations
www.drugscope.org.uk/wip/23/pdfs/journey.pdf

Harm Reduction Coalition
www.harmreduction.org

The Higher Education Center for Alcohol and Other Drug Prevention
www.edc.org/hec/pubs/policy.htm

The National Organization on Fetal Alcohol Syndrome (NOFAS)
www.nofas.org

National NORML Homepage
www.norml.org

Transform Drug Policy Foundation
www.tdpf.org.uk

he drug problem consistently competes with all major public
·licy issues, including the wars in Iraq and Afghanistan, the
·onomy, education, and foreign policy. Drug abuse is a seri-
·s national medical issue with profound social and legal con-
·quences. Formulating and implementing effective drug control
·licy is a troublesome task. Some would argue that the conse-
·ences of policy failures have been worse than the problems
·at the policies were attempting to address. Others would argue
·at although the world of shaping drug policy is an imperfect
·e, the process has worked generally as well as could be
·pected. The majority of Americans believe that failures and
·eakdowns in the fight against drug abuse have occurred in
·ite of various drug policies, not because of them. Although
·e last few years have produced softening attitudes and alter-
·tives for adjudicating cases of simple possession and use,
·e get-tough, stay-tough enforcement policies directed at ille-
·l drug trafficking remain firmly in place and widely supported.
·licy formulation is not a process of aimless wandering.

Various levels of government have responsibility for respond-
·g to problems of drug abuse. At the center of most policy
·bate is the premise that the manufacture, possession, use,
·d distribution of psychoactive drugs without government
·thorization is illegal. The federal posture of prohibition is an
·portant emphasis on state and local policymaking. Federal
·ug policy is, however, significantly linked to state-by-state
·ta, which suggests that illicit drug, alcohol, and tobacco use
·ry substantially among states and regions. The current fed-
·al drug strategy began in 2001 and set the goals of reduc-
·g drug use by young persons by 25 percent over five years.
·2008, President Bush announced that drug use by the pop-
·ation in this age group was down by 24 percent. President
·ama has continued the basic strategic constructs of the Bush
·licy. Core priorities of the overall plan continue to be to stop
·ug use before it starts, heal America's drug users, and disrupt
·e illegal market. These three core goals are re-enforced by
·jectives outlined in a policy statement produced by the White
·use Office of Drug Control Policy. All three goals reflect bud-
·t expenditures related to meeting goals of the overall policy.
·e current drug control policy, in terms of budget allocations,
·ntinues to provide for over $1.5 billion to prevent use before it
·rts, largely through education campaigns, which encourage
·cultural shift away from drugs, and more than $3.4 billion to
·al America's users. Each year produces modifications to the
·an as a result of analysis of trends and strategy impacts. Allo-
·tions for interdiction, largely a result of the attempt to secure
·e borders and frustrate alliances between drug traffickers and
·rorists, remain the most significant component of the budget
·$10 billion dollars.

One exception to prevailing views that generally support drug
·ohibition is the softening of attitudes regarding criminal sanc-
·ns that historically applied to cases of simple possession and
·e of drugs. There is much public consensus that incarcerating
·rsons for these offenses is unjustified unless they are related
·other criminal conduct. The federal funding of drug court pro-
·ams remains a priority with more than $38 million dedicated
·state and local operation. Drug courts provide alternatives to

Aaron Roeth Photography

incarceration by using the coercive power of the court to force
abstinence and alter behavior through a process of escalating
sanctions, mandatory drug testing, and outpatient programs.
Successful rehabilitation accompanies the re-entry to society
as a citizen, not a felon. The drug court program exists as one
important example of policy directed at treating users and deterring them from further involvement in the criminal justice system.
Drug courts are now in place in all 50 states.

The majority of Americans express the view that legalizing,
and in some cases even decriminalizing, dangerous drugs is
a bad idea. The fear of increased crime, increased drug use,
and the potential threat to children are the most often stated
reasons. Citing the devastating consequences of alcohol and
tobacco use, most Americans question society's ability to
use any addictive, mind-altering drug responsibly. Currently,
the public favors supply reduction, demand reduction, and an
increased emphasis on prevention, treatment, and rehabilitation
as effective strategies in combating the drug problem. Shaping

public policy is a critical function that greatly relies upon public input. The policymaking apparatus is influenced by public opinion, and public opinion is in turn influenced by public policy. When the president refers to drugs as threats to national security, the impact on public opinion is tremendous. Currently, record amounts of opium are being produced in Afghanistan, and the implications for its providing support for the Taliban and terrorism are clear. Opium production in Southwest Asia, an entrenched staple in the region's overall economic product, continues as a priority of U.S. national security. The resulting implications for sustaining enforcement-oriented U.S. drug policy are also clear; and in the minds of most Americans, they are absolutely necessary. The U.S. Department of State alone will receive $336 million for alternative crop production, diplomacy, interdiction, and enforcement.

Although the prevailing characteristic of most current drug policy still reflects a punitive, "get tough" approach to control, an added emphasis on treating and rehabilitating offenders is visible in policy changes occurring over the past 10 years. Correctional systems are reflecting with greater consistency the view that drug treatment made available to inmates is a critical component of rehabilitation. The California Department of Corrections, the largest in the nation, was recently renamed the California Department of Corrections and Rehabilitation. A prisoner with a history of drug abuse, who receives no drug treatment while in custody, is finally being recognized as a virtual guarantee to reoffend. In 2006, the National Institute of Drug Abuse published the first federal guidelines for administering drug treatment to criminal justice populations.

Another complicated aspect of creating national as well as local drug policy is consideration of the growing body of research on the subject. The past 20 years have produced numerous public and private investigations, surveys, and conclusions relative to the dynamics of drug use in U.S. society. Although an historical assessment of the influence of research on policy produces indirect relationships, policy decisions of the last few years can be directly related to evidence-based research findings and not just political views. One example is the consistently increasing commitment to treatment. This commitment comes as a direct result of research related to progress achieved in treating and rehabilitating users. Treatment, in terms of dollars spent, can compete with all other components of drug control policy.

One important issue affecting and sometimes complicating the research/policymaking relationship is that the policymaking community, at all levels of government, is largely composed of persons of diverse backgrounds, professional capacities, and political interests. Some are elected officials, others are civil servants, and many are private citizens from the medical, educational, and research communities. In some cases, such as with alcohol and tobacco, powerful industry players assert a tremendous influence on policy. As you read on, consider the new research-related applications for drug policy, such as those related to the rehabilitation of incarcerated drug offenders.

Catch and Release

California's prisons are packed with repeat nonviolent drug offenders. Folsom State Prison's Parolee Substance Abuse Program seeks to rehabilitate, not incarcerate.

JANELLE WEINER

For more than 20 years, Julius Johnson's life swung dangerously out of whack. Although he tried to attend school and hold down a job, plans for how and where to get his next drink or bag of weed crowded his mind. Constantly drunk, stoned or both, he landed in prison multiple times.

"You don't wanna know how many times I've been in," says Johnson, shaking his head. At 45, his face is still boyish, but the ache in his voice reveals a man who has suffered beyond his years. He's tried to walk the straight and narrow, but always loses his balance and winds up back "behind the wall."

This time it's different. After his most recent parole violation, Johnson was given a choice: Go back behind the wall, or enter the Parolee Substance Abuse Program, located in the Folsom Transitional Treatment Facility, in the shadow of the maximum-security state prison.

Johnson chose the latter, and now he says he's been "reborn."

Like Johnson, all of the 200 parolees participating in the recovery program have at least one nonserious, nonviolent felony on their records. Some have been in and out of custody for as long as they can remember. This time when they violated parole—many, but not all, for failing drug tests—they were given the same choice as Johnson: Return to prison for five months to a year or begin a 90-day substance-abuse and transitional living program at Folsom's minimum-security treatment facility.

With California's prisons facing unprecedented overcrowding and ballooning costs, proponents of parole reform are looking at programs like Folsom's to keep inmates from repeatedly returning to prison. Many experts say California's rigid parole policies result in parolees returning to prison at nearly twice the rate of the national average. They want more options for parole violators, including expanding rehabilitation and transitional services as an alternative to lengthy and costly prison terms for nonviolent offenders.

Nevertheless, systematic improvements have been met with resistance from government leaders, the public and the California Correctional Peace Officers Association. Gov. Arnold Schwarzenegger and the Legislature have repeatedly stricken reform measures from the budget, while voters and the CCPOA continue to hold fast to "three strikes."

The short of it? Unless the state takes immediate action, the three federal judges empowered in 2007 to reduce prison overcrowding may turn loose as many as 50,000 nonviolent offenders on the streets. Many won't have the skills to survive and will land right back in trouble. And thanks to the state's ongoing financial problems and lack of political will, recovery programs such as Folsom are in short supply exactly when they're needed the most.

"If no one addresses their substance abuse, even if they have a job, they're right back," insists Thomas Powers, director of the California Department of Corrections and Rehabilitation's Division of Addiction and Recovery Services. "The more risk and needs we can address in an inmate, the lower chance they have to recidivate."

The School of Drugs and Hard Knocks

In the cavernous room where Johnson and the other men sleep, a row of low concrete walls separates narrow beds from a section of the dorm used as a classroom for new arrivals. Battered lockers next to each bed provide some sense of individual space, and slivers of natural light fall from narrow windows. Outside the window, a fence topped with barbed wire and video cameras encloses the property.

The mattresses aren't soft, but it could be worse. The parolees could be behind the wall. A 2007 audit of CDCR's rehabilitative services labeled in-prison programs across the state "a complete waste." The program at the Folsom Transitional Treatment Facility, outside the main prison, offers a stark contrast to that assessment.

The Contra Costa County Office of Education runs the program; principal Shannon Swain monitors activities on site. She strolls across the linoleum floor in a long skirt, passing parolees who move aside and say, "Excuse me."

One guy looks up, his blue eyes dancing, and grins at Swain as she passes.

"Hey, you're the director or head coordinator or something, right?" he asks. The yellow lettering on his uniform reads "CDC Prisoner." Although the CDCR changed its name to include "Rehabilitation" in 2005, not all of the uniforms reflect the change.

"Principal," Swain says.

"I knew it was something like that."

Swain and project coordinator Sam Williams Jr. proceed across the enclosed outdoor common area to a classroom where parolees in their first 30 days of the program—Phase I—are reviewing the answers to a test on psychopharmacology. They sit around tables in small groups, folders, paper, pens and blue "Framework for Recovery" workbooks covering the surfaces in front of them. A few men chatter. One rests a foot on a chair.

The teacher, a small, peppy woman with graying hair moves back and forth to the whiteboard at the front of the room. She has written the objective at the top: "Student will classify drugs into categories and will be able to identify two withdrawal symptoms from each category." All of the teachers at PSAP are credentialed. They utilize structured lesson plans as wells as hands-on and cooperative learning to keep their students engaged.

"Under law, barbiturates are classified as . . . " she calls out, getting the ball rolling.

Answers pop up from around the room. A blond-haired guy calls out from the back row, "B—narcotics!"

The teacher writes the answer on the board and continues. The pace is quick. Participation is high.

"A lot of drugs make you impotent," she mentions at one point. A lanky college-age parolee whispers a question from his seat in the front.

"Not being able to rise to the occasion," answers the teacher.

The guy mouths, "Ohh."

Slumped in his seat in the back of the room, a short, muscular Latino man with tattoos under both eyes and above one eyebrow folds his arms tightly across his chest. His jaw is set and he looks tense, guarded, as if he's defending a one-man fortress. He's been staring straight ahead since Swain and Williams entered the room.

Swain asks to borrow his test packet momentarily. He nods.

"How are you doing?" she asks, gently lifting the packet from his hands.

The man's pained face softens into a smile. His shoulders drop. "Good, good," he says quietly. He has been here two weeks. The first days and weeks of Phase I are perhaps the most difficult. Detox, depending on the parolee's drug of

choice, can be physically demanding, and the intense psychological work needed to root out the addiction can be emotionally draining. At least two parolees per month drop out of the program and return to prison.

But Julius Johnson is no quitter. It was during Phase that he realized he'd been given a second chance. Outside the wall, Johnson spent most of his time trying to score Early mornings would find him passing by the same building where the same group of people always seemed to be standing outside, waiting to get in. Even when it was cold even when it was dark, they were there.

One day, returning with his stash, Johnson noticed the walk in front of the building was empty and decided to investigate. He pushed opened the door, stuck his head inside, and was greeted by a roomful of familiar faces turning to look at the man hovering in the doorway.

Johnson backed out of the silent room, away from the faces. Later that day, he asked a custodian what took place there in the mornings. It was an Alcoholics Anonymous meeting.

The next time he passed by, he could have walked in grabbed a cup of coffee and taken a seat. He could have told them his name and admitted he had a problem.

"That should have been my wake-up call," he says. "This is where I was supposed to go, but I didn't."

When his parole officer suggested he attend a rehabilitation program instead of returning to a prison cell, Johnson initially resisted. He knew how to do prison. He'd never attended recovery before, and he didn't believe in it.

"I knew I had a problem," he says. "But I always thought if a person wanted to stop, they would."

"The first week or so, they don't wanna be here," confirms project coordinator Williams, who passed on his powerful physique to his NFL player son. "Their parole officer did them an injustice. Then after about a week, it's 'Oh, this isn't as bad as I thought it was. I could learn something here.' We see that all the time."

Phase I opened doors for Johnson, teaching him how to raise his self-esteem and understand his emotions.

"It was like I was reborn," he says.

Later in Phase I, Johnson and his classmates cycled through lessons such as "The Process of Addiction" and "Cognitive Restructuring"—or as Williams calls it, "changing their stinkin' thinking."

The walls come down. Denial and grief are exposed. The men often keep it together in the classroom, only to break down in sessions with their independent-study teachers later. They reveal that a father abused them or that a mother taught them how to use drugs. To climb out of the hole, they've got to get to the bottom of it first.

In response to the 2007 audit, Gov. Schwarzenegger and prison leadership convened an expert panel to make recommendations for improving rehabilitation and reducing overcrowding. Among the numerous problems they found with existing in-prison programs were shoddily monitored care roviders, classes frequently interrupted by lockdowns and rison politics that distracted inmates from the mental and motional work of recovery.

Stephen Siscoe, a recovering methamphetamine addict currently going through Phase I, has experienced prison politics p close and personal. He says the continuous, often violent truggle between various gangs and factions behind the wall on't apply at Folsom's minimum-security program. After pending six hours a day in classes together, many of the men o back to the dorms and continue their conversations. Some lk about their pasts. Others prefer to focus on the future. here is almost always someone willing to offer support.

If Siscoe hadn't been sent to the program, he has no doubt e would still be on the streets, addicted and on the run.

"I would be out there cheating, lying, justifying my ehavior, looking behind my back," he says, elbows perched n a metal table bolted to the dormitory floor. Siscoe's large ands spill out of his denim uniform as he describes what anded him here. Family, adolescence, culture, choices.

"We're all adolescents inside," he says. In Phase I, he inally began to grow up.

reaking the Born-Bad Mold

he sign above the door of the Phase II classroom reads: Nothing Changes Until I Change." Williams and Swain enture into the classroom, where parolees continue to focus n unlocking negative thought and behavior patterns. They earn how to manage anger and maintain healthy relationhips, all the skills necessary to stay clean and sober outside he wall.

The room is packed with men sitting in pairs at rows of ables. An animated discussion in the classroom next door lters through the floor-to-ceiling room divider, but no one eems to notice. Someone jokes, "We're all crazy in here," but o one laughs.

Even with his beard, the teacher looks younger than he majority of men in the room. He's not intimidated, and nthusiastically leads a lesson on stereotypes.

"Is there such a thing as a 'bad' person?" he asks.

The room is quiet, and the teacher asks a thin young man vith a close-shaved head if he would like to answer.

The man says he's not sure, so the teacher presses him o share some things about himself that show he's a good erson.

"Playing with my kids, hanging out with my old lady, vorking. Those show I'm not bad."

A few others raise their hands. The discussion takes a hilosophical turn.

"Everyone does bad stuff, it's just some get caught," omes a voice from the back of the room.

Cedric McKinney reached his turning point one day durng the second phase. He and his classmates were asked to onsider the way substance abuse had affected their lives. he teacher told them to think of three things they had lost.

"I could think of more," he says.

McKinney wants to change. That increases his chances for success. But in a prison system where participation in some rehabilitation programs has actually been correlated with a higher recidivism rate, wanting to change isn't always enough. For McKinney, the difference is in the support he receives from the teachers at Folsom.

"The people who run the program give you all they have," says McKinney, who tutors fellow parolees for the GED in the evenings after class. "They don't just let you float through like it's prison."

James Ayres spent 31 months behind the wall and was released back to the community before coming to the program. On the outside, he informally counseled other addicts on the street. Then he got hooked again himself.

Ayres prefers to keep to himself in the dorms, but he has developed an admiration of teacher Mike Gray. Beyond helping him develop a transition plan for attending school, Gray has helped Ayres understand what the experience might be like.

In Gray's classroom, a detailed pencil drawing of Emiliano Zapata rests on a table. Gray encourages his students to explore and take pride in their cultures.

Throughout his 30 years of social work and teaching experience, Gray has worked to balance the need to maintain appropriate boundaries with his students and communicating to them that he knows where they've been.

To Ayres, Gray is "on the level."

As the lesson on stereotypes continues in the Phase II classroom, a common theme emerges.

"No one in society thinks we can be better," one parolee says soberly. "You find that out when you try to get a job."

"You begin to feel hopeless," another student chimes in.

From the front of the room, a heavy-set African-American man gets the floor.

"They don't care about us," he says. "Or they say they care, but they do it from a distance. If there were more programs, if we had more people advocating, we'd do better."

Tough on Crime, Weak on Justice

Dr. Barry Krisberg, director of the National Council on Crime and Delinquency, says there are limits to the effect rehabilitative programming can have on reducing recidivism. Nevertheless, he laments what he sees as a lack of reform in CDCR's rehabilitative policies and programs.

"The principal barrier has been political will," says Krisberg. "We added the 'R' [in CDCR], but the progress has been glacial."

The three-judge federal panel in the overcrowding case that recently wrapped up in San Francisco found that California could save $803 million to $906 million annually by instituting a system of earned credits and parole reform to reduce the prison population. That money could be used to implement the expert panel's recommendation to provide more evidence-based rehabilitation programs in the community.

CDCR currently provides 5,692 community treatment slots that deliver transitional services for recently released inmates. Some 2,028 slots are being utilized by parolees in another remedial sanction program for parole violators, the In Custody Drug Treatment Program. The three-judge panel left the door open for state officials to divert prisoners into rehabilitative programs rather than commit to a wholesale release of the estimated 50,000 prisoners it would take to bring the population to a safe level.

Nevertheless, in a March report, the California Rehabilitation Oversight Board noted none of the reforms *for rehabilitation programs* recommended by the expert panel were included in the governor's final budget, passed in February.

"The expert panel's report was basically thrown in the garbage," says Krisberg. "If we're unwilling to change because we're afraid of being seen as soft on crime, then we're locked into the same failure mode."

Back at the Folsom Transitional Treatment Facility, it's almost time for the head count. The parolees have lunch together and return to their classrooms for three more hours of instruction.

Tables are arranged conference style in the Phase III classroom, where Swain slips into an empty seat next to Johnson. All around her, parolees focus on teacher Vic Wedloe, a muscular former cop who leans against his desk and looks hard at the men as he lays out a situation they're likely to encounter once they're back home, around the old influences, the old temptations.

"It's the middle of the night," says Wedloe. "And you've got the craving. How do you get through it?"

Eyes flicker. The sea of blue uniforms shifts. The men seem to ponder, but no one raises a hand to answer. Wedloe calls on a wiry man a few seats down from Swain.

The man hesitates, but finally says, "If I can recognize it, I guess I can substitute drugs with something else."

His comment motivates others to speak up. They share stories and insights, chuckles and knowing nods. They articulate their plans: Turn on the television, rearrange the fridge, use positive self-talk. But Wedloe doesn't let them off easy. There are plans, and then there's the reality of facing a lifelong drug addiction.

When Johnson suggests he will call his sponsor, Wedloe challenges him.

"It's 3 in the morning. You wanna wake him up?"

Johnson pauses, looks down. "The way I understand it, he's gotta pick up. If he's a good sponsor, he'll pick up."

Wedloe nods, satisfied. If the men become familiar with their symptoms and have the tools to fight back, they can recover.

"That sensation's never gonna rule your life again?" asks Wedloe.

"Never," Johnson says.

Like 60 percent of the program's graduates, Johnson will attend a 90-day after-care program that includes transitional housing, recovery services and job assistance. Krisberg and other experts say aftercare is critically important—to increase the odds that a parolee will, in fact, stay clean.

Williams, the program's coordinator, is careful to point out that recovery, like addiction, is a process. Some of the parolees will return. Recently, a man who was part of the first group to attend the program approached Williams in the yard and asked if he remembered him.

Williams had to think a minute, but then recalled the man's stay. It wasn't a pleasant one, and the man didn't attend aftercare.

"I shoulda listened to you," he told Williams.

Revenge or Rehabilitation?

Although the price tag for a parole violator to attend substance-abuse classes is $50 higher per day than a prison stay, the program stands to save the state money since the stay is shorter and, at least anecdotally, the parolees who attend the Folsom program stay out of trouble longer, even if they do eventually recidivate.

"The old approach based on revenge needs to be replaced with something based on science," says Krisberg.

Williams isn't about revenge. He shakes his head when he talks about the parolee in the yard, but his voice is filled with understanding.

"We're not mad at them if they come back," he says. "If a lifelong addict can stay clean for six months to a year, it is counted as a success."

"Of course, we hope they stay out for longer," he adds.

Graduations occur on a rolling basis, since new parolees enter the program almost every day. CDCR director Powers says there are no current plans to expand the Parolee Substance Abuse Program, but he is optimistic that improving in-prison rehabilitative programs will lower recidivism rates. "What we're trying to do is make the whole yard a therapeutic yard," he says.

He also stresses the need to expand the number of openings in community-based transition programs for parolees beyond the current 5,692 slots. California currently releases more than 100,000 inmates back to the community each year.

With Assembly Bill 900, the Public Safety and Offender Rehabilitation Services Act of 2007, Gov. Schwarzenegger and legislators attempted to improve prison conditions and rehabilitation programs without releasing prisoners. Since the bill's passage, the number of in-prison drug-treatment slots has increased to nearly 10,000.

Powers, however, estimates 35,000 to 40,000 inmates could benefit from treatment. Many other experts, including Dr. Joan Petersilia, a professor of criminology at UC Irvine who served on the state's expert panel for prison reform, put the estimate at more than twice that.

Meanwhile, Stephen Siscoe will soon leave Folsom to enter a recovery program and take steps towards becoming a substance-abuse counselor himself.

"I've thought about it a lot," he says. "If I understand even more, I'll be more likely to stay away."

Ayres also plans to become a certified counselor. McKinney managed to enroll himself in a construction training course to begin the Monday immediately after his graduation.

Pastel-hued paper mobiles hang from the ceiling above Julius Johnson. The tags, with words like "hobbies," "family" and "respect" written on them, reflect the pieces individual parolees must juggle to lead balanced lives.

If he had been sent back to prison for his parole violation, Johnson would still be there, serving out his sentence and waiting for his "gate money," the $200 all prisoners are given on completion of their sentence. Instead, he will soon enter aftercare and start attending a school that will move him towards his goal of attaining a heavy-equipment operator's license.

At the Folsom facility, Johnson has been reborn. He's been given a second chance, and he knows it's up to him to restore balance to his life. He does not intend to go back behind the wall.

Critical Thinking

1. Why are politicians so resistant to drug rehabilitation programs?

2. Would it better serve our communities and states to focus on rehabilitating and treating these offenders instead of perpetuating the boomerang effect of prison sentences?

3. Do you think a time will come when we as a society decide to focus on treatment rather than punishment?

From *Sacramento News & Review*, April 2, 2009. Copyright © 2009 by Janelle Weiner. Reprinted by permission of the author.

Drugs: To Legalize or Not

Decriminalizing the possession and use of marijuana would raise billions in taxes and eliminate much of the profits that fuel bloodshed and violence in Mexico.

STEVEN B. DUKE

The drug-fueled murders and mayhem in Mexico bring to mind the Prohibition-era killings in Chicago. Although the Mexican violence dwarfs the bloodshed of the old bootleggers, both share a common motivation: profits. These are turf wars, fought between rival gangs trying to increase their share of the market for illegal drugs. Seventy-five years ago, we sensibly quelled the bootleggers' violence by repealing the prohibition of alcohol. The only long-term solution to the cartel-related murders in Mexico is to legalize the other illegal drugs we overlooked when we repealed Prohibition in 1933.

In 2000, the Mexican government disturbed a hornets' nest when it began arresting and prosecuting major distributors of marijuana, cocaine, heroin and amphetamines. Previously, the cartels had relied largely on bribery and corruption to maintain their peaceful co-existence with the Mexican government. Once this *pax Mexicana* ended, however, they began to fight not only the government but among themselves. The ensuing violence has claimed the lives of at least 10,000 in Mexico since 2005, and the carnage has even spilled north to the United States and south to Central and South America.

Some say that this killing spree—about 400 murders a month currently—threatens the survival of the Mexican government. Whether or not that is the exaggeration that Mexican President Felipe Calderón insists it is, Mexico is in crisis. The Mexicans have asked the Obama administration for help, and the president has obliged, offering material support and praising the integrity and courage of the Mexican government in taking on the cartels.

The U.S. should enforce its laws against murder and other atrocious crimes and we should cooperate with Mexican authorities in helping them arrest and prosecute drug traffickers hiding out here. But what more can and should we do?

Is gun control the answer? President Calderón asserts that the cartels get most of their guns from the U.S. We could virtually disarm the cartels, he implies, if we made it harder to buy guns here and smuggle them into Mexico. President Obama has bought into this claim and has made noises about reducing the availability of guns. However, even if the Obama administration were able to circumvent the political and constitutional impediments to restricting Americans' access to handguns, the effect on Mexican drug violence would be negligible. The cartels are heavily armed now, and handguns wear out very slowly.

Even if the Mexican gangsters lost their American supply line, they would probably not feel the loss for years. And when they did, they would simply turn to other suppliers. There is a world-wide black market in military weapons. If the Mexicans could not buy pistols and rifles, they might buy more bazookas, machine guns and bombs from the black market, thus escalating the violence.

Also hopeless is the notion—now believed by almost no one—that we can keep the drugs from coming into this country and thereby cut off the traffickers' major market. If we could effectively interdict smuggling through any of our 300-plus official border crossing points across the country and if we eventually build that fence along our entire border with Mexico—1,933 miles long—experience strongly suggests that the smugglers will get through it or over it. If not, they will tunnel under or fly over it. And there is always our 12,383 miles of virtually unguarded coastline.

Several proposals have been submitted in the Mexican congress to decriminalize illegal drugs. One was even passed in 2006 but, under pressure from the U.S., President Vicente Fox refused to sign it. The proposals rest on the notion that by eliminating the profit from illegal drug distribution, the cartels will die from the dearth of profits. A major weakness in such proposals, however, is that the main source of the cartels' profit is not Mexican but American. Mexican drug consumption is a mere trickle compared to the river that flows north. However laudable, proposals to decriminalize drugs in Mexico would have little impact on the current drug warfare.

Secretary of State Hillary Clinton recognized the heart of the matter when she told the Mexicans last month that the "insatiable demand for illegal drugs" in the U.S. is fueling the Mexican drug wars. Without that demand, there would be few illegal drug traffickers in Mexico.

Once we have recognized this root cause, we have few options. We can try to eliminate demand, we can attack the suppliers or we can attempt a combination of both. Thus far, the Obama administration, like every other U.S. administration since drug prohibition went into effect in 1914, seems bent on trying to defeat the drug traffickers militarily. Hopefully, President Obama will soon realize, if he does not already, that this approach will not work.

Suppose the U.S. were to "bail out" the Mexican government with tens of billions of dollars, including the provision of military personnel, expertise and equipment in an all-out concerted attack on the drug traffickers. After first escalating, the level of cartel-related violence would ultimately subside. Thousands more lives would be lost in the process, but Mexico could thereby be made less hospitable to the traffickers, as other areas, such as Colombia, Peru and Panama, were made less hospitable in the past. That, after all, is how the Mexicans got their start in the grisly business. Eventually, the traffic would simply move to another country in Latin America or in the Caribbean and the entire process would begin anew. This push-down, pop-up effect has been demonstrated time and again in efforts to curb black markets. It produces an illusion of success, but only an illusion.

An administration really open to "change" would consider a long-term solution to the problem—ending the market for illegal drugs by eliminating their illegality. We cannot destroy the appetite for psychotropic drugs. Both animals and humans have an innate desire for the altered consciousness obtainable through drugs. What we can and should do is eliminate the black market for the drugs by regulating and taxing them as we do our two most harmful recreational drugs, tobacco and alcohol.

Marijuana presents the strongest case for this approach. According to some estimates, marijuana comprises about 70% of the illegal product distributed by the Mexican cartels. Marijuana will grow anywhere. If the threat of criminal prosecution and forfeitures did not deter American marijuana farmers, America's entire supply of that drug would be home-grown. If we taxed the marijuana agribusiness at rates similar to that for tobacco and alcohol, we would raise about $10 billion in taxes per year and would save another $10 billion we now spend on law enforcement and imprisoning marijuana users and distributors.

Even with popular support, legalizing and regulating the distribution of marijuana in the U.S. would be neither easy nor quick. While imposing its prohibitionist will on the rest of the world for nearly a century, the U.S. has created a network of treaties and international agreements requiring drug prohibition. Those agreements would have to be revised. A sensible intermediate step would be to decriminalize the possession and use of marijuana and to exercise benign neglect of American marijuana growers. Doing both would puncture the market for imports from Mexico and elsewhere and would eliminate much of the profit that fuels the internecine warfare in Mexico.

After we reap the rewards from decriminalizing marijuana, we should move on to hard drugs. This will encounter strong resistance. Marijuana is a relatively safe drug. No one has ever died from a marijuana overdose nor has anyone gone on a violent rampage as a result of a marijuana high. Cocaine, heroin and amphetamines, on the other hand, can be highly addictive and harmful, both physically and psychologically. But prohibition makes those dangers worse, unleashing on vulnerable users chemicals of unknown content and potency, and deterring addicts from seeking help with their dependency. There is burgeoning recognition, in the U.S. and elsewhere, that the health benefits and the myriad social and economic advantages of substituting regulation of hard drugs for their prohibition deserves serious consideration.

A most impressive experiment has been underway in Portugal since 2001, when that country decriminalized the possession and personal use of all psychotropic drugs. According to a study just published by the Cato Institute, "judged by virtually every metric," the Portuguese decriminalization "has been a resounding success." Contrary to the prognostications of prohibitionists, the numbers of Portuguese drug users has not increased since decriminalization. Indeed, the percentage of the population who has ever used these drugs is lower in Portugal than virtually anywhere else in the European Union and is far below the percentage of users in the U.S. One explanation for this startling fact is that decriminalization has both freed up funds for drug treatment and, by lifting the threat of criminal charges, encouraged drug abusers to seek that treatment.

We can try to deal with the Mexican murderers as we first dealt with Al Capone and his minions, or we can apply the lessons we learned from alcohol prohibition and finish dismantling the destructive prohibition experiment. We should begin by decriminalizing marijuana now.

Critical Thinking

1. Is the answer to the violence which stems from illegal drugs simply to legalize them? Why do most people not believe in this?

2. Do you think the Portuguese strategy could work here in the United States?

STEVEN B. DUKE is a professor of law at Yale Law School.

Do No Harm

Sensible Goals for International Drug Policy

PETER REUTER

Drug policy has been an inconvenient issue for the national security apparatus of the United States, whether run by a Democratic or Republican administration. Even after 35 years of some sort of domestic "war on drugs", forcefully articulated by every President since Ronald Reagan, the international dimension of the issue remains distasteful to diplomats. It often involves dealing with law enforcement in corrupt countries and complicates many a U.S. Ambassador's life. The contending lobbies that care about it are loud, moralistic and well informed. If that were not enough, most of our principal allies, particularly in Europe, think there is a certain madness in the American belief that international interventions against the drug trade can accomplish much good.

Mere inconvenience is an insufficient reason to abandon a policy, of course, but in this case there are stronger arguments for change. The Obama Administration has an opportunity before it, for both history and argument show that U.S. international efforts to control drug production and trafficking cannot do much more than affect where and how coca and opium poppies are grown. The quantity produced is minimally affected, since suppression of production in one country almost invariably leads to expansion in another.

More important, control efforts often cause damage. Not only are such programs as spraying poppy and coca fields themselves harmful, but forcing the drug trade to move from one country to another may hurt the new producer country more than it helps the old one. Hence, the U.S. government should no longer push for "global containment", as the policy has been defined. Rather, it should focus attention and resources on supporting the few states both willing and able to do something about production or trafficking in their countries. Unfortunately, Afghanistan, the center of attention right now, is not one of those countries.

American Bull in the China Shop

The United States has been the principal driver of international drug control efforts since 1909, when it convened a meeting of the International Opium Commission (primarily aimed at helping China cut its opium consumption). The United States then pushed for the creation of a web of prohibitionist international treaties under the auspices first of the League of Nations and then the United Nations. Its voice is the dominant one at the annual meetings of the UN Commission on Narcotic Drugs. In that forum it has stood firm against any softening of existing policies. Most prominently, the United States has denounced

in recent years "harm reduction" interventions such as needle distribution programs aimed at reducing the spread of HIV.

Nor does it hesitate to scold even its closest neighbors for deviating from its hard-line, prohibitionist stance. In 2003, U.S. drug czar John Walters accused Canada of poisoning American youth when Ottawa proposed decriminalizing marijuana possession, a policy similar to that of a dozen U.S. states. The United States has even proven willing to barter specific foreign policy interests to influence other nations' drug policies. In the Clinton Administration senior State Department officials told Australia that trade negotiations would be dragged out if Canberra went ahead with a planned experiment in which the most troubled heroin addicts might be supplied with the drug (a program now routine in Switzerland and the Netherlands). Though not a lot of money (by the standards of the overall U.S. drug policy budget) is spent on overseas drug control Plan Colombia ($5 billion since 2001) is by far the largest U.S. foreign assistance program in Latin America, making Colombia the fourth largest recipient of U.S. aid.

These interventions have real consequences for U.S. foreign policy. Tensions with NATO allies in Afghanistan have been exacerbated by disagreements over how aggressively to act against opium production. Plan Colombia, which funds the civil rights-abusing Colombian military, causes much unease among neighboring countries. From 1986 until 2001, relations with Mexico were roiled by Mexican indignation at the U.S. annual "certification", in which the world's largest drug consumer decided whether its neighbors had done enough to reduce its own importation of drugs.

What these policies and programs seem not to have done is to reduce either the American or the global drug problems. That is not the consequence of badly designed programs or administrative incompetence, though there are plenty of both. Rather, it is a result of the fact that international programs like eradication or interdiction simply cannot make much of a difference because they aim at the wrong part of the problem: production and trafficking in source countries. The right part of the problem to aim at is demand in importing countries, including our own. But, of course, that is a difficult and uncertain task, and even successful programs take a long time to have much effect.[1]

It would not be wise to close up shop altogether. After all, there are some connections between the illicit drug trade and terrorist financing that Americans would be foolish to ignore, and there may occasionally be promising opportunities to help specific countries.

ut we should adopt more limited, common sense goals for U.S.
ternational drug policy.

Heroin and Cocaine

oday's mass market in illegal heroin is a new phenomenon. Before
965, the drug was a niche product and one of declining popu-
rity in the United States. Poppies were refined into opium and
ostly consumed in Asia. However, between 1965 and 1995 heroin
pidemics erupted in many rich industrialized countries from Aus-
alia to Norway. The loosening of social and economic controls
China in the late 1980s and the break-up of the Soviet Union
the early 1990s added a few more countries to the list of those
ith heroin problems. Iran, Pakistan, Thailand and other traditional
pium producers also became heroin-consuming countries, partly as
consequence of Western pressures to crack down on opium distri-
ution. Heroin use can't be found everywhere in the world these
ays, but it is certainly no longer just a niche problem. So serious
the challenge that there have even been times when the United
tates, Iran and Russia have quietly made common cause to deal
ith it.

While heroin use was spreading, heroin production became more
oncentrated. By the 1980s, Afghanistan and Burma had come to
ominate production, accounting for more than 90 percent of the
tal each year. Since 2002, Afghanistan has been the dominant
roducer: In 2007, with a new record output, it produced roughly
3 percent of the world total, about 8,000 tons. (Before the Tal-
an banned opium production in 2000, production had only once
xceeded 4,000 tons.)

Why do Afghanistan and Burma dominate? It's not because
ther is particularly well suited in terms of land or climate. Opium
as been produced in many countries; Australia and France are two
ig producers for the contemporary legal market, while Thailand
nd Macedonia were major producers in the past. So what accounts
r the current situation?

Afghanistan was not historically a large opium producer, but
iree major events combined to change that. The overthrow of
ie Shah in 1979 led to the installation of an Iranian regime much
nore concerned with drugs as a moral issue. The Islamic Repub-
c promptly cracked down on opium production in Iran. Willing
execute producers and growers after only minimal due process,
ran quickly eliminated domestic opium poppy cultivation. How-
ver, it was much less successful in reducing demand, and the result
vas a new market for Afghan exports. This happened at roughly
ie same time that the Soviet Union invaded Afghanistan, which
roded central government authority and led to the rise of warlords
or whom opium production was a major source of income. The
ivil war that broke out following the exit of the Soviet troops exac-
rbated the situation and made Afghanistan still more attractive for
pium growing and heroin refining.

For Burma the shaping events took place over an even longer
eriod. Those events relate partly to the political history of China.
Vhen the Communists took the Chinese Mainland in 1949, some
Luomintang army units retreated south into up-country Burma.
Now forced to support themselves, they put their military and
rganization skills to work in the opium industry. Then, in the
970s, the Burmese Communist Party, cut off from Chinese govrnment finance as China attempted to improve relationships with
ts neighbors, turned to the heroin trade as a way to finance its
ctivities. Thus Chinese anti-communists and Burmese commu-
ists alike helped raise Burma's heroin production profile—proof
f how deeply the drug trade is embedded in larger geopoliti-

cal processes. Drug production cannot be treated as just another
industry, responding primarily to economic influences. The Burmese and Afghan cases also illustrate how easily the location of
production can shift. There are many corrupt and poor countries
available for production if for some reason Afghanistan should
cut its production.

Cocaine lacks the global reach of heroin; it's still mostly a rich
nation's drug (though, of course, not mostly rich people in those
nations use it). What seemed in the 1980s a uniquely American
problem has now spread to Europe. Britain and Spain clearly have
substantial cocaine problems and others are vulnerable as well.
Eastern Europe is also catching up in heretofore Western vices as
its productivity and politics approach Western levels.

The production story here is straightforward. Bolivia,
Colombia and Peru are the only commercial producers of cocaine
for the illegal market. Whereas in the 1980s Colombia was the
third most important producer of coca leaves, for the past ten
years it has accounted for about two thirds of the total, as well
as the vast majority of refining. The shift of coca growing from
Peru and Bolivia to Colombia is probably the result both of massive rural flight in Colombia and tougher policies in the other two
countries. The violent conflict in Colombia's established rural
areas has forced farmers to frontiers within the country where
there is little infrastructure for legitimate agriculture, and coca
growing is very attractive in part because these areas are difficult
to monitor or police. Despite a massive eradication campaign,
production levels for the Andes as a whole have been fairly stable
over the past decade.

Ties to Terrorism

That U.S. policies over several decades now have not appre-
ciably affected the overall level of heroin and cocaine on the
market is a cause for some frustration. One reason it vexes U.S.
policymakers is that illegal drugs are funding some terrorist
organizations—though it would be counterproductive to exag-
gerate the extent of this funding. In 2003, the Office of National
Drug Control Policy attracted considerable derision with its
Super Bowl ads tying drug use to the promotion of international
terrorism. Since most U.S. drug use is limited to marijuana,
much of it produced domestically or in Canada, the connection
seemed flimsy. The ads disappeared quickly.

That said, the problem is not imaginary. Before it banned opium
production in 2000, the Taliban taxed it, though no more than it
taxed other agricultural products. Since it didn't provide much in
the way of government services, the estimated $30 million the Tal-
iban got from opium taxes was the second largest source of revenue,
after its taxation of consumer goods smuggled into Pakistan. Al-
Qaeda's sources of revenue are a matter of mystery, at least in the
unclassified literature, but it certainly has earned some money from
trafficking opium or heroin over the years. Nowadays its involvement in protecting (i.e., taxing) opium production in Afghanistan
may be an important activity. Secretary of Defense Robert Gates
has asserted that al-Qaeda receives $80–100 million annually from
the heroin trade. (Like all such figures, this one has no known prov-
enance and should be treated with some skepticism.)

Many other terrorist groups have known ties to drug trafficking. The FARC in Colombia taxes coca growing, the Kurdistan
People's Party in Turkey has some connection to drug traffickers among the Kurdish diaspora in Europe, and the Tamil Tigers

have been caught smuggling heroin. None of these groups are particularly important in the global drug trade, but the trade may be particularly important to them.

For policymakers the relevant question is whether attacking the drug trade is an efficient method for cutting terrorist finance. Given the fact that there are few successful examples of policies that generate large-scale reductions in drug revenues, the answer is generally no. While there might be specific opportunities in which, say, moving the drug trade from one route to another could help reduce the flow of funds to terrorists, in general these criminal problems are hardly twins joined at the hip. The drug trade is just one of many illegal activities for which terrorist organizations have some useful organizational assets. In short, we would not cripple terrorist financing even if we were successful in international drug policy efforts. But this is merely an academic point, for experience shows us why we cannot be successful.

Cutting Drug Exports

The United States has pushed three types of programs to cut source country production: eradication, alternative development and in-country enforcement. Eradication, usually involving aerial spraying, aims literally to limit the quantity of the drug available in the United States, raise the costs of those drugs, or otherwise discourage farmers from producing them. Alternative development is the soft version of the same basic idea. It encourages farmers growing coca or poppies to switch to legitimate crops by increasing earnings from these other products—for example, by introducing new and more productive strains of traditional crops, better transportation to get the crops to market or some form of marketing scheme. Finally, the United States pushes other countries to pursue traffickers and refiners more vigorously. None of the three methods has worked all that well.

Few countries are willing to allow aerial eradication, which may cause environmental damage. It is also politically unattractive because it targets peasant farmers, who are among the poorest citizens even when growing coca or poppy. Colombia and Mexico, neither one traditional producers of drugs, have been the producer countries most willing to allow spraying. Most others allow only manual eradication, a slow and cumbersome method.

The fundamental problem of source-country interventions aimed at producers of coca and poppy is easily described. These programs have always had a peculiar glamor and occupy a large share of the headlines about drug policy. But the fact that the actual production costs of coca or opium account for a trivial share of the retail price of cocaine or heroin dooms source-country interventions as ways of controlling the problem.

It costs approximately $300 to purchase enough coca leaves to produce a kilogram of cocaine, which retails for about $100,000 in the United States when sold in one-gram, two-thirds pure units for $70 per unit. The modest share of the agricultural costs associated with cocaine production is easily explained: Production involves cheap land and labor in poor countries, and it requires no expensive specialized inputs. (Even Bolivia, the smallest of the three producer countries, has more than 500,000 square miles of territory—much of it opaque to surveillance.) Assume that eradication efforts lead to a doubling of the price of coca leaf, so that cocaine refiners now must pay $600 for enough leaf to produce one kilogram of cocaine. Even if the full cost increase is passed along, the change in retail price will still be negligible. Indeed,

leaf prices have varied enormously over the past decade, whi the retail price of cocaine has fallen almost throughout the sam period. If retail prices do not rise, then total consumption in th United States will not decline as a consequence of eradication. I this scenario, there will be no reduction in total production—ju more land torn up in more places to plant an environmentally dam aging crop.

There is, of course, a less harsh option for policy in the sourc country: alternative development. Offer the farmers the opportuni to earn more money growing pineapples than coca, and they wi move to the legal crop, the argument goes.

Quite aside from the time and money it takes to implement successful alternative-crop program, the argument, alas, is subje to the same economic illogic as that for eradication. It assume that the price of coca leaf will not increase enough to tempt th peasants back to coca growing. But as long as the price of leaf so small compared to the street price of cocaine in Chicago, refi ers will offer a high enough price to get back the land and labo needed to meet the needs of the cocaine market. Peasants will b better off than before the alternative development, but only becaus they will make more money growing coca. Mexican peasants a substantially better off than those in Bolivia, but that has not kep them out of the drug business. Indeed, the same can be said fo Kentucky corn farmers, who are prominent in the marijuana trad in the United States.

Three Countries, Three Problems

For the United States the international drug problem is dominate by three countries: Afghanistan, Colombia and Mexico. Eac presents a different problem, both to the United States and to th producing country. But all three show why the elimination/inter diction approach to source country supply doesn't work.

The United States is trying to create an effective democrati state in Afghanistan and is demonstrably failing. Further, despi the presence of 60,000 NATO and U.S. troops, Afghanistan's ou put of opium has increased massively over the seven years since th Taliban fell. That has provided important funding for the Taliba and al-Qaeda as well as for warlords independent of the centra government. It has also worsened the country's deep-seated cor ruption. According to the former coordinator of U.S. counter-na cotics efforts in Afghanistan, there was much conflict within th Bush Administration about pursuing aggressive counter-narcotic efforts. Insiders argued over whether these efforts were neede to establish a strong state or, on the contrary, whether they woul threaten the very existence of the Karzai government.[2]

The drug hawks have usually won the rhetorical battles, but the have lost the programmatic wars. In October 2008, Defense Sec retary Gates declared that the U.S. military will go after trafficker and warlords but will not eradicate farmers' poppy fields. Give the relative invisibility of trafficking, this is effectively a truce. Bu better a truce than a "war" against poppies that cannot be won an might be counterproductive politically if it were won.

Colombia, unlike Afghanistan, is a principal producer of drug for the United States, most prominently cocaine but also heroin The United States has tried to strengthen a Colombian governmen long beleaguered by guerrilla conflict, and in this it has succeede reasonably well. But the primary goal of its assistance has been t reduce the flow of Colombian-produced cocaine into the Unite States, and in that task it has largely failed.

Mexico, occasionally described as a natural smuggling platform or the United States, has been the principal drug transshipment ountry into the United States for two decades. The bulk of America's imports of cocaine, heroin, marijuana and methamphetamine l come through Mexico. In the past two years the level of vionce associated with the U.S.-destined drug trade has skyrocketed. Iore than 5,000 people were killed in drug-related violence in 008; that included systematic terror killings of innocent individuals, honest police and reporters. This has happened partly because f changes in the trade itself and partly as a consequence of govrnment efforts to control the violence. The new U.S. program to elp Mexico—$400 million for training police and military—may stensibly be aimed at cutting down the flow of drugs to the United tates, but such low levels of funding are not likely to achieve uch. The money is more properly viewed as reparations: Mexico suffering from the consequences of our continued appetite for legal drugs, so the United States has an obligation to help amelioate those problems regardless of whether it cuts U.S. drug imports.

Strategic Consequences of the Balloon Effect

here is almost universal skepticism that international efforts y rich countries can reduce global production of cocaine and eroin. It is hard to find anyone outside of the State Department, the White House or Congress who argues otherwise. But fforts to curb production in specific places have had some effect. Ve noted previously that targeting Bolivian and Peruvian smuggling into Colombia helped make Colombia the dominant producer of coca. The Chinese government since about 1998 has ushed the United Wa State Army to successfully (and brutally) ut Burma's production of heroin. Spraying in Mexico in the 1970s hifted opium production from a five-state region in the north a much more dispersed set of states around the country.

Interdiction can also affect the routing of the trade. In the early 980s then-Vice President George H.W. Bush led the South Florida ask Force that successfully reduced smuggling through the Caribean. The traffic then shifted to Mexico, but the effort did help sevral Caribbean governments. Similarly, more heroin may now be lowing through Pakistan because the Iranian government has intenified its border control.

In recent years this kind of interaction has been most conspicuus with respect to cocaine trafficking. The Netherlands Antilles is conveniently located for Colombian traffickers shipping to urope, as there are many direct flights from Curaçao to Amsteram's Schiphol airport, one of the busiest in Europe. In response to vidence of growing cocaine trafficking to Amsterdam, the Dutch overnment implemented a 100 percent search policy for airline assengers from Curaçao in March 2004. Whereas cocaine seizures the Netherlands Antilles had not exceeded 1.3 tons before 2003, 2004 they reached nine tons, a remarkable figure for a jurisdicon with fewer than 200,000 inhabitants. (The United States seizes nly about 150 tons per year.) Shipments through Schiphol airport ave since fallen sharply.

Probably as a consequence, new trafficking routes have opened p from South America to Europe via West Africa. For example, uinea-Bissau is impoverished and small, it has no military or olice capacity to deal with smugglers, and its government is eas-y corrupted. Smugglers have begun using landing strips there for large shipments. In 2007, there was one seizure of three-quarters of a ton, and it is believed that an even larger quantity from that shipment made it out of the country.

Ghana, a larger nation but one with fragile institutions, has also seen a sudden influx of cocaine traffickers. In 2005, flights from Accra accounted for more seized cocaine at London's Heathrow airport than from flights from any other city. There are now regular reports of multi-kilo seizures of the drug either in Ghana itself or at airports receiving flights from Ghana.

Assuming that Ghana and Guinea-Bissau are serving as trafficking platforms at least in part because of the effective crackdown on an existing route through Curaçao, is the world better off? Certainly the Netherlands has helped itself. One can hardly be critical of a country making a strong effort to minimize its involvement in the drug trade. However, one can reasonably ask whether, in making these decisions, the Netherlands should take into account the likely effects of its actions on other, more vulnerable countries.

This analysis also applies to Afghanistan, assuming that it will for the foreseeable future be the most attractive location for opium production. The U.S. government continues to press the Karzai Administration to begin eradication activities in the areas it controls. At the same time, the United States emphasizes the importance of opium production to the Taliban. If farmers in government-controlled areas are forced out of business, it is likely that more of the growing activity, and probably more refining as well, will shift to areas controlled by the Taliban. The result may be to increase Taliban strength, both politically and financially—obviously not a result we would ever intend.

Awkward Choices

International drug policy will not be high on the Obama Administration's list of priorities, given that the U.S. drug problem itself is gradually declining. It has indeed not been a major issue for the Bush Administration. Congress was fairly passive on the issue during the past eight years, but those members who have been vocal have all been drug hawks, passionately arguing that this nation has a moral obligation to fight one of the great scourges of modern times on a worldwide scale. The public is apparently indifferent, seeing the drug problem as one for which every measure (tough enforcement, prevention or more treatment slots) is fairly hopeless. This, in turn, has not encouraged liberal members of Congress to take on the issue.

Drug policy is one of many areas of international policy in which the Obama Administration would benefit from adopting a more humble attitude. The arrogance with which U.S. delegations at the annual Commission on Narcotic Drugs lecture the rest of the world would be laughable if it weren't for the fact that many nations are still cowed by the sheer scale of U.S. efforts. There is no evidence that the United States knows how to help reduce the world's drug problems or to affect the ease with which cocaine, heroin and methamphetamine are procured and trafficked. Moreover, the harm that some of our interventions cause is more apparent than their benefits. For example, spraying coca fields in Colombia clearly has adverse environmental consequences if only because it spreads production further, and it also probably sharpens conflict between the Colombian government and its citizens. Pressing the Karzai government to spray poppy fields increases tensions with our allies. Our attack on drug policy initiatives in other countries exacerbates the U.S. reputation for bullying and disinterestedness in true multilateral collaboration.

Doing less about a problem is rarely an attractive policy recommendation. But for international drug policy it is the only recommendation one can make with confidence. It is perhaps true, as Simone Weil once said, that "it is better to fail than to succeed in doing harm."

Notes

1. See, for example, Jonathan Caulkins and Peter Reuter, "Re-orienting Drug Policy", *Issues in Science and Technology* (Fall 2006); David Boyum and Peter Reuter, *An Analytic Assessment of U.S. Drug Policy* (American Enterprise Institute Press, 2005); and Mark A.R. Kleiman, "Dopey, Boozy, Smoky— and Stupid", *The American Interest* (January/February 2007).

2. Thomas Schweich, "Is Afghanistan a Narco-State?" *New York Times Magazine,* July 27, 2008.

Reference

Reuter, Peter. (2009, March/April). The American Interest: Do No Harm. *Sensible Goads for International Drug Policy,* Vol. IV. No. 4, 46-52.

Critical Thinking

1. Should we continue with our current international drug policy? Why?

2. Some argue that current strategies to counter global drug issues are not working. What suggestions would you make?

PETER REUTER is a professor of public policy and criminology the University of Maryland. He is co-author (with Letizia Paoli a Victoria Greenfield) of the forthcoming *The World Heroin Marke Can Supply Be Cut?* (Oxford University Press).

New Drug Control Strategy Signals Policy Shift

AM Hananel

The White House is putting more resources into **drug prevention** and treatment, part of President Barack Obama's pledge to treat illegal drug use more as a public health issue than a criminal justice problem.

The new drug control strategy to be released Tuesday boosts community-based anti-drug programs, encourages health care providers to screen for drug problems before addiction sets in, and expands treatment beyond specialty centers to mainstream health care facilities.

"It changes the whole discussion about ending the war on drugs and recognizes that we have a responsibility to reduce our own drug use in this country," Gil Kerlikowske, the White House drug czar, said in an interview.

The first drug plan unveiled by the Obama White House calls for reducing the rate of youth drug use by 15 percent over the next five years and for similar reductions in chronic drug use, drug abuse deaths, and drugged driving.

Kerlikowske criticized past drug strategies for measuring success by counting the number of children and teens who have not tried marijuana. At the same time, he said, the number of deaths from illegal and prescription drug overdoses was rising.

"Us facing that issue and dealing with it head on is important," Kerlikowske said.

The new drug plan encourages health care professionals to ask patients questions about drug use even during routine treatment so that early intervention is possible. It also helps more states set up electronic databases to identify doctors who are overprescribing addictive pain killers.

"Putting treatment into the primary health care discussion is critical," Kerlikowske said.

The policy shift comes in the wake of several other drug policy reforms since Obama took office. Obama signed a measure repealing a two-decade-old ban on the use of federal money for needle-exchange programs to reduce the spread of HIV.

His administration also said it won't target medical marijuana patients or caregivers as long as they comply with state laws and aren't fronts for drug traffickers.

Earlier this year, Obama called on Congress to eliminate the disparity in sentencing that punishes crack crimes more heavily than those involving powder cocaine.

Some drug reform advocates like the direction Obama is heading, but question whether the administration's focus on treatment and prevention programs is more rhetoric than reality at this point. They point to the national drug control budget proposal released earlier this year, for example, which continues to spend about twice as much money on enforcement as it does on programs to reduce demand.

"The improved rhetoric is not matched by any fundamental shift in the budget or the broader thrust of the drug policy," said Ethan Nadelmann, executive director of the Drug Policy Alliance, which favors drug policy reform.

Nadelmann praised some of Obama's changes, but said he is disappointed with the continued focus on arresting, prosecuting, and incarcerating large numbers of people.

Kerlikowske rejected that as "inside the Beltway discussion," and said there are many programs that combine interdiction and prevention.

The drug control office's budget request does include a 13 percent increase in spending on alcohol and **drug prevention** programs, along with a 3.7 percent increase for addiction treatment.

Critical Thinking

1. What changes do you expect to see as a result of this policy change?

2. What are your thoughts if this is "more rhetoric than reality?"

Beyond Supply and Demand: Obama's Drug Wars in Latin America

Suzanna Reiss

In its first years, the Obama Administration has embraced and even extended its predecessors' militaristic counternarcotics policies in the Americas. In doing so, it has also adopted the basic tenets and priorities that have shaped U.S. drug control policies for decades. Among the most prominent examples are the administration's decision to deploy U.S. military personnel to Colombian bases, the decertification of Bolivia and Venezuela as having "failed demonstrably" in upholding counternarcotics agreements, the continued funding for Plan Colombia (an estimated $672 million in 2009), and Obama's expansion of the Merida Initiative, the "regional security partnership" brokered by the Bush administration with Mexico in October 2007.Under Obama's watch, funding for the Mexican initiative almost doubled in 2009 to $830 million, making it the largest U.S. foreign aid program.

All of this unfolded even as the director of National Drug Control Policy, R. Gil Kerlikowske, suggested on various occasions that the new administration was making a historic shift on drug policy. In October, for example, Kerlikowske told the Association of Chiefs of Police that "it's become increasingly clear that the metaphor and philosophy of a 'War on Drugs' is flawed. . . . . it's time to adopt a different approach." This echoed sentiments he expressed in June, when he emphasized the need to move away from "divisive 'drug war' rhetoric" as part of a broader U.S.-led effort "to reduce the demand for drugs which fuels crime and violence around the world."

The Obama administration has made some gestures in this direction, most significantly making it a low priority for federal law enforcement to go after state-authorized medical marijuana retailers and suggesting a new orientation toward prevention and treatment. But to genuinely change the philosophy animating the so-called War on Drugs, it is essential to understand and question the international political and economic foundations of U.S. drug policy. These much-neglected foundations continue to fuel violence, repression, and economic coercion both within and beyond the United States' borders.

The drug war has failed to achieve even its stated goals, as critics have long emphasized—there has been no net decrease in illicit drug production and trafficking, even while the devastating human and environmental costs of drug war militarism continue to rise. Meanwhile, rarely discussed is the drug war's great success in helping to achieve unstated goals: extending global U.S. military hegemony and extending the reach of the legal U.S. drug economy, which often depends on raw materials and consumer markets in the very same territories forced to participate in the U.S.-led drug control regime.

This analysis gets submerged by the language of supply and demand and the notions of legality that permeate drug policy discourse. Both indicate capitalism's shaping influence on the ideology of U.S. drug war policies. This obfuscating language—and the idea that regulating the drug trade is a question of effectively policing supply and demand—is itself a legacy of the economic and imperial logic that created an international drug control apparatus, which rests on the unquestioned power of the United States to designate players in the drug trade as either legal or illegal. Rather than presuming that the international flow of drugs is a consequence of the natural workings of a mythical, though often naturalized, free market, it is more useful to ask: Who gets to supply what and who gets to demand? Inequities between the global North and the South have historically structured the answer to these questions.

The language of supply and demand, much like the designation of legal or illegal, must be understood as a political and historical construction rather than as a set of neutral descriptive categories. The system of drug control itself has given these categories and labels substantive power. Attempts to control coca in the Andes provide an instructive example, since the region has been on the international drug control radar since the aftermath of World War II. In 1949, the UN Committee on Narcotic Drugs sent a commission to Peru and Bolivia (at that time the two primary producers of the coca leaf) as part of a broader effort to regulate "raw materials." Arguing that indigenous people's consumption of coca was addictive and destructive, the UN commissioners recommended that it be abolished. The only "legal" market for Andean coca leaves would be their primary international market, the United States. This goal was codified in the 1961 Single Drug Convention, which dictated that all traditional domestic coca consumption be eradicated in 25 years and that the export market be carefully monitored to ensure supplies remained in "licit" channels. Thus, the international drug control regime itself structured Andean countries' participation within the drug trade as a "supply side" source of raw materials.

To this day, coca leaves are processed by pharmaceutical companies authorized by the U.S. government to produce a flavoring extract for Coca-Cola (the biggest coca "consumer") and to manufacture cocaine for use in research laboratories and as a local anesthetic in medicine. The drug control regime that emerged in the 1950s was just that, a system of control—not outright prohibition. Drugs themselves were not illegal. Cocaine and other controlled substances straddled the licit–illicit divide, since their legal status depended on their circulation within the marketplace and on the question of who grew, manufactured, sold, and consumed them.

One of the more dramatic, and mostly unquestioned, contradictions is that while the United States spends billions of dollars attacking "drugs," the legal drug industry is regularly among the top five most profitable industries in the country. North Americans are notoriously quick to turn

ugs to answer their ailments, medical or otherwise; meanwhile, through
rect marketing, the pharmaceutical industry encourages the excessive
nsumption of drugs that are often of questionable medical value.

Internationally, drugs have always served as a measure of the United
ates' wealth and influence. According to the U.S. Census Bureau, phar-
aceutical preparations represent by far the most profitable U.S. exports,
hich is partly the result of free trade agreements, like the Andean Trade
omotion and Drug Eradication Act (ATDPEA), whose title alone indi-
tes the intimate connection between economic relations and U.S. police
d military collaboration. Beyond chemicals' prominent and controver-
al role in drug crop fumigation campaigns, these agreements establish
eferential access for legal U.S. drugs in foreign markets, extend their
tents, and include a number of other measures that propel the domi-
nce of the U.S. pharmaceutical industry around the world.

The United States does not so much wage war on drugs as wage
ar with drugs. Throughout the 20th century, the U.S. government has
nsidered certain drugs, including most recently flu vaccines strate-
c materials and has subsidized their mass-production and stockpiling
the interests of national security. Drugs, among other things, can
mb a soldier's pain, stimulate and ease labor, and vaccinate against
sease, giving them special strategic value. Obama's continuation
the U.S. embargo against Cuba, including policies that limit the
ailability of critical medicines, shows how drugs' medicinal value
s also been deployed to exert coercive diplomatic leverage. A U.S.
mpany selling drugs to Cuba would in this context be committing a
ime, revealing the limits of drug war rhetoric focused on an under-
orld of "illicit" drug profiteering.

This dynamic interplay between the legal and illegal drug econo-
ies and political and economic interests continues to determine drug
forcement's focus. The Obama administration's handling of the con-
rrent crises in Mexico of drug trafficking and the swine flu, or H1N1
rus, is emblematic. On April 30, congressional hearings on the presi-
nt's fiscal year 2009 War Supplemental Request included a discus-
on that linked the two issues: The U.S. government would provide
fficient resources and support for the mass production of (privately
tented) flu vaccines (especially ensuring adequate supplies to the U.S.
ilitary), while waging war against drug cartels. Senator Patrick Leahy
.-Vt.) reflected the consensus in government when he strongly sup-
rted "helping Mexico, which is facing real threats from heavily armed
ug cartels and is now dealing with the H1N1 virus." Secretary of State
llary Clinton explained that USAID had given $5 million to the World
ealth Organization (WHO) and the Pan-American Health Organiza-
n to "help detect and contain the disease in Mexico," an insignificant
iount when compared to the some $2 billion the Obama administra-
n has spent stockpiling vaccines for U.S. citizens.

These efforts at "helping" Mexico reflect broader political and eco-
mic inequities in access to legal drugs. Linked to the U.S. practice
securing adequate national drug supplies is the power to determine
io gets to consume them—a politically charged issue on tumultu-
s display recently regarding the H1N1 vaccine. U.S. (and European)
ug patents price most of the world's population out of the market,
d power dictates who receives the drugs that are produced and dis-
buted, even in the context of the swine flu "emergency." The WHO
s warned that there will be a critical shortage of the H1N1 vaccine in
e developing world, since some 90% of it has already been pledged
"high income countries." On the domestic front, Michigan Demo-
atic representative Bart Stupak, referring to plans to vaccinate pris-
ers at Guantánamo (presumably to protect their U.S. guardians from
fection), complained in October that "while much of America waits
line to receive their H1N1 vaccination, the Pentagon is giving prior-
status to accused terrorists."

Perhaps without knowing it, Stupak seemed to intimate how some
ople are more worthy of medical care than others. Obama chillingly

echoed these sentiments when giving his own assurance that health
care provision will "not apply to those who are here illegally." The
president also indicated that he might allow an exception for "children
who may be here illegally but are still in playgrounds or at schools, and
potentially are passing on illnesses and communicable diseases," presumably to "legal" children—a distinction that dramatically embodies
the dehumanizing impact of U.S. drug wars.

Drug Warriors in the United States and at the United Nations,
the main international body regulating the drug trade, typically divide the countries of the world into drug suppliers
(mostly in Latin America and Central and Southeast Asia) and consumers (primarily North America and Europe). This formulation has
had a definitive impact on both the thrust of drug control initiatives,
and on the arguments presented by their opponents. So, for example, the United States spends the vast majority of drug war funding
on interdiction campaigns in "supply" countries—constituting some
65% of federal drug control expenditures. Some governments in Latin
America have welcomed this funding, in particular the presidents of
Colombia, Mexico, and Peru, who have all embraced the drug war
as a powerful tool in their efforts to consolidate political control and
finance counter-insurgency wars against political and economic dis-
sidents. But there have also been demands from across the region,
including among the United States' allies, that the U.S. government do
more to limit domestic consumption, as well as to limit its involvement
in supplying the precursor chemicals and weapons that are essential to
illicit production and distribution.

The Obama administration has had a somewhat novel response to
this diplomatic challenge. Unlike his predecessor, Obama acknowledged a deeper U.S. role in the illicit drug trade. In April, when a number of administration officials, including the president and secretary of
state, traveled to Mexico to show support for President Felipe Calderón and his war on the cartels, Obama declared he would not pretend
that combating drugs "is Mexico's responsibility alone." He continued: "A demand for these drugs in the United States is what is helping
to keep these cartels in business. This war is being waged with guns
purchased not here, but in the United States."

Yet the administration's acknowledgement of "shared responsibilities" has helped only to cement the ongoing militarization of the
region. The devastating impact of this approach has been well documented: increased levels of violence, political corruption, and a blur-
ring of the line between the police, the military, and drug cartels in
ways that profoundly undermine democracy and human rights. The
limits of a supply–demand framework extend to the weapons deployed
in the conflict. The Obama administration provides Mexico with billions of dollars to buy U.S.-manufactured weapons, Black Hawk heli-
copters, surveillance equipment, and police training, making the U.S.
the major source of both legal and illegal weapons that are flooding
the streets of Mexico.

Embodying the U.S. orientation toward "supply-side" interdiction,
the U.S. president each year identifies "major" illicit drug "producing"
as well as "transit" countries and then determines whether they cooperate
with international drug control. In September, Obama identified 20 countries as "major drug transit or major illicit drug producing countries"; of
these, 15 were in Latin America and the Caribbean, including the Baha-
mas, Bolivia, Brazil, Colombia, the Dominican Republic, Ecuador, Guatemala, Haiti, Jamaica, Mexico, Panama, Paraguay, Peru, and Venezuela
(the rest included Afghanistan, Burma, India, Laos, and Pakistan).

Of the "major" supplying countries, Obama designated three—
Bolivia, Burma, and Venezuela—"as countries that have failed demonstrably during the previous 12 months to adhere to their obligations
under international counternarcotics agreements." This designation, or

"decertification," as it is known, empowers the United States to with-hold aid and deny preferential treatment under existing trade agree-ments with those countries. The supply–demand formulation deployed in this context, together with the selective designation of countries as "major" drug suppliers and as having "failed" by assessing their will-ingness to collaborate with a particular system of international drug control, recasts diplomatic struggles not as political or economic but as conflicts over the pursuit of criminality and terrorism.

The political ideologies associated with governments in the hemisphere—not the actual health consequences or "violence" ema-nating from struggles over control of the drug trade—have deter-mined the certification process. If this were not the case, Colombia and Mexico, as the major "producer" country and the largest "tran-sit" country, respectively, would undoubtedly top the blacklist of drug war failures with their thousands of displaced peoples, environ-mental devastation, and documented human rights abuses. Yet it is Bolivia and Venezuela that have been branded as drug-control rogue states, primarily as an outcome of political tensions between these nations and the United States.

Bolivia again provides a useful example of how drug war spectacle masks political conflict and how decertification is used as a tool to criminalize challenges to U.S. hegemony. The Obama administration's decertification of Bolivia, continuing the Bush administration's policy by maintaining Bolivia's suspension from the ATDPEA, defies any ratio-nal, fact-based justification. It seems instead to be a retaliatory move for actions the Bolivian government took in the fall of 2008, when it did not renew USAID contracts, accused the DEA of spying, expelled the U.S. ambassador, and alleged that the United States was providing covert sup-port to the violent and economically powerful U.S.-aligned opposition.

After the White House said Bolivia had failed to live up to its "shared responsibility," Bolivian president Evo Morales fired back, accusing Obama of having "lied to Latin America" at the Summit of the Ameri-cas in April, when the U.S. president said "there is no senior partner and junior partner" in the United States' hemispheric relations. Further chal-lenging the inequality built into the economic roles assigned to various countries in the drug economy, the Bolivian government formally sub-mitted a request, now under review before the United Nations, to have coca leaf removed from the 1961 Single Drug Convention.

The convention's "restrictions on and prohibition of coca leaf chewing," the Morales administration argued, violates the UN Decla-ration on the Rights of Indigenous Peoples (among other international treaties), which maintains that "indigenous peoples have the right to maintain, control, protect, and develop their cultural heritage, tradi-tional knowledge, and traditional cultural expressions, as well as the manifestations of their sciences, technologies, and cultures, including human and genetic resources, seeds, medicines, and knowledge of the properties of fauna and flora. . . . "

Morales, reelected to a second term in December, is not alone in challenging the U.S. drug war. Leaders across Latin America are seeking not only to expand their right to participate in the legal drug market, but also to question the validity of the control and enforce-ment regime. They increasingly question U.S. drug control priorities, emphasizing its many failures. In August, the First Latin-American Conference on Drug Policy, which brought together representatives from an array of the region's governments, international organizations, and community groups, concluded that "Bolivia, Peru, and Colombia, the three countries that together produce the entirety of the world pro-duction of cocaine, did not manage in 10 years to reduce the acres of [coca] cultivation, but instead gained 2 million refugees, put peasants in jail, and sprayed pesticide that degrades the environment."

The capitalist ideology that sustains the United States' ongoi drug war in the Americas manifests not only in the assum tions built into the supply–demand model. It is also present the very notion that drugs themselves "cause crime and violence," Kerlikowske said when he announced the administration's professed forward-thinking and practical approach to drug policy.

Focusing on the commodity overshadows the people and politi struggles at the heart of the "drug" conflict. It is not drugs per se, rather competition to control their production, distribution, and cc sumption that has generated violence over the last half-century. P sonifying drugs themselves as criminal, violent agents has served a useful mechanism for obscuring the real human impact of drug cont policy since well before the Nixon administration, which officia launched the drug "war." Despite the frequently staged spectacles drug enforcement officers burning marijuana fields in California airplanes fumigating coca fields in the Andes, it is necessary to rest the obvious: The United States has never waged a "war on drug Rather, it has waged various "wars" on specific groups of people.

Take, for example, African Americans, who are disproportionat represented in the U.S. prison population, even though most illicit (a licit) drug users in the United States are white. The domestic drug w since the introduction of the first mandatory minimum sentences in United States in the 1950s, has always been structured by racial and ec nomic bias. Similarly, the burdens of U.S.-led drug wars in Latin Amer have fallen disproportionately on indigenous communities, many of wh have fled drug war violence or lost access to their economic means survival—caught in the political crossfire between governments and ins gencies, which both capitalize on the drug trade as a means of waging w

The Obama administration's early rhetorical shift away from d war rhetoric continues the government's dishonest assessment of wl fuels drug production and consumption. It fails to acknowledge violence that maximizing profits and monopolizing international d flows require. Domestically, in the country with the world's high incarceration rate, the fact that most imprisoned people are serving ti for drug-related offenses has yet to become a serious topic in the Oba administration's deliberations on drug policy. On the international sta the power hierarchies of who gets to supply and who gets to dema also ripple through racial, economic, and social disparities.

Until the administration pays attention to the structural origins the drug war, as well as the profound international dependencies up which it has always rested, it will be fated to continue pursuing ill-conceived, destructive, and failed policy under which the value drugs is determined by violence and economic inequality.

Critical Thinking

1. Explain the dichotomy of how the United States is one of the leaders in drug interdiction yet is also one of the world's largest consumers.

2. Explain how political ideologies, and not public health consequences, impact the decertification process. Why might this be an issue?

3. After reading this article, do you think the current administra-tion has changed their domestic and international drug policies?

SUZANNA REISS teaches history at the University of Hawaii, Man and is a Fellow at the Charles Warren Center for Studies in Americ History at Harvard University. She is the author of Policing for Pro U.S. Imperialism and the International Drug Economy (forthcomin

Drug Courts: Conceptual Foundation, Empirical Findings, and Policy Implications

Jeanne B. Stinchcomb

Introduction

In America's elusive search for more productive responses to the drug abuse epidemic that has been clogging court facilities since the late 1970s, drug courts emerged on the public policy-making agenda with considerable fanfare, prompting renewed hope for breaking the cycle of drug-related crime. Less than two decades ago, the concept of a 'drug court' was simply nonexistent. It took the zero-tolerance crackdown of the war on drugs initiated in the early 1970s to so overburden the capacity of the criminal justice system that the necessity to explore creative alternatives became the driving force behind implementation of the first drug court in Miami, Florida, in 1989. From this grass-roots beginning, the concept spread across the USA with the judicial equivalent of wildfire, in what has since been described as a driving 'spirit of fanaticism' (Dodge, 2001, quoting Mark Kleiman). By December, 2007, some 2147 fully-operating drug courts were operating throughout all fifty states, with 284 more in the planning phases (Office of Drug Control Policy, 2008; see Figure 1). In fact, when federal and state expenditures are combined, it has been estimated that American drug courts represent an economic investment of more than one billion dollars (Roman, Butts, & Rebeck, 2004). While similar figures are not available worldwide, the International Association of Drug Treatment Courts has observed that in the past decade since Canada opened the first drug court outside of the USA, additional courts have been established in over a dozen countries, ranging from Australia to Macedonia (see http://www.iadtc law.ecu.edu.au/about/index.html).

Despite their phenomenal growth and the investment of substantial fiscal resources, however, it has been noted as recently as 2003 that evaluation research investigating the impact of drug courts has 'lagged considerably behind' their exponential expansion (Goldkamp, 2003; see also US Government Accountability Office, 2002). Moreover, even among those studies that have been conducted, many have been criticized for lack of methodological rigor, and/or a somewhat premature focus on the criminal behavior of participants during their participation in the program, rather than upon its completion (Jensen & Mosher, 2006). Additionally, such studies generally focus on a single site, or, at most, embrace a small handful of programs for comparative purposes.

For these and many other reasons, the drug court evaluation literature thus far has not established the firm foundation of confidence that can serve as a definitive empirical springboard from which incremental knowledge building can emerge.

Yet outcome evaluations of policy initiatives can be a powerful tool, particularly in terms of their potential to cast doubt upon presumed assumptions and 'reframe' issues that were once thought to have been resolved by policy-makers (Gerston, 1997, p. 120). As a result, it is worthwhile to analyze the results of drug court research somewhat more closely, particularly in the context of the drug-court movement's historical development, conceptual foundation, theoretical underpinnings, and related public policy implications.[1]

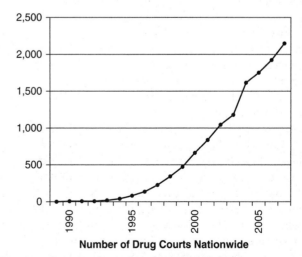

Figure 1   Growth of drug courts, 1990–2008.

(Source: National Drug Court Institute, 2008. Retrieved 28 April 2008, from http://www.whitehousedrugpolicy.gov/dfc/files/drug%5Fcourts.pdf).

Defying Tradition: The Drug Court Model

Unlike their counterparts in the juvenile justice system, criminal courts in the United States have traditionally operated on the basis of an adversarial model of jurisprudence, with the prosecutor and defense serving incompatible interests, and the judge officiating to rule on legal issues, assure due process, and maintain courtroom decorum. Ultimately, the goal of this traditional model of jurisprudence is to determine a defendant's guilt or innocence within the framework of constitutional protections, and, in the case of a conviction, to impose a suitable penalty. From the role of the judge to the nature of the interactions, goals of the proceedings, and outcome of the process, this model bears little resemblance to that of a drug court—where 'formal adversarial rules generally do not apply' (Goldkamp, 2000, p. 952).

Most fundamentally, many drug courts are not technically an adjudicatory process in the typical sense. Although some models require eligible clients to plead guilty and receive a suspended sentence before enrolling in drug court (with the conviction expunged upon successful completion)[2], many others operate on a diversionary (pre-plea) basis (Peters & Murrin, 2000, p. 73; Wilson, Mitchell, & MacKenzie, 2006). In diversionary drug courts, a defendant who is drug- or alcohol-dependent has the option to avoid prosecution (and eventually have charges dropped; see Drug Strategies, 1997) in exchange for participation in a rigorous treatment regimen. In such cases, the defendant is essentially on 'judicial probation' until successfully completing the drug court program (usually, within two years), withdrawing, or being expelled (Fischer, 2003, p. 240).

Either way, the defendant is provided with a powerful, judicially-enforced incentive to complete the program. By the same token, however, the stipulations that drug courts require of participating clients in terms of everything from attending counseling sessions to remaining substance free, submitting to periodic urine analysis, becoming gainfully employed, reporting progress periodically to the court, and so on, can be viewed by some as so excessively demanding that the personal investment is not worth the dispositional trade-off, especially for a defendant facing a relatively short sentence, with credit for time served in pretrial status[3]. In that regard, it has been noted that the 'traditional tools of punishment' have not been eliminated from the repertoire of drug courts, but rather, punishment has been recast into constructive terminologies such as 'motivational sanctions' or 'incentives for ensuring compliance' (Chiodo, 2002, p. 86).

Moreover, penalties for non-compliance can produce more time behind bars than would have been assigned if the case had been traditionally adjudicated (Goldkamp, 2000, p. 953).

An additional characteristic that delineates drug courts from more traditional judicial proceedings is their non-adversarial approach that focuses on helping the client in a coordinated manner, emphasizing teamwork among the judge, prosecution, defense counsel, case managers, and treatment providers. In this atmosphere, the defense counsel becomes an integrated component of the treatment team (Boldt, 1998, p. 1245) rather than an independent legal advocate. In contrast to traditional responses to criminal offenses, the drug court model provide access to a continuum of treatment and rehabilitation service with abstinence monitored by frequent testing (Drug Cou Programs Office, 1997). In fact, it is this intensive monitorin function, coupled with the threat of graduated sanctions f non-compliance, that perhaps most clearly distinguishes bo the interactive judicial role and the personal accountability the defendant from that of traditional courtroom proceedings where the judge maintains a neutrally-detached distance fro the defendant, who, in turn, passively submits to punishme without any personal investment in either assuming responsibi ity for past failures or making behavioral changes in the futur In a traditional courtroom, judges have been anecdotally note for 'playing God,' holding the offender's future destiny in the enlightened hands in a manner that is perhaps respected, b often not fully comprehended, by those who are subjected such far-reaching judicial authority. In contrast, the judge's ro in drug court is more analogous to the hands-on interactio of a 'guardian angel,' who is continually keeping watch ov transgressors to assure that they are maintaining agreed-upo commitments to redirect their lives, and poised to dispen either praise for compliance or sanctions for violations—bo delivered in an atmosphere of compassionate concern.

The result has been nothing less than a major paradig shift—from 'court practices designed for speed and efficienc in dispensing penalties' to problem-solving courts designe to 'prevent future crime by addressing problems that increa the risk of criminal activity' (Harrell, 2003, p. 207). As suc drug courts have been described as 'the most significant crim nal justice initiative in the last century' (Huddleston, Freema Wilson, & Boone, 2004, p. 1). As Goldkamp (2003, p. 197) h noted, however, not everyone has embraced this widesprea departure from tradition, with some viewing it as conflictin with the judicial mission to serve as 'neutral arbiter,' and unde mining the 'professional detachment' needed to dispense ju tice in an equitable manner.

Given the fact that many drug-related offenders have pa histories of frequently recycling into and out of treatment pr grams (Huddleston et al., 2004), they are not well noted for the steadfast ability to fulfill commitments or their staunch tena ity in pursuing rehabilitative goals. As a result, drug courts ofte enter into a shaky therapeutic relationship with somewhat relu tant clients, many of whom have experienced the discourag ment of previous failures. In this setting, the unique power an authority of a judge represents an essential ingredient to comp compliance with treatment (Wilson et al., 2006, pp. 460–461 Moreover, because of their treatment focus, an integral featu of drug courts is their ability to mobilize community support an resources through a team-oriented approach to building partne ships with key stakeholders (Drug Court Programs Office, 1997

Nurturing a New Paradigm in Unfertile Ground

In retrospect, it is easy to dismiss what a 'dramatic a depa ture from prevailing judicial philosophy' the first drug court Miami actually represented (Goldkamp, 2003, p. 197). Sinc adition has a tenacious way of becoming entrenched in the riminal justice system, the question is how such a distinctly on-traditional approach as drug courts not only emerged, but ctually flourished, in a relatively inhospitable public-policy nvironment.

In that regard, it is notable that more than thirty years have assed since the paradigms guiding American jurisprudence hifted from the rehabilitative focus of the medical model to renewed emphasis on the retributive and deterrent emphasis f the more punitive practices associated with the contempo- ry justice model (Stinchcomb, 2005a, pp. 17–19). While cur- nt social policy tends to reaffirm a traditionally adversarial pproach to the pursuit of justice, drug courts appear to be an utlying anomaly that clearly contradicts modern trends. Just ow did such a needs-based initiative, rooted in the theoretical asis of the medical model that had been politically and con- eptually cast aside years ago, become a prevalent practice in ne contemporary era of free-choice-based rationality charac- ristic of the justice model? The answer largely points toward ne failure of prevailing efforts, combined with 'improved nowledge about the nature of addiction and its treatment' Listwan, Sundt, Holsinger, & Latessa, 2003, p. 392) and the nanticipated burdensome fiscal consequences of pursuing an ncreasingly punitive public-policy agenda.

he Shifting Sands
of Drug-Related Public Policy

mericans are notable for their public-policy ambivalence, par- cularly in terms of criminal justice, where policy paradigms have wung dramatically in widely differing directions over recent ecades: Community-based alternatives go out—intermediate anctions come in. Rehabilitation goes out—accountability comes . Soft-on-crime goes out—zero tolerance comes in (Stinch- omb, 2000, p. vi). But perhaps nowhere has US policy-making mbivalence found greater expression than in America's diver- ent responses over the years to drug-related crime and substance buse.

In fact, today it is difficult to imagine that in the early twen- eth century, cocaine was legal but alcohol was not. More ecently, US drug policy, along with the legislative enactments nd fiscal investments associated with it, has shifted dramati- ally, from zero-tolerance enforcement—and even the threat f capital punishment at one point—to faith-based initiatives nd the provision of voluntary treatment programs. In 1956, for xample, the federal Narcotic Control Act was passed in the nidst of what was then thought to be 'the height of the drug care' (Stinchcomb, 2005a, p. 41). Although this legislation stablished the death penalty for a second conviction of selling rugs to a minor, its implementation revealed our discomfort vith the disproportionately punitive nature of such drug-related olicies, since not a single person was ever sentenced to death nder this law (Carney, 1980, p. 7).

In subsequent years, America's ongoing struggle to develop coherent public policy in response to the escalating threat f illicit drugs has witnessed wide-ranging shifts, from zero- lerance enforcement to therapeutic interventions. By the

early 1990s, studies were emerging that began to identify drug addiction as a 'chronic, relapsing condition that is not effec- tively addressed by sanctions, enhanced monitoring, or lon- ger prison sentences' (Andrews & Bonta, 1998; Fagan, 1994; Listwan et al., 2003, p. 391, citing Belenko, Mara-Drita, & McElroy, 1992). Particularly in light of research demonstrating that drug abuse may have genetic origins that can mitigate the impact of free choice (Maes et al., 1999; Saah, 2005; Tsuang et al., 1998), the logic of empirical evidence coincided with an inherent distaste for excessively harsh sanctions in response to addiction-related behavior, producing contemporary social policies that have promoted preventive approaches and treat- ment-oriented initiatives. Enter, the therapeutic jurisprudence of drug courts.

The etiology of drug-addiction research notwithstanding, it is somewhat ironic that such a non-traditional, utilitarian strategy as the drug court concept can trace its genesis to the unrelenting arrests and immitigable sentencing provisions of the war on drugs that characterized public policy during the 1980s (see Figure 2). Certainly, it was not merely the result of a 'nostalgic swing of the pendulum back to the philosophy of the 1960s,' or a 'simple reincarnation of rehabilitation' (Goldkamp, 2003, p. 198). As the crack-cocaine epidemic spread through- out a country firmly committed to conservative political agen- das, 'just say no' became the rallying cry and zero-tolerance the enforcement weapon in this metaphoric war. At the same time, the shift toward legislatively structured guidelines based on the determinate sentencing mandates of the justice model significantly reduced judicial discretion (Stinchcomb & Hip- pensteel, 2001; Wallace, 1993), resulting in the confinement of escalating numbers of drug-addicted offenders in correctional facilities (Anonymous, 1992; Mauer, 2006).

As this double-barreled punch of increasingly intensive enforcement and progressively punitive sanctions ultimately produced crowded court dockets and sky-rocketing correctional populations (with much of the increase attributed to drug offend- ers),[4] public policies in support of the war-on-drugs crackdown came face to face with conservative political commitments to avoid the imposition of new taxes. Since there are no punish- ment options more costly than secure confinement in correc- tional facilities, it was apparent that something had to give.

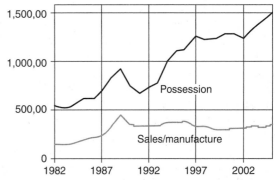

Figure 2 Number of arrests by type of drug law violations, 1982–2005.

(Source: Federal Bureau of Investigation, **Uniform Crime Reports, Crime in the United States**, annually. Retrieved 28 April 2008, from http://www.ojp.usdoj.gov /bjs/dcf/enforce.htm).

The New Paradigm: Merging Alternatives with Accountability

Thus, it was a desperate search for feasible solutions to the enormous caseloads, unyielding court backlogs, and unrelenting jail crowding, which were paralyzing the justice system, that promoted development of the first drug court in Miami in 1989 (Goldkamp, 2003). By the mid-1980s, officials at the Miami–Dade Department of Corrections and Rehabilitation were facing fiscal demands from a persistently-escalating jail population, along with orders from a federal court to reduce the daily population to acceptable limits, while having virtually exhausted their options in terms of such pretrial release alternatives as standard bonds, release on recognizance, and electronic monitoring[5]. At the same time, local judges were expressing extreme frustration with sentencing more and more offenders to probation, only to later revoke their community supervision and incarcerate them in a seemingly endlessly repetitive cycle (Drug Strategies, 1997). The observation that 'necessity is the mother of invention' clearly applied here. As a result, the first drug court came into existence—designed as a judicially sanctioned alternative process incorporating a treatment-oriented approach, which redefined relevant defendants from offenders destined for incarceration to addicts targeted for treatment[6]. Ultimately, as the movement spread across the country, drug courts came to be defined by the following parameters:

A specially designed court calendar or docket, the purposes of which are to achieve a reduction in recidivism and substance abuse among non-violent substance-abusing offenders and to increase the offender's likelihood of successful habilitation through early, continuous, and intense judicially supervised treatment, mandatory periodic drug testing, community supervision and use of appropriate sanctions and other habilitation services (Bureau of Justice Assistance, 2003).

Grounded in an ideology with broad-based political appeal, it is not surprising that drug courts have become so widely popular, inasmuch as they are attractive to both liberals endorsing treatment alternatives to incarceration and conservatives supportive of enforcing offender accountability through close supervision and sanctions for non-compliance[7]. In addition to ardent supporters, much of their explosive growth has been stimulated by federal funding that was initiated through the 1994 Violent Crime Control and Law Enforcement Act. Ultimately, this legislation translated into the distribution of $40 million through the Drug Court Discretionary Grant Program. Given the drug court's origins in Miami under Janet Reno's tenure as state attorney, following her appointment to the position of US Attorney General, it was predictable that she would establish the Drug Court Program Office in the US Department of Justice to support the growing momentum throughout the country (Goldkamp, 2003, p. 201).

In more recent years, however, the drug court appropriation was eliminated from President Bush's proposed budget for fiscal year 2008, prompting the National Association of Drug Court Professionals to raise an alarm, urging their membership to launch a telephone petition calling for the restoration of the Drug Court Discretionary Grant Program at its historic funding level of $40 million (National Association of Drug Court Professionals, 2007). While considerably less ($15.2 million) wa ultimately authorized, it represented a 50% increase over th $10 million that had been appropriated in fiscal years 200 and 2007 (National Association of Drug Court Professionals, 2008). Whether drug courts will continue to proliferate federal funding is curtailed remains to be seen, although it ha been observed that they have 'moved in status from isolated grant-funded projects' to integral components of the criminal justice system (Goldkamp, 2003, p. 201).

Drug Courts and Therapeutic Jurisprudence

Regardless of their underlying political ideology or pragmati idiosyncrasy, drug courts reflect the theoretical foundation of a burgeoning initiative known as therapeutic jurisprudence Originally defined by Wexler and Winick (1991), therapeuti jurisprudence focuses on the 'socio-psychological ways i which laws and legal processes affect individuals involved i the legal system' (Hora, Schma, & Rosenthal, 1999, p. 441 particularly in terms of whether they produce therapeutic anti-therapeutic results for those involved. In fact, it is thi emphasis on outcomes that clearly distinguishes therapeuti from traditional jurisprudence:

The latter largely concerns itself with whether the correc law or legal interpretation has been applied in a particular case but not with the consequences of the decision. Therapeuti jurisprudence brings the effect of the legal system's actions o the welfare of the defendant . . . squarely into the jurispruden tial equation (Reed, 2001, p. 1).

Above and beyond traditional adjudicatory and sentencin responsibilities, courts operating according to this perspectiv use their power to enforce legal rules and procedures to pro mote the psychological and physical wellbeing of stakeholder (Harrell, 2003; Senjo & Leip, 2001; Wexler & Winick, 1991 with the court playing a key role as 'an active therapeutic agen in the recovery process' (Lerner-Wren, 2000, p. 6). Sinc courtrooms are obviously not drug-treatment centers, thi requires multidisciplinary input into the application of lega processes in a manner that can most effectively produce thera peutic outcomes. Instead of relying exclusively on the statutor substance of the law in decision making, therapeutic jurispru dence therefore incorporates knowledge from other relevar disciplines (such as psychology and the social sciences), 't inform what legal practices may best lead to healing result (Reed, 2001, p. 2). Essentially, the fundamental intent is t pursue 'treatment, justice, and public safety,' in a manner tha reflects 'a synthesis of therapeutic treatment and the judici process' (Hora et al., 1999, pp. 449 & 453).

Problem-solving courts based on the concept of therapeu tic jurisprudence have been adapted to address any number c social and interpersonal issues, from mental health to domesti violence, drunk driving, and even homelessness. In that regarc drug courts in particular have been praised for adding a 'ric and humane dimension to traditional jurisprudence,' and fc recognizing drug-related crimes as 'public health as well a iminal justice problems' (Reed, 2001, pp. 1–2). But questions ve also been raised in terms of whether the ends justify the eans—i.e. whether their use of legal pressure is justified in e interest of therapeutic effects (Harrell, 2003, p. 210). For .ample, it has been noted that the very presence of drug courts generating more arrests and prosecutorial filings in the kinds ' low-level drug cases 'that the system simply would not have othered with before,' and that drug courts are actually 'sending bstantially more drug defendants to prison' (Hoffman, 2001– 002, p. 174). Such net-widening consequences have caused least one judge to question whether 'frustration over the war n drugs' combined with 'powerful hopes for workable reha- litation' may have 'clouded our judgment' (Hoffman, 2001– 002, pp. 173–174). Likewise, others have observed that the ghly stigmatizing nature of drug courts might, in accordance ith labeling theory, potentially be doing more harm than good Miethe, Lu, & Reese, 2000). In that regard, it has been noted at the fundamental question that should be asked is:

Why drug offenders are in the criminal justice system rather an in treatment in the first place? The answer to this question ppears to lie in the socio-racially and enforcement driven gen- sis and evolution of drug control laws . . . Drug courts obscure e fact that punishment is the persistent and predominant mode addiction control (Fischer, 2003, p. 244).

Along the same lines, doubts have been raised about the ompatibility of the principles of criminal justice and those of habilitative treatment. Particularly under the justice model of ublic policy making—with its emphatic emphasis on free will, dividual choice, and personal accountability—the contempo- ry criminal justice paradigm appears to be in direct contra- ction to the deterministic, pathological, and even biological asis from which drug addiction treatment flows. In fact, it has een noted that these contrasting perspectives are 'not only ndamentally different, but contradictory and exclusionary' Fischer, 2003, p. 235).

Systematic Reviews nd Meta-Analyses of Drug Court Evaluation Literature

evertheless, the community-based, problem-solving nature f therapeutic jurisprudence has invoked significant symbolic ppeal as well as widespread sentimental support and political opularity throughout the United States (Fischer, 2003, p. 242). et the critical substantive question is whether drug courts are chieving an impact on reducing criminal behavior, inasmuch s 'neither prevalence nor popularity' should substitute for olid empirical evidence (Goldkamp, 2003, p. 202). In response that question, interpretations of empirical evidence have fluc- ated widely, ranging from assertions that drug court success as been definitively established (e.g. Marlowe, 2004; Meyer Ritter, 2001–2002), to concerns that they are essentially sham perpetuated by irrational believers' (Marlowe, 2004, ferring to Anderson, 2001, and Hoffman, 2001–2002). On the ne hand, there is a 'strong sense of enthusiasm and conviction' bout the ability of drug courts to 'deliver on their ambitious

promises,' but on the other hand, there is 'very limited evi- dence' documenting their superior effectiveness, especially when taking into account the substantial methodological prob- lems that are often characteristic of their assessments (Fischer, 2003, p. 231).

In an effort to more precisely assess the drug court evalua- tion literature, four systematic reviews have been reported in the current literature on this topic (Belenko, 2001; Jensen & Mosher, 2006; US Government Accountability Office, 2005; Wilson et al., 2006), with the latter also incorporating meta- analytical techniques. In addition, two meta-analytic reviews were conducted in recent years, one published (Lowenkamp, Holsinger, & Latessa, 2005), and one as-yet unpublished (Shaf- fer, 2006). Although overall findings of these studies lean toward endorsing the beneficial effects of drug courts, they are neither universally nor unconditionally positive, as outlined in the following summarized descriptions.

Belenko's (2001) review of 37 published and unpublished evaluations of drug courts produced between 1999 and April, 2001, reports that they have 'achieved considerable local sup- port and have provided intensive, long-term treatment ser- vices to offenders with long histories of drug use and criminal justice contacts, previous treatment failures, and high rates of health and social problems.' His findings indicate that drug use and criminal activity are 'relatively reduced' during program participation, but with an average of 47% graduat- ing, 'the long-term, post-program impacts' are 'less clear' (Belenko, 2001, p. 1). In four of the six studies that examined one-year post-program recidivism, a reduction was found, but the size of the reduction varied[8]. Among the three studies that used random assignment, all reported a reduction in recidi- vism, but none distinguished between in-program and post- program rearrests.

As a result, Belenko (2001, p. 2) concludes that his review 'suggests a continuing need for better precision in describ- ing data sources,' particularly in terms of clearly identifying whether the population is being studied during or after drug court participation. Additionally, he points out that 'findings from several evaluations suggest that drug court impacts may fluctuate over time,' thus requiring multi-year replication stud- ies to accurately determine long-term outcomes (Belenko, 2001, p. 2). Goldkamp (2003, p. 199) further affirms this obser- vation, noting that his research likewise revealed 'some pretty strong years, some not-so-strong years, and some years in which significant differences in outcomes between participants and comparisons could not be found.'

In an effort to update Belenko's review, Jensen and Mosher (2006) searched criminology and criminal justice research sources for adult criminal drug court outcome evaluations published in refereed journals from 2001 through June 2005. They uncovered only eleven studies that met their requirements for scientific rigor that had not been reviewed previously by Belenko. In response to the methodological concerns expressed by Belenko, their findings are separated into two distinct cate- gories: (1) those studies that mix in-program and post-program follow-up periods; and (2) those that measure post-program outcomes only.

Among the first (mixed) group, three studies found that drug courts reduced recidivism, one found a small reduction in reconvictions (but it was not statistically significant), and in one results were mixed. Among the second group (post-program outcomes only), three studies found that drug courts resulted in lower recidivism rates. Given these differences in follow-up designs, they conclude that ten of the eleven evaluations reviewed were found to reduce criminal recidivism, although the reduction in one was small, and another reported mixed results (Jensen & Mosher, 2006, p. 464). Like Belenko, these researchers also denounced the lack of methodological consistency, particularly in terms of 'how recidivism is measured, the length and scope of the study, and the use of non-equivalent comparison groups' (Jensen & Mosher, 2006, p. 464). Additionally, they pointed out that peer-reviewed journals are considerably more likely to publish studies that find positive results, thus concluding that 'a selection bias may exist' that would modify their findings (Jensen & Mosher, 2006, p. 464).

The research conducted by the US Government Accountability Office (GAO) began by noting that determining whether drug courts reduce recidivism and substance use has been challenging because so much of the empirical evidence is weak (US Government Accountability Office, 2005). Nevertheless, GAO was mandated by the Department of Justice Appropriations Authorization Act to assess drug court program effectiveness. To meet this mandate, a systematic review of drug court research was conducted, which identified 117 evaluations that reported outcome data and were published between May 1997 and January 2004. However, when additional criteria for methodological soundness were applied, only 27 evaluations were ultimately selected (just five of which employed random assignment).

GAO's analysis of 'within-program' recidivism data (i.e. recidivism during program participation) showed that participants had fewer incidents of rearrests or reconvictions and a longer time until rearrest or reconviction than comparison group members (these reductions were observed for any felony offense and for drug offenses). Moreover, GAO's evidence suggests that recidivism reductions observed during the program endured when post-program recidivism was measured for up to one year after completion (US Government Accountability Office, 2005)[9].

With regard to substance use, results were somewhat less consistent. While drug test results generally showed significant reductions in use during program participation, self-reported results did not. From a fiscal perspective, however, among the seven evaluations that provided sufficient cost and benefit data, all yielded positive net benefits (US Government Accountability Office, 2005). Since completion rates ranged from 27% to 66%, and inasmuch as program completion was associated with compliance with requirements, GAO concluded that 'practices that encourage program completion may enhance the success of drug court programs in relation to recidivism' (US Government Accountability Office, 2005, p. 7). As another researcher observed in this regard, 'we know that drug courts reduce recidivism and drug use among participants when they are in drug court, though we don't know how long the effect lasts' (Fo 2004, p. 6, quoting John Roman).

The systematic literature review conducted by Wils et al. (2006) differed from those previously cited on at lea two significant dimensions—i.e. it included both publishe and unpublished reports, as well as a statistical meta-analysi thereby enabling them to estimate overall effect across studie Their search strategy was designed to locate all eligible dr court evaluations—whether published or not—that used a con parison group and experimental or quasi-experimental desig Sixty-eight documents representing 50 studies met the eligibi ity criteria, the majority of which (62%) were actually unpul lished, thereby addressing the potential selection bias issu raised by Jensen and Mosher (2006).

Findings reported by Wilson et al. (2006, p. 479) 'tentative suggest that drug offenders participating in a drug court are le likely to reoffend than similar offenders sentenced to tradition correctional options.' More specifically, they found the redu tion in overall offending was approximately 26% across a studies (14% for two high-quality randomized studies). Ne ertheless, they qualify their results as 'tentative,' explaining tl equivocation in their conclusions as resulting from the 'ger erally weak nature of the research designs' employed by tl studies they reviewed (Wilson et al., 2006, p. 479). Althoug they maintain that 'evidence is supportive of the hypothesis th drug courts are effective at reducing future drug use and oth criminal behavior,' it is 'not convincing from a social scientif standpoint' (Wilson et al., 2006, p. 479).

The research conducted by Lowenkamp et al. (2005) likewi included both published and unpublished evaluations, alor with meta-analytic techniques. They identified 22 outcon evaluations that met their criteria for inclusion of a compar son group and utilization of some measure of criminal beha ior as an outcome measure. Looking at long-term results, the determined that studies using a follow-up period of more tha two years actually demonstrated the greatest reductions recidivism (with each twelve-month increase in follow-up tin increasing the average recidivism reduction). This prompted tl authors to conclude that their findings 'may indicate that lons term behavioral changes are an outcome of the drug court pr grams and that these changes do not begin to dissipate with three years' (Lowenkamp et al., 2005, p. 10). One of the mo unique features of this meta-analysis, however, was its focus c offender risk level, which was found to be a significant predict associated with a doubling of the effect size—i.e. 'studies whe less than 50% of the participants had a prior record produced a average reduction in recidivism of 5%,' compared 'to an ave age 10% reduction associated with studies where half or mo of the participants had a prior record', thus apparently valida ing the notion that treatment programs should be reserved f higher-risk cases (Lowenkamp et al., 2005, pp. 10 & 28).

Finally, in her meta-analysis, Shaffer (2006) collecte data from 60 outcome evaluations, representing 76 distin drug courts and six multi-site evaluations[10]. Overall, her fin ings indicate that drug courts in general reduce recidivism t approximately 9%, although this average masks considerab ifferences between adult drug courts (10%) and juvenile drug ourts (5%). Differences in effect size were also noted on the asis of methodological quality and program length (Shaffer, 006), with those lasting between eight and sixteen months gnificantly more effective than those lasting less than eight onths or longer than sixteen months.

It is also noteworthy that, while empirically qualifying as either a systematic review nor a meta-analysis, Fischer's 2003, p. 232) analysis of the literature identified the follow- g key issues as illustrating 'the state of limited effectiveness r research quality' in drug court evaluations (Fischer, 2003, . 232):

1. **Limited program retention**—i.e. several dozen evaluation reviews suggest that drug courts retain (for at least one year) about 40–60% of eligible offenders. Particularly in light of the correlation between participation and positive outcomes, this is interpreted as 'a key indicator' of limitations in terms of establishing the effectiveness of drug courts.

2. **Skimming practices**—i.e. many drug courts carefully select the 'most treatable' or 'lowest risk' offenders, making them vulnerable to 'self-selection bias.' Since most of their evaluations are based on control groups (rather than random assignment), comparing the experimental group to either dropouts who are expelled for rule violations or high-risk offenders who are ineligible to participant results in comparing 'not so bad apples' with 'very bad apples,' thus skewing results in favor of the intervention.

3. **No long-term, post-intervention follow-up**—i.e. focusing the evaluation on those remaining in the program (and therefore under the supervision of the criminal justice system), who are, by default, in compliance with the very program rules and regulations that serve as effectiveness indicators, thereby creating a tautological effect.

Conclusions from Empirical Findings

As is illustrated by this review of the literature, researchers have ome to rather divergent opinions about evidence reflecting on he impact of drug courts. In that regard, Marlowe (2004) rhe- orically questions why this field has continued to languish in serious dispute about whether drug courts work,' in light of xtensive empirical results. His assessment of the answer relates o the likelihood that, as the literature is expanded, it is inevi- ably going to contain more conflicting findings, inadequate methodologies, and differential standards of proof, but that these ssues should not detract from the scientific integrity of well- designed studies that 'prove the efficacy of drug courts' beyond he standard of evidence needed to establish the efficacy of a ew medication in clinical trials (Marlowe, 2004, p. 3). In fact, anet Reno herself has remarked that she did not expect to see fairy tale' results showing dramatic reductions in reoffending,

but rather, appeared to be more impressed with the finding that, when drug court participants did recidivate, they took two to three times longer to be rearrested than their counterparts (Gold- kamp, White, & Robinson, 2001, p. 32).

At the opposite extreme, another researcher describes drug courts as 'unproven mandatory treatment programs . . . that rely on legal coercion' (Anderson, 2001, p. 469), and at least one judge clearly denounces their efficacy (i.e. 'drug courts don't work, and never have'), criticizing them for massive net-widening, as well as creating 'a dangerous psycho-judicial branch [of government] populated by judges who think they are doctors, who think drug addiction is a treatable disease, and who send their patients to prison when they fail to respond to treatment' (Hoffman, 201–2002, p. 172). Still others take a more neutral position, concluding that drug courts are 'prom- ising but understudied,' (Marlowe, DeMatteo, & Festinger, 2003), and expressing concern that 'what we know [about drug courts] is very small . . . what we think we know is much big- ger' (Fox, 2004, p. 3, quoting John Roman).

Policy-Related Conclusions and Implications

Reviewing the findings reported herein helps to illustrate why evaluation research often does not contribute significantly to public policy development. Not only do empirical studies tend to produce ambivalent results (Petersilia, 1996) that can lead to the widely-differing conclusions expressed above, but even when definitive findings are forthcoming, they often do little to identify why change did or did not occur in the anticipated direction (Stinchcomb, 2005b). The resulting lack of specific- ity is among the reasons that at least one public policy analyst has observed that he has been unable to identify a single gov- ernmental program that has been 'terminated solely as a con- sequence of an unfavorable systematic evaluation' (Anderson, 1994, p. 250). The dynamic environment of ongoing debate over the efficacy of drug courts therefore continues to raise questions concerning the strength of their conceptual foun- dation, the execution of their implementation strategies, and, ultimately, the future potential of their ability to maintain a prominent position on the public-policy agenda.

With regard to their conceptual basis, the therapeutic juris- prudence foundation of drug courts perhaps most closely resembles the non-traditional judicial approaches that have characterized the contemporary restorative justice movement (see Bazemore & Griffiths, 1997; Perry, 2002; Zehr, 1991). Founded in the midst of disenchantment with the capability of punishment alone to reduce drug-related crimes (Stinchcomb, 2000), drug courts to a considerable extent share a common theoretical basis with restorative justice initiatives, which emerged in the United States at approximately the same time, as a result of similar frustrations with existing practices. In that respect, both approaches attempt to hold offenders accountable for their actions, while at the same time incorporating into the judicial decision-making equation a tough-love-oriented con- cern for addressing whatever underlying condition prompted their law-violating behavior. Likewise, both rely on a multi-disciplinary team-focused intervention that, in contrast to traditional judicial practices, represents a relatively unstructured and unstandardized initiative that is based on the unique circumstances of each case (Stinchcomb, 2005a, p. 37).

While a certain degree of 'shaming' is inherent in both, restorative justice emphasizes reintegrative rather than stigmatic shaming (Braithwaite, 1989), whereas drug courts have been criticized for actually being more stigmatizing than conventional courts [emphasis added] and 'not reintegrative enough' in their orientation toward punishment (Miethe et al., 2000, p. 522). This may be a reflection of the fact that restorative justice practices appear to be grounded on somewhat more solid theoretical underpinnings (see, for example, Bazemore & Stinchcomb, 2004) than drug courts, which seem to have emerged more atheoretically as an opportunistic reaction to fiscal and political realities. As Scheirer (1981) has observed in that regard, opportunistic public policies are substantially less likely to succeed in fulfilling their mission than those based more on analytical problem solving. Without theory-driven parameters to serve as directional guideposts, public policy has a tendency to drift through the shifting sands of popular opinion and political ideology, which does not provide 'fertile soil in which to plant productive policy paradigms' (Stinchcomb, 2000, p. viii).

Whether theoretically grounded or politically driven, however, policy ultimately must be translated into practice. In that process, some degree of reshaping and redefinition is always necessary in order to enable the broad-based nature of policy to be specifically applied in response to local needs (Levine, Musheno, & Palumbo, 1980, p. 118). Nevertheless, it is well known that even the best policy intentions are not always converted effectively into operational practices. Consider, for instance, the so-called 'medical model' that ostensibly dominated correctional policy (and by inference, practice) from the 1930s to the mid-1970s (Archambeault & Archambeault, 1982, p. 165). While widespread rehabilitative rhetoric surrounded this policy, the reality of its implementation reflected little of its theoretical assumptions.

[O]ne might assume that treatment services were widely available in prisons under the medical model. That, however, was not the case. Even at the height of the medical model, in-depth psychological counseling, social casework, and psychiatric therapy were never prominent features of correctional institutions . . . In the mid-1950s, for example, there were only twenty-three full-time psychiatrists in US correctional institutions . . . The psychological staff numbered sixty-seven. The 257 caseworkers [in prisons throughout the country] averaged less than sixteen minutes per inmate each month. (Stinchcomb, 2005a, pp. 276–77, citing data from Schnur, 1958).

Moreover, drug-court evaluations that focus exclusively on outcome measures such as recidivism often fail to explore implementation procedures representing the 'black box' that intervenes between policy intentions and operational outcomes. Such evaluations are insensitive to political and organizational contexts within which the drug court emerged and neglect such issues as the relationship between planned and delivered treatment, official and operative goals, intended and unintended effects, etc. (Chen,

1990; Stinchcomb, 2001). Although most drug-court evaluations reflect outcome-focused summative assessments, some have opened the black box, discovering, for example, a 'wide disparity' between the court's 'organizational rhetoric and actual practices' (Miethe et al., 2000, p. 536). Until more empirical assessments explore this level of analysis through a combination of formative and summative assessments, the reasons underlying either positive or negative results will remain obscured.

In the final analysis, the challenge for drug courts in terms of their potential to maintain a prominent position on the public policy agenda is intimately related to each of the issues discussed above—i.e. the strength of their conceptual foundation and the execution of their implementation strategies, both of which are encompassed within a politically charged policy development environment. As Lindblom (1980, p. 12) has noted in that regard:

On the one hand, people want policy to be informed and well-analyzed. On the other hand, they want policy-making to be democratic, hence necessarily political. In slightly different words, on the one hand, they want policy-making to be more scientific; on the other, they want it to remain in the world of politics.

Whether emerging from theoretical, political, or simply pragmatic considerations, drug courts ultimately must be able to demonstrate their operational utility, empirical benefits, and comparative superiority to traditional practices. That is more likely to be achieved for public policies that are based on solid theoretical grounding than those that are floundering in conceptual uncertainty. For although people may want public policy to encompass the diametrically opposed attributes of scientific inquiry and political reality, the question for both policy makers and practitioners is what happens when political support diminishes or ideological paradigms shift, leaving public policy that was dependent on these frail foundations floating in a sea of ambiguity. It is only when theory is solidly anchored to policy—and subsequently, policy to practice, and ultimately, practice to methodologically rigorous evidence-based outcomes—that a protective causal chain can be convincingly mounted to guard against the destructive repercussions of unanticipated idiosyncrasies ranging from political reactions to public indifference.

Declaration of Interest

The author reports no conflicts of interest. The author alone is responsible for the content and writing of the paper.

Notes

1. Although the research in this article is based on the widespread empirical results that have been generated in conjunction with the US drug court experience over the past two decades, findings are in most cases likewise relevant to similar initiatives in other countries without benefit of an extensive empirical foundation on which to rely in shaping their developmental drug court initiatives.

2. In such post-adjudication drug courts, the defendant pleads guilty, and the sentence is suspended in lieu of successfully completing drug court programming, at which point the

sentence is waived, and often the conviction is expunged as well (or if the client is unsuccessful, the suspension is lifted and the sentence imposed).

3. Between 40% and 80% of drug abusers drop out of treatment prior to the ninety-day threshold of effective treatment length, . . . and 80 to 90% drop out in fewer than twelve months (Huddleston et al., 2004, p. 4).

4. For example, between 1985 and 1995, the population of drug offenders in state prisons increased by 478%, more than double the increase for any other offense category (Mauer, 1999, p. 35). Moreover, in terms of the fiscal impact, a comparative study of two groups of low-level drug traffickers sentenced before and after the adoption of mandatory minimums and sentencing guidelines concluded that the additional time spent in prison for the second group would cost taxpayers approximately $515 million (Harer, 1994).

5. These insights reflect the fact that during this period of time, the author was on the management staff of the Miami–Dade Department of Corrections and Rehabilitation.

6. In an ironic twist of fate, as of mid-April, 2007, Miami–Dade's drug court had placed a moratorium on accepting new defendants in order to reduce the load of 2000 cases, which had become unmanageable for its solitary judge (Arthur, 2007).

7. In fact, the same perspectives are held among drug court opponents—some of whom believe that they are 'soft on crime' by offering offenders a means of avoiding punishment, while others view them as too coercive, thereby increasing the risk of incarceration for participants, among which minorities are overrepresented (Harrell, 2003, p. 209).

8. Another study independent of Belenko's research found that, based on a sample of 2020 drug-court graduates (designed to represent approximately 17,000 graduates), 16.4% had been arrested and charged with a serious offense within one year of graduation. Within two years, the figure rises to 27.5% (Roman, Townsend, & Bhati, 2003).

9. These findings are in contrast to an earlier GAO analysis of the literature, which, on the basis of evidence available at that time, concluded that 'some studies showed positive effects of the drug court programs during the period offenders participated in them, while others showed no effects, or effects that were mixed and difficult to interpret. Similarly, some studies showed positive effects for offenders after completing the programs, while others showed no effects, or small and insignificant effects' (US Government Accounting Office, 1997, p. 85).

10. Additionally, she surveyed and conducted telephone interviews with the targeted courts.

References

Anderson, J. E. (1994). *Public policymaking: An introduction.* Geneva, IL: Houghton Mifflin.

Anderson, J. F. (2001). What to do about 'much ado' about drug courts? *International Journal of Drug Policy, 12,* 469–475.

Andrews, D. A., & Bonta, J. (1998). *The psychology of criminal conduct.* Cincinnati, OH: Anderson.

Anonymous. (1992). Emphasis on enforcement not the answer to the drug crisis. *Narcotics Control Digest,* January 29, 4.

Archambeault, W. G., & Archambeault, B. J. (1982). *Correctional supervisory management: Principles of organization, policy, and law.* Englewood Cliffs, NJ: Prentice Hall.

Arthur, L. (2007). Drug court puts new cases on hold. *The Miami Herald,* April 15, 1B.

Bazemore, G., & Griffiths, C. T. (1997). Conferences, circles, boards, and mediations: The 'new wave:' of community justice decision making. *Federal Probation,* June 25, 25–37.

Bazemore, G., & Stinchcomb, J. B. (2004). Civic engagement and reintegration: Toward a community-focused theory and practice. *Columbia Human Rights Law Review, 36*(1), 241–286.

Belenko, S. (2001, June). *Research on drug courts: A critical review, 2001 update.* New York: National Center on Addiction and Substance Abuse, Columbia University.

Belenko, S., Mara-Drita, I., & McElroy, J. (1992). Pre-arraignment drug tests in the pretrial release decision: Predicting defendant failure to appear. *Crime and Delinquency, 38*(4), 554–582.

Boldt, R. C. (1998). Rehabilitative punishment and the drug treatment court movement. *Washington University Law Quarterly, 76,* 1205–1306.

Braithwaite, J. (1989). *Crime, shame, and reintegration.* Cambridge, UK: Cambridge University Press.

Bureau of Justice Assistance. (2003). *Competitive grant announcement: Adult drug court implementation grants.* Washington, DC: US Department of Justice.

Carney, L. P. (1980). *Corrections: Treatment and philosophy.* Englewood Cliffs, NJ: Prentice Hall.

Chen, H.-T. (1990). *Theory-driven evaluations.* Newbury Park, CA: Sage.

Chiodo, A. L. (2002). Sentencing drug-addicted offenders and the Toronto Drug Court. *Criminal Law Quarterly, 45,* 53–100.

Dodge, M. (2001). Drug courts as an alternative treatment modality: Preface. *Journal of Drug Issues, 31*(1), i–iii.

Drug Court Programs Office, Office of Justice Programs. (1997). *Defining drug courts: The key components.* Washington, DC: US Department of Justice.

Drug Strategies. (1997). *Cutting crime: Drug courts in action.* Washington, DC: Drug Strategies. (Available at: www.drugstrategies.org).

Fagan, J. A. (1994). Do criminal sanctions deter drug crimes? In D. L. MacKenzie, & C. D. Uchida (Eds.), *Drugs and crime: Evaluating public policy initiatives* (pp. 89–131). Thousand Oaks, CA: Sage.

Fischer, B. (2003). Doing good with a vengeance: A critical assessment of the practices, effects, and implications of drug treatment courts in North America. *Criminology and Criminal Justice, 3*(3), 227–248.

Fox, A. (Ed.), (2004). *Bridging the gap: Researchers, practitioners, and the future of drug courts.* New York: Center for Court Innovation.

Gerston, L. N. (1997). *Public policy making: Process and principles.* Armonk, NY: ME Sharpe.

Goldkamp, J. S. (2000). The drug court response: Issues and implications for justice change. *Albany Law Review, 63,* 923–961.

Goldkamp, J. S. (2003, March). The impact of drug courts. Criminology and Public Policy, 2(2), 197–205.

Goldkamp, J. S., White, M. D., & Robinson, J. B. (2001). Do drug courts work? Getting inside the drug court black box. *Journal of Drug Issues, 31*(1), 27–72.

Harer, M. D. (1994). Do guideline sentences for low-risk traffickers achieve their stated purpose? *Federal Sentencing Reporter, 7*(1), 22–27.

Harrell, A. (2003, March). Judging drug courts: Balancing the evidence. *Criminology and Public Policy, 2*(2), 207–212.

Hoffman, M. B. (2001, November–2002, February). The rehabilitative ideal and the drug court reality. *Federal Sentencing Reporter,* 14(3–4), 172–177.

Hora, P. F., Schma, W. G., & Rosenthal, J. (1999). Therapeutic jurisprudence and the drug treatment court movement: Revolutionizing the criminal justice system's response to drug abuse and crime in America. *Notre Dame Law Review, 74*(2), 439–527.

Huddleston, C. W., Freeman-Wilson, K., & Boone, D. L. (2004, May). *Painting the current picture: A national report card on drug courts and other problem solving court programs in the US.* Alexandria, VA: National Drug Court Institute.

Jensen, E., & Mosher, C. (2006). Adult drug courts: Emergence, growth, outcome evaluations, and the need for a continuum of care. *Idaho Law Review, 42*(2), 443–470.

Lerner-Wren, G. (2000). Broward's mental health court: An innovative approach to the mentally disabled in the criminal justice system. *Community Mental Health Report, 1*(1), 5–6, 16.

Levine, J. P., Musheno, M. C., & Palumbo, D. J. (1980). *Criminal justice: A public policy approach.* New York: Harcourt Brace Jovanovich.

Lindblom, C. E. (1980). *The policy-making process.* Englewood Cliffs, NJ: Prentice Hall.

Listwan, S. J., Sundt, J. L., Holsinger, A. M., & Latessa, E. J. (2003, July). The effect of drug court programming on recidivism: The Cincinnati experience. *Crime and Delinquency, 49*(3), 389–411.

Lowenkamp, C. T., Holsinger, A. M., & Latessa, E. J. (2005). Are drug courts effective: A metaanalytic review. *Journal of Community Corrections,* Fall, 5–10, 28.

Maes, H. H., Woodard, C. E., Muordle, L., Meyer, J. M., Silberg, J. L., Hewitt, J. K., Rutter, M., et al. (1999). Tobacco, alcohol, and drug use in 8 to 16 year-old twins: The Virginia twin study of adolescent behavioral development. *Journal of Studies on Alcohol, 60,* 293–305.

Marlowe, D. B., DeMatteo, D. S. & Destinger, D. S. (2003). A sober assessment of drug courts. F*ederal Sentencing Reporter, 16,* 153–157.

Marlowe, D. B. (2004). *Drug court efficacy vs. effectiveness.* (Available at: http://www.jointogether.org/news/yourturtn/commentary/2004/durg-court-efficacy-vs.html)

Mauer, M. (2006). *Race to incarcerate.* New York: The New Press, 1999.

Meyer, W. G., & Ritter, A. W. (2001, November–2002, February). Drug courts work. *Federal Sentencing Reporter, 14*(3–4), 179–185.

Miethe, T. D., Lu, H., & Reese, E. (2000, October). Reintegrative shaming and recidivism risks in drug court: Explanations for some unexpected findings. *Crime and Delinquency, 46*(4), 522–541.

National Association of Drug Court Professionals. (2007, March 5). *Help save drug courts: Action alert.* (Previously available at: http://www.jointogether.org/getinvolved/actionalerts/nadcp-helpsave-drug-courts.html)

National Association of Drug Court Professionals. (2008, January 7). *Drug court grant receives a 50% increase in funding* [press release]. (Available at: http://www.nadcp.org/publicrelations/)

Office of National Drug Control Policy. (2008). Drug Courts: *Providing Treatment instead of Jail for Nonviolent Offenders.* Washington, DC: ONDCP. (Available at: http://www.whitehousedrugpolicy.gov/ dfc/files/drug%5Fcourts.pdf)

Perry, J. (Ed.)., (2002). *Repairing communities through restorative justice.* Lanham, MD: American Correctional Association.

Peters, R. H., & Murrin, M. R. (2000, February). Effectiveness of treatment-based drug courts in reducing criminal recidivism. *Criminal Justice and Behavior,* 27(1), 72–96.

Petersilia, J. (1996). Improving corrections policy: The importance of researchers and practitioners working together. In A. T. Harland (Ed.), *Choosing correctional options that work: Defining the demand and evaluating the supply* (pp. 223–231). Thousand Oaks, CA: Sage.

Reed, D. (2001, May/June). Therapeutic jurisprudence: Looking at developments in mental health law through a caring lens. *Community Mental Health Report, 1*(4), 1–3.

Roman, J., Butts, J. A., & Rebeck, A. S. (2004). American drug policy and the evolution of drug treatment courts. In J. Roman, & J. A. Butts (Eds.), *Juvenile drug courts and teen substance abuse.* Washington, DC: Urban Institute Press.

Roman, J., Townsend, W., & Bhati, A. S. (2003, July). *Recidivism rates for drug court graduates: Nationally based estimates* (Final Report, OJP document #201299). Washington, DC: US Department of Justice.

Saah, T. (2005, June). The evolutionary origins and significance of drug addiction. *Harm Reduction Journal, 2*(8), 2–8.

Scheirer, M. A. (1981). *Program implementation: The organizationa context.* Beverly Hills, CA: Sage.

Schnur, A. C. (1958). The new penology: Fact or fiction? Journal of Criminal Law, *Criminology and Police Science, 49* (November/December), 331–334.

Senjo, S., & Leip, L. A. (2001). Testing therapeutic jurisprudence theory: An empirical assessment of the drug court process. *Western Criminology Review, 3*(1). (Available at: http://wcr.sonoma. edu/v3n1/senjo.html)

Shaffer, D. K. (2006, October). *Reconsidering drug court effectiveness: A meta-analytic review.* Executive summary. Unpublished dissertation. Las Vegas: University of Nevada.

Stinchcomb, J. B. (2000). Corrections and public policy: Where we've been, where we're going. *Corrections Management Quarterly,* 4(4), vi–viii.

Stinchcomb, J. B. (2001). Using logic modeling to focus evaluation efforts: Translating operational theories into practical measures. *Journal of Offender Rehabilitation, 33*(2), 47–65.

Stinchcomb, J. B. (2005a). Corrections: Past, present, and future. Lanham, MD: American Correctional Association.

Stinchcomb, J. B. (2005b). From optimistic policies to pessimistic outcomes: Why won't boot camps either succeed pragmatically or succumb politically? *Journal of Offender Rehabilitation, 40*(3), 27–52.

Stinchcomb, J. B., & Hippensteel, D. (2001). Presentence investigation reports: A relevant justice model tool or a medical model relic? *Criminal Justice Policy Review, 12*(2), 164–177.

Tsuang, M. T., Lyons, M. J., Eisen, S. A., Goldberg, J., True, W., Lin, N., Toomey, R., & Eaves, L. (1993, December). Genetic influences on DSM-III-R drug abuse and dependence: A study of 3,372 twin pairs. *Neuropsychiatric Genetics, 67*(5), 473–477.

US Government Accountability Office. (2002). *Drug courts: Better DOJ data collection and evaluation efforts needed to measure impact of drug court programs.* Washington, DC: US Government Accountability Office.

US Government Accountability Office. (2005). *Adult drug courts: Evidence indicates recidivism reductions and mixed results for other outcomes.* Washington, DC: US Government Accountability Office.

S Government Accounting Office. (1997). *Drug courts: Overview of growth, characteristics, and results.* Washington, DC: US Government Accounting Office.

allace, H. S. (1993, September). Mandatory minimums and the betrayal of sentencing reform: A legislative Dr. Jekyll and Mr. Hyde. *Federal Probation, 54*(3), 13–15.

exler, D. B., & Winick, B. J. (1991). Therapeutic jurisprudence as a new approach to mental health law, policy analysis and research. *University of Miami Law Review, 45,* 979–1004.

ilson, D. B., Mitchell, O., & MacKenzie, D. L. (2006, November). A systematic review of drug court effects on recidivism. *Journal of Experimental Criminology, 2*(4), 459–487.

Zehr, H. (1991). Restorative justice. *International Association of Residential and Community Alternatives Journal,* March, 7.

Critical Thinking

1. Describe the shift in American public policy since the early twentieth century related to illicit drug use.

2. What is meant by therapeutic jurisprudence?

3. Given the author's presentation of the literature, would you argue in favor or against the use of drug courts? Please support your position.

UNIT 7

Prevention, Treatment, and Education

Unit Selections

Learning Outcomes

After reading this Unit, you should be able to:

- Explain how the drug problem can be impacted by targeting demand and not supply.

- Understand what harm reduction is in the context of drug policy and treatment and how harm reduction differs from the American model of criminalization and punishment for drug using behaviors.

- Discuss correctional systems' involvement in treating drug dependency of prisoners. Explain why this practice should exist or not

Student Website
www.mhhe.com/cls

Internet References

American Council for Drug Education
www.acde.org
D.A.R.E.
www.dare-america.com
The Drug Reform Coordination Network (DRC)
www.drcnet.org
Drug Watch International
www.drugwatch.org
Hazelden
www.hazelden.org
Join Together
www.jointogether.org

KCI (Koch Crime Institute) The Anit-Meth Site
www.kci.org/meth_info/faq_meth.htm
Marijuana Policy Project
www.mpp.org
National Institute on Drug Abuse
www.nida.nih.gov/Infofacts/TreatMeth.html
Office of National Drug Control Policy (ONDCP)
www.whitehousedrugpolicy.gov
The Partnership for Drug-Free America
www.drugfree.org/#
United Nations International Drug Control Program (UNDCP
www.undcp.org

There are no magic bullets for preventing drug abuse and treating drug-dependent persons. Currently, more than 22 million Americans are classified as drug dependent on illicit drugs and/or alcohol. Males continue to be twice as likely to be classified as drug dependent as females. Research continues to establish and strengthen the role of treatment as a critical component in the fight against drug abuse. Some drug treatment programs have been shown to dramatically reduce the costs associated with high-risk populations of users. For example, recidivism associated with drug-related criminal justice populations has been shown to decrease by 50 percent after treatment. Treatment is a critical component in the fight against drug abuse but it is not a panacea. Society cannot "treat" drug abuse away just as it cannot "arrest" it away.

Drug prevention and treatment philosophies subscribe to a multitude of modalities. Everything seems to work a little and nothing seems to work completely. The articles in this unit illustrate the diversity of methods utilized in prevention and treatment programs. Special emphasis is given to treating the drug problems of those who are under the supervision of the criminal justice system. All education, prevention, and treatment programs compete for local, state, and federal resources. Current treatment efforts at all public and private levels are struggling to meet the demands for service due to the impacts from the U.S. economic crisis of the past few years.

Education: One critical component of drug education is the ability to rapidly translate research findings into practice, and today's drug policy continues to emphasize this in its overall budget allocations. Funding for educational research and grants is generally strong with the trend being toward administering funds to local communities and schools to fund local proposals. For example, in 2011 more than $50 million was again made available to schools for research-based assistance for drug prevention and school safety programs. Another example is the refunding of the $120 million National Youth Media Campaign designed to help coach parents in processes of early recognition and intervention. Encouraging successful parenting is one primary emphasis in current federal drug policy. Other significant research efforts continue to support important education, prevention, and treatment programs such as The National Prevention Research Initiative, Interventions and Treatment for Current Drug Users Who Are Not Yet Addicted, the National Drug Abuse Treatment Clinical Trial Network, and Research Based Treatment Approaches for Drug Abusing Criminal Offenders. In 2011, federal research-related grants totaling almost $100 million were made available to local and state school jurisdictions.

Prevention: A primary strategy of drug prevention programs is to prevent and/or delay initial drug use. A secondary strategy is to discourage use by persons minimally involved with drugs. Both strategies include (1) educating users and potential users; (2) teaching adolescents how to resist peer pressure; (3) addressing problems associated with drug abuse such as teen pregnancy, failure in school, and lawbreaking; (4) creating community support and involvement for prevention activities; and (5) involving parents in deterring drug use by children. Prevention and education programs are administered through

© The McGraw-Hill Companies, Inc./John Flournoy, photographer

a variety of mechanisms, typically amidst controversy relative to what works best. Schools have been an important delivery apparatus. Funding for school prevention programs is an important emphasis within the efforts to reduce the demand for drugs. Subsequently, an increase in federal money was dedicated to expanding the number of high school programs that implement student drug testing. Drug testing in high schools, authorized by the Supreme Court in a 2002 court decision, has produced a positive and measurable deterrent to drug use. Despite its controversy, school drug testing is expanding as a positive way to reinforce actions of parents to educate and deter their children from use. The testing program provides for subsequent assessment, referral, and intervention process in situations where parents and educators deem it necessary.

In addition, in 2011, approximately $90 million in grant funds were again dedicated to support the federal Drug-Free Communities Program, which provides funds at the community level to anti-drug coalitions working to prevent substance abuse among young people and in local neighborhoods. There are currently more than 700 local community coalitions working under this program nationwide. Also, there are community-based drug prevention programs sponsored by civic organizations, church groups, and private corporations. All programs pursue funding through public grants and private endowments. Federal grants to local, state, and private programs are critical components to program solvency. The multifaceted nature of prevention programs makes them difficult to assess categorically. School programs that emphasize the development of skills to resist social and peer pressure generally produce varying degrees of positive results. Research continues to make more evident the need to focus prevention programs with specific populations in mind.

Treatment: Like prevention programs, drug treatment programs enlist a variety of methods to treat persons dependent upon legal and illegal drugs. There is no single-pronged approach to treatment for drug abuse. Treatment modality may differ radically from one user to the other. The user's background, physical and mental health, personal motivation, and support structure all have serious implications for treatment type. Lumping together the diverse needs of chemically dependent persons for purposes of applying a generic treatment process does not work. In addition, most persons needing and seeking treatment have problems with more than one drug—polydrug use. Current research also correlates drug use with serious mental illness (SMI). Current research by the federal Substance Abuse and Mental Health Services Administration (SAMHSA) reports that adults with a drug problem are three times more likely to suffer from a serious mental illness. The existing harmful drug

use and mental health nexus is exacerbated by the fact that using certain powerful drugs such as methamphetamine push otherwise functioning persons into the dysfunctional realm of mental illness. Although treatment programs differ in methods most provide a combination of key services. These include drug counseling, drug education, pharmacological therapy, psychotherapy, relapse prevention, and assistance with support structures. Treatment programs may be outpatient oriented or residential in nature. Residential programs require patients to live at the facility for a prescribed period of time. These residential programs, often described as therapeutic communities emphasize the development of social, vocational, and educational skills. The current trend is to increase the availability of treatment programs. One key component of federal drug strategy is to continue to fund and expand the Access to Recovery treatment initiative that began in 2004. This program uses voucher system to fund drug treatment for individuals otherwise unable to obtain it. This program, now operational in 14 states and one Native American community, allows dependent persons to personally choose care providers, including faith-based care providers. It is hoped that this program will encourage states to provide a wider array of treatment and recovery options. As one example, the state of Missouri has transformed all public drug treatment within the state to an "Access to Recovery-Like" program in which involved persons choose their providers and pay with state vouchers. It is hoped that this and similar programs will allow a more flexible delivery of services that will target large populations of dependent persons who are not reached through other treatment efforts.

Crime and Treatment

Overcrowded Prisons and Addicted Inmates Are a Tough Challenge for Lawmakers

DONNA LYONS

With a prison population that surged 12 percent from 2007 to 2008, Kentucky lawmakers are looking for solutions.

They think they have found one in a measure passed last year that offers some felony offenders the option of substance abuse treatment in lieu of criminal charges.

"This represents a culture change in dealing with addicted offenders," says former Senator Dan Kelly, the key sponsor of the measure who has since taken a circuit court judgeship.

> **This represents a culture change in dealing with addicted offenders.**
>
> —Former Kentucky Senator Dan Kelly

The policy is expected to save millions of dollars by diverting offenders from prison and also could save the lives of those who complete the treatment. "It's one of those fairly small changes to law that will have significant policy impact," Kelly says.

Kentucky's problem is also a national one. Substance abuse offenders make up 20 percent of inmates in state prisons. Abuse and addiction, however, play a much larger role. Some 80 percent of offenders abuse drugs and alcohol, and nearly half of jail and prison inmates are thought to be clinically addicted.

Two-Pronged Approach

Kentucky's approach is to screen felony defendants for substance abuse. Some are diverted to community-based services; others with more serious problems and criminal records are referred to an intensive, secure substance abuse treatment program run by the department of corrections.

"There would be a sense of justice denied if there was no secure confinement option in this," Kelly says. "This gives those serious offenders an opportunity for pretrial diversion if they demonstrate commitment to treatment."

About 200 felons can be held in secure treatment at a time for an estimated savings of $1.4 million in the first year.

Long-term supporters of the legislation say cost savings will be about $40 million.

Kentucky currently has 20 corrections-based substance abuse treatment programs in prisons and jails. A study of the programs started in 2005 found reductions in recidivism and substance abuse among the participants. Reported drug use drops more than 50 percent during the 12 months following release as compared with before treatment. And more than two-thirds of participants are not in prison or jail 12 months later.

"It pays for itself," said Senator Ed Worley, who was among sponsors of the legislation aimed at stopping the revolving door for repeat drug offenders. "There are too many repeat offenders with drug problems filling up our jails and prisons. We need to rehabilitate them so they can contribute to society, rather than repeatedly drain our revenues."

In 2007, the Texas Legislature authorized 5,000 more beds for short-term treatment in the state's corrections system. At the time, the state was facing prison growth projections that would require 17,000 new prison beds by 2012. The treatment beds and other community-based substance abuse and mental health treatment programs were approved as an alternative to prison construction. Texas is now seeing its prison population decline along with fewer probation and parole revocations.

Representative Jerry Madden of Texas calls state funds spent for drug, alcohol, and mental health programs a "reinvestment strategy" that pays off.

"If we provide reentry services that work, the public is safer. If we provide drug treatment that works, the public is safer," Madden says. Not only that, he said the state is approaching $1 billion in savings as a result of the reinvestment begun three years ago.

Explosive Growth

States also have turned to specialty drug courts to help break the cycle of drugs and crime. The growth of these courts is nothing short of amazing.

The first drug court began in 1989 in Dade County, Fla., at a time when crack cocaine was overwhelming criminal justice systems elsewhere. Florida officials, including then-Florida Attorney General Janet Reno, developed and piloted the model of drug treatment under close judicial supervision. Two decades later, there are more than 2,100 operating drug courts around the country in all states, with more planned.

Florida's programs, funded largely by local and state money, are presently expanding in nine counties using federal stimulus money. Each year, about 10,000 Florida offenders enter drug court supervision, and current expansion will add as many as 2,000 people statewide.

Drug court professionals hail the ability of specialty courts to get and keep people in treatment while saving corrections money. But others advocate that addiction should be treated as a public health concern rather than a criminal justice matter.

Hawaii Offers Hope

In 2004, Hawaiian Circuit Court Judge Steve Alm took a new approach to dealing with "high-risk" drug offenders on probation.

The pilot program, Hawaii's Opportunity Probation with Enforcement, or HOPE, provided 35 offenders on the verge of being sent back to prison with one final chance to get clean and comply with the rules.

Offenders considered at high risk attended a formal "warning hearing" and were notified that violations would result in swift and certain sanctions. When a violation—missed appointment, drug use, or other violation of probation—occurred, the person on probation was immediately summoned before the judge and given a sanction, such as a short jail term served on the weekend, progressing in length for additional violations. Drug treatment was not mandatory and was ordered only if the person requested it or had repeated violations related to drug use.

Research comparing HOPE probationers to "probation-as-usual" caseloads found reduced drug use, better compliance with rules and reduced recidivism. During the first six months of participation in HOPE, the rate of positive drug tests fell by 93 percent and missed probation officer appointments dropped from 14 percent to 1 percent. Research also concluded that "probation-as-usual" offenders were three times more likely to be sent to prison than HOPE probationers.

Judge Alm's leadership in the development of HOPE led to early success. In 2007, the Hawaii Legislature appropriated funds to continue and expand the program. By 2009, the program had more than 1,500 participants and now permits domestic violence and sex offenders to participate.

Sustained success has been attributed to these factors:

- The basic tenets of the program—clear behavior expectations, swift action upon violation, certainty of punishment, and the least amount of punishment necessary for the violation—mean that offenders must change their behavior to succeed.
- Coordination, cooperation, and buy-in from agencies involved in running the program—the court, probation, law enforcement, attorneys, and treatment providers—are crucial, and some question if other programs will work as well without it.

Drug Abuse: By the Numbers

$11.3 Billion
Growth in federal drug control budget from FY 1988 to FY 2009—$2.8 billion to $14.1 billion.

2,147
Total number of drug courts in the United States since the first opened in 1989.

1.7 Million
Drug abuse violation arrests in 2008, 12.2 percent of all arrests that year.

More than 1 Million
Number of people in specialized alcohol or drug treatment on any given day.

$135.8 Billion
Amount states spent on substance abuse and addiction in 2005.

Sources: FBI Uniform Crime Reports, National Center on Addiction and Substance Abuse at Columbia University, National Drug Court Institute, Substance Abuse and Mental Health Services Administration, White House Office of National Drug Control Policy.

Programs with similar principles have been replicated in other jurisdictions around the country. The South Dakota court-based 24/7 Sobriety Project applies "swift, certain, and meaningful consequences" to people who are repeatedly arrested for driving under the influence. A planned replication in Clark County, Nev., also is in the works.

The success of HOPE and additional efforts throughout the country on policies that aim to reduce spending on corrections, control growth in the prison population, and increase public safety have gained attention at the national level. In November 2009, two bills were introduced in Congress. One would authorize a national HOPE program, and a second would provide grants to states for "justice reinvestment," a strategy currently underway in a number of states that analyze criminal justice data to identify and implement cost-saving policies.

—*Alison Lawrence, NCSL*

The National Association of Criminal Defense Lawyers issued a report in late 2009 after a task force spent two years studying the courts. Its findings question the effect of drug courts and assert that minorities, immigrants, and the poor are often under-represented in drug courts.

"Drug courts have not slowed the rise in either drug abuse or prison costs," says Cynthia Orr, president of the group. She says it's time to ask if our national drug policy is working and look at shifting focus to a public health-centered approach.

Drug courts have not slowed the rise in either drug abuse or prison costs.

—Cynthia Orr, President, National Association
of Criminal Defense Lawyers

California Collaboration

The largest scale criminal justice–drug treatment collaboration to date is underway in California.

Proposition 36, approved by voters in 2000, provides treatment instead of incarceration for nonviolent drug offenders. From 2002 through mid-2008, 340,000 drug offenders were referred and 242,000 were placed in treatment under the policy.

California Assemblyman Tom Ammiano, who chairs the Committee on Public Safety, says treatment policy is a sensible way to stretch limited criminal justice resources. "California's budget and prison overcrowding crises are invariably linked—and so are their solutions," he says. Ammiano says public safety and rehabilitation can be successfully integrated, and he's interested in back-end policies, as well, like improving access to treatment for drug-addicted parolees.

Proposition 36 programs have evolved to include graduated levels of service to meet a variety of substance abuse needs, says Millicent Gomes, the deputy director of the Office of Criminal Justice Collaboration in the California Department of Alcohol and Drug Programs. She notes that after 30 months, arrest rates of those who complete treatment are lower than for others who do not receive treatment.

"Jail and prison costs are offset," Gomes says. "There are benefits and costs avoided in many other areas, such as emergency rooms and family services."

Most state-level drug court funding has been sustained in California, but many county-level diversion programs have suffered from the state's fiscal crisis. A 2008 study by the University of California, Los Angeles, found the effectiveness of the policy was undermined by inadequate funding, even while it has saved taxpayers millions of dollars. The principal investigator on UCLA's Proposition 36 studies, Darren Urada, said it was exciting to find a tool like this in a current climate of budget cuts. The researchers warned, however, that shrinking and unpredictable funding will erode the benefits.

Even so, Gomes says the nearly decade-old policy in California has created the kind of culture change other states seek in dealing with offender addicts. She said Proposition 36 has institutionalized a continuum of care model that can withstand tough economic times.

Despite the tough fiscal situation facing California, Gomes says, support remains strong from many lawmakers and the public for the diversion approach.

In Kentucky, the diversion legislation quickly garnered bipartisan support in both chambers and from other branches of government, Kelly says. He points to two reasons because of which the policy passed unanimously in both houses.

"There is a clear recognition that our criminal justice system can do better with addicted offenders," he says. "And, I don't know of any family that isn't affected in some way by addiction. So there is a great deal of understanding and emotion about this."

Critical Thinking

1. How would you argue as an advocate for Kentucky's solution? How could it be applied elsewhere?
2. Are the drug courts helping or hurting, and why?

DONNA LYONS heads NCSL's criminal justice program.

Fetal Alcohol Spectrum Disorders: When Science, Medicine, Public Policy, and Laws Collide

Kenneth R. Warren and Brenda G. Hewitt

Historically, alcohol has been used for different purposes, including as a part of religious observances, as a food, at times as a medicine, and its well-known use as a beverage, often in place of uncertain water sources [Vallee 1994, 1998]. It is alcohol's use as a beverage and to some extent as a medicine that has most often come into social and legal conflict, partly as interest in the effects of alcohol on the social fabric of society has waxed and waned and partly due to increasing scientific evidence of alcohol's benefits and risks. While the literature on alcohol's many uses over the millennia is fascinating and growing, we will limit our comments in this article to cyclic waxing and waning of concern for the effects of prenatal alcohol use, primarily focusing on changing views of alcohol's prenatal and antenatal effects.

Historical Reflections: What Did We Know and When Did We Know It?

As noted by Jones and Smith, "historical reports indicate that the observation of an adverse effect on the fetus of chronic maternal alcoholism is not new" [Jones et al., 1978]. As many authors have concluded, mention of adverse pregnancy outcomes associated with alcohol use has been noted by Aristotle, Plutarch, and Diogenes [Lemoine et al. 2003], in the Bible [Randall, 2001], in 18th Century England [Warner and Rosett, 1975], and in 19th century medical and temperance literature [Warner and Rosett, 1975]. For example, Aristotle's warning about the effects of drinking on progeny ("foolish, drunken, and harebrained women most often bring forth children like unto themselves, morose, and languid") is often cited as one of the earliest observations of alcohol's effect on pregnancy and pregnancy outcomes. Another often cited reference is Judges 13:7 in which an angel appears to Manoah and his wife and states "Behold, thou shall conceive, and bear a son, and now drink no wine or strong drink. . . ." The couple obeys the admonition an Manoah's wife bears a son, Sampson, who becomes renowne for his physical strength and wisdom. However, much of th literature on alcohol use and pregnancy begins within the 18t century and the "London Gin Epidemic" which is considere by many authors to be the genesis of the first medical warning about the dire consequences of drinking during pregnancy.

London Gin Epidemic (~1720–1750)

The "London Gin Epidemic" occurred at a time when newe distillation technologies entered England from the Netherland simultaneous with the ascent of William and Mary (from th same country) to the throne of England. Bans were placed o the importation of French wines, England experienced bumpe crops of wheat, and taxes were lowered on gin (distilled fror wheat) for the benefit of wealthy landowners. These condition created what amounted to the "perfect storm" for the produc tion, distribution, and consumption of "cheap, plentiful" gi [Warner and Rosett, 1975]. In his often quoted treatise on th excesses of gin drinking as the underlying cause of increase criminal behavior in 18th century London, the English autho and magistrate, Henry Fielding, addressed a number of socia moral, and health ills he and other members of the upper socia strata attributed to the excess drinking of gin. According t Fielding, "the consumption of [gin] is almost wholly confine to the lowest Order of the People [Fielding, 1751]." Amon the ills he described were those inflicted on unborn childre and future generations: . . . What must become of the Infar who is conceived in Gin? with the poisonous distillations c which it is nourished both in the Womb and the Breast [Field ing, 1751]." Other contemporaries of Fielding made simila observations. For example, customs administrator and note economist Corbyn Morris observed that the significant deat rate relative to births in London was particularly attributable t the enormous use of spirituous liquors . . . which render suc as are born meager and sickly and unable to pass through th irst stages of life [Morris, 1751]. William Hogarth's depiction f the horrors of gin drinking by the lower classes in his famous iin Lane [1751] has been described by some authors (but not y all) as depicting the fetal alcohol syndrome [Rodin, 1981; Abel, 2001b].

By 1725 the damage that was attributed to alcohol was so reat that the London College of Physicians presented its con-erns about the medical and social problems occasioned by xcessive alcohol use in a petition to the House of Commons. mong the concerns expressed was that

". . . the frequent use of several sorts of distilled Spiritu-us Liquors . . . [is] too often the cause of weak, feeble, dis-empered children, who must be instead of an advantage and trength, a charge to their Country." Whether prompted by ear of losing the common worker, fear for self and property, r medical concerns about alcohol's effects including those on regnancy outcome, the observations made by influential Lon-oners, including Fielding, Morris, and Hogarth, are widely redited as contributing to the eventual repeal of laws that elped fuel the cheap production of gin and the "gin epidemic" Coffey, 1966].

Not All Agree

Examples of historic knowledge of alcohol's effects on preg-ancy such as those described above are presented in many rticles on alcohol and pregnancy. The most comprehensive f the earliest reviews of historic observations was an excel-ent account from ancient times to the early 1970s [Warner nd Rosett, 1975]. This article was subsequently criticized in number of publications [Abel 1997, 1999, 2001a,b; Arm-trong and Abel, 2000] for over interpretation and imputing the eaning of historical events to imply that the earlier centuries ruly understood alcohol teratogenesis and had seen FAS. For xample, while Warner and Rosett suggest that the entry in udges is a recognition of the harm alcohol can cause during regnancy, Abel notes that there are other explanations in the iblical text, for example, membership of Manoah in a sect that ras abstinent (meaning that Samson should also be abstinent) account for this admonition without invoking a knowledge of eratology [Abel, 1997]. We would also suggest that it may well ave simply reflected an acknowledgement of warnings handed own from antiquity concerning the use of alcohol at the time f conception (by men and women) to prevent damage to the hild or to the pregnancy. In this interpretation, both parents vere judged capable of damaging a child due to alcohol use. As pointed out by Lemoine, "unfortunately, two errors have ersisted throughout time . . . very often paternal alcoholism ras blamed . . ."; and "exaggerations led to accusing alcohol or many unidentified physical and psychological anomalies" Lemoine, 2003].

Alcohol, Medicine, and Politics: Temperance to Prohibition

The abuse of alcohol is so mixed up with morals, science, and conomics that it is impossible to disentangle the effects of the

chemical substance itself from its associated social complexi-ties" [Boycott, 1923].

"Our society's conceptions of disease are often weighted by moral valences as well as biological realities" [Armstrong, 1998].

That alcohol has an effect on pregnancy outcome is well documented in 19th and early 20th Century literature [Warner and Rosett, 1975]. However, scientific findings were inter-preted through the lens of then contemporary public attitudes about alcohol, its linking to a wide variety of social ills by the temperance movement, and by a lack of basic scientific under-standing, particularly with regard to the differences between heredity and prenatal effects [Katcher, 1993].

That alcohol has an effect on pregnancy outcome is well-documented in 19th and early 20th Century literature.

Reviewing 19th century scientific/medical literature, it is difficult to determine whether deficits in children are attributed to alcohol consumption in pregnancy, male and/or female alco-hol use at the time of conception or before conception, damage to genetic factors (germ cells); toxic damage to the fetus from alcohol exposure in the womb; alcohol exposure post preg-nancy through breast milk, or even the direct feeding of alcohol to the infant in place of breast milk.

One often cited reason for this difficulty is the involvement of a large number of physicians in the temperance movement (primarily in the United States and England) and the subse-quent influence of this movement on medical views of alco-hol's injurious effects on health in general and on pregnancy outcome in particular.

Another complicating factor with the early literature was a lack of modern (20th century) understanding of genetics, heredity, toxicity, and teratology. In the preMendel period, even knowledgeable physicians were unaware of the heredity principles of Mendelian genetics, and the distinction between genetic inheritance (DNA), damage to the "germ line" (sperm and ova), and direct toxic damage to developing tissues and organs. The Lamarckian view that traits acquired by either par-ent during his or her lifetime can be passed on to offspring (like inebriety or alcoholism) was not uncommon. Consistent with Lamarck, Robert MacNish of Glasgow wrote in 1835: "the children (of confirmed drunkards) are in general neither numer-ous nor healthy. From the general defect of vital power in the parental system, they are apt to be puny and emaciated" [Mac-Nish, 1835]. Ironically, we now understand that some aspects of Lamarckian inheritance do indeed exist via mechanisms of epigenetics. This view was somewhat modified by WC Sulli-van in his observations on 600 births to female prison inmates. Sullivan found 335 pregnancies ended in stillbirth or death to surviving children before age 2 and 80 women had three or more such infant deaths. He concluded that although inebriety could be transmitted by either parent to his or her offspring, "maternal inebriety is a condition peculiarly unfavorable to the vitality and to the normal development of the offspring a large part [of which] depends on the primary action of the poison" [Sullivan, 1899].

Between 1912 and 1920 Charles Stockard (Cornell University) conducted what for the time were very careful experiments on pregnancy outcomes in a guinea pig model. Both male and female guinea pigs were exposed to alcohol via an inhalation model before conception. Stockard found effects on growth and viability (liveborn, stillborn) in the offspring. These effects on viability persisted when the 1st generation offspring were mated with guinea pigs without a heritage of alcohol exposure but diminished with each subsequent generation. After four generations, the initial alcohol-exposed line had returned to the values of the control group [Stockard, 1918]. Stockard's findings appear very consistent with the 21st century understanding of epigenetics. MacDowell reproduced Stockard's results with rats finding reduced viability in the first generation and increased litters in the second generation [MacDowell and Vicari 1917; MacDowell, 1922]. He attributed the reduced viability in alcoholized rats to the effect of alcohol on "germplasm bearing factors detrimental to litter production" and "increased litters in the second generation to the elimination of the litters in the first generation that bore the less fertile germinal material" [MacDowell, 1922].

The following passage from an article appearing in the British Journal of Inebriety in 1923 sums up 19th and early 20th century thought on alcohol and pregnancy: "I think it is not an exaggeration to state that alcohol is a poison, and that the fetus of a chronic alcoholic mother is itself a chronic alcoholic, absorbing alcohol from the mother's blood and subsequently from her milk . . ." That is, they knew it did damage to the fetus if not exactly how. This knowledge appears to have been widely held among physicians and scientists during this time.

Nascent research progress that had begun during the heyday of early alcohol research came to an abrupt halt in 1919 with the passage of the Volstead Act and the ratification of the 18th Amendment to the U.S. Constitution prohibiting "the manufacture, sale, or transportation of intoxicating liquors . . . for beverage purposes" ushering in the era known as Prohibition. From the mid-1850s until Prohibition, many physicians were "temperance" advocates supporting total abstinence from alcohol use [Varma and Sharma, 1981]. By the time Prohibition became a reality, public opinion, largely stimulated by the temperance movement, had shifted from a view of inebriety as being an individual problem to one that found alcohol at the root of most health and social ills. With alcohol ostensibly no longer available, problems related to its use were viewed as less urgent. When Prohibition ended in the United States in 1933, temperance leaders and temperance tenets were by and large denounced. The country had swung away from the view of alcohol as villain to one that viewed alcoholism, rather than alcohol use, as the problem. A new era in alcohol science resulted, in which alcohol's harmful effects were minimized, and the study of alcoholism (once again an individual problem) became the prime scientific/ medical focus [Katcher, 1993].

Alcohol and Pregnancy Research: Postprohibition and Beyond

A clear cycle can be seen between the large attention to drinking during pregnancy that occurred during the late 19th and early 20th centuries, and the "forgetfulness" of the harmful consequences of alcohol use [Warner and Rosett, 1975]. The country that had seen Prohibition turn into one of the deadliest crime waves then known, wanted nothing to do with alcohol as a problem. Not only did the country repudiate the prohibition of alcohol, but also the large body of science that had been generated during the late 19th and early 20th centuries likely because much of it was associated with temperance movement "moralism." Many of the physicians and scientists who had been involved in generating much of this science were so integrally identified with the temperance movement that most of their research was dismissed as reflecting a no longer fashionable "moral" view of alcohol [Katcher, 1993]. This carried over in the 1940s as scientists began, once more, to address concerns about harmful alcohol use [Warner and Rosett, 1975]. These scientists made it perfectly clear that their problem was not with alcohol use in the main but in what has come to be known as chronic late stage alcohol dependence. In an interesting chapter-by chapter repudiation of late 19th and early 20th century temperance "science" on alcohol, Haggard and Jellinek sought to distance the neo-science of "chronic intolerance" (alcoholism) from the temperance-colored science published in the earlier century. They wanted the focus on alcoholism, not on alcohol. Writing in a 1942 book covering what was then known about the biological and psychological effects of alcohol, Haggard and Jellinek addressed the temperance view of alcohol's damage to the "germ" or the egg of the mother and/ or sperm of the father, thus affecting the physical/mental status of the child. According to Haggard and Jellinek, ascribing damage to the child as a result of drinking alcohol was a "belief, reflected in myth and custom . . ." that has "maintained itself up to present times." Thus, they approached alcohol not in terms of alcohol as a teratogen, but in terms of alcohol's effect on reproduction and associated organs. While acknowledging that the appearance of feeblemindedness, epilepsy, and mental disorders is more frequent among the offspring of abnormal drinkers, they stated unequivocally that this was not a direct effect of alcohol, but of "bad stock" or defects inherited by offspring "which predispose to alcoholism" [Haggard and Jellinek, 1942].

Even then, vestiges of the country's dislike of the temperance movement and Prohibition remained and Jellinek, often referenced as the father of the modern era of alcoholism research, and others who were at the head of alcohol's rediscovery as a researchable topic, did not believe that maternal alcohol use was detrimental to the fetus. In fact, Haggard and Jellinek wrote, "the fact is that no acceptable evidence has ever been offered to show that acute alcoholic intoxication has any effect whatsoever on the human germ or . . . in altering heredity" [Warner and Rosett, 1975]. They posited that the damaged children of alcoholic parents were the result of poor nutrition; alcohol exposure in the womb as the agent responsible for causing physical and mental abnormalities in children did not appear to be a possibility.

Modern Recognition of Alcohol as a Teratogen

We now know that alcohol, certainly when consumed at doses consistent with the lowest thresholds of legal intoxication (0.08% blood alcohol concentration), is an agent capable of causing not only a variety of health problems but also birth defects. Alcohol is a teratogen. Because of its common availability and usage, alcohol is more than just a teratogen; it is the most prominent behavioral teratogen in the world. Indeed, alcohol may be viewed as having introduced an entirely new discipline—that of behavioral teratology.

> **Because of its common availability and usage, alcohol is more than just a teratogen; it is the most prominent behavioral teratogen in the world.**

FAS as a Modern Diagnosis

In 1970, Christine Ulleland, a medical student at the University of Washington, undertook a thesis project to study children hospitalized for failure to thrive. In reviewing the medical charts, she observed that a common element in the medical records was an indication of alcoholism in over 41% of the mothers noting, "these observations indicate that infants of alcoholic mothers are at high risk for pre- and postnatal growth and developmental failure," and suggesting that "greater attention should be given to alcoholic women during the child bearing years" [Ulleland, 1970].

When the prominent dysmorphologist, David Smith, and his associate, Kenneth Lyons Jones, examined a group of these children they immediately recognized the subtle, but important, pattern we now know as FAS. The physical and behavioral characteristics of these children were subsequently published [Jones et al., 1973], ushering in the modern era of research on fetal alcohol syndrome.

In their search for other evidence of the adverse effects of alcohol on fetal outcome, Jones and Smith discovered a paper published in 1968 in France, by Lemoine et al., [1968] describing virtually the identical physical and behavioral problems among 127 children of alcoholic mothers from Roubaix, France. The Lemoine paper had likely escaped attention because it appeared in a minor journal and was published in French [Warner and Rosett, 1975]. Subsequently, an earlier doctoral dissertation on the influence of parental alcoholic intoxication on the physical development of young babies by Jacqueline Rouquette, published in Paris in 1957, came to the attention of FAS researchers [Barrison et al., 1985]. In their second publication, David Smith introduced the name "fetal alcohol syndrome" to describe their clinical observations [Jones and Smith, 1973]. It was often the case that a new syndrome would be named after the scientists or physicians who first describe the condition (e.g., Williams's Syndrome). The authors chose to assign the name fetal alcohol syndrome (FAS) because they believed that the name would call attention to alcohol as a teratogen, alert women to the dangers of drinking in pregnancy, and aid in the elimination of this disorder. While the name FAS does garner attention in the medical community and public, some argue that the name FAS today may actually be more problematic due to the stigma associated with alcohol problems than if a neutral name like "Smith and Jones" or "Lemoine" syndrome had been applied.

No Immediate Acceptance

Despite the Lemoine and Jones and Smith reports, much skepticism as to whether alcohol could cause birth defects existed in the 1970s. For example, if it truly existed, why did we not know about it before in this era of modern medicine? How did we know that alcohol was indeed the agent rather than nutrition, other drug use, or the "deviant lifestyle" of the alcoholic woman?

The answer to these questions required the undertaking of animal and epidemiological research and a funding agency to support that research.

The National Institute on Alcohol Abuse and Alcoholism and FAS: The Story of a Science Success

In the late 1960s, a United States Senator, Harold E. Hughes, himself a recovering alcoholic, along with a group of influential recovering alcoholics with business and political acumen and ties, began advocating for legislation to create a federal focal point for alcoholism. At this time, medicine had little if any concern for alcoholics who were seen as morally deficient, or suffering from weak wills or character defects (shades of the earlier 19th/20th centuries temperance movement). Treatment for alcoholism was mainly accomplished through Alcoholics Anonymous, and to a much smaller extent within state mental health systems (a small center for the control and prevention of alcoholism in the National Institute of Mental Health was tasked with helping to create a federal alcoholism presence mainly within the existing federal and state mental health services system).

Many early alcohol investigators noted that alcohol research was as stigmatized as alcoholism itself [Lieber, 1988]. The National Institutes of Health supported very limited alcohol research; what was supported was often disguised as something else, e.g., using alcohol as a "probe" to study other types of liver disease. Indeed, a major epidemiological study of birth defects undertaken in the late 1960s did not ask any questions on alcohol use [Jones et al., 1974]. This attitude changed with the passage of the landmark Comprehensive Alcohol Abuse and Alcoholism Prevention, Treatment and Rehabilitation Act of 1970 (P.L. 91–616) which established the National Institute on Alcohol Abuse and Alcoholism (NIAAA) and provided national visibility and funds to understand, prevent, and treat alcoholism and problems related to alcoholism. NIAAA, with its newly minted research mandate, supported the research that helped to validate the existence of FAS and what we now recognize as the full spectrum of fetal alcohol spectrum disorders (FASD).

The 1970s alcohol and pregnancy research took two forms: animal research and human epidemiological research. Animal research established the nature of FAS teratogenesis by verifying that the same deficits reported by Lemoine and Jones and Smith could be seen in animals (rodents, dogs, and later primates); and that alcohol and not other confounding factors were responsible. Human epidemiological research prospectively examining the outcomes of children exposed to alcohol in pregnancy demonstrated the range of physical and behavioral deficits in children exposed to alcohol in pregnancy. By 1977, NIAAA sponsored the first international research conference on FAS. Though not an original intent of the meeting, those attending were so impressed with the findings to date that they collectively recommended that NIAAA issue the first government health advisory on FAS.

Warning the Public

Doing anything the first time in Government presents numerous challenges. In this instance, NIAAA was attempting to have the Federal Government put its imprimatur on a warning about drinking during pregnancy that ran counter to prevailing medical and social practices. Resistance from within the US Department of Health, Education and Welfare (now the US Department of Health and Human Services), NIAAA's administrative home, and from non-Federal groups and organizations was expected. Federal skepticism was overcome primarily due to the strength of the science, and the first governmental advisory about alcohol use during pregnancy was published by NIAAA in 1977 [Warren and Foudin, 2001]. Taking a "conservative approach" this first ever advisory stated that more than six drinks a day was dangerous and recommended a "2-Drink Limit" per day. Unlike today's warnings against any use until proven safe, implicit in this first warning was the notion that alcohol use is "safe" within the given guidelines until proven dangerous.

The response was as varied (and as vocal) as expected. For example, the recommendation in the advisory was supported by the American College of Pediatrics, but not immediately by the American College of Obstetrics and Gynecology. Some medical and patient advocacy organizations criticized NIAAA for going too far, and some for not going far enough, by not recommending abstinence during pregnancy. However, the 1977 Health Advisory did focus sufficient attention on the issue of alcohol and pregnancy that Senate hearings were held for the purpose of considering legislation requiring warning labels related to alcohol and pregnancy risks. The outcome of the hearings was the call for a Report to the President and Congress on *Health Hazards Associated with Alcohol and Methods to Inform the General Public of these Hazards* prepared jointly by the Departments of Health and Human Services and Treasury [US Department of Transportation and US Department of Health and Human Services, 1980]. The report did not immediately call for alcoholic beverage labeling but did recommend the issuance of a Surgeon General's Advisory on Alcohol and Pregnancy that was subsequently issued in 1981 [FDA Drug Bulletin 1981]. Unlike the previous Advisory, the 1981 Advisory recommended that women who are pregnant or planning to become pregnant avoid alcohol. In 1988 Congress considered the issue of alcoholic beverage labeling as a means to warn of the dangers of alcohol exposure in the womb and enacted the Alcoholic Beverage Labeling Act of 1988 (Public Law 100690) which became effective in 1989. In 2005, the Surgeon General reissued an updated advisory on alcohol use and pregnancy that warned against FASD, the full spectrum of birth defects caused by prenatal alcohol exposure (US Surgeon General, 2005].

Conclusion: Promises of Current Research

Although today there is little disagreement about the existence of FASD, we are again embroiled in determinations that are as much about policy as medicine. What does a physician tell his/her patient who is either pregnant or may become pregnant? The US Surgeon General's Advisory on Alcohol and Pregnancy is clear. We do not know the dose at which we can unequivocally state that the fetus will not be harmed. It is therefore prudent advice to avoid all drinking during these time periods. Yet there is not full agreement on this issue. Recently, for example, a medical ethicist likened this message to "medical paternalism" [Gavaghan, 2009]. As science continues to refine our knowledge of the consequences of exposure to alcohol during gestation, we are hopeful that public health policies and practice can reach closure on what advice will best serve pregnant women and their future offspring.

As concluded by Clarren and Smith, alcohol exposure during gestation "appears to be the most frequent known teratogenic cause of mental deficiency in the Western world" which "through accurate understanding . . . and widespread public awareness could be largely reduced and, ideally, eliminated" [Clarren and Smith, 1978]. This was the goal of the early pioneers in describing FAS and FASD, and it remains the goal of committed scientists, patients, and their families today.

References

Abel EL. 1997. Was the fetal alcohol syndrome recognized in the ancient Near East? Alcohol Alcohol 32:3–7.

Abel EL. 1999. Was the fetal alcohol syndrome recognized by the Greeks and Romans? Alcohol Alcohol 34:868–872.

Abel EL. 2001a. The gin epidemic: much ado about what? Alcohol Alcohol 36:401–405.

Abel EL. 2001b. Gin lane: did Hogarth know about fetal alcohol syndrome? Alcohol Alcohol 36:131–134.

Armstrong EM. 1998. Diagnosing moral disorder: the discovery and evolution of fetal alcohol syndrome. Soc Sci Med 47:2025–2042.

Armstrong EM, Abel EL. 2000. Fetal alcohol syndrome: the origins of a moral panic. Alcohol Alcohol 35:276–282.

Barrison IG, Waterson EJ, Murray-Lyon IM. 1985. Adverse effects of alcohol in pregnancy. Addiction 80:11–22.

Boycott AE. 1923. The action of alcohol on man. Lancet 202:1055–1056.

larren SK, Smith DW. 1978. The fetal alcohol syndrome. N Engl J Med 298:1063–1067.

offey T. 1966. Beer street—Gin lane—some views of 18th-century drinking. Quart J Stud Alcohol 27:669–692.

DA Drug Bulletin. 1981. Surgeon genera's advisory on alcohol and pregnancy. Washington, DC: FDA Drug Bulletin. p 9–10.

ielding H. 1751. An enquiry into the causes of the late increase of robbers, etc.: with some proposals for remedying this growing evil. London: printed for A. Millar. 203 p.

avaghan C. 2009. "You can't handle the truth"; medical paternalism and prenatal alcohol use. J Med Ethics 35:300–303.

aggard HW, Jellinek EM. 1942. Alcohol explored. Garden City: Doubleday, Doran and Company. 297 p.

ones KL, Hanson JW, Smith DW. 1978. Palpebral fissure size in newborn infants. J Pediatr 92:787.

ones KL, Smith DW. 1973. Recognition of the fetal alcohol syndrome in early infancy. Lancet 302:999–1001.

ones K, Smith D, Streissguth A, et al. 1974. Outcome in offspring of chronic alcoholic women. Lancet 303:1076–1078.

ones K, Smith D, Ulleland C, et al. 1973. Pattern of malformation in offspring of chronic alcoholic mothers. Lancet 301:1267–1271.

atcher BS. 1993. The post-repeal eclipse in knowledge about the harmful effects of alcohol. Addiction 88:729–744.

emoine P. 2003. The history of alcoholic fetopathies (1997). J FAS Int 1:e2.

emoine P, Harousse H, Borteyru JP, et al. 1968. Children of alcoholic parents—anomalies in 127 cases. Arch Francaises De Pediatr 25: 830–832.

emoine P, Harousseau H, Borteyru JP, et al. 2003. Children of alcoholic parents—observed anomalies: discussion of 127 cases. Ther Drug Monit 25:132–136.

ieber C. 1988. NIAAA and alcohol research: a researcher's view—National Institute on alcohol abuse and alcoholism. Perspectives on current research. Alcohol Health Res World 12:306–307.

MacDowell EC. 1922. The influence of alcohol on the fertility of white rats. Genetics 7:117–141.

MacDowell EC, Vicari EM. 1917. On the growth and fecundity of alcoholized rats. Proc Natl Acad Sci USA 3:577–579.

MacNish R. 1835. The anatomy of drunkenness. New York: D. Appleton. 227.

Morris C. 1751. Observation on the past growth and present state of the city of London. London.

Randall CL. 2001. Alcohol and pregnancy: highlights from three decades of research. J Stud Alcohol 62:554–561.

Rodin AE. 1981. Infants and Gin mania in 18th century London. JAMA 245:1237–1239.

Stockard CR, GNP. 1918. Further studies on the modification of the germ-cells in mammals: the effect of alcohol on treated guinea-pigs and their descendants. J Exp Zool 26: 119–226.

Sullivan WC. 1899. A note on the influence of maternal inebriety on the offspring. J Mental Sci 45:489–503.

Ulleland C. 1970. Offspring of alcoholic mothers. Pediatr Res 4:474.

US Department of Transportation, US Department of Health and Human Services. 1980. Report to the president and congress on health hazards associated with alcohol and methods to inform the general public of these hazards. Washington, DC.

US Surgeon General. 2005. Surgeon general's advisory on alcohol and pregnancy. Washington, DC: US Department of Health and Human Services.

Vallee BL. 1994. Alcohol in human history. EXS 71:1–8.

Vallee BL. 1998. Alcohol in the western world. Sci Am 278:80–85.

Varma SK, Sharma BB. 1981. Fetal alcohol syndrome. Prog Biochem Pharmacol 18: 122–129.

Warner RH, Rosett HL. 1975. The effects of drinking on offspring: an historical survey of the American and British literature. J Stud Alcohol 36:1395–1420.

Warren KR, Foudin LL. 2001. Alcohol-related birth defects—the past, present, and future. Alcohol Res Health 25:153–158.

Critical Thinking

1. To date, scientists have not been able to determine the dose level at which the fetus will be harmed by alcohol. What factors must a pregnant mother consider when deciding whether to drink during pregnancy?

2. What do you think is the best advice a doctor can give his or her patient concerning alcohol consumption during pregnancy?

3. How should policymakers approach this topic to reduce the incidence rate of FAS?

U.S. and Europe Split Over Drugs Policy

LUKE BAKER

United Nations sponsored negotiations on a new global drugs strategy are close to breaking down, with profound divisions between Europe and the United States on key policy issues, participants at the talks in Vienna say.

The problem is that U.S. negotiators are trying to push through anti-drug programmes that were promoted during the former Bush administration but which are no longer advocated by President Barack Obama, they said.

Whereas former President George W. Bush believed in a zero-tolerance approach in the war on drugs, one of Obama's first moves was to back the lifting of a ban on federal funding for needle-exchange programmes. He also gave tacit support to so-called "harm-reduction" strategies that are seen as crucial in the fight against drug-related diseases such as HIV/AIDS.

The Vienna stand-off, which threatens to scupper a March summit at which the new drug policy declaration is to be signed, has prompted Democrats in Congress to write to the new U.S. ambassador to the United Nations calling for intervention.

Drug policy campaigners say that without a change in the U.S. position, anti-drug strategies could be set back for the next decade and have a knock-on impact on the spread of HIV/AIDS and other diseases.

"We understand that the U.S. delegation in Vienna has been actively blocking the efforts of some of our closest allies—including the European Union—to incorporate in the declaration reference to harm reduction measures, such as needle exchange," read the letter, sent to Susan Rice on Wednesday and signed by California Congressman Henry Waxman, among others.

The U.S. delegation should be given new instructions from the new administration, it said.

"Otherwise, we risk crafting a U.N. declaration that is at odds with our own national policies and interests, even as we needlessly alienate our nation's allies in Europe."

Officials close to the U.S. negotiators in Vienna denied that Bush-era policies were being "rammed through" but said instructions from Obama administration had not been received.

"We are currently hearing out proposals, keeping options open and Washington informed. Our new administration will continue to review and develop our negotiating positions," a spokeswoman for the U.S. mission in Vienna said.

The Needle and the Damage Done

The Vienna negotiations, under the auspices of the U.N. Office on Drugs and Crime, have been going on intermittently for several months but are due to wrap up before a summit on March 12–13 when the new declaration is due to be signed.

While the United States is the chief proponent of a zero tolerance approach to the estimated $160 billion (111.9 billion pound) illegal drugs industry, it has support from Russia and Japan, neither of whom support 'harm reduction' policies, which can include medication-assisted therapy and drug legalisation.

The European Union's policy position is supported by Australia, Latin America and Iran, among others, all of whom favour policies that include harm-reduction measures.

Drug policy campaigners believe that if the United States could be brought closer to the European position, Japan, Russia and others including China and India would follow, potentially producing consensus on a new global drugs strategy.

"Time is very tight and the race is now on to change the instructions from U.S. officials before the ink dries on the previous administration's line," said Danny Kushlick, head of policy at Transform, a British drug policy foundation.

"The implications of changing the political line is enormous for those who have suffered under the U.S. administration's refusal to support basic harm reduction measures."

U.S. sources said that while it was not impossible that the negotiating position could be changed, it would only happen once new instructions were issued from Washington.

At the same time, while the Obama administration differs from Bush, it does not advocate all 'harm reduction' strategies, which can include drug consumption rooms, safe-injecting rooms, and providing heroin and needles in prisons.

Critical Thinking

1. What is a "zero tolerance" approach to drug use?
2. What is one important component of harm reduction drug policy?
3. How big an international "industry" are illegal drugs?

Portugal's Drug Policy Pays off; U.S. Eyes Lessons

These days, Casal Ventoso is an ordinary blue-collar community— mothers push baby strollers, men smoke outside cafes, buses chug up and down the cobbled main street.

BARRY HATTON AND MARTHA MENDOZA

These days, Casal Ventoso is an ordinary blue-collar community—mothers push baby strollers, men smoke outside cafes, buses chug up and down the cobbled main street.

Ten years ago, the Lisbon neighborhood was a hellhole, a "drug supermarket" where some 5,000 users lined up every day to buy heroin and sneaked into a hillside honeycomb of derelict housing to shoot up. In dark, stinking corners, addicts—some with maggots squirming under track marks—staggered between the occasional corpse, scavenging used, bloody needles.

At that time, Portugal, like the junkies of Casal Ventoso, had hit rock bottom: An estimated 100,000 people—an astonishing percent of the population—were addicted to illegal drugs. So, like anyone with little to lose, the Portuguese took a risky leap: they decriminalized the use of all drugs in a groundbreaking law in 2000.

Now, the United States, which has waged a 40-year, $1 trillion war on drugs, is looking for answers in tiny Portugal, which is reaping the benefits of what once looked like a dangerous gamble. White House drug czar Gil Kerlikowske visited Portugal in September to learn about its drug reforms, and other countries—including Norway, Denmark, Australia and Peru—have taken interest, too.

"The disasters that were predicted by critics didn't happen," said University of Kent professor Alex Stevens, who has studied Portugal's program. "The answer was simple: Provide treatment."

Drugs in Portugal are still illegal. But here's what Portugal did: It changed the law so that users are sent to counseling and sometimes treatment instead of criminal courts and prison. The switch from drugs as a criminal issue to a public health one was aimed at preventing users from going underground.

Other European countries treat drugs as a public health problem, too, but Portugal stands out as the only one that has written that approach into law. The result: More people tried drugs, but fewer ended up addicted.

Here's what happened between 2000 and 2008:

- There were small increases in illicit drug use among adults, but decreases for adolescents and problem users, such as drug addicts and prisoners.
- Drug-related court cases dropped 66 percent.
- Drug-related HIV cases dropped 75 percent. In 2002, 49 percent of people with AIDS were addicts; by 2008 that number fell to 28 percent.
- The number of regular users held steady at less than 3 percent of the population for marijuana and less than 0.3 percent for heroin and cocaine—figures which show decriminalization brought no surge in drug use.
- The number of people treated for drug addiction rose 20 percent from 2001 to 2008.

Portuguese Prime Minister Jose Socrates, one of the chief architects of Portugal's new drug strategy, says he was inspired partly by his own experience of helping his brother beat addiction.

"It was a very hard change to make at the time because the drug issue involves lots of prejudices," he said. "You just need to rid yourselves of prejudice and take an intelligent approach."

Officials have not yet worked out the cost of the program, but they expect no increase in spending, since most of the money was diverted from the justice system to the public health service.

In Portugal today, outreach health workers provide addicts with fresh needles, swabs, little dishes to cook up the injectable mixture, disinfectant and condoms. But anyone caught with even a small amount of drugs is automatically sent to what is known as a Dissuasion Committee for counseling. The committees include legal experts, psychologists and social workers.

Failure to turn up can result in fines, mandatory treatment or other sanctions. In serious cases, the panel recommends the user be sent to a treatment center.

Health works shepherd some addicts off the streets directly into treatment. That's what happened to 33-year-old Tiago, who is struggling to kick heroin at a Lisbon rehab facility.

Tiago, who requested his first name only be used to protect his privacy, started taking heroin when he was 20. He shot up four or five times a day, sleeping for years in an abandoned car where, with his addicted girlfriend, he fathered a child he has never seen.

At the airy Lisbon treatment center where he now lives, Tiago plays table tennis, surfs the Internet and watches TV. He helps with cleaning and other odd jobs. And he's back to his normal weight after dropping to 50 kilograms (110 pounds) during his addiction.

After almost six months on methadone, each day trimming his intake, he brims with hope about his upcoming move to a home run by the Catholic church where recovered addicts are offered a fresh start.

"I just ask God that it'll be the first and last time—the first time I go to a home and the last time I go through detox," he said.

Portugal's program is widely seen as effective, but some say it has shortcomings.

Antonio Lourenco Martins, a former Portuguese Supreme Court judge who sat on a 1998 commission that drafted the new drug strategy and was one of two on the nine-member panel who voted against decriminalization, admits the law has done some good, but complains that its approach is too soft.

Francisco Chaves, who runs a Lisbon treatment center, also recognizes that addicts might exploit good will.

"We know that (when there is) a lack of pressure, none of us change or are willing to change," Chaves said.

Worldwide, a record 93 countries offered alternatives to jail time for drug abuse in 2010, according to the International Harm Reduction Association. They range from needle exchanges in Cambodia to methadone treatment in Poland.

Vancouver, Canada, has North America's first legal drug consumption room—dubbed as "a safe, health-focused place where people inject drugs and connect to health care services." Brazil and Uruguay have eliminated jail time for people carrying small amounts of drugs for personal use.

Whether the alternative approaches work seems to depend on how they are carried out. In the Netherlands, where police ignore the peaceful consumption of illegal drugs, drug use and dealing are rising, according to the European Monitoring Centre for Drugs and Drug Addiction. Five Dutch cities are implementing new restrictions on marijuana cafes after a wave of drug-related gang violence.

However, in Switzerland, where addicts are supervised as they inject heroin, addiction has steadily declined. No one has died from an overdose since the program began in 1994, according to medical studies. The program is credited with reducing crime and improving addicts' health.

The Obama administration firmly opposes the legalization of drugs, saying that it would increase access and promote acceptance, according to drug czar Kerlikowske. The U.S. is spending $74 billion this year on criminal and court proceedings for drug offenders, compared with $3.6 billion for treatment.

But even the U.S. has taken small steps toward Portugal's approach of more intervention and treatment programs. And Kerlikowske has called for an end to the "War on Drugs" rhetoric.

"Calling it a war really limits your resources," he said. "Looking at this as both a public safety problem and a public health problem seems to make a lot more sense."

There is no guarantee that Portugal's approach would work in the U.S. For one, the U.S. population is 29 times larger than Portugal's 10.6 million.

Still, an increasing number of American cities are offering nonviolent drug offenders a chance to choose treatment over jail, and the approach appears to be working.

In San Francisco's gritty Tenderloin neighborhood, Tyrone Cooper, a 52-year-old lifelong drug addict, can't stop laughing at how a system that has put him in jail a dozen times now has him on the road to recovery.

"Instead of going to smoke crack, I went to a rehab meeting," he said. "Can you believe it? Me! A meeting! I mean, there were my boys, right there smoking crack, and Tyrone walked right past them. 'Sorry,' I told them, 'I gotta get to this meeting.'"

Cooper is one of hundreds of San Franciscans who landed in a cour[t] program this year where judges offered them a chance to go to rehab get jobs, move into houses, find primary care physicians, even remove their tattoos. There is enough data now to show that these alternative courts reduce recidivism and save money.

Nationally, between 4 and 29 percent of drug court participants wil[l] get caught using drugs again, compared with 48 percent of those wh[o] go through traditional courts.

San Francisco's drug court saves the city $14,297 per offender officials said. Expanding drug courts to all 1.5 million drug offenders in the U.S. would cost more than $13 billion annually, but would return more than $40 billion, according to a study by John Roman, senior researcher at the Urban Institute's Justice Policy Center.

The first drug court opened in the U.S. 21 years ago. By 1999, there were 472; by 2005, 1,250.

This year, new drug courts opened every week around the U.S., a[s] states faced budget crises exarcebated by the high rate of incarceratio[n] on drug offenses. There are now drug courts in every state, more tha[n] 2,400 serving 120,000 people.

Last year, New York lawmakers followed counterparts across th[e] U.S. who have tossed out tough, 40-year-old drug laws and manda[]tory sentences, giving judges unprecedented sentencing options. Also the Department of Health and Human Services is training doctors t[o] screen patients for potential addiction, and reimbursing Medicare an[d] Medicaid providers who do so.

Arizona recently became the 15th state in the nation to approv[e] medical use of marijuana, following California's 2006 legislation.

In Portugal, the blight that once destroyed the Casal Ventoso neigh[]borhood is a distant memory.

Americo Nave, a 39-year-old psychologist, remembers the chillin[g] stories his colleagues brought back after Portuguese authorities sent first team of health workers into the Casal Ventoso neighborhood i[n] the late 1990s. Some addicts had gangrene, and their arms had to b[e] amputated.

Those days are past, though there are vestiges. About a dozen frai[l] mostly unkempt men recently gathered next to a bus stop to get ne[w] needles and swabs in small green plastic bags from health worker[s] as part of a twice-weekly program. Some ducked out of sight behin[d] walls to shoot up, and one crouched behind trash cans, trying to shiel[d] his lighter flame from the wind.

A 37-year-old man who would only identify himself as Joao sai[d] he's been using heroin for 22 years. He has contracted Hepatitis C, an[d] recalls picking up used, bloody needles from the sidewalk. Now h[e] comes regularly to the needle exchange.

"These teams . . . have helped a lot of people," he said, strugglin[g] to concentrate as he draws on a cigarette.

The decayed housing that once hid addicts has long since bee[n] bulldozed. And this year, Lisbon's city council planted 600 trees an[d] 16,500 bushes on the hillside.

This spring they're expected to bloom.

Critical Thinking

1. What percentage of the Portuguese population were addicted to illegal drugs eleven years ago?

2. How exactly did the Portuguese change their drug laws?

3. How much does the United States spend each year on criminal proceedings for drug offenders? How much on treatment?

Transcending the Medical Frontiers: Exploring the Future of Psychedelic Drug Research

David Jay Brown

When I was in graduate school studying behavioral neuroscience I wanted nothing more than to be able to conduct psychedelic drug research. However, in the mid-1980s, this was impossible to do at any academic institution on Earth. There wasn't a single government on the entire planet that legally allowed clinical research with psychedelic drugs. However, this worldwide research ban started to recede in the early 1990s, and we're currently witnessing a renaissance of medical research into psychedelic drugs.

Working with the Multidisciplinary Association for Psychedelic Studies (MAPS) for the past four years as their guest editor has been an extremely exciting and tremendously fruitful endeavor for me. It's a great joy to see how MDMA can help people suffering from posttraumatic stress disorder (PTSD), how LSD can help advanced-stage cancer patients come to peace with the dying process, and how ibogaine can help opiate addicts overcome their addiction. There appears to be enormous potential for the development of psychedelic drugs into effective treatments for a whole range of difficult-to-treat psychiatric disorders.

However, as thrilled as I am by all the new clinical studies exploring the medical potential of psychedelic drugs, I still long for the day when our best minds and resources can be applied to the study of these extraordinary substances with an eye that looks beyond their medical applications, toward their ability to enhance human potential and explore new realities.

This article explores these possibilities. But first, let's take a look at how we got to be where we are.

A Brief History of Time-Dilation Studies

Contemporary Western psychedelic drug research began in 1897, when the German chemist Arthur Heffter first isolated mescaline, the primary psychoactive compound in the peyote cactus. In 1943 Swiss chemist Albert Hofmann discovered the hallucinogenic effects of LSD (lysergic acid diethylamide) at Sandoz Pharmaceuticals in Basel while studying ergot, a fungus that grows on rye. Then, 15 years later, in 1958, he was the first to isolate psilocybin and psilocin—the psychoactive components of the Mexican "magic mushroom," Psilocybe mexicana.

Before 1972, nearly 700 studies with LSD and other psychedelic drugs were conducted. This research suggested that LSD has remarkable medical potential. LSD-assisted psychotherapy was shown to safely reduce the anxiety of terminal cancer patients, alcoholism, and the symptoms of many difficult-to-treat psychiatric illnesses.

Between 1972 and 1990 there were no human studies with psychedelic drugs. Their disappearance was the result of a political backlash that followed the promotion of these drugs by the 1960s counterculture. This reaction not only made these substances illegal for personal use, but also made it extremely difficult for researchers to get government approval to study them.

The New Wave of Psychedelic Drug Research

The political climate began to change in 1990, with the approval of Rick Strassman's DMT study at the University of New Mexico. According to public policy expert and MAPS president Rick Doblin this change occurred because, "open-minded regulators at the FDA decided to put science before politics when it came to psychedelic and medical marijuana research. FDA openness to research is really the key factor. Also, senior researchers who were influenced by psychedelics in the sixties now are speaking up before they retire and have earned credibility."

The past 18 years have seen a bold resurgence of psychedelic drug research, as scientists all over the world have come to recognize the long-underappreciated potential of these drugs. In the past few years, a growing number of studies using human volunteers have begun to explore the possible therapeutic benefits of drugs such as LSD, psilocybin, DMT, MDMA, ibogaine and ketamine.

Current studies are focusing on psychedelic treatments for cluster headaches, PTSD, depression, obsessive-compulsive disorder (OCD), severe anxiety in terminal cancer patients, alcoholism, and opiate addiction. The results so far look quite promising, and more studies are being planned by MAPS and other private psychedelic research organizations, with the eventual goal of turning MDMA, LSD, psilocybin, and other psychedelics into legally available prescription drugs.

As excited as I am that psychedelic drugs are finally being studied for their medical and healing potential, I'm eagerly anticipating the day when psychedelic drug research can really take off, and move beyond its therapeutic applications in medicine. I look forward to the day when researchers can explore the potential of psychedelics as advanced learning tools, relationship builders, creativity enhancers, pleasure magnifiers, vehicles for self-improvement, reliable catalysts for spiritual or mystical experiences, a stimulus for telepathy and other psychic abilities, windows into other dimensions, and for their ability to possibly shed light on the reality of parallel universes and nonhuman entity contact.

Let's take a look at some of these exciting possibilities.

The Science of Pleasure

Almost all medical research to date has been focused on curing diseases and treating illnesses, while little attention has been paid to increasing human potential, let alone to the enhancement of pleasure. However, one can envision a time in the not-too-distant future when we will have cured all of our most challenging physical ailments and have more time and resources on our hands to explore post-survival activities. It's likely that we'll then focus our research efforts on discovering new ways to improve our physical and mental performance.

A science devoted purely to enhancing pleasure might come next, and psychedelics could play a major role in this new field. Maverick physicist Nick Herbert's "Pleasure Dome" project seeks to explore this possibility, and although this is little more than an idea at this point, it may be the first step toward turning the enhancement of pleasure into a true science.

According to surveys done by the U.S. National Institute of Drug Abuse, the number one reason why people do LSD is because "it's fun." Tim Leary helped to popularize the use of LSD with the help of the word "ecstasy," and sex expert Annie Sprinkle has been outspoken about the ecstatic possibilities available from combining sex and psychedelics. Countless psychedelic trip reports have described long periods of appreciating extraordinary beauty and savoring ecstatic bliss, experiences that were many orders of magnitude more intense than the subjects previously thought possible.

With all the current research emphasis on the medical applications and therapeutic potential of psychedelics, the unspoken and obvious truth about these extraordinary substances is that, when done properly, they're generally safe and healthy ways to have an enormous amount of fun. There's good reason why, they're so popular recreationally, despite their illegality.

When psychedelic research begins to integrate with applied neuroscience and advanced nanotechnology in the future, we can begin to establish a serious science of pleasure and fun. Most likely this would begin with a study of sensory enhancement and time dilation, which are two of the primary effects that psychedelics reliably produce.

Perhaps one day our brightest researchers and best resources will be devoted to finding new ways to enhance sexual, auditory, visual, olfactory, gustatory, and tactile sensations, and create undreamed of new pleasures and truly unearthly delights. Scientific studies could explore ways to improve sexual performance and enhance sensory sensitivity, elongate and intensify our orgasms, enlarge the spectrum of our perceptions, and deepen every dimension of our experience. Massage therapy, Tantra, music, culinary crafting, and other pleasure-producing techniques could be systematically explored with psychedelics, and universities could have applied research centers devoted to the study of ecstasy, tickling, and laughter.

The neurochemistry of aesthetic appreciation, happiness, humor, euphoria, and bliss could be carefully explored with an eye toward improvement. Serious research and development could be used to create new drugs, and integrate neurochemically heightened states with enhanced environments, such as technologically advanced amusement parks and extraordinary virtual realities. In this area of research, it seems that psychedelics may prove to be extremely useful, and countless new psychedelic drugs are just waiting to be discovered.

In addition to enhancing pleasure, psychedelics also stimulate the imagination in extraordinary ways.

Creativity Problem-Solving

A number of early studies suggest that psychedelic drugs may stimulate creativity and improve problem-solving abilities. In 1955, Louis Berlin investigated the effects of mescaline and LSD on the painting abilities of four nationally recognized graphic artists. Although the study showed that there was some impairment of technical ability among the artists, a panel of independent art critics judged the experimental paintings as having "greater aesthetic value" than the artists' usual work.

In 1959, Los Angeles psychiatrist Oscar Janiger asked sixty prominent artists to paint a Native American doll before taking LSD and then again while under its influence. A panel of independent art critics and historians then evaluated these 120 paintings. As with Berlin's study, there was a general agreement by the judges that the craftsmanship of the LSD paintings suffered; however, many received higher marks for imagination than the pre-LSD paintings.

In 1965, at San Francisco State College, James Fadiman and Willis Harman administered mescaline to professional workers in various fields to explore its creative problem-solving abilities. The subjects were instructed to bring a professional problem requiring a creative solution to their sessions. After some psychological preparation, subjects worked individually on their problem throughout their mescaline session. The creative output of each subject was evaluated by psychological tests, subjective reports, and the eventual industrial or commercial validation and acceptance of the finished product or final solution. Virtually all subjects produced solutions judged highly creative and satisfactory by these standards.

In addition to the scientific studies that have been conducted here are also a number of compelling anecdotal examples that suggest a link between creativity and psychedelic drugs. For example, architect Kyosho Izumi's LSD-inspired design of the ideal psychiatric hospital won him a commendation for outstanding achievement from the American Psychiatric Association, and Apple cofounder Steve Jobs attributes some of the insights which lead to the development of the personal computer to his use of LSD. Additionally, a number of renowned scientists have personally attributed their breakthrough scientific insights to their use of psychedelic drugs—including Nobel Prize winners Francis Crick and Kary Mullis.

There hasn't been a formal creativity study with psychedelics since 1965, although there are countless anecdotal reports of artists, writers, musicians, filmmakers, and other people who attribute a portion of their creativity and inspiration to their use of psychedelics. This is an area that is more than ripe for study. Anecdotal reports suggest that very low doses of LSD—threshold level doses, around 20 micrograms—are especially effective as creativity enhancers. For example, Francis Crick was reported to be using low doses of LSD when he discovered the double-helix structure of the DNA molecule.

I'd love to see a whole series of new studies exploring how cannabis, LSD, psilocybin, and mescaline can enhance the imagination, improve problem-solving abilities, and stimulate creativity. As advances in robotics automates more of our activities, I suspect that creativity will eventually become the most valuable commodity of all. Much of the creativity in Hollywood and Silicon Valley is already fueled by psychedelics and research into how these extraordinary tools could enhance creativity even more effectively may become a booming enterprise in the not-too-distant future.

However, creativity isn't the only valuable psychological ability that psychedelics appear to enhance.

ESP Psychic Phenomena

Few people are aware that there have been numerous, carefully controlled scientific experiments with telepathy, psychokinesis, remote viewing, and other types of psychic phenomena, which have consistently produced compelling, statistically significant results that conventional science is at a loss to explain. Even most scientists are currently unaware of the vast abundance of compelling scientific evidence for psychic phenomena, which has resulted from over a century of parapsychological research. Hundreds of carefully controlled studies—in which psi researchers continuously redesigned experiments to address the comments from their critics—have produced results that demonstrate small, but statistically significant effects for psi phenomena, such as telepathy, precognition, and psychokinesis.

According to Dean Radin, a meta-analysis of this research demonstrates that the positive results from these studies are significant with odds in the order of many billions to one. Princeton University, the Stanford Research Institute, Duke University, the Institute of Noetic Science, the U.S. and Russian governments, and many other respectable institutions, have spent years researching these mysterious phenomena, and conventional science is at a loss to explain the results. This research is summarized Radin's remarkable book *The Conscious Universe.*

Just as fascinating as the research into psychic phenomena is the controversy that surrounds it. In my own experience researching the possibility of telepathy in animals, and other unexplained phenomena with British biologist Rupert Sheldrake, I discovered that many people are eager to share personal anecdotes about psychic events in their life—such as remarkable coincidences, uncanny premonitions, precognitive dreams, and seemingly telepathic communications. In these cases, the scientific studies simply confirm life experiences. Yet many scientists that I've spoken with haven't reviewed the evidence and remain doubtful that there is any reality to psychic phenomenon. However, surveys conducted by British biologist Rupert Sheldrake and myself reveal that around 78% of the population has had unexplainable "psychic" experiences, and the scientific evidence supports the validity of these experiences.

It's also interesting to note that many people have reported experiencing meaningful psychic experiences with psychedelics—not to mention a wide range of paranormal events and synchronicities, which seem extremely difficult to explain by means of conventional reasoning.

A questionnaire study conducted by psychologist Charles Tart, PhD. of 150 experienced marijuana users found that 76% believed in extrasensory perception (ESP), with frequent reports of experiences while intoxicated that were interpreted as psychic. Psychiatrist Stanislav Grof, M.D., and psychologist Stanley Krippner, PhD., have collected numerous anecdotes about psychic phenomena that were reported by people under the influence of psychedelics, and several small scientific studies have looked at how LSD, psilocybin, and mescaline might effect telepathy and remote viewing.

For example, according to psychologist Jean Millay, PhD., in 1997, students at the University of Amsterdam in the Netherlands did research to establish whether the use of psilocybin could influence remote viewing. This was a small experiment, with only 12 test-subjects, but the results of the study indicated that those subjects who were under the influence of psilocybin achieved a success rate of 58.3 percent, which was statistically significant.

A great review article by Krippner and psychologist David Luke, PhD. that summarizes all of the psychedelic research into psychic phenomena can be found in the Spring, 2011 MAPS Bulletin that I edited about psychedelics and the mind/body connection.

When I conducted the California-based research for two of Sheldrake's books about unexplained phenomena in science, *Dogs That Know When Their Owners Are Coming Home* and *The Sense of Being Stared At*, one of the experiments that I ran involved testing blindfolded subjects to see if they could sense being stared at from behind. One of the subjects that I worked with reported an unusually high number of correct trials while under the influence of MDMA. I'd love to run a whole study to see if MDMA-sensitized subjects are more aware of when they're being stared at.

It is especially common for people to report experiences with telepathy, clairvoyance, precognition, remote viewing, and psychokinesis while using ayahuasca, the potent hallucinogenic jungle juice from the Amazon. There have only been several studies with ayahuasca which demonstrate health benefits, but this is an area that is just crying out to be explored carefully and in depth. Future studies could examine ayahuasca's potential and accuracy as a catalyst for psychic phenomena, and all of the traditional studies that have been done with psychic phenomena, which generated positive results, could be redone with subjects dosed with different psychedelics to see if test scores can be improved.

Increasing our psychic abilities may open up the human mind to new, unimagined possibilities–and if you think that harnessing telepathic and clairvoyant abilities is pretty wild, then hold on to your hats for what's likely to come next.

Higher Dimensions and Nonhuman Entity Contact

A primary ingredient in ayahuasca is DMT, and users claim that this remarkable substance has the extraordinary power to open up an interdimensional portal into another universe. Some of the most fascinating psychedelic research has been done with this incredible compound.

DMT is a mystery. One of the strangest puzzles in all of nature—in the same league as questions like "What existed before the Big Bang?" and "How did life begin?"—revolves around the fact that the unusually powerful psychedelic DMT is naturally found in the human body, as well as in many species of animals and plants, and nobody knows what it does, or what function it might serve, in any of these places.

Because natural DMT levels tend to rise while we're asleep at night, it has been suggested that it may have a role in dreaming. But this is pure speculation, and even if true, it may do much more. Because of its endogenous status and unusually potent effects, many people have considered DMT to be the quintessential psychedelic. DMT has effects of such strength and magnitude that it easily dwarfs the titanic quality of even the most powerful LSD trips, and it appears to transport one into an entirely new world—a world that seems more bizarre than our wildest imaginings, yet, somehow, is also strangely familiar.

Psychiatric researcher Rick Strassman, PhD., who conducted a five year study with DMT at the University of New Mexico, has suggested that naturally elevated DMT levels in the brain may be responsible for such unexplained mental phenomena as spontaneous mystical experiences, near-death experiences, nonhuman entity contact, and schizophrenia. Strassman and others have even gone so far as to speculate about the possibility that elevated DMT levels in the brain might be responsible for ushering the soul into the body before birth, and out of the body after death.

But perhaps what's most interesting about DMT is that, with great consistency, it appears to allow human beings to communicate with other intelligent life forms. When I interviewed Strassman, I asked him if he thought that there was an objective reality to the worlds visited by people when they're under the influence of DMT, and if he thought that the entities that so many people have encountered on DMT actually have an independent existence or not. Rick replied:

I myself think so. My colleagues think I've gone woolly brained over this, but I think it's as good a working hypothesis as any other. I tried all other hypotheses with our volunteers, and with myself. The "this is your brain on drugs" model; the Freudian "this is your unconscious playing out repressed wishes and fears;" the Jungian "these are archetypal images symbolizing your unmet potential;" the "this is a dream;" etc. Volunteers had powerful objections to all of these explanatory models—and they were a very sophisticated group of volunteers, with decades of psychotherapy, spiritual practice, and previous psychedelic experiences. I tried a thought-experiment, asking myself, "What if these were real worlds and real entities? Where would they reside, and why would they care to interact with us?" This led me to some interesting speculations about parallel universes, dark matter, etc. All because we can't prove these ideas right now (lacking the proper technology) doesn't mean they should be dismissed out of hand as incorrect.

A 2006 scientific paper by computer scientist Marko A Rodriguez called "A Methodology for Studying Various Interpretations of the N,N-dimethyltryptamine-Induced Alternate Reality" explores how to possibly determine if the entities experienced by people on DMT are indeed independently existing intelligent beings or just projections of our hallucinating brains. Rodriguez suggests a test that involves asking the entities to perform a complex mathematical task involving prime numbers to verify their independent existence. While it seems like a long shot that this method could lead to fruitful results, I think that any serious speculation about establishing communication channels with these mysterious beings is constructive.

Strassman's work could represent the very beginning of a scientific field that systematically explores the possibility of communicating with higher dimensional entities, and this might prove to be a more fruitful endeavor for establishing extraterrestrial contact than the SETI project. What they can teach us we can only imagine.

My own experiences with DMT lead me to suspect that Strassman's studies would have yielded far more fruitful results had the subjects been dosed with harmaline prior to receiving the DMT injections. Harmaline is an MAO-inhibiting enzyme that is found in a number of plants. It's found in the famous South American vine known as Banisteriopsis cappi, which composes half of the mixture in the sacred hallucinogenic jungle juice ayahuasca, which has been used for healing purposes by indigenous peoples in the Amazon basin for thousands of years. Harmaline is widely known as the chemical that allows the DMT in other plants, like Psychotria viridis, to become orally active.

Orally consumed DMT is destroyed in the stomach by an enzyme called monoamine oxidase (MAO), which harmaline inhibits. However, it does much more than just make the DMT orally active. I've discovered that drinking a tea made from yrian rue seeds–which also contain harmaline–two hours rior to smoking DMT dramatically alters the experience. armaline has interesting psychoactive properties of its own at are somewhat psychedelic, and it slows down the speed f the DMT experience considerably, rendering it more comrehensible, less frightening, and easier to understand. For ousands of years indigenous peoples in the Amazon jungles ombined harmaline and DMT, and this long history has culvated a powerful synergism between how the two molecules act in our body.

In future studies harmaline could be used in conjunction ith DMT, to more accurately simulate the ayahuasca experince that strikes such a powerful primordial chord in our spees. This would allow for the experience to become much more omprehensible, and last for a greater duration of time, which ould allow for more ability to examine the phenomenon of onhuman entity communication.

Some readers may have noticed that this article has loosely ollowed a Christian theological progression, from the ego eath and bodily resurrection of the medical studies with sychedelics, to the paradisiacal pleasures of Heaven, where e discovered our godlike powers and met with the angels. ltimately, it appears, this research will lead us to the source of vinity itself.

he Study of Divine Intelligence

erhaps the most vital function of psychedelics is their abil-y to reliably produce spiritual or mystical experiences. These anspersonal experiences of inseparability often result in an creased sense of ecological awareness, a greater sense of terconnection, a transcendence of the fear of death, a sense the sacred or divine, and identification with something much rger than one's body or personal life.

Many people suspect that this experience lies at the heart the healing potential of psychedelics—and they believe that aking this experience available to people is essential for the rvival of our species. I agree that we need a compassion-e vision of our interconnection with the biosphere to guide r technological evolution and without it we might destroy rselves.

In his book *The Physics of Immortality*, physicist Frank pler introduces the idea that if a conscious designing intel-gence is genuinely a part of this universe, then ultimately

religion—or the study of this designer intelligence—will become a branch of physics. Psychedelic drug research may offer one pathway toward establishing this future science.

Recent studies by Roland Griffiths and colleagues at Johns Hopkins have confirmed that psilocybin can indeed cause religious experiences that are indistinguishable from religious experiences reported by mystics throughout the ages—and that substantial health benefits can result from these experiences.

These new studies echo the findings of an earlier study done in 1962 by Walter Pahnke of the Harvard Divinity School, and it's certainly not news to anyone who has had a full-blown psychedelic experience. R.U. Sirius responded to this seemingly redundant research by saying that "Wow! Scientists Discover Ass Not Elbow!" Nonetheless, this may represent the beginning of a whole new field of academic inquiry, which explores those realms that have been previously declared off-limits to science.

It appears that the integration of science and spirituality could be the next event horizon—our next adventure as a species. Our future evolution may depend on it. Without a transpersonal perspective of interconnection to guide our evolutionary direction, we seem to be firmly set on a path toward inevitable self-destruction. I personally believe psychedelics can help us get back on track, and help us heal the damage that we've done to ourselves and to the Earth. This is why I believe so strongly in psychedelic drug research.

There isn't much time left before our biosphere starts to unravel, and we may only have a small window of opportunity to save our fragile world. I think that MAPS—and sister organizations, like the Beckley Foundation and the Heffter Research Institute—are industrialized society's best hope for transforming the planet's ancient shamanic plants into the respectable scientific medicines of tomorrows and, in so doing, bring psychedelic therapy to all who need it. This may not only help to heal a number of difficult-to-treat medical disorders and increase ecological harmony on the planet, but it may also open up a doorway to untold and unimagined new worlds of possibility.

Critical Thinking

1. Discuss the benefits and the challenges in the use of psychedelic drugs.

2. Provide an argument for or against legalizing psychedelics for medical reasons.

Test-Your-Knowledge Form

We encourage you to photocopy and use this page as a tool to assess how the articles in *Annual Editions* expand on the informatio in your textbook. By reflecting on the articles you will gain enhanced text information. You can also access this useful form on product's book support website at www.mhhe.com/cls

NAME: DATE:

TITLE AND NUMBER OF ARTICLE:

BRIEFLY STATE THE MAIN IDEA OF THIS ARTICLE:

LIST THREE IMPORTANT FACTS THAT THE AUTHOR USES TO SUPPORT THE MAIN IDEA:

WHAT INFORMATION OR IDEAS DISCUSSED IN THIS ARTICLE ARE ALSO DISCUSSED IN YOUR TEXTBOOK OR OTHE READINGS THAT YOU HAVE DONE? LIST THE TEXTBOOK CHAPTERS AND PAGE NUMBERS:

LIST ANY EXAMPLES OF BIAS OR FAULTY REASONING THAT YOU FOUND IN THE ARTICLE:

LIST ANY NEW TERMS/CONCEPTS THAT WERE DISCUSSED IN THE ARTICLE, AND WRITE A SHORT DEFINITION:

4 1 16